Posthuman Ecologies

Posthuman Ecologies

Complexity and Process
after Deleuze

Edited by
Rosi Braidotti and Simone Bignall

ROWMAN &
LITTLEFIELD
——————— INTERNATIONAL
New York • London

Published by Rowman & Littlefield International Ltd
6 Tinworth Street, London SE11 5AL, United Kingdom
www.rowmaninternational.com

Rowman & Littlefield International Ltd.is an affiliate of Rowman & Littlefield
4501 Forbes Boulevard, Suite 200, Lanham, Maryland 20706, USA
With additional offices in Boulder, New York, Toronto (Canada), and Plymouth (UK)
www.rowman.com

British Library Cataloguing in Publication Data
A catalogue record for this book is available from the British Library

ISBN: HB 978-1-7866-0822-2
     PB 978-1-7866-0823-9

Library of Congress Cataloging-in-Publication Data Is Available

ISBN 978-1-78660-822-2 (cloth: alk. paper)
ISBN 978-1-78660-823-9 (pbk: alk. paper)
ISBN 978-1-78660-824-6 (electronic)

♾™ The paper used in this publication meets the minimum requirements of American
National Standard for Information Sciences—Permanence of Paper for Printed Library
Materials, ANSI/NISO Z39.48-1992.

Printed in the United States of America

Contents

List of Figures

Acknowledgements

Viewed from a Deleuzian perspective, knowledge-production is a multiple and collective affair that emerges 'alongside' the creative act of composition when conceptual elements are drawn together into novel combinations. We sincerely thank everyone who has contributed to this book as a complex assemblage of parts. Together we have created a loosely bound and mobile system of ideas for understanding the posthuman condition. In diverse renditions, the chapters situate posthumanist concepts transversally across fields of enquiry or in practices of disciplinary encounter, to describe an interactive ecology without closure or fixity. The outcome is not an ending, but provocative of further beginnings, future thoughts: new formations of knowledge for worlds yet to come.

We are especially grateful to Natalie Linh Bolderston and Isobel Cowper-Coles at Rowman and Littlefield International; their good advice and encouragement continually lightened for us the burden of the editorial process. Sincere thanks to Gry Ulstein and Evelien Geerts for their editorial and administrative assistance. We thank all the chapter authors for their participation, and for their ever-willingness to accommodate our suggestions and requests. We owe special thanks to Jussi Parikka, Iris van der Tuin and James Williams, for enduring a longer-than-expected haul to the finish line.

An earlier version of Jussi Parikka's chapter was published as 'Cartographies of Environmental Arts' in *The Midden*, edited by Jenni Nurmenniemi and Tracey Warr and published by Garret Publications in 2018. We are grateful for the permission generously granted by Garret Publications to reprint a revised version of this work. Parikka's chapter references works of art by Helen Hunter, Tuula Närhinen, Elena Mazzi & Sara Tirelli, Mirko Nikolić, and Nabb+Teeri. We thank the artists for allowing us to include images of their work. The image by Helena Hunter appears courtesy of the Natural

History Museum, London. All other images in Parikka's chapter are used by kind permission of the curators of the Frontiers in Retreat project as part of the Helsinki International Artist Programme.

Chapter 1

Posthuman Systems

Simone Bignall and Rosi Braidotti

The 'posthuman turn'—defined as the convergence of posthumanism with postanthropocentrism—is a complex and multidirectional discursive and material event. It encourages us to build on the generative potential of the critiques of humanism developed by radical epistemologies that aim at a more inclusive practice of becoming-human. And it also supports an opening out of our conceptual imagination, the power (*potentia*) of thinking beyond the established anthropocentric frame, towards becoming-world. Deleuze's geo-zoe-ethological philosophy, resting on the vital materialism he draws from revisiting Spinoza, Nietzsche and Bergson, is particularly useful in stressing that we should abandon hierarchical comparisons in deciding the value or operative potential of humanity or a plant or a fly (for example), since these life-forms inhabit, or comprise, mutually affective 'inter-kingdoms'. At the same time, Deleuzian materialism offers an important framework for understanding how these interlaced assemblages of life exist also in inextricable and constitutive connection to the nonliving forms and forces that factor in any particular framing of the earth for the emergence of a provisional stability.[1] Félix Guattari adds his own specific contribution to this intensive philosophy of life, difference and the project of becoming 'otherwise other', by highlighting the constitutive effects of media and technological mediation, both on our self-understanding and on our relational capacity. What emerges from the posthuman convergence thus defined therefore is a qualitative leap based on the need to think in zoe/geo/techno-oriented frames.

This focus on trans-species formations, on technological mediation and 'geophilosophy' characterises an important strand of contemporary feminist thought observed, for example, in work by Elizabeth Grosz, Karen Barad, Donna Haraway and Elizabeth Povinelli.[2] This collection of essays is situated in relation to such enquiries. Feminist epistemology, notably the materialist tradition of differential feminism that runs through 'standpoint theory', 'situated knowledges' and embedded, embodied nomadic subjectivity,[3] stresses the importance of specific and accountable perspectives. This approach criticises the Eurocentric, masculinist universalism that is still operative in most knowledge production scientific systems, while proposing robust alternatives. Perspectivism is at work in feminist theory, not as a form of fragmentation and relativism, but rather as the source of counter knowledges and alternative values. It offers a point of encounter and intersection with the highly defined forms of perspectivism currently formalised by Indigenous philosophy. We recognise, therefore, that contemporary posthuman and ecofeminist efforts to describe a mode of thought adequate to the complex material energies of the earth—in geo/zoe-techno mediated ways—sits alongside a far older tradition of Indigenous philosophy, which likewise understands the power and potentiality of thought as being materially embedded in the geoformations and trans-species influences that shape and define existence in relational terms.[4]

Such grounded, accountable and perspectivist approaches inform the thinking in this collection of essays, which in their various ways continue the project of a materialist theorisation of posthumanist affirmative ethics.[5] The chapters in this book respond philosophically and affirmatively to the ethical and political fractures and challenges that ensue as a result of the ex/implosion of a unitary and falsely universal notion of the 'human' and of the system of moral values and human rights that rest upon it. The posthuman paradigm as an analytic tool for understanding the perspectival nature of knowledge, and for drawing attention to the primacy of nonhuman influences in formative processes, can be misunderstood as celebrating an 'inhuman' system, potentially also expressing lack of concern or care for humans. We suggest this is not the case, however, with the posthuman convergence being best understood as an epistemological framework for supporting the elaboration of alternative values and new codes of inter-relation that extend beyond human influence and cognisance, but do not discount it.

This is an imperative task for academic teaching and research as well, since the role of the 'inhuman' in reconceiving the humanities is ambivalent in its critical and creative potential. On the one hand, attention paid to the pre-individual and impersonal earth-forces that affectively condition terrestrial becomings and territorial beings opens a pathway to 'the outside' of current arrangements of social life.[6] Insofar as these arrangements are most often orchestrated through a globally dominant paradigm of liberal subjectivation that takes its conceptual moorings from the compass of modern European thought, a less territorially constrained focus on geophilosophical forces of creativity and the 'inhumanism' of global processes creates new possibilities for reconceiving humanity and human responsibility beyond the circumscribed limits of (modern Western) sovereign entitlement. But on the other/hand, 'inhumanism' conjures the spectre of premodern cruelty historically associated with the unchecked exercise of sovereign might; or else it references the merciless modes of social alienation and self-subjectivation that are pervasive postmodern consequences of diffuse global technologies of discipline and control, so characteristic of biopolitical operations in late capitalism. Each of these epochal political formations was, of course, strikingly analysed by Foucault in his lecture series at the Collège de France and developed further by Deleuze and Guattari's neo-materialist philosophy.[7] In light of this escalating *problem* of inhumanism, which in fact threatens to submerge and subvert the liberating potential of nonhuman forces of becoming, we insist the posthuman convergence of nonanthropocentrism and nonhumanism is not best conceived as a manifesto for inhumane indifference, nor does it point to a single direction for knowledge and freedom. It is, rather, a multidirectional appeal that resists and yet is in dialogue with the critical tendency to steer analysis towards a paradigm of 'inhumanism'. Instead of proposing a single counter-paradigm to modern humanism and anthropocentrism, conceived under the banner of 'the inhuman', posthumanism is a wake-up call that aims at building on the generative potential of already existing critiques of both humanism and anthropocentrism, in order to deal with the complexity of the present juncture.

Furthermore, as Dipesh Chakrabarty points out, 'our common predicament' of climate change and the threat of environmental collapse impacts differentially upon the various classes of humanity inhabiting 'developed' and 'developing' countries, which may be differently rich or poor, vulnerable or resilient, according to a range of measures—and not all of them economic. This complexity means that not all humans are equally placed to respond effectively to the social and economic impacts of the inhuman earth-forces of natural disaster. An 'inhuman' approach would be all the more unacceptable considering that the devolved and dispersed character of human agency and moral responsibility induced by the posthuman condition takes place in a context of diffuse geopolitical arrangements and biopolitical technologies, subtending a contemporary necro-political regime of extermination of species and extinction of multiple life-forms, both human and nonhuman. The uncertain future faced by all of humanity—and by nonhuman life—in the contemporary era of ecological crisis that prominently defines the Anthropocene is *both* a unifying factor, *and* a prospect of uneven fallout that threatens to engulf more precarious life-forms more quickly, or more completely, than others. This raises difficult questions about distributive justice that 'pose a challenge to the categories upon which our traditions of political thought are based'.[8]

As we have already suggested, one aspect of this challenge involves resisting the tendency to work with a single new paradigm—such as inhumanism—that would reduce posthumanism and postanthropocentrism to a relation of equivalence, despite their notable convergences.[9] Whereas critiques of anthropocentrism denounce the species hierarchy that culminates in human exceptionalism and privilege, posthumanism more specifically engages a critique of the humanist ideal of 'Man', and the political and philosophical programmes of progressive Enlightenment (or 'civilisation') that rest upon this ideal. We believe the preservation of discontinuities and divergences between these two perspectives (despite their obvious conjunctions) enables a more nuanced critical and ethical response to our contemporary condition: it should be possible to decry human exceptionalism as the basis for species privilege, while also attending to the specificity of human responsibility and potentiality in conceptualising adequate forms of response to the damages arising significantly from human activity. At the same time, the effective performance and institutionalisation of such responsive understandings involves acknowledging how the experiences and perspectives defining humanity are not the universal prerogative of European Man as the normative measure of all excellence and inspiration. Rather, embodied and embedded experiences of humanity—our varied sexed and enculturated experiences of 'being human'—are differential; and human differences may create diverse contextual solutions to global problems. Local and perspectival solutions to universal crises, developed contextually through human ingenuity in pragmatic relation to specific materialities, can be mobilised in innovative ways towards the development of practical measures with an emergent effect, potentially bringing general benefit.

The reclamation of diverse human agencies and accountabilities in the context of faceless phenomena of exploitation and inhuman(e) processes of production in late or cognitive capitalism—and perhaps also the potential redemption of humanity in the era of 'the Anthropocene'—suggests there is an urgent need for new thinking about the differential nature of human influences in complex interactional systems, and about the nature of such systems and of agency within them, when such phenomena are conceived in nonanthropocentric ways. Indeed, the question of what human-actioned systems would look like beyond anthropocentrism haunts a range of contemporary enquiries into the nature of the diverse phenomena that interact in complex affective ecologies. How can human thought adequately conceive nonhuman temporality and spatiality? What are the nature, value and impact of nonhumanist productivity in natural, social and economic systems? What is a posthuman system of language, or of perception and subjectivity? How would a posthuman sensibility transform legal, political and educational systems? When it conceives subjectivity apart from intentionality or integrated moral selfhood directed actively towards discrete end purposes, can posthumanism offer an adequate framework for theorising responsiveness in complex interactive ecologies?

In response to such questions, the chapter contributions to this book explore the posthumanist implications of Deleuze's assertion that 'the system must not only be in perpetual heterogeneity, it must also be a heterogenesis'.[10] The authors draw resources from Deleuze's philosophy to examine the operation of spatial, temporal, political, legal, economic, aesthetic, informational, epistemological, conceptual and educational 'systems', conceived as posthuman ecologies whose processual characters and complex relations are constituted by circulations of affect. Through specific readings and uses of Deleuze's conceptual apparatus, each chapter extends nonhumanist concepts for understanding reality, agency and ethical interaction in dynamic ecologies of reciprocal determination and influence. Inquiry across a broad range of topics, traversing the traditional disciplines of the Humanities, offers new potential to expand contemporary discussions about the recomposition of the human as an enhanced and revised subject in the posthuman era, and of human-actioned systems as complex arenas of heterogeneous ethical concern and accountability. In drawing together such ideas, we hope this book will open new pathways for vital new theorisations of human scope, responsibility and potential in the posthuman condition.

'The posthuman, as a dynamic, creative convergence phenomenon, is creating new fields of scholarship'.[11] Based on the parallelism that Deleuze and Guattari establish between philosophy, science and the arts, this collection addresses posthuman systems in a diffractive and trans-disciplinary manner. The chapters traverse studies of earth processes, philosophical ideas, cultural texts, political practices, digital and geographical mediation, and pedagogy. In bringing such diverse topics of discussion together in a single volume, our primary aim is not to unify them by identifying commonalities that bridge their differences under the banner of a singularly defined 'posthumanism'. Rather, our key intention in presenting such a clamorous and multiperspectival set of discussions taking place across and within the hybrid and marginal disciplinary terrains of 'the new Humanities'—in chapters ranging across vastly varied topics—is to facilitate a methodological opportunity for diffractive reading as defined by Karen Barad, and elaborated here by Iris van der Tuin in chapter 2.[12] Van der Tuin considers the encounter between Deleuze and Bergson in the light of contemporary interlocutions by Leonard Lawlor and Valentine Moulard-Leonard. For van der Tuin, this set of encounters provides an entry point for presenting diffractive reading as a methodology of indeterminacy, appropriate both for Deleuze studies and for the new Humanities. The practice of reading diffractively involves an effort to understand the complex and multiscalar consequences of productive encounters between differences when they are brought into affective relationships, always in particular and contingent circumstances of engagement. Iris van der Tuin argues that diffractive reading is an exemplary posthumanist methodology: 'both in terms of how the philosophical canon is dealt with (transversally), and how the humanities and the sciences are traversed in the same stroke'. The diffractive reader is less animated by questions of definition ('*what is* a posthuman ecology?') than by questions of performative operation or orchestration and relational consequence ('*what happens* when x meets y, and how does their encounter influence the way in which y impacts upon z to transform the relationship with a such that effects b and c might emerge?').[13] For example, in our case, we are interested by *what happens* to understandings of spatial construction, and to frameworks of education and pedagogy, when the reader encounters Radman (chapter 4) alongside de Freitas (chapter 5), to conceive how a change in affect produced by altered environmental or architectural conditions can influence an individual capacity for creative thought, for active learning and enhanced agential potentiality. Or, *what happens* when the reader forges new conceptual associations upon encountering theories of temporality (chapter 6) and nonhumanist agency (chapters 7 and 8), alongside an account of the geophysical shifts of the earth arising from the complex interplay of living and nonliving forces over aeons of time before (and likely beyond) human existence and earthly influence (chapter 14)? Taken together, the chapters relate to one another in various and shifting ways depending on the purpose or serendipity of their association, the perspective of the reader, and the order in which they are read.

While the chapters are diverse in their content and focus, and are best approached diffractively, they overall produce an interactive ecology of concepts and frameworks that 'opens up the way to a general logic'[14] for reconceiving and reconstructing the posthumanities. Chapter 3 by Jussi Parikka articulates some general geophilosophical principles that help us to think the operation of posthuman systems as complex ecologies, which always-already take their bearings in relation to the material situation of their genesis and their agendas. Parikka undertakes a cartographical analysis of the environmental arts, in this context encompassing a range of projects that traverse traditional boundaries between geography, philosophy, institutional mediation, artistic practice and science. His chapter is an exercise in mapping the practices and processes that make up an 'operating system', and he identifies a series of analytic strategies for understanding such systems. They involve cognisance of the principle of 'survol' or height, which enables a beyond-individual, trans-localised perspective for considering how a system of elements connect;[15] the framing act or art of establishing a 'frontier' by carving out a situated or localised 'territory' from a boundless plane of consistency or composition; the institutional frameworks or technologies

that engender (or constrain) this practice; and the temporality of the operating system as a process of organisation or a nonlinear series of operations,
rather than a structure. These analytic strategies or cartographic techniques
reveal how environmental art practices involve complex relational processes
that constitute what Deleuze and Guattari describe as 'eccentric' models 'of
becoming and heterogeneity', in which 'flux is reality itself, or consistency'
and the model is 'problematic, rather than theorematic: figures are considered
from the viewpoint of the *affections* that befall them'. In contrast to the
teleological linear progressions of modern humanist systems, a posthuman
system, though genetically situated in a particular material or environmental
context of formation, 'operates in an open space throughout which things-
flows are distributed, rather than plotting out a closed space for linear and
solid things'.[16]

Indeed, this book is engaged by the subject of 'posthuman ecologies', and
is itself a network of posthuman concepts; but it is more narrowly subtitled
'complexity and process after Deleuze'. In this respect, the collection is
geared towards an enhanced understanding of the contribution made by
Deleuzian philosophy to the emergence of the contemporary posthumanities.
Returning once again to van der Tuin's chapter on method, we recognise
that reading Deleuze's own philosophical oeuvre *diffractively* seems especially important when we consider the process of its genesis, its internal
shifts and its indeterminate quality, in terms of Deleuze's encounters with
other thinkers. Although Deleuze's works are impressive in part because
of the erudition evidenced in his vast bibliographies, especially prominent
among his philosophical engagements are persistent trysts with Spinoza,
Nietzsche, Bergson, Simondon—and of course, especially, Guattari. In fact,
if Deleuze is named in our title as a preeminent source for the emergence of
a posthuman 'ecosophy', this can only be because of his long and productive
association with the 'ecological' thinking of Guattari, whose late work, *The
Three Ecologies*, describes the interactive relational systems of environment,
economic society and subjectivity and defines a geophilosophical-political-
ethical approach that has come to characterise various posthumanisms.[17] If
the current collection takes Deleuze, and not Guattari, as its philosophical
focus, this is not, then, because we downplay the significance of Guattari's
thought in the Deleuze-Guattari assemblage, or deny Guattari's prominent
influence in shaping contemporary understandings of what it means to think
ecologically. Rather, we take Deleuze as our focus because his important
influence on posthumanist frameworks emerges not only from his collaboration with Guattari, but also from his other individual and highly idiosyncratic
readings of Spinoza, Nietzsche, Bergson and Simondon. And subsequent
interlocutors with Deleuze have themselves become elements in a new series
of philosophical assemblages that also describe the conceptual apparatus of

posthumanism. Concepts produced (selectively and differentially) through this complex and dynamic array of philosophical assemblages are taken up in this collection in various ways, and put to various uses.

By focusing on the qualities of a posthumanist architectural practice in his chapter 4, Andrej Radman continues the analysis of the genetic power of affective encounters begun by Iris van der Tuin in her opening chapter, and by Jussi Parikka in his geophilosophical analysis of the emergent consequences of constitutive relations for the operation of posthuman systems. Radman argues that the recomposition of what Guattari refers to as 'architectural enunciation' profoundly transforms the role of the architect, who becomes its relay by assuming the analytic and pragmatic responsibility for the production not merely of the environment, but of subjectivation itself. Following Deleuze's Spinozism, and continuing the affective corporeal emphasis subsequently given to this in work by Brian Massumi, Radman suggests that if to think differently one has to feel differently, and if the sole purpose of design is to change us, then architecture is effectively a 'psychotropic practice' that modulates and compels routines of experience.

Chapter 5 by Elizabeth de Freitas shifts the reader's attention to the developmental potentialities enabled by a posthuman approach to learning. Like Radman, she turns to Deleuze's Spinoza, and to Massumi's interpretation of this, to help think the nonhuman forces at work in learning. Her chapter discusses the use of sensory data in current learning sciences, and explores the ways this might be folded into an 'amorous' learning encounter that intensifies the enjoyment of the heterogeneity of life. De Freitas sees this as an attempt to rethink the refrain 'love of learning' in a way that seeks the inorganic potentialities of the nonhuman forces by which a body can 'branch out into territories beyond its own self-maintenance'.[18] The aim of her chapter is to show how Spinoza's ontology, coupled with Simondon's account of 'thought networks', can be mobilised to rethink and reclaim active learning in the context of today's data industries. The industries generate excessive amounts of sensory information applied in education research through the massive proliferation of micro-digital body sensors. According to de Freitas, posthumanism helps us theorise this data in new ways. Rather than conceive biodata as that which belongs to the individuated and well-bounded body, and likely pathologises it, we can begin to imagine this surplus sensory data as that which circumvents consciousness and plugs into the textured richness of a 'more-than-human' thought, as evidence of a love of learning that is postphenomenological.

Concepts of processual expansion and the affective development of agentic capabilities are likewise taken up for discussion in following chapters on the topics of temporality and posthuman agency. Indeed, these topics raise urgent questions regarding progress, human experience and responsibility in 'the time of the now', while also querying the possibility and desirability of conceiving posthumanist and nonanthropocentric notions of time and temporality. How, for example, might we respond sanely to the contemporary posthuman situation of instantaneous and proliferating information overload driving cognitive capitalism, without reinforcing accelerationism by normalising presumptions of Anthropocene apocalypse as a symptom and effect of 'catastrophic time'?[19] Is it possible to hold fast to modern notions of progressive politics, while also abandoning conceptualisations of linear temporality in favour of a notion of history as multiple and simultaneous, ambivalent, fragmented, ephemeral, discontinuous and dissonant, registering the posthuman reality that diverse entities live diverse histories that travel incompossible lines of time? What happens to chrononormativity and chronobiopolitics when bodies are augmented for alternative reproductive capabilities? How do some Indigenous and non-European models of time and temporalisation resist the 'homogenous empty time' of universal History to affirm the ways in which experiences of time and history are shaped by places, and what happens to such experiences of temporal existence when ancestral places are destroyed by colonial histories of devastation?[20]

In chapter 6, James Williams connects Deleuze's philosophy of time to an opposition between two recent ways of taking up his philosophy over the question of posthumanism. He argues that one way, described by Rosi Braidotti, adopts Deleuze's philosophy as a starting point for an exploration of a posthuman future, which leads to posthumanism in the humanities. By contrast, the other way—developed by A. W. Moore—develops a sympathetic interpretation of Deleuze's work, but then departs from it critically around the idea of the need for philosophy to be anthropocentric. Williams shows how Deleuze's philosophy of time supports Braidotti's posthumanist approach, and he sheds light on the forms posthumanism might take. For Williams, Deleuze's philosophy of time provides a set of rejoinders to Moore and to his strong defence of anthropocentrism in thought and experience.

Chapter 7 by Sean Bowden takes as its focus the temporal structure of action and agential responsibility, conceived in the light of a posthumanist sensibility. With reference to Deleuze's work on the 'third synthesis of time' in *Difference and Repetition*, Bowden investigates what it means to be an agent of an action when, as agents, we are lodged in a 'caesura' between past and future, and when our actions, in their very temporal structure, outstrip what we intend and can foresee? He answers this question by elaborating an 'expressive' account of agency that is very different to the Hegelian one. Bowden draws not only on resources found in Deleuze's oeuvre, but also in the work of Hölderlin, who is identified as an important reference in Deleuze's exposition of the third synthesis of time. Hölderlin sketches an account of thought and agency that does not depend on the ideal or achievement of an agent's full self-understanding of what is expressed in their activity, as it does in Hegel, and that is capable of bearing the 'momentarily incomplete' without denying the very notion of agential responsibility. Bowden expands conceptual resources evident in Deleuze's work on time and temporalisation, which he uses to extend Hölderlin's account and provide a conception of agency appropriate to the posthuman condition.

Chapter 8, by Suzanne McCullagh, also investigates genetic conditions of emergence underlying the capacity to act, but her chapter is located more firmly in the context of the political sphere. She develops the concept of heterogeneous political space for the purpose of better conceptualising the systemic political requirements, and agentic capacities, of nonhumans. Bringing Hannah Arendt's humanist political philosophy of the pluralist public sphere into contact with Deleuze and Guattari's notions of heterogeneous assemblage, McCullagh advances posthumanist modes of thinking about collective action and justice. Heterogeneous political spaces are constituted by compositions of material, affect and desire, features which are obscured by humanist and individualist theories of action. Traditional theories of collective action provide accounts of a macro-political order made up of unified rational subjects with clear intentions and commitments, whereas Deleuze and Guattari's concepts of 'assembling' and 'becoming' describe a micro-political register composed of heterogeneous collectivities in complex processes of composition and co-emergence. In their insistence that human action cannot be separated from the productions of nature, we find that heterogeneity, rather than human plurality, is given as a condition of action. More explicitly, human-nonhuman assemblages form the genetic conditions for action. All capabilities for action can thus be seen as emerging from constellations where humans are assembled with material and incorporeal elements (plant, animal, mineral, technological bodies and statements, utterances, expressions, affects, moods, gestures, and so forth). The breakdown of human exclusivity in constructions of political subjectivity allows us to register nonhuman forms of influence and activity. This shift not only places humans within a system of nature but also brings nonhumans into focus as relevant 'subjects' of ethics and politics. The concept of heterogeneous political space therefore helps us to 'renaturalise' justice.

The following chapter 9, by Simone Bignall and Daryle Rigney, also contends with the notion of a heterogeneous political space potentially opened up by posthumanist frameworks. Their starting point is the problematic legacy of colonialist systems on philosophical thinking after the Enlightenment, which bears also upon the contemporary development of Continental posthumanism. As an Indigenous political sociologist and a non-Indigenous philosopher, Rigney and Bignall bring together Indigenous conceptualisations of 'more-than-human' being with notions of 'posthumanity' arising in

Continental philosophy. They argue that some posthumanist theory, like most European philosophy, risks the elision of Indigenous cultural and intellectual authority by remaining blind to the ancient presence and contemporary force of Indigenous philosophies of human being, which are typically materialist, naturalist and expressivist. This exclusion allows Continental European philosophy to claim the 'new Humanities' as its current 'discovery' after modern humanism, but this apparently 'new' intellectual frontier in fact traces an ancient philosophical terrain already occupied by Indigenous epistemologies and associated modes of human experience. Insofar as posthumanism has emerged strongly influenced by the philosophy of Deleuze and Guattari, the authors enquire about the role of their philosophy in the continuing elision of Indigenous ontologies in the emerging posthumanities. They argue that the potential usefulness of Deleuzian 'nomadic thought' is by no means unambiguous when viewed from a postcolonial perspective. It may indeed have multiple potentialities: some appear colonialist in effect, others decolonising in outcome; for this reason it is necessary to interrogate the intersection that Deleuze forges between indigeneity, nomadology and the creative exercise of thought. Bignall and Rigney ultimately affirm how contemporary renditions of Deleuze's philosophical nomadology, notably by Rosi Braidotti, are engaged in advancing a non-imperial posthumanism.

Chapter 10 continues a posthumanist focus on political systems. Thomas Nail uses elements of a Deleuzian framework to explain how the most defining feature of any system is its movement. In contrast to essences, forms and structures—which are defined by stasis, immutability and fixity—systems are defined by their flux, mobility and circulation. Accordingly, a system is not just an assembly of heterogeneous elements, but a kinetic pattern or regime of circulation through which elements are continuously reproduced and transformed. For Nail, there are numerous strengths and implications of shifting our understanding of politics from one of anthropocentric forms and cultural structures to one of material kinetic systems. If political systems are defined and distinguished not by their anthropocentric and ideological content (authoritarianism, liberalism, Marxism, and so on) but more fundamentally by their patterns of motion, then political theory ought to provide a much closer analysis of the nonhuman material and kinetic systems within which ideology itself emerges. Nail's chapter analyses the mobile nature of borders to illuminate how posthumanist perspectives help us to think responsively about the contemporary politics of migration.

In chapter 11, Gregory Flaxman takes up Deleuze's essay on 'Control Societies' to consider the vexed relationship between Deleuze's views on political economy and his occasional, more hopeful, suggestions regarding political ecology associated with a vitalist or affirmative ethics. As Deleuze foresaw, contemporary societies have undergone a rapid and radical transformation: over the last twenty years, the institutions of disciplinarity—the structures of the welfare state—have increasingly given way to an age of 'control'. Flaxman's chapter lays out the problem that this regime entails: while it introduces a smooth, digitised and altogether posthuman regime, control also describes a digital economy that capitalises on 'freedom' because it optimalises choice, but only in order to track our movements, manipulate our desires, feed our addictions, and invent a supple new system of domination. This diagnosis forms the basis for the two elements of Flaxman's argument. The first is that control, as Deleuze characterises it, ought to be read in tandem with Foucault's *Birth of Biopolitics*; control is rooted in the posthumanist constituents of neoliberalism. But second, Deleuze's analysis of 'control' must be read literally as a 'postscript' signalling what Deleuze left unsaid, at the point where he broke off the analysis at the end of his own book on *Foucault*. For Flaxman, Deleuze's thinking regarding a political economy of control is at once a counterpoint to, and the formative impetus for, that which Deleuze calls 'life'.

Like Flaxman's contribution, the chapter by Jon Roffe is focussed at the nexus of political and economic processes in posthumanist systems. Following Bataille's famous analysis in *The Accursed Share*, Roffe explains that any attempt to define a discrete set of activities and processes as the economic sphere confronts a problem of delimitation. Since all activity involves loss, gain and circulation, restricting the definition of economics to commercial activity indexed to a currency is illegitimate. At the limit, then, the category of the economic tends to absorb the entirety of reality. In the work of Gilles Deleuze, Roffe finds two solutions to this problem. In *Difference and Repetition*, the economic names only the virtual facet of society, which is actualised in turn concrete (extra-economic) social relations. Consequently, 'there are only economic social problems',[21] and society is the creative and contingent response to these problems. However, in both *Anti-Oedipus* and *A Thousand Plateaus*, Deleuze and Guattari instead claim that only specific forms of society possess an economy. In this second model, the economic names a particular form of social organisation structured around infinite debt. In this way, it belongs to social-production and the plane of organisation rather than to desiring-production and the plane of consistency which are infraeconomic. In this sense, the account in the volumes of *Capitalism and Schizophrenia* advances an implicit rejection of Bataille's position, given that the capitalist economy functions to deal with the troubling excess he identifies, by taking it as fuel. Roffe's chapter elaborates on these differing accounts of what constitutes the economy. He finally proposes a certain syntheses of the two in relation to capitalism, on the basis of the concept of price. Prices, Roffe suggests, are the intensive features of social organisation that problematise existing regimes of evaluation.

Shifting our attention to the realm of law, Edward Mussawir points out in chapter 13 that Deleuze's work is sometimes acknowledged for its affinity both for certain kinds of animals or 'becomings-animal' as well as for jurisprudence as a mode of thought in relation to law. Mussawir's contribution explores the close connection that Deleuze's 'casuistic' conception of jurisprudence has with the method and technique of the classical Roman jurists. Mussawir attends especially to the appearance of the animal (the bees) in a fragment concerning liability under the *lex Aquilia*. A rather atypical and awkwardly phrased 'case', the example of the bees in Ulpian's text reveals how the animal can occupy a remarkable centrality in the thought of law: not so much as metaphor but as jurisprudential 'diagram' capable of refining and extending juridical institutions. Offering a conception of law that can, in Deleuze's words, 'do without any subject of rights',[22] Mussawir explains how the casuistry of Roman law provides some unexpected avenues into the contemporary projects of antihumanism and nonanthropocentrism in law.

It seems appropriate that our final focus is trained upon the Earth processes that shape and define interactional ecologies to produce new forms of emergence. These complex relational geo-systems comprise not only life forces, but also the influences of nonliving materials: minerals, metals, acids, complex polymers and so forth. In chapter 14 by Myra Hird and Kathryn Yusoff, we learn how microbes have newly begun to digest toxic waste at the Berkeley Pit, a dump site filled with acidic and metal-laden toxic waste from copper mining in Butte, Montana. The artificial lake that is a mile wide and a mile-and-a-half long is breeding a new form of life that has scientists bioprospecting for unusual bacteria to fulfil evermore intricate forms of inhuman labour, from antivirals to anticancer drugs. Among the new forms of life, one bacterial agent—found only in the rectum of geese—has the ability to digest metal waste. This bacteria had evidently found its way into the pit after the mass die off of migrating snow geese stumbled into the toxic lake, impacting its ecology. This chapter maps out the multidirectional and nonhuman trajectories of the interstratum of life and nonlife. Attending to insistent and opportunistic bacterial innovation and the emerging science of mineralogical evolution, the chapter argues for a form of mineral-microbial heterogenesis; an interlocking stratum that has consequences for thinking the multipersectival dimensions of becoming across geologic and biologic strata in post-Anthropocene worlds.

Taken together, the contributions to this volume advance our understanding of the new transdisciplinary knowledge systems emerging today, as traditional academic disciplines transform and blend to accommodate and reflect posthuman paradigms. The change of focus is both thematic and methodological, traversing concepts of geology, biology, power, law, economy, technology, learning, animality, communality and creativity. The chapters describe for us core elements of, or possibilities for, posthuman life and alternative ways of producing knowledge. The posthuman convergence rests upon and coproduces a vital materialist method that is illustrated throughout this volume. It approaches differences as modulations within a common matter, linked in a relational political economy that is framed by relations of power as both restrictive and empowering. This is no 'flat ontology', but rather embedded and embodied material perspectivism at work in addressing real-life issues.

Viewing these emergent knowledge formations as Deleuzian 'systems', whose processes are complex, relational, nonlinear, heterogeneous and heterogenetic, enables a clearer vision of the 'three ecologies'—environmental, socioeconomic and subjective—of the posthuman condition. This is at once a planetary consequence of the era of the Anthropocene, and a culturally and biologically differential experience, inflected by diverse materialities and vitalities. In turn, the understanding thus generated enables an ethological understanding of how knowledge may be put to use towards an affirmative posthumanist ethics that responds to trenchant inequalities, exacerbated now by cognitive capitalism. And this achievement, for us, refocuses the true purpose of knowledge: not to control, nor merely to describe the world; but to transform it for the betterment of all.

NOTES

1. Bonta and Protevi 2004.
2. For example, Grosz 2011; Povinelli 2016; Barad 2007; Haraway 2016.
3. For example, Harding 1991; Haraway 1988; Braidotti 1994.
4. See, for example, Cajete 2000; Simpson 2011; Bentarrak, Muecke and Roe 2014; Bignall, Hemming and Rigney 2016; Viveiros de Castro 2017. On the potential of the posthumanities for enhanced receptivity to historically marginalised knowledges (and subjects of knowledge), see Braidotti 2018 and 2016.
5. This project has been advanced by Rosi Braidotti over several decades. See, for example, Braidotti 1994 and 2013.
6. Grosz 2011; see also her interview in Grosz, Yusoff and Clark 2017.
7. Foucault 1995, 2008; see also Deleuze 1988, 1995.
8. Chakrabarty 2017, 25. See Birch 2018 for a discussion of the intellectual resources—scientific and philosophical—that Indigenous custodians of knowledge offer for working towards environmental and social resilience in the face of climate change.
9. Braidotti 2018.
10. Deleuze 2007, 365.
11. Braidotti 2018, 8.
12. See Barad 2007 (forerunning her many other recent writings on this topic).

13. Deleuze 2004.

14. Deleuze 2007, 177.

15. See Deleuze and Guattari's (1994) references to 'overflight' and the concept as existing 'in a state of survey [survol] in relation to its components' on page 20 and the closing pages of *What Is Philosophy?*

16. Deleuze and Guattari 1987, 361–62.

17. Guattari 2000.

18. Colebrook 2014, 138.

19. Colebrook 2017.

20. Barad 2017; for an Indigenous account of temporality see, for example, Deloria 1972.

21. Deleuze 1994, 186.

22. Deleuze 2007, 354.

REFERENCES

Barad, K. (2007). *Meeting the Universe Halfway: Quantum Physics and the Entanglement of Matter and Meaning.* Durham, NC: Duke University Press.

Barad, K. (2017). 'Troubling Time/s and Ecologies of Nothingness: Re-Turning, Re-Membering, and Facing the Incalculable', *New Formations* 92, 56–86.

Bentarrak, K. Muecke, S., and Roe, P. (2014). *Reading the Country: Introduction to Nomadology.* Melbourne: Re.Press.

Bignall, S., Hemming, S., and Rigney, D. (2016). 'Three Ecosophies for the Anthropocene: Environmental Governance, Continental Posthumanism, and Indigenous Expressivism', *Deleuze Studies* 10(4), 455–78.

Birch, T. (2018). '"On What Terms Can We Speak?": Refusal, Resurgence and Climate Justice', *Coolabah* 24 & 25, 2–16.

Bonta, M., and Protevi, J. (2004). *Deleuze and Geophilosophy: A Guide and Glossary.* Edinburgh: Edinburgh University Press.

Braidotti, R. (1994). *Nomadic Subjects: Embodiment and Sexual Difference in Contemporary Feminist Theory.* New York: Columbia University Press.

Braidotti, R. (2013). *The Posthuman.* Cambridge: Polity Press.

Braidotti, R. (2016). 'The Contested Posthumanities'. In *Contesting Humanities*, R. Braidotti and P. Gilroy, eds. London: Bloomsbury.

Braidotti, R. (2018). 'A Theoretical Framework for the Critical Posthumanities', *Theory, Culture and Society*, 1–31.

Cajete, G. (2000). *Native Science: Natural Laws of Interdependence.* New York: Clear Light.

Chakrabarty, D. (2017). 'The Politics of Climate Change Is More Than the Politics of Capitalism', *Theory, Culture and Society* 34(2–3), 25–37.

Colebrook, C. (2014). *The Death of the Posthuman: Essays on Extinction, Volume I.* Ann Arbor, MI: Open Humanities Press.

Colebrook, C. (2017). 'Anti-Catastrophic Time', *New Formations* 92, 102–19.

Deleuze, G. (1988). *Foucault*. Translated by Séan Hand. Minneapolis: University of Minnesota Press.

Deleuze, G. (1994). *Difference and Repetition*. Translated by Paul Patton. London: Athlone.

Deleuze, G. (1995). 'Postscript on Control Societies' in *Negotiations, 1972–1990*. Translated by Martin Joughin. New York: Columbia University Press.

Deleuze, G. (2004). 'The Method of Dramatisation' in *Desert Islands and Other Texts 1953–1974*, D. Lapoujade, ed.; Translated by M. Taormina. New York: Semiotext(e).

Deleuze, G. (2007). *Two Regimes of Madness: Texts and Interviews 1975–1995*, ed. David Lapoujade, Translated by Ames Hodhges and Mike Taormina. New York: Semiotext(e).

Deleuze, G., and Guattari, F. (1994). *What Is Philosophy?* Translated by G. Burchell and H. Tomlinson. London: Verso.

Deleuze, G., and Guattari, F. (1987). *A Thousand Plateaus*. Translated by Brian Massumi. Minneapolis: University of Minnesota Press.

Deloria, V. (1972). *God is Red: A Native View of Religion*. Golden, CO: Fulcrum.

Foucault, M. (1995). *Discipline and Punish: The Birth of the Prison*. Translated by Alan Sheridan. New York: Vintage Books.

Foucault, M. (2008). *The Birth of Biopolitics: Lectures at the Collège de France, 1978–1979*. Translated by Graham Burchell. New York: Palgrave Macmillan.

Grosz, E. (2011). *Becoming Undone: Darwinian reflections on Life, Politics and Art.* Durham, NC: Duke University Press.

Grosz, E., Yusoff, K., and Clark, N. (2017). 'An Interview with Elizabeth Grosz: Geopower, Inhumanism and the Biopolitical', *Theory, Culture and Society*, 34(2–3), 129–46.

Guattari, F. (2000) *The Three Ecologies*. London: Athlone.

Haraway, D. (1988). 'Situated Knowledges: The Science Question in Feminism and the Privilege of Partial Perspective', *Feminist Studies* 14(3), 575–99.

Haraway, D. (2016). *Staying with the Trouble: Making Kin in the Chthulucene*. Durham, NC: Duke University Press.

Harding, S. (1991). *Whose Science? Whose Knowledge?* Ithaca, NY: Cornell University Press.

Povinelli, E. (2016). *Geontologies: A Requiem to Late Liberalism*. Durham, NC: Duke University Press.

Simpson, L. (2011). *Dancing on Our Turtle's Back. Stories of Nishnaabeg Re-Creation, Resurgence, and a New Emergence*. Winnipeg: ARP Books.

Viveiros de Castro, E. (2017). *Cannibal Metaphysics*. Minneapolis: University of Minnesota Press.

Chapter 2

Deleuze and Diffraction[1]

Iris van der Tuin

In my recent philosophical writings I have been making use of the method-ology of 'diffractive reading' so as to prevent the dialectic from slipping into my work. The dialectic 'reduces philosophy to interminable discussion'.[2] After all, Henri Bergson, whom Gilles Deleuze and Félix Guattari cite in *What Is Philosophy?* in relation to 'the nature of philosophical problems',[3] stated in *Introduction to Metaphysics* that:

> divergences are striking between the schools, that is to say, in short, between the groups of disciples formed around certain of the great masters. But would one find them as clear-cut between the masters themselves? Something here dominates the diversity of systems, something, I repeat, simple and definite like a sounding of which one feels that it has more or less reached the bottom of a same ocean, even though it brings each time to the surface very different materials. It is on these materials that disciples normally work: in that is the role of analysis. And the master, in so far as he formulates, develops, translates into abstract ideas what he brings, is already, as it were, his own disciple. But *the simple act which has set analysis in motion and which hides behind analysis, emanates from a faculty quite different from that of analyzing.*[4]

Bergson's intuitive method is meant to reach 'the whole of experience (*l'expérience intégrale*)'.[5] I argue that diffractive reading is connected precisely to the methodological issue of intuition-reaching-the-whole-of-experience, and indeed the term diffraction is to be found in the work of Bergson. As I write in the volume *Bergson and the Art of Immanence: Painting, Photography, Film*: 'Distinguishing acting freely from automaton-mode, Bergson hints at interference patterns or 'diffraction' as a tool to think with',[6] precisely because experiencing one's deepest self implies '[a] disturb[ance of] my whole consciousness like a stone which falls into the water of a pond'.[7] This stone produces a series of waves circling into infinity. In addition, diffractive reading can be said to be exemplary for the new humanities both in terms of how the philosophical canon is dealt with (i.e., transversally) and how the humanities and the sciences are traversed in the same stroke. Diffraction, and diffractive reading in particular, play a central role in transversal methodology. This method derives from classical *and* quantum physics and partakes in a discussion about the fact that the quantum physical notion of diffraction can explain the classical one, whereas classical physics cannot explain the quantum definition because—and this is very Bergsonian—parts cannot be used to reconstruct or understand the whole.

'Diffraction' features in Deleuze's philosophy and in Deleuzian scholarship. Arkady Plotnitsky has commented on this in terms of the conceptual engagement created by the crossover of quantum physical phenomena, (feminist) quantum physical conceptual tools, and a most general understanding of process-philosophies of becoming.[8] Plotnitsky has also demonstrated that diffraction features in Deleuze and Guattari's *What Is Philosophy?* when they argue that '[c]oncepts are like multiple waves, rising and falling, but the plane of immanence is the single wave that rolls them up and unrolls them'.[9] However, so far this peculiarity hasn't been studied or evaluated in *methodological* terms: what does diffraction do in, or for, Deleuze scholarship? Diffraction has made a methodological appearance in the Deleuze field: Leonard Lawlor has put to use *Foucault*'s 'points of diffraction'—formulated in the latter's *The Archaeology of Knowledge*.[10] One of his former students, Valentine Moulard-Leonard, has done the same in her monograph *Bergson-Deleuze Encounters: Transcendental Experience and the Thought of the Virtual*. Through a critical reading of Moulard-Leonard's work, this chapter asks whether the potentialities of diffraction, in particular reading diffractively, are sufficiently utilised in Deleuze Studies, given that the methodology is so successfully employed in the field of Gender Studies at the moment.[11] I argue that whereas Moulard-Leonard's engagement with diffraction through Deleuze and Guattari's concept of *interference* is not in line with the methodological implementation of the Foucaultian notion, it is nonetheless possible to remedy this situation. This becomes clear in the feminist implementation and conceptualisation of diffraction, where we find Deleuze's *Foucault* next to Foucault's *Archaeology of Knowledge*.

THE POINT OF DIFFRACTION AS Y-CROSSING DIVERGENCE?

This chapter is less interested in Moulard-Leonard's (or Lawlor's, for that matter) own contribution to philosophical debates than in the way in which she journeys through the oeuvres of Bergson and Deleuze. I am interested in what the mode of their encounter—to use Moulard-Leonard's own term—is able to actualise. *What can an encounter be* given the specific utilisation of 'points of diffraction' in play?

Diffraction appears first on page 5 of *Bergson-Deleuze Encounters* and always without a footnote. Although diffraction is never defined, the argumentative line with which the term is entangled demonstrates that diffraction must have something to do with a Y-crossing divergence: a parting of ways. Moulard-Leonard argues that Deleuze's reading of Proust's *A la recherche du temps perdu* introduces this forking (and whereas the differences and similarities between Proust and Bergson are well documented,[12] these are not footnoted by Moulard-Leonard either). Indeed, on page 7 we find the term 'point of indiscernibility', contrasted on the next page with 'point of diffraction'. The argument is that transcendental, virtual or superior empiricism can be found in the work of *both* Bergson and Deleuze,[13] *whereas* in the work of Deleuze

> the pre–World War II humanist hope for progress still held by Bergson is replaced with the postwar vision of a world reduced to chaos and crumbs. The whole has been shattered, the human has been demoted from its pedestal, and the only junction between the human and the world now lies in their shared positive fragmentation. But for Deleuze, this transcendental experience is also the experience of becoming, because it coincides with experimentation *as* the very force of time (and not only its effects): the empirical cycles of creation and destruction are shown to be conditioned by deeper, 'machinic' processes governed by a necessary absence of unity. And of course we must keep in mind that for Deleuze this fundamental fragmentation of the world, the self, and time also coincides with the future, with the untimely event of A life.[14]

The methodological aspect of this quote reveals quite a lot about Moulard-Leonard's conceptualisation of diffraction. We see that whereas Moulard-Leonard makes a distinction between unity (Bergson) and fragmentation (Deleuze), this dualism immediately proves to be uncontainable: '*But for Deleuze* … ' Deleuze demonstrates that unity and fragmentation are *both* effects of machinic processes. As confirmed by the author herself on page 9, the dualism is pushed to the extreme, which is precisely an instantiation of Bergson's methodological formula from *Matter and Memory*: dualisms (unreal oppositions) are dealt with correctly—that is, metaphysically—when pushed to an extreme.[15] We see this too when, somewhat later in the book, Moulard-Leonard focusses on Deleuze's cinema books in her attempt to locate the presupposed point of diffraction—Y-crossing divergence—that causes Deleuze to depart from Bergson. Here, Moulard-Leonard tries to argue that Bergson has stayed with the movement-image while Deleuze has advanced to the time-image,[16] whereas it immediately becomes clear that this situation of moving from a representational logic of recognition to the direct presentation of time *without a standpoint* has an excess that is likely to stem from the optical analogy that is employed here. In line with diffraction as such—and this is not taken up by Moulard-Leonard—the representational logic of recognition (in other words: classical physics) can be understood by the direct presentation of time, whereas the reverse relation does not hold. Representational logics (for instance logics of reflection) start from parts and will never reach the whole, whereas the time-image *is* the whole. Once we have established this point we are directed by Moulard-Leonard to the famous concluding section of *Cinema 2: The Time-Image*: 'It is at the level of the *interference* of many practices that things happen, beings, images, concepts, all the kinds of events'.[17] This interference can be read productively along the lines of the three interferences that are distinguished in the conclusion of *What Is Philosophy?*, namely: extrinsic, intrinsic, and nonlocalisable interferences.[18] It appears that Deleuze at this point favours intrinsic interference, given that he states at the end of *Cinema 2*: '*no* technical determination, whether *applied* (psychoanalysis, linguistics) or *reflexive*, is sufficient to constitute the concepts of cinema itself'.[19] Here we see a leaping into philosophy of cinema, as a kind of intrinsic interference.

My question is, therefore, whether Moulard-Leonard has *reduced* the possibilities enabled by the Bergson-Deleuze encounter. I am left with many questions when differentiations are made between Bergson and Deleuze, and hope to respond to some with my meditation on diffraction in this chapter. First, Moulard-Leonard's conclusion seems to be that Bergson ultimately uses the intellect to open to intuition, which implies the wrong—the impossible—part-to-whole relation. But when she states that 'Bergson remains committed to an otherwise conventional conception of truth as the *stable—* though not immutable—*accord with reality*',[20] I ask whether this is not what I will call, in the following text, a performative correspondence, along the lines of the immanent interference patterns mentioned earlier? In line with this, when Moulard-Leonard argues that 'Bergson has opened up avenues for what one may call, following Gregg Lambert's insight, Deleuze's non-philosophy',[21] yet that he did not manage to reach 'the spark that provides the reason for the continual yet fortuitous genesis of a thought that must not be equated with knowledge or representation',[22] what is again eclipsed is something that *also*, nonetheless, appears in Moulard-Leonard's book. This is the relation between Bergson and Deleuze as a 'creative involution',[23] on the one hand, and, on the other, the very positive claim—well-phrased in the light of the current trending of Object Oriented Ontology—that 'Bergson shows that the intelligence's negative activity must be negative of something, and that this something we must grasp [*intuit*] in some sense in order to delimit it in the first place'.[24] Intelligence's dis-identification with intuition—the fact that *even intelligence* experiences the whole before it starts analysing—implies that Moulard-Leonard's conclusions cannot be sustained. Indeed, '[t]o regress is to move in the direction of something less differentiated. But to involve is to form a block that runs its own line "between" the terms in play and beneath assignable relations'.[25] This chapter discusses this 'between' or 'beneath', with respect to the method of diffraction.

Let me therefore end this part of the chapter by claiming that Moulard-Leonard's search for 'the man Henri Bergson'[26] is futile; and whereas a solution might have led to the why and how of Bergson's thought, it would certainly not have provided insight to its event. Attending especially both to the conclusion of *What Is Philosophy?* and to Deleuze's early and later Bergson-texts, Lambert provides further clues about the nature of Deleuzian interferences:

> [I]t is the brain that thinks, not man. A brain is not in your head, any more than it is in the next thought, or the next perception, association, or memory; it is all of these at once and more. What is more is the plane on which all of these take place at once, as if simultaneously, even though this plane never appears as an object of representation, that is to say, does not refer to any external point of view. Thus, the brain is not opposed to the world, but rather the world is composed of a special type of brain-matter ... each time new images are created, like new circuits in the brain, they also first become possible in a world, enlarging our sense of reality.[27]

This point is important because whereas Deleuze and Guattari argue that it is 'chaos into which the brain plunges',[28] they also formulate specific modes of interference.

DELEUZE AND GUATTARI'S THREE INTERFERENCES

As indicated, Plotnitsky has written about interference as a concept from physics, which enters the philosophy of Deleuze, and of Deleuze and Guattari. Plotnitsky argues that we must make a distinction between the way in which 'resonance' features in the early work of Deleuze in *Difference and Repetition* and *The Logic of Sense*, and how 'interference' characterises the work of Deleuze and Guattari from *Anti-Oedipus* onwards.[29] Resonance comes from classical physics and therefore deals with predetermined and predeterminable entities even as it differentiates waves—obstruction or amplification—from particles. Interference comes from quantum physics and whereas it includes resonance as an actualisation, its workings are not exhaustively classifiable as either–or situations: the co-production of entirely new waves, and the wave-like behaviour of *single* particles, must each be taken into account here. Nevertheless, resonance is both object (there can be 'extrinsic interference between philosophy and science [physics]')[30] and concept (this would then be 'an interference that leaves the resulting concept within a given field, in this case, philosophy');[31] for instance, the artistic production of a sensation based on engagement with a philosophical text. The interference is *extrinsic*; it is a *resonance* between two entities related externally. When it comes to the other two kinds of interference—intrinsic and nonlocalisable—we instead observe how '[c]oncepts are like multiple waves, rising and falling, but the plane of immanence is the single wave that rolls them up and unrolls them'.[32] Plotnitsky argues especially that nonlocalisable interferences take on a quantum-physical reality, and we can therefore mention—next to 'THE plane of immanence' of Spinoza—'the ultimate nature of quantum objects, such as electrons and photons, [which] must be thought and yet cannot be thought by quantum theory' as exemplary nonlocalisable interferences.[33] Intrinsic interference, however, would involve a sliding of art into philosophy, a sliding of science into philosophy, and so on.[34] Another example of a nonlocalisable interference given by Plotnitsky affirms that 'Heisenberg's and Bohr's unthinkable quantum objects are nonlocalisable interferences which are themselves quantum-like as we can no longer describe, or even conceive of, the ultimate nature of quantum objects, even though we must still work with these inconceivable objects which must be thought and cannot be thought'.[35]

Whereas this may seem to be a detour, Plotnitsky's work is important for the argument that I wish to make about methodology as he uses the three interferences as a yardstick in order to make diagnostic statements about phases in the work of Deleuze (and Guattari). A definition of diffractive reading from Barad's *Meeting the Universe Halfway: Quantum Physics and the Entanglement of Matter and Meaning* reads as follows: 'Diffractively reading Bohr's and Butler's insights through one another for the patterns of resonance and dissonance they coproduce usefully illuminates the questions at hand'.[36] What we see here is description of a more or less conscious act (of reading) on the part of Barad, who disrupts the terms of extrinsic interference in order to describe a sliding of feminist theory into philosophy of science, and vice versa. In other words, what she formulates is an intrinsic interference. Another example comes from the article 'Posthumanist Performativity: Toward an Understanding of How Matter Comes to Matter' in which Barad famously formulates diffractive reading for the first time:

> Diffractively reading the insights of feminist and queer theory and science studies approaches through one another entails thinking the 'social' and the 'scientific' together in an illuminating way. What often appears as separate

entities (and separate sets of concerns) with sharp edges does not actually entail a relation of absolute exteriority at all. Like the diffraction patterns illuminating the indefinite nature of boundaries—displaying shadows in 'light' regions and bright spots in 'dark' regions—the relation of the social and the scientific is a relation of 'exteriority within.' This is not a static relationality but a doing—the enactment of boundaries—that always entails constitutive exclusions and therefore requisite questions of accountability.[37]

We see here that even the element of exclusion taken on by Barad hints at nonlocalisable interference! What I wish to do now is follow in Plotnitsky's footsteps and discuss the 'point of diffraction' in Foucault's *Archaeology of Knowledge*. Following the analysis of Moulard-Leonard's work, we have seen that the concept needs work in order to reach something like the notion of interference that we find in *What Is Philosophy?* Barad's reading of Foucault's *Archaeology* next to Deleuze's *Foucault* is key to this operation of specification.

FOUCAULT'S POINT OF DIFFRACTION AND THE SPECULATIVE DIMENSION

The two scholars who have put the so-called diffractive reading methodology on the agenda of feminist scholarship—Donna Haraway and Karen Barad—each have an ambiguous relationship with the philosophies of Foucault and Deleuze (and Guattari).[38] However, Barad refers to both Deleuze's *Foucault* and Foucault's *Archaeology of Knowledge* in her seminal monograph *Meeting the Universe Halfway*. In fact, quotes from both books are used as epigraphs to a section dealing with juridical and epistemological individualism, and the related issue of the gap between epistemology and ontology. Barad writes:

> [R]epresentationalism is the belief in the ontological distinction between representations and that which they purport to represent; in particular, that which is represented is held to be independent of all practices of representing.[39]

She specifies that the assumption of objectivity in the mediating function of a representation—whether a legal, scientific, or literary text—does not solve but rather continues the trend of ontologically separating word and world by having subjects begin and end at the surface of the skin, which becomes impermeable. Distinguishing representationalism from practices of representing makes clear that some work on representation is done in unawareness of the assumed gap, and therefore cannot study how 'the represented' participates in the entangled, material-semiotic or material-discursive process of its own representation. Foucault's *Archaeology* is referenced in this context for its problematisation of 'discourses as groups of signs', and Deleuze's *Foucault* is noted for its 'rais[ing of words and sight] to a higher exercise that is *a priori*'. The Foucault reference is especially important for our purposes, because it is precisely *The Archaeology*'s notion of diffraction that has been introduced to Deleuze scholarship. However, the way in which this has been done by Lawlor and by Moulard-Leonard is not in line with Barad's (and Haraway's) methodological innovation. Furthermore, Foucault's own concept can advance the feminist new materialist implementation, but only provided that we read it with a focus on Deleuze's rewriting of the concept in his book on Foucault.

Let us first look at the way in which Foucault conceptualises and implements diffraction. Barad quotes Foucault:

> 'Words and things' is the entirely serious title of a problem; it is the ironic title of a work that modifies its own form, displaces its own data, and reveals, at the end of the day, a quite different task. A task that consists of not—of no longer—treating discourses as groups of signs (signifying elements referring to contents or representations) but as practices that systematically form the objects of which they speak. Of course, discourses are composed of signs; but what they do is more than use these signs to designate things. It is this *more* that renders them irreducible to the language (*langue*) and to speech. It is this 'more' that we must reveal and describe.[40]

Journeying towards the development of a methodology for revealing and describing this 'more', Foucault's chapter on 'The Formation of Strategies' places objects in conjunction with concepts and enunciative types, which are all formed by discourses-as-practices and together they form theories or themes (such as linguistic kinship in nineteenth-century philology and species evolution in biology a century earlier). Foucault is interested in designing the study of discursive formations multidimensionally and he argues that the starting point could be to '[d]etermine the possible *points of diffraction* of discourse'.[41] At first sight, this study seems to continue the trend of Foucault's predecessors/teachers Gaston Bachelard and Georges Canguilhem; that is, to argue for an epistemological history of the sciences. But this, as *The Archaeology* itself affirms, is only one of *four* types of history of science.[42] More specifically, with 'points of diffraction' we are talking about an analysis of points of incompatibility which turn out to designate points of equivalence (thus establishing the epistemological form of either–or logics) and indicate link points of systematisation:

> [O]n the basis of each of these equivalent, yet incompatible elements, a coherent series of objects, forms of statement, and concepts has been derived (with, in each series, possible new points of incompatibility) ... [which o]ne describes

… as a unity of distribution that opens a field of possible options, and enables various mutually exclusive architectures to appear side by side or in turn.[43]

The important point made here is underlined in the next section of Foucault's text, where he makes clear that the description of the process of branching-off has a *speculative dimension* while at the same time making clear that the analysis is—in spite of feminist critique[44]—thoroughly *materialist*. By using the term 'speculation' here, I want to indicate that not only does Foucault speak of an endless list of sheer points of diffraction, but he also identifies the task of analysis being to project imaginatively the 'field of possible options' alongside the specific architectures that 'appear', but whose sense as such relies upon their discrete differentiation from that field. In addition, we may want to argue that Foucault here approaches Deleuze's own method of 'transcendental empiricism', which then substantiates Barad's bringing together of the two philosophers. But let us first refine our reading of Foucault's 'points of diffraction', and make sure to come back to the latter observations later.

Gary Gutting makes the same analysis: the pairs of either–or 'represent forks within the discursive formation from which different theoretical turns *can* be taken, leading to very different theoretical developments'.[45] Whereas the rules of the discursive formation may afford some diffraction points, not all of these points may actualise owing to the work of certain 'authorities' (among them are the ones mentioned in the next quote, but also relations between discursive formations, an 'authority' I will deal with somewhat later in this chapter). In Foucault's terms:

> In any case, the analysis of this authority must show that neither the relation of discourse to desire, nor the processes of its appropriation, nor its role among non-discursive practices is extrinsic to its unity, its characterization, and the laws of its formation. *They are not disturbing elements* which, superposing themselves upon its pure, neutral, atemporal, silent form, suppress its true voice and emit in its place a travestied discourse, but, on the contrary, its *formative elements*.[46]

The material institutional analysis seems to be preceded by a speculation that is to be found in the considering of all possible options, while 'all the possible alternatives are not in fact realized: there are a good many partial groups, regional compatibilities, and coherent architectures that might have emerged, yet did not do so'.[47] The materialism is not founded upon a naïve realism (a representationalism?), which can be said to be the opposite of a speculative philosophy. In order to come to an understanding of the nature of this entanglement of material genealogy and speculation—especially since Deleuze, too, argues that 'the task of archaeology is double',[48]—I wish to suggest that the important feature of note is that the point of diffraction operates as a 'threshold' in *The Order of Things*:

> Perhaps knowledge succeeds in engendering knowledge, ideas in transforming themselves and actively modifying one another (but how?—historians have not yet enlightened us on this point); one thing, in any case, is certain: archaeology, addressing itself to the general space of knowledge, to its configurations, and to the mode of being of the things that appear in it, defines systems of simultaneity, as well as the series of mutations necessary and sufficient to circumscribe the threshold of a new positivity.[49]

In concrete terms, this 'threshold' is evident also in observations like: 'Possibly *Justine* and *Juliette* [of De Sade] are in the same position on the threshold of modern culture as that occupied by *Don Quixote* [of Cervantes] between the Renaissance and Classicism'.[50] The importance of this claim resides in the fact that other texts existed too and it *could have been other texts* that had leapt into the future! Having been trained in the specifically French tradition of historical epistemology, which suffered from a 'chronological empiricism' just like any naïve realism,[51] what we see Foucault do here is consistently argue for critical attention paid *both* to the realised (or, in fact, actualised; Foucault's word choice is suggestive for the careful Bergsonian) *and* to the possible (the virtual). These stand in a relation to one another that can best be explained with reference to Deleuze, who guides us to the closing section of *Archaeology of Knowledge*, even if the concept of 'threshold' was also formulated by Foucault's colleague Gilbert Simondon. Interesting also for our discussion of points of diffraction and diffractive reading in the Baradian sense is that Simondon's threshold-concept was informed by quantum physics, which field of expertise as we have seen has been influential for Barad's formulation of the diffractive method. In the words of Brian Massumi:

> Simondon's bitter critique of 'holism' in the 'Technical Mentality' essay applies to philosophies which replace the diversity of conditions from which an effect arises with the nondecomposability of the arising whole, annulling their diversity and attributing a foundational ontological priority to the whole rather than rightly placing it on the level of emergent effect. This is one example of one of the most original aspects of Simondon's thought: his endeavoring to always think discontinuity and continuity *together*… . This endeavor is encapsulated in his emphasis on the *quantum*, borrowing from physics. A quantum leap in physics is non-decomposable as a movement across a threshold. But its nondecomposability takes off from one set of diverse and decomposable conditions (a collection of particles in a particular configuration) and leads to another (a collection of particles in a changed configuration). The dynamic

wholeness of the quantum event (the all-or-nothingness of its occurrence) interposes itself between two diversities, whose discontinuity it marks by a change in level accompanied by a qualitative change in the defining properties of the system (a passage, for example, from one element of the periodic table to another). For Simondon, all transition, all change, all becoming, is quantum.[52]

Later we will see that Barad also shares these insights, and also Deleuze, evident especially when he discusses 'the whole and the part'. Furthermore, despite how my linking of Foucault to Deleuze adds to Foucault's celebration (or was it jokingly, that he said it?) of a Deleuzian century,[53] we must not forget that in *The Order of Things* a particularly Nietzschean episteme was pronounced by using the word threshold,[54] signalling a threshold between modern and—what was later called—'postmodern' philosophy.[55] Additionally, we must ask ourselves to what extent our discussion is situated on the level of historical ages at all. After having specified the four gradations of thresholds—the thresholds of positivity, epistemologisation, scientificity and formalisation[56]—Foucault argues:

> If one recognizes in science only the linear accumulation of truths or the ortho-genesis of reason, and fails to recognize it in a discursive practice that has its own levels, its own thresholds, its own various ruptures, one can describe only a single historical division, which one adopts as a model to be applied at all times and for all forms of knowledge: a division between what is definitively or what is not yet scientific. All the density of the disconnections, the dispersion of the ruptures, the shifts in their effects, the play of the interdependence are reduced to the monotonous act of an endlessly repeated foundation.[57]

Foucault is here revealed as a Bergsonian, because in addition to making the important point about thresholds (or diffractions) in discursive practices (which appear much freer from their historical age than we tend to think of them), he argues that we must not mould science according to the predetermined format of linear time, which approaches Bergson's 'retrograde movement', '[f]rom [which] results an error which vitiates our conception of the past; from this arises our claim to anticipate the future on every occasion'.[58]

It is here that we should insert the second epigraph used by Barad: the quote from Deleuze's *Foucault*. This is what Deleuze argues:

> As long as we stick to things and words we can believe that we are speaking of what we see, that we see what we are speaking of, and that the two are linked: in this way we remain on the level of an empirical exercise. But as soon as we open up words and things, as soon as we discover statements and visibilities, words and sight are raised to a higher exercise that is *a priori*, so that each reaches its

own unique limit which separates it from the other, a visible element that can only be seen, an articulable element that can only be spoken. And yet the unique level that separates each one is also the common limit that links one to the other, a limit with two irregular faces, a blind word and a mute vision.[59]

It is important to note that whereas Foucault has famously asked himself whether the archaeological project had been successful at all, Deleuze attends to the fact that 'the question of primacy' is key to *The Archaeology*. He insists: 'The question of primacy is essential: the statement has primacy. ... But primacy has never meant reduction'.[60] Deleuze affirms the fact that the statement's *primacy has never meant reduction* plays out on the levels of rhythm, history, and form (of expression). This means not only that form pertains to the differing of 'fields of statements' and 'places of visibility', but also that whole and part, or system and individuation get their proper place, *and* that 'the primacy of the statement will be valuable only in this way, to the extent that it brings itself to bear on something irreducible'.[61] This irreducibility is played out only with regards to the thresholds of epistemologisation, scientificity and formalisation.

The third step in this chapter then involves taking up the 'threshold' of positivity, which is performed in Deleuze's *Foucault* with the 'subject-function' and another discussion of the virtual and the actual, but is announced by Foucault only in the conclusion to *The Archaeology*, where he posits that the positivity-threshold deals with individuation[62] and that he is '[a]t the moment ... not sufficiently advanced in [his] task to answer this question'.[63] The notion of 'interference' (synonymous of diffraction) appears a few pages later as the *modus operandi*, the *doings* of ethics (e.g., the talk about sexuality), aesthetics (e.g., the making of a painting) and politics (e.g., the tactics of the revolutionary).[64]

THE THRESHOLD OF POSITIVITY

Let me now explain, with reference to Deleuze, the difference between the intermediary step of 'irreduction'—to borrow a concept from Bruno Latour[65]—and the threshold of positivity, which does not come out well in Foucault's work. Indeed, the points of diffraction in Foucault are less straightforward than 'applicable'. Diffraction implies that realised theoretical options and all possible other forkings *relate to one another*. Theoretical possibilities that are available but have not been seized were cut off by 'authorities' which must not be seen as disturbances but, on the contrary, as *formative* (here we recognise Foucault's double face of power: *potestas* and *potentia*). One additional quote by Foucault—describing the role of authority in shaping relations between discursive formations—will lead us back to the heart of the matter:

> A discursive formation does not occupy therefore all the possible volume that is opened up to it of right by the systems of formation of its objects, its enunciations, and its concepts; it is essentially incomplete, owing to the system of formation of its strategic choices. Hence the fact that, taken up again, placed, and interpreted in a new constellation, a given discursive formation may reveal new possibilities ... but we are not dealing with a silent content that has remained implicit, that has been said and yet not said, and which constitutes beneath manifest statements a sort of sub-discourse that is more fundamental, and which is now emerging at last into the light of day.[66]

This quote demonstrates the extent to which Foucault works in agreement with the Simondonian interpretation of thresholding: the point of diffraction is a nondecomposable *event*, but what is effectuated on both sides of the threshold (this is the *effect* of the diffraction) is decomposable (either–or).

In *Foucault* Deleuze takes the leap to the threshold of positivity and explains what is at stake with regards to this threshold, in a much more explicit manner than the Foucault of *Archaeology of Knowledge* has been capable of. With the claim that *The Archaeology* 'analyses the subject-function'[67] Deleuze wants to explain how—and differently in different ages—'we cannot say that the individual pre-exists the subject-function, the projection of a psyche, or the normalizing agency'.[68] Dis-connected from psychiatric discourse, this is about 'individuation', to use a Simondonian concept. Deleuze explains:

> [T]he subject is a place or position which varies greatly according to its type and the threshold of the statement, and the 'author' himself is merely one of these possible positions in certain cases. A single statement can even have several positions. So much so that what comes first is a ONE SPEAKS, an anonymous murmur in which positions are laid out for possible subjects: 'the great relentless disordered drone of discourse'.[69]

The thresholding is now fully positioned at the level of *one* statement and a lot is bypassed (some of this bypassing we have seen as if announced in this quote): the Cogito, the structuralism of the generation of 1890, and phenomenology's all-too-easy equalisation of world and word.[70] Of crucial importance is the Foucaultian point—made also earlier—that individuation has a *history*, knows specific *moments* of effectuation, and is in *transformation* (through history, form and rhythm). Risking making a neo-Kantian out of Foucault, but successfully circumventing an equalisation act, Deleuze concludes that Foucault's work 'is neither a history of mentality, nor of behaviour. Speaking and seeing, or rather statements and visibilities, are pure Elements, *a priori* conditions under which all ideas are formulated and behaviour displayed, *at some moment or other*'.[71] I wish to call this latter moment the point of diffraction, which demonstrates how a diffraction is not a Euclidean, circumscribed point that exists in stillness and isolation, but rather an event that exists in a spatial (*potestas-potentia*) and durational (actual-virtual; transformative) field. But how should we best deal with the historical, the systemic and the individuated, levels or layers which have been intermingling in the text produced so far? Since diffraction was introduced as a methodology that sidesteps epistemological individualism, we must simply continue our quest.

DO NOT REDUCE

Reminding ourselves of the fact that 'diffraction' was introduced by Haraway and Barad in a discussion about the presuppositions of representation (these were spelled out by Trinh T. Minh-ha)[72] allows us to move away from René Descartes (the classical age) and Immanuel Kant (the modern age), and towards Deleuze. Also referring to Foucault's discussion about the episteme to come,[73] Lambert in *In Search of a New Image of Thought* has argued:

> Today ... the only thing that the faculties can be said to share in common is a notion of difference that remains abstract, because it is now understood or presupposed in nonrepresentational terms. It no longer works, at least according to the rules previously prescribed to it by Representation ... does this not accurately depict the situation of contemporary philosophy ... for which in place of presupposing the world and the self as objects of natural representation, philosophy presupposes a pure plane of immanence that it is not yet capable of thinking according to a framework of representation?[74]

Affirming a subject that is becoming, not Being (or identitarian), Lambert directs the reader to Deleuze and Guattari's *Anti-Oedipus* (a volume prefaced by Foucault), and precisely to the section 'The Whole and Its Parts' of the chapter 'The Desiring-Machines'. Here, the complex intra-action—to borrow a conceptual tool coined by Barad—between the actualised and the virtual, and the formative nature of the closing off of paths, is stated in a manner that Lambert calls 'most crucial' and 'in the most material and even historical of terms'.[75] Indeed, converging with the argumentative field opened up above, the claim is that breaks in a seeming whole are productive, and that assembling, disassembly, and reassembling may happen at the same time and in multiple ways. A whole must not be seen as holistic, but simply as a machine in, and with which, a great number of antagonistic, different or differing movements happen simultaneously. The point is to move way from a 'logic of One', and the insight must be that a romantic, nostalgic or naturalising holism is nothing but a reaffirmation of the predetermination coming from dialectics. This is the (Simondonian) reading offered by Deleuze and Guattari:

> We live today in the age of partial objects, bricks that have been shattered to bits, and leftovers. We no longer believe in the myth of the existence of fragments that, like pieces of an antique statue, are merely waiting for the last one to be turned up, so that they may all be glued back together to create a unity that is precisely the same as the original unity. We no longer believe in a primordial totality that once existed, or in a final totality that awaits us at some future date. We no longer believe in the dull grey outlines of a dreary, colorless dialectic of evolution, aimed at forming a harmonious whole out of heterogeneous bits by rounding off their rough edges. We believe only in totalities that are peripheral. And if we discover such a totality alongside various separate parts, it is a whole *of* these particular parts but does not totalize them; it is a unity *of* all of these particular parts but does not unify them; rather, it is added to them as a new part fabricated separately.[76]

Complicating the unity-fragmentation distinction emphasised by Moulard-Leonard, for Lambert the task of the philosopher today is 'to know how to assemble a multiplicity from all the parts that have no relation to the Whole, to create a real multiplicity out of nothing but differences'.[77] For us, this exposé is necessary, because Foucault gives us no clue about the nature of diffraction (the term is not footnoted), and yet we know that there are at least four interpretations possible: the classical and the quantum interpretation, and (leaving Albert Einstein out) the debate between Bohr and Heisenberg. This takes us to the third step of our discussion, a step we began previously but which was hindered by the limitations of Foucault's *Archaeology of Knowledge*, in which the point of diffraction is not brought to the fullest fruition.

Earlier I argued: 'Diffraction implies that realised theoretical options and all possible other forkings *relate to one another*. Theoretical possibilities that are available but have not been seized were cut off by 'authorities' *which must not be seen as disturbances but, on the contrary, as formative* (here we recognise Foucault's double face of power: *potestas* and *potentia*)'. The issue of 'nondisturbance' has direct bearing on the issue of diffraction, because (non) disturbance is key to the famous debate in the 1940s between Heisenberg (who opted for uncertainty and disturbance) and Bohr (who chose for indeterminacy, nondisturbance and complementarity). The notion of diffraction that we find after Plotnitsky and Barad, in particular, is Bohrian:

> The lesson that Bohr takes from quantum physics is very deep and profound: there aren't little things wandering aimlessly in the void that possess

the complete set of properties that Newtonian physics assumes (e.g., position and momentum); rather, there is something fundamental about the nature of measurement interactions such that, given a particular measuring apparatus, certain properties become determinate, while others are specifically excluded. Which properties become determinate is not governed by the desires or will of the experimenter but rather by the specificity of the experimental apparatus.[78]

Hence, again we see the interplay of the empirical and the speculative, whereby the speculative—and this is of course an importation of a philosophical notion into the text of Barad here, a text that is differently philosophical at this point—does not undo the empirical or vice versa. Precisely the point of complementarity, for instance, is that one entity can be objectively measured to be both A and non-A or B, which does not imply an uncertainty, but rather the *entanglement* of subject, object and instrument. Therefore, '[i]n absence of a given apparatus there is no unambiguous way to differentiate between the object and the agencies of observation [subject + instrument], but then the apparatus must be understood as part of what is being described'.[79] My favourite example pertains to an experiment described by Barad, who concludes: 'Among the particulars are a warm bed, a bad cigar, a timely postcard, a railroad strike, and an uncanny conspiracy of Nature'.[80] The point of Bohrian diffraction is simple: do not reduce.

THE FIELD-NATURE OF THE DIFFRACTION

In order to bring the discussion to a close, we must return to the way in which 'point of diffraction' features in Deleuze Studies and repeat the analysis I made of Moulard-Leonard now with her teacher, Lawlor. It is in the final section of this chapter that I will work with Foucault's notion itself and with Deleuze's *Foucault*. Although Lawlor's analysis is philosophically more complex than Moulard-Leonard's, I will be able to be more concise about his work.

Lawlor does not define diffraction either, yet his line of argumentation also is about disjunction. In addition, Lawlor argues from the start that the diffraction may be absorbed by similarity. Both 'The Beginnings of Thought' and *Thinking Through French Philosophy* uphold a definition of diffraction that is threefold: first, diffraction deals with a disjunction between thinkers/ philosophical systems; second, diffraction is a point: 'Always the diffraction [the disjunction] threatens to disappear into the point [of convergence];'[81] and third, a point of diffraction is sought or constructed *on purpose* by the commentator, or the philosopher, or both.[82] The convergence, on the one hand, seems to 'happen'. This has to do with the fact that in the end, diffraction is a *field* rather than a point (albeit that in the following formulation, the term 'point' pops up again):

> If one used, not Merleau-Ponty, but Sartre or Lacan or Lévi-Strauss as a partner in the dialogue, one might be required to construct the French Sixties philosophical system differently. Undoubtedly changing the partner would bring to light a different aspect of the point of diffraction.[83]

The field-nature of the diffraction—which indicates how what is diffractive involves more than what is documented between the covers of the book—is hard to reconcile with the demand of being 'required to construct'. This reveals much about the nature of the diffractive methodology of Lawlor: wherever partners in dialogue come from, their presence—in movement—is not without consequences. In sum, Lawlor states:

> I was seeking a point—like a glimmering star—on which to focus; I was seeking a point—like a knot—to disentangle. The point that I found has, I think, to speak like Deleuze, the power on the basis of which one creates new concepts. Because of this power concentrated in this point, I have come to call this system of thought 'the great French philosophy of the Sixties.'[84]

Lawlor argues that diffraction is an optics that consists of several aspects. First, it involves constructing a schema that 'always focuses on a lack (powerlessness)',[85] which has to do with the fact that the French sixties philosophy he is interested in is a philosophy of interrogation. Second, it involves establishing oppositions: 'I was interested in that fine point where one kind of thought turns into its opposite just as white turns into black'.[86] And a final step causes Lawlor 'to determine, with precision, the gradual change of the "more and less"',[87] which is about the infinitesimal nature of change. Before this, however, when Lawlor states that Maurice Merleau-Ponty 'had already found the point of diffraction in the experience of the question'[88] *in his uncompleted last book*, the three characteristics of the point of diffraction (including diffraction *as a point*) are compromised: we do not know whether it is a disjunction we are talking about; the point-nature of diffraction comes out transformed; and the purposeful quest is still continuing. The same happens in the work of Lawlor, about whom we may ask whether he has actually succeeded in writing up a system, since the system is a philosophy of interrogation and the conclusion—reached after documenting a myriad of oppositions (this or that) and gradual changes (more or less)—reads:

> [J]ust as a question lacks an answer, it also demands an answer. Thus the question opens out onto *an excess of answers*, potentiality of voices, responsibility. Where time is out of joint, the untimely (*l'intemporel*) is generated as an

excess of life. The question implies: life in death, death in life. The doubling of life in death and of death in life is a paradox. The paradox of the double is what finally enables the genuine movement of thought. The paradox of the double is the point of diffraction.[89]

So, finally, what we find in Lawlor is next to convergence and opposition, a graduation and a movement 'from white to black' *even in the point of diffraction*, which suggests something like a quantum understanding of the diffractive point. Take the example of a razor blade, about which Barad has stated:

> If you look at the image carefully, you'll see that the shadow cast by the razor blade is not the sharply delineated geometrical image one might expect. In particular, there is not a single solid dark area in the shape of the blade surrounded on all sides by a uniformly bright background. Rather, a careful examination reveals an indeterminate outline around each of the edges: along both the inside and outside edges there are alternating lines of dark and light that make the determination of a 'real' boundary quite tricky. Perhaps even more surprisingly there are lines of alternating dark and light even into the very center that corresponds to the notched-out part of the blade. Shouldn't that entire area be light? How can there be dark lines in the center at all? How can we understand this pattern that is produced?[90]

Lawlor argues that his system was written up ultimately as a 'claim [which] could be tested',[91] suggesting that he is speaking here of an empirical exercise that does not 'rais[e words and sight] to a higher exercise that is *a priori*'. However, we find a doubleness in the Merleau-Ponty quote from *The Visible and the Invisible*, which Lawlor is so fond of and which does demand a 'higher exercise', because the question is, just like in Deleuze's *Foucault*, 'a question as to how the "ideas of the intelligence" are initiated over and beyond'.[92] Should we say that Lawlor's historical-systemic account tries not to change the parameters of either historical or systemic philosophy, and that it does not make sense in the context of diffraction? That the excess in the text itself demonstrates the soundness of the double nature of diffraction, a doubling up also confirmed by Merleau-Ponty?[93]

The conclusion at this point could be that my exposé is in the end about Hélène Metzger's solution to the chronological empiricism that she argued was shared by the two extremes of logical positivism and historical epistemology, the two competing paradigms of her time (the 1930s). This is what she argues: the historian of thought does not prejudge what he or she has found, because this historian is aware of the difficulties of scientific research. Constantly searching for a deepened understanding of the past, the historian tries to penetrate with greater certainty and more active sympathy the creative thinking of the past in which he infuses new life, that he revives for a moment. Moreover, there is a personal, subjective factor ... which is impossible to eliminate completely; it is better to admit it honestly than to deny it *a priori*. Historians, like all philosophers, like all scientists and like all humans have innate tendencies, individual, but imperceptible ways of thinking that are themselves not yet opinions or even systems of thought, but that can and do engender such opinions and systems. ... And instead of rebelling against the nature of things to achieve a fake objectivity placed outside of the world and outside of science, [the historian] tries to find or recreate, for a moment in itself, the forces underlying the works that are the object of his meditation.[94]

Intuitive metaphysics is not a move either stirred by (under the spell of) intellectualism, or moving away from it (thus reaffirming it by negation), because intuition can also pertain to thinking, to *epistemology*. In the *a priori* exercise of Deleuze there is no place for reduction.

NOTES

1. This text was originally delivered as a keynote lecture at the conference *Deleuze's Cultural Encounters with the New Humanities* (June 9–12, 2014; Hong Kong).
2. Deleuze and Guattari 1994 [1991], 79.
3. Ibid., 8.
4. Bergson 2007 [1934], 168; emphasis added.
5. Ibid., 169.
6. van der Tuin 2013, 233.
7. Bergson 1913 [1889], 168.
8. Plotnitsky 2012.
9. Deleuze and Guattari 1994 [1991], 36.
10. Lawlor 2003a, 2003b.
11. See, for example, Kaiser and Thiele 2014; Hickey-Moody et al. 2016.
12. Gunter 2012.
13. Moulard-Leonard 2008, 7.
14. Ibid., 8, emphasis in original.
15. Bergson 2004 [1896], 236.
16. Moulard-Leonard 2008, 106ff.
17. Deleuze 2000 [1985], 280, emphasis added. In French this reads: "C'est au niveau de l'interférence de beaucoup de pratiques que les choses se font, les êtres, les images, les concepts, tous les genres d'événement" (p. 365 *Cinéma II*).
18. Deleuze and Guattari 1994 [1991], 216–18.
19. Deleuze 2000 [1985], 280, emphasis added.
20. Moulard-Leonard 2008, 125.
21. Ibid., 127.

22. Ibid.
23. Ibid., 2.
24. Ibid., 7.
25. Deleuze and Guattari 1987 [1980], 238–39.
26. Moulard-Leonard 2008, 128.
27. Lambert 2012, 205–8.
28. Deleuze and Guattari 1994 [1991], 218.
29. Plotnitsky 2012.
30. Plotnitsky 2012, 23.
31. Ibid.; cf. pages 26, 28–29.
32. Deleuze and Guattari 1994 [1991], 36.
33. Plotnitsky 2012, 28.
34. Ibid., 29.
35. Ibid., 30.
36. Barad 2007, 195.
37. Barad 2003, 803.
38. With regards to Foucault, Barad's point is that he has been prone to predeter-mining the (causal) relation between matter and signs (e.g., Barad 2003, 809–10). Haraway (2008, 27ff) has been critical about Deleuze and Guattari's 'fantasy' of the wolf pack and Barad (2007, 436–37 n.80) about the privileging of the virtual-actual coupling to the real and the possible. Haraway says: 'My Deleuze is Rosi Braidotti's feminist trans-mutant' (in Gane 2006, 156) and Barad has said that she wants to take Braidotti's Deleuze Seminar (personal communication).
39. Barad 2007, 46.
40. Foucault 1972 [1969], 49; emphasis in original.
41. Ibid., 65, emphasis in original. The French text—*L'archéologie du savoir*—speaks of '*points de diffraction*' (Foucault 1969, 87). The concept is not footnoted.
42. Ibid., 189ff.
43. Ibid., 66.
44. For example, Barad 2003, 803–11.
45. Gutting 1989, 237; emphasis added.
46. Foucault 1972 [1969], 68; emphasis added.
47. Ibid., 66.
48. Deleuze 1999 [1986], 45.
49. Foucault 1994 [1966], xxiii.
50. Ibid., 210.
51. Metzger 1987 [1937], 58.
52. In De Boever et al. 2009, 40–41.
53. Foucault 1998 [1970], 343.
54. Foucault 1994 [1966], 342.
55. See Gutting 1989, 207.
56. Foucault 1972 [1969], 186–87.
57. Ibid., 188.
58. Bergson 2007 [1934], 11.
59. Deleuze 1999 [1986], 55.

60. Ibid., 43. Only the first sentence—up to the colon—appears in the work of Barad.

61. Ibid.

62. Foucault 1972 [1969], 186.

63. Ibid., 192.

64. He says: 'interference and mutual transformation' (Foucault 1972 [1969], 195). The French edition speaks of 'l'interférence et la mutuelle transformation' (Foucault 1969, 255).

65. Latour 1988 [1984].

66. Foucault 1972 [1969], 67.

67. Deleuze 1999 [1986], 47.

68. Foucault 2006 [2003], 56.

69. Deleuze 1999 [1986], 47.

70. Note that some contemporary new materialisms repeat the evaluation of phenomenology as 'the "World speaks"' [Ibid., 48].

71. Ibid., 51; emphasis added.

72. Minh-ha 1997, 1996.

73. Lambert 2012, 11.

74. Ibid., 21.

75. Ibid.

76. Deleuze and Guattari 1983 [1972], 42; emphasis in original.

77. Lambert 2012, 22.

78. Barad 2007, 19.

79. Ibid., 118.

80. Friedrich and Herschbach 2003 in Barad 2007, 164.

81. Lawlor 2003a, 81.

82. Lawlor 2003b, 1–2.

83. Ibid., 179 n.6.

84. Ibid., 1.

85. Ibid., 3.

86. Ibid.

87. Ibid., 4.

88. Ibid., 2.

89. Ibid., 143; emphasis added.

90. Barad 2003, 75.

91. Lawlor 2003b, 1.

92. Merleau-Ponty 1968, 152 cited in Lawlor 2003b, 3; Deleuze 1999 [1986], 55.

93. Cf. Kirby 2011, chapter 6.

94. Metzger 1987 [1933], 11.

REFERENCES

Barad, K. (2003). 'Posthumanist Performativity: Toward an Understanding of How Matter Comes to Matter'. *Signs: Journal of Women in Culture and Society* 28(3), 801–31.

Barad, K. (2007). *Meeting the Universe Halfway: Quantum Physics and the Entanglement of Matter and Meaning*. Durham, NC: Duke University Press.

Bergson, H. (1913) [1889]. *Time and Free Will: An Essay on the Immediate Data of Consciousness*. Translated by F. L. Pogson, 3rd ed. London: George Allen.

Bergson, H. (2004) [1896]. *Matter and Memory*. Translated by Nancy Margaret Paul and W. Scott Palmer. 5th ed. Mineola, NY: Dover Publications.

Bergson, H. (2007) [1934]. *The Creative Mind: An Introduction to Metaphysics*. Translated by Mabelle L. Andison. Mineola, NY: Dover Publications.

De Boever, A., Murray, A., and Roffe, J. (2009). 'Technical Mentality' Revisited: Brian Massumi on Gilbert Simondon'. *Parrhesia: A Journal of Critical Philosophy*, 7, 36–45.

Deleuze, G. (1999) [1986]. *Foucault*. Translated by S. Hand. London: Continuum.

Deleuze, G. (2000) [1985]. *Cinema 2: The Time-Image*. Translated by H. Tomlinson and R. Galeta. Minneapolis: University of Minnesota Press.

Deleuze, G., and Guattari, F. (1983) [1972]. *Anti-Oedipus: Capitalism and Schizophrenia*. Translated by R. Hurley, M. Seem, and H. R. Lane. Minneapolis: University of Minnesota Press.

Deleuze, G., and Guattari, F. (1987) [1980]. *A Thousand Plateaus: Capitalism and Schizophrenia*. Translated by B. Massumi. Minneapolis: University of Minnesota Press.

Deleuze, G., and Guattari, F. (1994) [1991]. *What Is Philosophy?* Translated by H. Tomlinson and G. Burchell. New York: Columbia University Press.

Foucault, M. (1969). *L'archéologie du savoir*. Paris: Gallimard.

Foucault, M. (1972) [1969]. *The Archaeology of Knowledge*. Translated by A. M. Sheridan Smith. London: Routledge.

Foucault, M. (1994) [1966]. *The Order of Things: An Archaeology of Human Sciences*. New York: Vintage Books.

Foucault, M. (1998) [1970]. 'Theatrum Philosophicum'. *Essential Works of Foucault, 1954–1984, Vol 2: Aesthetics, Method, and Epistemology*, J. D. Faubion and P. Rabinow. eds. New York: New Press, pp. 343–68.

Foucault, M. (2006) [2003]. *Psychiatric Power: Lectures at the Collège de France, 1973–74*. Translated by G. Burchell. Basingstoke: Palgrave Macmillan.

Gane, N. (2006). 'When We Have Never Been Human, What Is to Be Done?' *Theory, Culture & Society* 23(7–8), 135–58.

Gunter, P. A. Y. (2012). 'Bergson and Proust: A Question of Influence'. In *Understanding Bergson, Understanding Modernism*. P. Ardoin, S. E. Gontarski, and L. Mattison, eds. New York: Bloomsbury, 157–76.

Gutting, G. (1989). *Michel Foucault's Archaeology of Scientific Reason*. Cambridge: Cambridge University Press.

Haraway, D. (2008). *When Species Meet*. Minneapolis: University of Minnesota Press.

Hickey-Moody, A., Palmer, H., and Sayers, E. (2016). 'Diffractive Pedagogies: Dancing across New Materialist Imaginaries', *Gender and Education* 28:2, 213–29.

Kaiser, B. M., and Thiele, K., eds. (2014). 'Diffracted Worlds—Diffractive Readings: Onto-Epistemologies and the Critical Humanities'. Special issue of *Parallax* 20.3.

Kirby, V. (2011). *Quantum Anthropologies: Life at Large*. Durham, NC: Duke University Press.

Lambert, G. (2012). *In Search of a New Image of Thought: Gilles Deleuze and Philosophical Expressionism*. Minneapolis: University of Minnesota Press.

Latour, B. (1988) [1984]. 'Irreductions'. In *The Pasteurization of France*. Cambridge, MA: Harvard University Press, 152–235.

Lawlor, L. (2003a). 'The Beginnings of Thought: The Fundamental Experience in Derrida and Deleuze'. In *Between Deleuze and Derrida*. Paul Patton and John Protevi, eds. London: Continuum. 67–83.

Lawlor, L. (2003b). *Thinking Through French Philosophy: The Being of the Question*. Bloomington: Indiana University Press.

Metzger, Hélène. 1987 [1933]. 'L'historien des sciences doit-il se faire le contemporain des savants don't il parle?', in G. Freudenthal (ed.), *La méthode philosophique en histoire des sciences: Textes 1914–1939*. Corpus des Oeuvres de Philosophie en Langue Française. Fayard, pp. 9–21.

Metzger, Hélène. (1987) [1937]. 'La méthode philosophique dans l'histoire des sciences'. [The Philosophical Method in the History of Science.] *La méthode philosophique en histoire des sciences: Textes 1914–1939* [The Philosophical Method in the History of Science: Texts 1914–1939], ed. Gad Freudenthal, 57–73. Corpus des Oeuvres de Philosophie en Langue Française. Paris: Fayard.

Minh-ha, T. (1996). 'An Acoustic Journey'. In *Rethinking Borders*, John C. Welchman, ed. Minneapolis: University of Minnesota Press, 1–17.

Minh-ha, T. (1997). 'Not You/Like You: Postcolonial Women and the Interlocking Questions of Identity and Difference'. In *Dangerous Liaisons: Gender, Nation, and Postcolonial Perspectives*, A. McClintock, A. Mufti, and E. Shohat, eds. Minneapolis: University of Minnesota Press, 415–49.

Moulard-Leonard, V. (2008). *Bergson-Deleuze Encounters: Transcendental Experience and the Thought of the Virtual*. New York: SUNY Press.

Plotnitsky, A. (2012). 'From Resonance to Interference: The Architecture of Concepts and the Relationships among Philosophy, Art and Science in Deleuze and Deleuze and Guattari'. *parallax* 18(1): 19–32.

van der Tuin, I. (2013). 'The Untimeliness of Bergson's Metaphysics: Reading Diffractively'. In *Bergson and the Art of Immanence: Painting, Photography, Film*, John Mullarkey and Charlotte de Mille, eds. Edinburgh: Edinburgh University Press.

Chapter 3

Cartographies of Environmental Arts

Jussi Parikka

> Because the concept in its unrestrained usage is a set of circumstances, at a volatile juncture. It is a vector: the point of application of a force moving through a space at a given velocity in a given direction. The concept has no subject or object other than itself. It is an act. —Brian Massumi.[1]

This text functions as a cartography that is also an operating system. It is an exercise in how concepts migrate across art practices that deal with the environment and inform and condition the practices as ways of being involved in different material situations across differing scales. While it works in the midst of selected art works, Gilles Deleuze and Félix Guattari's philosophy is one underlying reference point even if at times left more implicit. Their work is particularly useful however as it facilitates the encounters of concepts with art practices and the sort of vectors that the epigraph from Massumi also points to: concepts map velocities that take place in territories and movements in and across territories, including passages in multiple other directions that extend the forms of sense and sensation that art practices are very good at producing. Hence, as expressed by Matthew Fuller who has already earlier summarised the possibilities of art methodologies in a precise way: 'Art methodologies convey art's capacities to enact a live process in the world, launching sensorial particles and other conjunctions in ways and combinations that renew their powers of disturbance and vision'.[2] The short sections in this chapter explore the various processes and dynamics, situations and localisations, planes of composition as well as institutional frameworks—even technologies—in which artistic practices unfold: in short, the sections map the temporality of the operating system as a process of organisation or a series of operations, rather than a structure.

PRACTICES, AN OPERATING SYSTEM

Textual practice—or what we can call conceptual practice to emphasise its material, locatable nature that itself can be a form of art methodology—becomes a way to tease out some of the qualities that are central in the visual, sonic, performative accounts that this chapter attends to as examples from current environmental art practices providing entry points to posthuman ecologies.[3] The projects discussed in this short chapter express artistic relations to times, materials and political territory as ways to map the shifting dynamic scales of local and global, speeds and slownesses. These are forms of thinking that emerge in practice and their material situations. It's the practices that enable the emergence of conceptual territories as centres of concerns and of interest. In many ways, art projects become flexible, moving and collaborative exercises in mapping 'what is out there': these are the words used by Anna Tsing, Heather Swanson, Elaine Gan and Nils Bubandt in their introductory text to the volume *Arts of Living on a Damaged Planet* and in their use relate to the 'on-the-ground observations' and 'varied historical diffractions' in which we are constantly enfolded.[4] Such arts of learning things 'out there' and 'in here' are also practical exercises about particular grounds, undergrounds, and the above-grounds of atmosphere and aerial vision. They are practices concerning companion species, some of which might be already long gone and dead. Practice binds these various sites into a circuit.

It is by now a truism to state that our environments are complex and constituted of multiple scales of reference, agency and time. Hence to speak of 'the environment' already starts off as too broad, so one must be quick to add: the place of practice involves the productive possibility of specifying, situating and allowing somewhat unexpected qualities to emerge, whether this comes out as a thing, a collective, an expression, or something else. And all this, the forms of practice—to be exercising, practising and engaging—sometimes take the form of a residency, sometimes the form of a temporary group, sometimes a dialogue, sometimes an encounter with other materials than humans. Artistic practice is often located in techniques such as focusing but it can benefit as immeasurably from *unfocusing*;[5] to train oneself to observe what appears out of sight so as to cultivate an understanding of the structural complexity and agency of our environment and its various layers of activity.

To observe situations of space and place is often important for both artistic and conceptual practice too: to mark a territory in its dynamics. Tsing and colleagues write of landscapes as 'overlaid arrangements of human and nonhuman living spaces',[6] and it is this sort of an involved relation to the landscape that, to me, feels most apt for thinking about the practices I am concerned with. Landscapes as places and spaces, as technological and biological, signal an attachment to situated ways of doing. Naturally, not all landscapes are natural frontiers, and indeed in this chapter landscapes are treated more as mixed arrangements of knowledge and ecology. Laboratories, observatories and other institutional forms are referred to as particular historical models where perception or experimentation might take place, but also as places recreated, as adopted for artistic uses. These models seem particularly useful for understanding artistic practice in terms of posthuman ecology, as they are, traditionally, associated with the possibilities of rescaling, like Alice in Wonderland as the laboratory subject, as the observatory scientist par excellence. They take us higher, lower, deeper, involve us speaking to minerals, taking a breath of air with the wind, and seeing differently.

Figure 3.1: Helena Hunter. Photo from the collections of the Natural History Museum, London.

Consider Helena Hunter's (2018) writing-with-minerals as an example:

> unseen
> uncertain frequency
> hear it cracking
> these fragments
> sustaining shouts
>
> what language
> for your atoms?
> slow in speech
> to reach you
>
> time pressures
> issues of strength
>
> what if we garnet
> a question for the sky?
> How to write interruption
> Ways of seeing variance
> not writing as a tool
> of measurement

The words that become concepts are situated in places and acknowledge the importance of 'where'—of geographies, places, and spaces. They also act as part of cartographies that draw a 'micro-geography of power relations that are simultaneously local and global'.[7] Hunter's text performs a work of conceptual cartography that is not only about local/global but also about the various other sorts of condensations of time, movement, place and art practices as forms of ecological knowing. I argue that this is where environmental art practice—art methods—can engage in dialogue with work in environmental humanities to complement their understanding of what is at stake in the topics that are, well, for the lack of a better word, about ecologies. Many of the examples presented in this chapter give insights into what fieldwork entails in situations where the artist or the collective is acutely aware of the field they enter, transform, listen to and move with.

One of the insights emerging from theoretical and artistic activity in recent years has been that ecology is less a word or an analytical term denoting a thing than it is a way of looking at things in their relations, conceptualising and making sense of their multiple scales. In other words, diverse things and relations can be coined as ecology. Ecology is more like an operation. This realisation opens up a world: a world of relations, abstractions, spaces that turn into movements, import and export operations, materials and how they are made data, then calculated, operated upon and made into further things. Ecology is productive, and it becomes an onto-epistemological framework, to think with Karen Barad. This stance does not work at a distance but is involved: 'knowing is a material practice of engagement as part of the world in its differential becoming'.[8]

As involvements, ecology can be seen in words, interactions, political institutions, art practices, environmental situations, financial systems, and it can also bind all of those together in what becomes the insight of ecological practice: to establish relations. There is an 'ecology of practices' that is not merely a description of the current state of how things are done but an identification of potentials and novel forms of emergent knowing.[9] There are political ecologies and there are conceptual ecologies that are abstract yet connote a completely material force.[10] Cultural ecologies allow literary texts to move from them being merely words.[11] Ecology can be general in its relational operation, and there can be thousands of particular and distinct material ecologies embodying a general operation.[12] Digital ecologies can be our infrastructure, and media ecologies embody worlds of techniques, technologies, relations and processes.[13] What is not amenable to being named as ecology?

In the context of ecology in art practices, the evaluative criteria of who, where, when, how connect to ethical issues of why, why not; art connects to assumed liberties of experimentation, which are still constrained by their situations and infrastructures as conditions of the very same experiments.[14] We could name many of them, but for example: funding systems, places, travel, time and lack of time. This sort of an ecology is where landscape and the laboratory are entangled,[15] as some practices in bioart have demonstrated. But those terms of landscape—frontier, laboratory, museum, observatory and more—carry with them a whole range of connotations that are important when considering the wider field of knowledge about, and in, those border zones where geopolitics and environmental issues meet.

These brief parameters are an attempt to speak to the operations and even implicit operating principles. If preferable, we can even call them methods that are at play in the organisation of ecologies. Keller Easterling's thoughts are helpful here. She writes about cities as operative forms, and how one particularly useful method for understanding urban life is to train the eye to unfocus from the immediately visible elements of buildings to their slightly less visible operating principles, to better observe their operating systems and infrastructure.[16] Transport this beyond the context Easterling means it primarily for. Consider it in relation to our topic at hand and consider it in relation to the particular operating systems, principles and, indeed, cartographies that are also formative of art methods. What are the modes of operating, being involved, thinking and reporting that form the backbone for these operations?

HEIGHTS, IN-DEPTH

Any kind of frontier, geographic space and place is anyway multiple.[17] It is multiple and it is further multiplied in various visual forms many of which are not, increasingly, human readable. To detach the observation of such situations from that pair of human eyes and sensorium is somewhat necessary for a full grasp of the multiple scales that define those situations one enters, including in rural settings. It also means asking: how do we become multiple and multiply our points of view into movement of views? This is a good reminder that not merely the more recent inventions relating to machine vision and other automated and technological systems detach from the usual human perspectives, but we also can make use of other techniques that shift us in place.

To lift upwards. Observation takes off from the ground we usually have stabilised most of human perception on. Landscapes are primarily horizontal[18] but sometimes the aerial is where one starts to survey a different perspective than the normalised human inhabitant. This survey is not merely one of controlling birds'-eye views (even if birds are perhaps in many ways apt references for philosophies of surveying immanence, including a brief appearance in *What Is Philosophy?* of the 'ironical soliloquy bird'). As Deleuze and Guattari point out, spatio-temporal dynamics of a concept's path of survey relates to how it is constantly 'in relation to its components'.[19] The survey becomes then a term for this immanence of the field in which and of which concepts emerge; and it also becomes a term for the operation that does not presuppose subjects surveying their objects, but the co-constitution of both—a dynamics of formation as an act itself.[20]

Geographies are constantly surveyed and mapped from higher up, from realities of satellites and drones but also other ways of moving upwards and in-depth. A more DIY version is to use kites. Tuula Närhinen speaks of her *LOCAL* project at the Centre d'Art i Natura in Farrera in the Pyrenees:

> I let the turbulent mountain winds carry my DIY kite equipped with a video camera; painted and catalogued colour perceptions in an archive of water colours and photographs; extracted minerals from the rocks and used them as paint and followed the meandering creeks on their way from the high sources of melting snow through the meadows into the deep river valley. Walking, climbing and flying over the mountains turned my body into an instrument of observation as well: I felt the terrain under my feet, breathed in the air and absorbed the scenery through my eyes.[21]

While she is speaking about the body as an instrument, it appears there is more at play. It concerns a body that becomes moving, uplifted and somewhat

Figure 3.2:   Tuula Närhinen, 'Local Winds' (2015). Courtesy of the artist.

equipped with an added awareness of what is more than just above our heads as if heads were always stable and resident at the same level of vision. With a change in perspective, or a change in its usual situation or relation to the world, the body becomes assembled as a vehicle that allows us to be moved outside the assumption that it is a stable centre of attention and more akin to a force field which allows us to understand and perceive other sorts of scales too. The body becomes less a substance than a hinge that itself enables more than meets the eye at first. Bodies jump, walk, accelerate, decelerate, ascend, descend and more. Thoughts follow a path of movement. I feel that this is also the point expressed by Rebecca Solnit writing about walking as this back and forth play between the body and the world, a shape-shifting in movement: 'Moving on foot seems to make it easier to move in time; the mind wanders from plans to recollections to observations'.[22] Walking is one way—and a very good example—of moving the body and its thoughts, but there are also other activities that take us into different speeds and heights.

A process is set off that also launches more than a body that is normalised. There is always more to perception and what it can become, as Elizabeth Grosz writes in her account of the Earth and the emergence of arts as a territorial framing about this multiplication of the Earth. The Earth is enveloped in this potentiality to become always more:

> The Earth can be infinitely divided, territorialized, framed. ... Framing is how chaos becomes territory. Framing is the means by which objects are delimited, qualities unleashed and art is made possible.[23]

Indeed, the Earth is less discovered as a ground than constantly in creation; it is ontogenetic. The Earth creates its own potentials for discovery. It becomes a potential dynamics of ungrounding that sets in process much more than just something easily returnable to a body. Grosz continues by way of emphasising that what emerges is not merely the body—one's own body as such—but a force that pushes something else to emerge: 'exactly the opposite: it is linked to those processes of distancing and the production of a plane of composition that abstracts sensation from the body'.[24] In these ways, the body becomes one part of a longer chain of operations that starts to understand the varieties where perception takes place and at times is returned to one's own body. One sees with much more than one's own eyes, one sees higher up, from particular perspectives that open up a landscape.

Higher up, Elena Mazzi with Sara Tirelli start to unfold the morphogenetic and dynamic understanding of a landscape in their work, *A fragmented world*. The work unfolds as a mediation between moving images taken from a geo-database used by geography and volcanology researchers, and what emerges as a simple hint of a narrative structure when the camera starts to zoom into a lone figure running through the landscape.[25] The breathing, movement and the bird's-eye view targeting of the subject itself becomes reminiscent of the ways in which aerial vision is a targeting vision while also resonating

Figure 3.3:   Elena Mazzi and Sara Tirelli, *A fragmented world*, 2017. Installation view from the exhibition Edge Effects: Active Earth, Art Sonje Center, Seoul. Photo: Yeonje Kim. Used with permission.

with the point about shifting perspectives: higher, lower, slower, faster. An understanding of space and embodiment is also something that moves on different levels than the body itself, or where the body is an instrument that surveys, lives, moves across but also is enabled by the various geographies and localities. Large-scale stories such as the Anthropocene or the increasing human creation of uninhabitable wastelands come in smaller-scale versions, and in particular situations, or as Gan and colleagues put it:

> Yet the Great Acceleration is best understood through immersion in many small and situated rhythms. Big stories take theirs from seemingly minor contingencies, asymmetrical encounters, and moments of indeterminacy. Landscapes show us.[26]

Could one follow this line of thought to the other direction here too? Any extreme, even uninhabited landscape is never devoid of life and always part of the cultural techniques of geopolitical mapping. The Earth, as Benjamin Bratton[27] reminds us, is considered humanly important in terms of its territorial control as well as its particular resources that open up the underground to such depths of material excavation. These sorts of maps about frontiers were for their modern duration linked to colonialism and resource extraction. So, they are now too, as forms of neocolonialism in mining for fuel and nonfuel minerals for example.[28]

So, what you see as the landscape is contingent upon how you visualise it. As scientific maps of resources, volumetric insights into the ground as harbouring gas or oil, as geologic strata that are quite literally fractured by hydraulic fracturing, making the landscape, the earth, to scream?[29] The unfocusing from the landscape to its constituent elements both upwards and downwards is one significant (and also rather literal) movement where bodies entangle with technological capacities. Perception is set in motion, while materials, but also their political ecologies, unfold as part and as co-constituent of that movement.

Downwards, one finds the other aspects of the geophysical environment, some of which are left as remnants of modern technological culture. To take these questions to geographies such as old agricultural sites, architectural ruins or old copper mines (as Mirko Nikolić does in '*earth wants to be free*')[30] starts to address a particular story about questions of geographic and legal territories and particular political technologies of inclusion and exclusion. But it also by necessity engages us in heightened perceptions of locality or localisation: we are exposed to histories of material transportation, use and resourcing of abstractions from legal questions of ownership to extending rights for nonhumans, and then questions of geopolitical lineages as well as speculative possibilities in art practice, all themes that emerge in Nikolić's practice too.

Figure 3.4: Mirko Nikolić, *earth wants to be free, a 2-day camp symposium in Kemiö, Finland,* May 2016. Photo: Salla Lahtinen / Frontiers in Retreat; HIAP.

FRONTIER, RETREAT

The shift from urban to the rural has entered many disciplines recently. Besides the usual suspects, media studies is refocusing on the infrastructures and political ecologies of landscapes outside the urban,[31] geographical formations, and such. Similarly, parallel fields such as forensic architecture offer particularly apt tools to reveal the extended visual conditioning of legal and political struggles at the thresholds of usual political geographies.[32] In art practices, this, for sure, is not a new feature but has been carried forward with many possible earlier reference points, not least Earth Arts.[33]

Taru Elfving explains the centrality of the nonurban for art practices: the move outside the white cube is where the landscape, the terrain and the dynamic nature become part of the experimentation 'within the frontier between the semiotic and the sensible, or between deconstructive and embodied/embedded methodologies, to name but a few'.[34] But less than deconstructive, one can coin these practices as additive: they add words, proposals, ideas, future trajectories, potentials and materials.[35] They survey the locations and landscapes in which they take place.

From the art market and discourse to cultural and political history, there is a lot at stake. At least since the emergence of the satellite era, frontiers have also been tightly marked for their geopolitical importance and for possible resources (energy, minerals, etc.). Contemporary art and bioart practices have in this sense had to acknowledge that the local and the rural were already also marked by this particular history of planetary geopolitics. Frontiers carry with them the legacy of colonial expeditions and settlers moving in on indigenous lands—a frontier is what is declared as *res nullius*, whether such ever existed or not—and frontiers carry with them the connotation of military troop operations. Another concept of 'front' is borrowed from meteorology with some deliberate remediation of the military use of the term: 'the interface or transition zone between two air masses of different density and temperature' (as the *Encyclopedia Britannica* puts it). Political, military, meteorological terms mix. Similarly, art practices can be formative of what we perceive as frontiers of densities, intensities, masses and transformations. Art can be understood as a geographical concept constituted in particular zones, areas, sometimes rural and often uninhabited but always ecologically significant by virtue of their situatedness.[36]

Traditionally frontiers such as forests have been central to the political definition of the territory and the polis. The foundation of the city has to do with techniques of managing the surrounding forests, and hence defining the borders of the political regime from what resided for such a long time as the imaginary of the forest, as the wild, uncontrolled multiplicity, 'anarchy, shadows and the inhuman'.[37] What is important to note is that instead of merely marking the threshold of political order and its other, the frontier (such as forests but also other natural formations that are not necessarily inhabited by humans) are actually constantly produced, cultivated as such,[38] both in terms of their resources as well as landscapes, geopolitical zones, part of contemporary routes of transport, logistics, energy and so on.

Frontier is a particular situation that starts to open up as a political ecology, a spatial imaginary particular to the political history of liberalism (and its inherent link to colonialism).[39] And one can see how essential this is for decolonising and humanitarian projects that relate to European frontiers: for example, water frontiers, islands in the Mediterranean and other border zones, are intensively the places where the current geopolitical surveillance turns into the biopolitical control of refugees. In grim ways, some of this contemporary crisis is indeed about patterns of seeing and unseeing. Which capsized boat is being reported, or even rescued, is a matter of perception of liquid frontiers. Another aspect concerns mobility, represented by the different wall and fence formations and patterns of movement and preventing movement. Also retreat, a term easily understood only in its military connotations, becomes one way to think political and collective subjectivity while avoiding romanticising it.

To retreat is then not only a defensive gesture but marks a particular way of moving into a space and its political ecology. Retreat is then a sort of a temporally involved way of marking, inhabiting, experiencing and sensing a space but also starting to address its multiple elements. These are not merely linguistic connotations or personal feelings about the space but an awareness of what it might mean as a meshwork of multiple forces: spaces are landscapes in the way outlined by Tsing et al.,[40] and they are entered more ethically with awareness of the onto-epistemological practices that acknowledge how knowing is materially involved in situations.

For some, to retreat is to focalise—a particular way of localising too, which extends to a set of practices. The artist duo, Nabb+Teeri, pitch such practices as a particular collective exercise in locations:

Focal practices gather human being around a focus that demands skills, traditions, and sociality. An example may be heating with wood since it engenders a bodily and skilful gathering around a meaningful practice that can be socially transmitted over generations. Focal practices mesh the practitioners into a collective and also non-human field of experience.[41]

But this exercise becomes more than mere phenomenological retuning. Nabb+Teeri ground their interest through the work of Antti Salminen and Tere Vadén who mobilise focality and related themes in their work on energy.[42] Nabb+Teeri explain in more depth what focality means in terms of practice that relates to particular places but also is itself more akin to a co-determining practice in that material situation:

Figure 3.5:   Nabb+Teeri, *Focal Exercises* (2015–2016). Photo: Courtesy of the artist.

Like localism, focality functions against con-distancing. Through training, a focal practice builds up a holistic skill, makes stronger its connections and centrifugal tendencies. A forester is challenged by the forest, and the forest in turn is challenged by the forester; the forester reacts with the store and the hearth, which in their turn change the timber and so on. If this mutual challenge can go on for generations, sustainable skills may be developed so that humans can live with their environments in ways that are both socially and ecologically sound. In this way, also, the human part of the challenge can be meaningful: it is not any more a technological enframing, but a developed part of the life of the local landbase.[43]

But what is local? Here, local cannot, or should not, be set *against* global and as such, one needs to be aware of the complex cartographies where all entities (if one can call them such) are co-determining. Hence there is an interesting twist to continue to think how focality can be exercised as cartography in its own right. Collective practice starts to work around particular ways of making sense of areas—topographic maps, images, diagrams and such demonstrate how a territory can also turn into ways of passing on, connecting and collectively entering another visual level of what space is.

To retreat can mean to enter the multiple layers that define a space, including ones that escape the sensorium at first, and can then become images that continue a life of their own. The local itself then becomes understood as more than just what is here, catered to my senses. Indeed, this sort of an understanding is also necessary to avoid one of the seeming risks where retreat becomes a gesture of defensive bunkerism, as a sort of a version of survivalism where locality turns into an enclosure. Hence, a further question is necessary to guide the ethics of environmental art practice: how can situations of locality function as sorts of strategies for an engagement with the wider planetary situation? How is it possible to develop the cartography in ways where the local becomes more than its particular situation as self-enclosed entity?

LABORATORY, MUSEUM

What sort of institutional terms, practices and situations can multiply the local, or ensure it can scale up and down? Laboratories have acted as such places in many ways, while other sorts of scenes, such as tweaking the legacy of museums (Terike Haapoja and Laura Gustafsson's *Museum of Nonhumanity* for instance)[44] also challenges the assumed privileged of human history. Both 'human' and 'theory' are of course terms that were central to the modern institutional practices of the purification of nature out of culture[45] but they also carry with them other possibilities as situations where classifications are rethought, histories are rearticulated and the rather messy situation of humans, animals, natural formations, geological durations and transdisciplinary forms of knowledge can pick up on the scalar effects and stage that either the lab or the museum offer.

'Lab' has become a term that has started to frame artistic activity too. The *Zooetics* project, a 'cross-disciplinary exploration of future environmental fictions and models',[46] is a particularly apt example of creating situations that work as laboratories—perhaps nodding to the lineage of art+technology that inaugurated this model during the twentieth century. But it also functions as a way of recreating situations where transdisciplinary knowledge is circulated while not contained inside institutional walls.[47] Laboratories were often anyway more than completely controlled and rationalised spaces. As historians of science have noted, the lab as *elaboratory* was one formative lab activity. Elaborating materials for medicine and chemistry, working with the variety of materials in ways that was not merely under human control; the elaboratory was a place to let things unfold in their own way, even if offering a stage by way of the thermomedia control[48] that allowed material transformations to be accelerated from Earth time to lab time.

For a longer period, laboratories also included an etymologically bootstrapped link to natural formations too—in other words, they were not necessarily seen as two separate spheres of messy nature versus the ordered laboratory, even if in many ways the lab took that place gradually. Considered ecologically, the laboratory was already in the landscapes, always-already before the current fever involving living laboratories.

In 1815 Sir Humphry Davy stated that 'the soil is the laboratory in which the food is prepared'. In 1860, in a very different scientific context regarding the physical geographies of the sea, Louis Ferdinand Alfred Maury spoke of the sea as 'a laboratory in which wonders by processes the most exquisite are continually going on', as a sort of a model for understanding atmospheric movements.[49] One is tempted to start unfolding the story of contemporary islands, water routes and more through such ideas.

Indeed, reverse from our current laboratory fever some one hundred years and a bit more and shift the focus to Bangor in Wales and to Sir William Thomson, 1st Baron Kelvin of, indeed, *the* kelvin fame of temperature measurement, but who also worked with maritime compasses (as an early example of planetary media). When opening the new physics and chemistry labs in 1885 at the University of Bangor, Thomson seemed to be offering a rather extended way of understanding the link between emerging forms of knowledge and nature:

The laboratory of a scientific man is his place of work. The laboratory of the geologist and naturalist is the face of this beautiful world. The geologist's laboratory is the mountain, the ravine, and the seashore. The naturalist and the botanist go to foreign lands, to study the wonders of nature, and describe and classify the results of their observations.[50]

Of course, one has to be aware that maps and knowledge of foreign lands, frontiers and wonders of nature were tightly integrated into the power systems of empires, colonial trade routes and outposts and capitalist mechanisms of profit and security. Following on from that particular modern legacy, there are several interesting developments that link the laboratory to a particular stance of resistance to modernity, embracing interdisciplinary knowledge and interested in a particular way of ensuring the global circulation of that knowledge. More recently and in artistic contexts, Bureau d'Etudes speak of the Laboratory Planet as the particular twentieth-century inaugurated global network of research sites, governance, military and surveillance, resource extraction and supply routes and such that offer a different way of looking at questions of planetary scale.[51] The Laboratory Planet is one way of narrating the effects of capitalism and technological forms of knowledge as a global system that establishes natural formations and localities as part of its circulation. Laboratories were always already the place where nonhumans made an entry to modern forms of knowledge. Could it also be adapted as a counterforce, a stance to interrogate such forms of operation knowledge, mobilisation of natural resources, and possible interventions into the assumed planetary systems that also reshape localities?

The Laboratory maps across planetary space and becomes one way of articulating what forms of knowledge are necessary for us to 'scale up' to respond to the particular difficult, complex and multilayered problems of the Anthropocene. In critical contexts, the laboratory might be a useful term to understand how scales can shift and local and global are conditions of each other. Concerns, methods, practices can become transportable. Situations and knowledge about them can be refocalised in other situations. A hinge emerges. Laboratories are, as such, not merely enclosures but a term for this movement across situations as well as in many cases across disciplinary knowledge. The sort of experimental practice that the lab seemed to denote becomes spread out in those situations at frontiers, in localities and in other sites that connect to a network of circulation of ideas and practices.

WHEN AND UNTIL WHEN?

This chapter has mostly spoken of places and sites, and how particular situated practices are articulations of multiple ecologies: ecologies of terminology and institutions, natural histories and cultural sites, embodiment and technology. But they also embody time while mapping the emerging potential of what is to come, instead of mere descriptions of what is already in existence.[52] These are ecologies of practices in landscapes which unfold in time, and hence also are practices which are by necessity involved in rescaling the temporal: they involve the artist or the practitioner interrogating not just what, but when and how slow, how fast, for how long?

Across institutional situations, poached terms, local uses articulating planetary routes, and many other affordances of contemporary environmental art practices, ecologies also articulate times. What time does one occupy? In contemporary art theory, the issue of time or contemporaneity has become central again, with the emergence of various material notions of time. As Cox and Lund put it, time has become more complex and problematised:

> Temporality under these conditions becomes a more open process, less deterministic, or straightforwardly causal in activating the movement from cause to effect, more performative and open ended in the production of meanings.[53]

The different slownesses and accelerations of art practices are worthy of attention as they also reach out to thinking the nonhuman through time. Dynamic natural formations have a different sort of a temporality that is at stake in many of the environmental art practices, and in order to reach out to the planetary scales, one also feels through time. The Anthropocene, one could argue, is a particular way of experiencing social time through geological durations that have become accelerated. Mineral durations are part of how historical sites of mining are brought into contemporary aesthetic-political discussions. Historical sites are opened up not merely through human narratives but through their nonhuman inhabitants of flora and fauna. One narrates through figures that occupy a different scale, and hence a different rate of perception. As Joanna Zylinska has articulated, scale is central to the ways in which our spatiotemporal dimensions, perceptions and observations can move the ladder up and down, shift across different registers of matter and allow us to shift back and forth between what is assumed to be our perception and other perceptions, or durations.[54]

In which ways are temporal coordinates part of the operating system and the methodology of environmental arts? To acknowledge the alternative rhythms and temporalities of the environments of practice is also to acknowledge the intensive dynamics of the nonhuman world. Places, spaces and situations do not solidify only into stable matter or things but are also active as environments that have a time of their own, a theme that forms a central part of how we should consider posthuman ecologies: multiple layers of time, dynamics and duration that extend much further than the anthropocentric bias would allow.

NOTES

1. Massumi 1992, 5–6.
2. Fuller 2008, 45.
3. The text draws on work created as part of the Frontiers in Retreat project (http://www.frontiersinretreat.org/) that ran in 2013–2018 and with a central node of the project in Finland, at the Helsinki International Arts Programme (HIAP). The project description emphasises the forms of collaborative and multiscalar operations that are also the focus of this article: 'the five-year long collaborative enquiry into the intersections of art and ecology, is entering its final year. During its first four years, the Frontiers network of remote residencies has strived to generate a more complex understanding of the entanglements unfolding between locally articulated ecological concerns and larger, systemic, global processes'. (quoted from the project website).
4. Tsing, Swanson, Gan and Bubandt 2017, G3.
5. Easterling 2014.
6. Tsing et al. 2017, G3.
7. Braidotti 2006, 91.
8. Barad 2007, 89.
9. Stengers 2010, 2017.
10. Guattari 2000.
11. Zapf 2016.
12. Hörl 2017.
13. Fuller 2005.
14. See Deleuze 2004, 98. Deleuze refers to the method of dramatisation as the nonrepresentational form of spatio-temporal dynamism that can be seen as the generative aspect of Ideas as differentiation; the intense life of concepts.
15. Beloff, Berger and Haapoja 2013.
16. Easterling 2014.
17. Massey 2005.
18. Lippard 2014, 10.
19. Deleuze and Guattari 1994, 20.
20. See Massumi 1992, 5–6.
21. Närhinen 2014.
22. Solnit 2002, 22 on ebook version.
23. Grosz 2008, 17.
24. Ibid., 11.
25. Mazzi and Tirelli, 2016.

26. Tsing et al., 2017, G5.
27. Bratton 2015.
28. Cubitt 2016.
29. See Parikka 2014.
30. Nikolić 2016.
31. See, for example, Starosielski 2015.
32. Weizman, 2017.
33. See the work of Robert Smithson, Lucy Lippard, and others.
34. Elfving 2018, 65.
35. cf. Stengers 2017.
36. I am here also thinking of Richard Skelton's *No Frontier* (2017) art work, http://www.frontiersinretreat.org/activities/richard_skelton_no_frontier.
37. Tavares 2018, 163.
38. Tavares 2018, 166.
39. Povinelli 2018.
40. Tsing et al. 2017, G4.
41. Nabb+Teeri 2015.
42. Salminen and Vadén 2015.
43. Nabb+Teeri 2015.
44. Haapoja and Gustafsson 2016.
45. van der Tuin 2018, 270.
46. See the project description online at http://www.frontiersinretreat.org/activities/zooetics.
47. Jutempus 2014–2018.
48. On temperature and media, see Starosielski 2016.
49. Gooday 2008, 789.
50. Quoted in Gooday 2008, 789.
51. Bureau d'Etudes 2018.
52. Stengers 2010.
53. Cox and Lund 2016, 31.
54. Zylinska 2014, 26.

REFERENCES

Barad, K. (2007). *Meeting the Universe Halfway*. Durham, NC: Duke University Press.
Beloff, L., Berger, E., and Haapoja, T., eds. (2013). *Field Notes: From Landscape to Laboratory—Maisemasta Laboratorioon*. Helsinki: The Finnish Society of Bioart.
Braidotti, R. (2006). *Transpositions. On Nomadic Ethics*. Cambridge, MA: Polity.
Bratton, B. (2015). *The Stack*. Cambridge, MA: MIT Press.
Bureau d'Etudes. (2018). *The Laboratory Planet.* https://laboratoryplanet.org/en/. Accessed April 6, 2018.
Cox, G., and Lund, J. (2016). *The Contemporary Condition: Introductory Thoughts on Contemporaneity and Contemporary Art*. Berlin: Sternberg.
Cubitt, S. (2016). *Finite Media*. Durham, NC: Duke University Press.

Deleuze, G. (2004). 'The Method of Dramatization'. In *Desert Islands and Other Texts 1953–1974*, G. Deleuze, ed. Translated by M. Taormina. Los Angeles: Semiotext(e), 94–116.

Deleuze, G., and Guattari, F. (1994). *What Is Philosophy?* London: Verso.

Easterling, K. (2014). *Extrastatecraft*. London: Verso.

Elfving, T. (2018). 'How to Retreat in/to the Frontiers'. In *The Midden*, J. Nurmenniemi and T. Warr eds. Helsinki, Garret, 46–83.

Fuller, M. (2005). *Media Ecologies. Materialist Energies in Art and Technoculture.* Cambridge, MA: MIT Press.

Fuller, M. (2008). 'Art Methodologies in a Media Ecology'. In S. O'Sullivan and S. Zepke, eds. *Deleuze, Guattari and the Production of the New*. London: Continuum, 45–55.

Gooday, G. (2008). 'Placing or Replacing the Laboratory in the History of Science?', *Isis*, 99(4), 783–95.

Grosz, E. (2008). *Chaos, Territory, Art: Deleuze and the Framing of the Earth.* New York: Columbia University Press.

Guattari, F. (2000). *The Three Ecologies*. Translated by Ian Pindar and Paul Sutton. London: Athlone Press.

Happoja, T., and Gustafsson, L. (2016). *Museum of Nonhumanity.* http://www.historyofothers.org/upcoming-the-museum-of-the-history-of-non-humanity/. Accessed April 4, 2018.

Hörl, E., ed. (2017). *General Ecology. The New Ecological Paradigm.* London: Bloomsbury.

Hunter, H. (2018). 'With-out-Sound', *Something Other. Collective Writing, Performance & Their Others blog*, https://somethingother.blog/2018/03/24/with-out-sound/. Accessed April 4, 2018.

Lippard, L. (2014). *Undermining: A Wild Ride through Land Use, Politics, and Art in the Changing West.* New York: New Press.

Jutempus. (2014–2018). *Zooetics.* http://www.zooetics.net. Accessed April 4, 2018.

Massey, D. (2005). *For Space*. London: Sage.

Massumi, B. (1992). *A User's Guide to Capitalism and Schizophrenia. Deviations from Deleuze and Guattari*. Cambridge, MA: MIT Press.

Mazzi, E., and Tirelli, S. (2016). *A Fragmented World.* http://elenamazzi.com/works/a-fragmented-world/. Accessed April 4, 2018.

Nabb, J., and Teeri, M. (2015). *Focal exercises.* http://www.fronticrsinretreat.org/activities/janne_nabb_amp_maria_teeri_focal_exercises. Accessed April 4, 2018.

Närhinen, T. (2014). *LOCAL.* http://www.frontiersinretreat.org/activities/tuula_n_rhinen_local. Accessed 4 April 2018.

Nikolić, M. (2016). *<< earth wants to be free >>.* http://www.frontiersinretreat.org/activities/mirko_nikolic_gt. Accessed April 4, 2018.

Parikka, J. (2014). *The Anthrobscene*. Minneapolis: University of Minnesota Press.

Povinelli, E. (2018). "Horizons and Frontiers, Late Liberal Territoriality, and Toxic Habitats." *E-Flux* #80, April 2018, http://www.e-flux.com/journal/90/191186/horizons-and-frontiers-late-liberal-territoriality-and-toxic-habitats/. Accessed April 14, 2018.

Salminen, A., and Vadén, T. (2015). *Energy and Experience: An Essay in Nafthology.* *Chicago: MCM' Publishing.* http://www.mcmprime.com/files/Energy-and-Experience.pdf. Accessed April 4, 2018.

Skelton, R. (2017). *No Frontier.* http://www.frontiersinretreat.org/activities/richard_skelton_no_frontier. Accessed April 4, 2018.

Solnit R. (2002). *Wanderlust. A History of Walking.* New York: Penguin. (ebook version).

Starosielski, N. (2015). *The Undersea Network.* Durham, NC: Duke University Press.

Starosielski, N. (2016). 'Thermocultures of Geological Media', *Cultural Politics*, 12(3), 293–309.

Stengers, I. (2010). *Cosmopolitics.* Minneapolis: University of Minnesota Press.

Stengers, I. (2017). 'Matters of Concern All the Way Down', *Ctrl-Z*, Issue 7, http://www.ctrl-z.net.au/articles/issue-7/stengers-matters-of-concern-all-the-way-down/. Accessed April 6, 2018.

Tavares, P. (2018). 'Forests'. In *The Posthuman Glossary*, Braidotti and Hlavajova, eds., London: Bloomsbury, 162–67.

Tsing, A. L., Swanson, H. A., Gan, E., and Bubandt, N., Eds. (2017). *Arts of Living on a Damaged Planet: Ghosts and Monsters of the Anthropocene.* Minneapolis: University of Minnesota Press.

van der Tuin, I. (2018). 'Naturecultures'. In *The Posthuman Glossary*, Braidotti and Hlavajova, eds. London: Bloomsbury, 269–70.

Weizman, E. (2017). *Forensic Architecture.* Cambridge, MA: MIT Press.

Zapf, H. (2016). *Literature as Cultural Ecology: Sustainable Texts.* London: Bloomsbury.

Zylinska, J. (2014). *Minimal Ethics for the Anthropocene.* Ann Arbor, MI: Open Humanities Press.

Chapter 4

Involutionary Architecture
Unyoking Coherence from Congruence

Andrej Radman

Men are conscious of their own desire, but are ignorant of the causes whereby that desire has been determined. —Baruch Spinoza[1]

In solipsism, you are ultimately isolated and alone, isolated by the premise "I make it all up." But at the other extreme, the opposite of solipsism, you would cease to exist, becoming nothing but a metaphoric feather blown by the winds of external "reality." (But in that region there are no metaphors!) Somewhere between these two is a region where you are partly blown by the winds of reality and partly an artist creating a composite out of the inner and outer events. —Gregory Bateson[2]

It would no longer involve raising to infinity or finitude but an unlimited finity, thereby evoking every situation of force in which a finite number of components yields a practically unlimited diversity of combinations. It would be neither the fold nor the unfold that would constitute the active mechanism, but something like the Superfold. ... And is this unlimited finity or superfold not what Nietzsche had already designated with the name of eternal return? The forces within man enter into a relation with forces from thc outside. —Gilles Deleuze[3]

ANNEXED MILIEU AS A SITE OF RESISTANCE TO THE PRESENT

This chapter is devoted to the 'involutionary' relation of the forces from within with the forces from without.[4] It starts from the premise that the interior as a given needs to be set aside until the issue of *how* the given is given has been addressed. Only then will it be possible to make sense of the Superfold's (eternal) giving. When the explanatory ladder is turned upside down, what has figured as an explanation—namely interiority as a *datum*—becomes that which begs the question. To give due prominence to interiorisation it is necessary to stop treating structure and agency independently. To discount the facile rejoinder that evolution is imposed design, focus must be given to the mutation of boundary conditions.[5] In the words of Didier Debaise: 'It is as if the universe, in its creative advance, never ceases to create new constraints, which are the existents themselves, canalizing how they inherit what is possible, in a new way'.[6]

To think the moving by way of the unmovable is to privilege homeo*stasis* over and above homeo*dynamics*. This is a misconception, since the latter bears the capacity to learn. The idea of a progressive constraint, as captured in Félix Guattari's concept of ethico-aesthetics, will require a step further in order to substitute the gregarious *morpho*dynamics for the parochial metabolic concerns of *homeo*dynamics.[7] As Guattari's radical empiricist predecessor William James surmised, only if sentience is involved do ethical considerations come into play.[8] Sentience inevitably implies a valence ('response-ability'),[9] and that raises the question of immanent normativity. Physics may be value-free, but ecology is certainly not.[10] By positing that there are good and bad encounters, Spinoza paved the road for such a nomadic version of normativity. The encounters can be distinguished as the empowering powers *of* life and the hindering powers *over* life.[11] His ethics equals ethology. Consequently, niche construction could have taken another course because no thing is logically necessary but only ever contingently obligatory.

The truth of the relative, which is not to be confused with the (postmodern) relativity of truth, has profound consequences for design in general and architecture in particular. In his preface to Bernard Cache's *Earth Moves*, Michael Speaks draws a diagram of architecture's enabling constraints. Building a wall is to *dis*connect first and then *re*connect differently by punching holes in it.[12] Crucially and somewhat paradoxically, architectural relation is always antecedent to its '*relata*', the interior and exterior. While the interior and exterior are interior to the actualised systems of strata, the process of dividing remains exterior to both regardless of whether they are inorganic (geological), organic (biological), or alloplastic (cultural).[13]

The thesis of Gerald Raunig's recent book, aptly named *Dividuum*, rests on a kindred premise.[14] By introducing a third term, namely the *singular-one*, Raunig overcomes the impasse of the binary opposition between the *individual-one* and the *all-one*. In his *Cartography of Exhaustion: Nihilism Inside Out*, Peter Pál Pelbart joins Raunig in refusing to take sides between (what effectively is the conceptual double of) individualism and communalism. As he puts it, 'neither fusion, nor intersubjective dialectic, nor metaphysics of alterity, but rather an enveloping composition, a disjunctive synthesis, a polyphonic game'.[15] For our own purposes it is worth emphasising that interiority does not entail detachment from the world. Rather, the interior is inconceivable as nonreciprocally presupposed with, or nonmutually constitutive of, the exterior.

Notoriously, Deleuze and Guattari never settled for diacritical solutions either. That is why they proposed a further 'con-division' of every stratum into metastable epistrata and parastrata.[16] The former relate to territorialities and movements of de-re-territorialisation, while the latter relate to codes and processes of de-re-coding. Material and discursive *activity* is all there is.[17] The epistrata are just as inseparable from the movements that constitute them as are the parastrata from their processes of semiosis. The entanglement of epistrata and parastrata is known as the Ecumenon. This unity of composition is opposed to the plane of consistency, or the Planomenon.

To bring the concept of the Ecumenon down from a high register of abstraction, the authors of *Deleuze and Geophilosophy* provide a helpful diagram.[18] In the case of religion, the unity of composition is not established solely by the faithful who make up the interior and the unfaithful from the exterior. It also includes the membrane that both protects the Ecumenon's integrity and projects its messages. In this particular diagram (the Ecumenon need not be religious), the epistrata are different internal stable states or organisational nuances and the parastrata are different affects, or capacities for becomings when encountering other assemblages.

Drawing on Gilbert Simondon's work, Deleuze and Guattari do not merely distinguish between the interior and exterior milieus mediated by the milieu of the membrane. They introduce the fourth—annexed—milieu, whereby sources of energy, different from the material that will make up the interior, are annexed to the organism. Crucially for our thesis, apart from being defined by the capture of energy sources, the fourth milieu is related to action-perceptions.[19]

According to Deleuze and Guattari, the development of associated milieus with all their active-perceptive and energetic characteristics culminates in the *umwelt* of Jacob von Uexküll.[20] They provide a graphic example which was also the favourite of Gregory Bateson's.[21] The annexed milieu of the tick is 'three-fold' and consists of (1) the gravitational pull (climbing the tree), (2) olfactory field (perception: scenting the prey), and (3) haptic sense (action: locating a hairless spot to latch on). Although much more is to be found there, it is blatantly disregarded because it matters not for the life of ticks. Here one recognises a Bergsonian trope where perception is a function of *ascesis*, and not of enrichment.[22] Existential niches are subtracted from the intensive space (*spatium*).[23] In contrast to phenomenology, which maintains the isomorphic symmetry between the two prongs of the empirico-transcendental

double, we ought to insist on the 'vital' asymmetry between the actual territory and the virtual milieu-of-milieus. The disparation is literally ontogenetic
(in this region there are no metaphors!).

Deleuze never tires of expressing his preference for lines over points. This
is his subtle way of distinguishing between the milieu's dimensions that are
directional (topological) and those of territories that are dimensional (metric).
While accepting multiple scales of reality, this view opposes the alleged primacy of the 'physical' world. What we cope with is the *umwelt*. The *umwelt* is
an ethological concept insofar as it is defined by capacities or affects. Affect
is shorthand for to-affect-and-be-affected. The animal is prone to fight as
much as it is to flight. By this curious assertion Deleuze and Guattari target
the vulgar view of the supposed evolutionary drive known as the 'survival of
the fittest'. Flights of those 'less fit' are also conquests and creations in their
own right:

> A ... kind of line of flight arises when the associated milieu is rocked by blows
> from the exterior, forcing the animal to abandon it and strike up an association
> with new portions of exteriority, this time leaning on its interior milieus like fra-
> gile crutches. When the seas dried, the primitive Fish left its associated milieu
> to explore land, forced to "stand on its own legs," now carrying water only on
> the inside, in the amniotic membranes protecting the embryo.[24]

Although the process of natural selection decreases variety and increases
constraints on form and function, the resultant consistency provides a certain
resilience that in turn allows new forms of 'cultural' variety to emerge in parallel to the 'natural'. The new means by which new information—defined as
difference that makes a difference—can emerge open up new higher-order
combinatorial possibilities. These new possibilities, however, come under
the constraining influence of the natural selection process. In the words of
the biological anthropologist Terry Deacon: 'such back-and-forth interplay
between [evolutionary] selection and [involutionary] morphodynamics thus
opens the door to indefinite complexification and ever higher-order forms
of teleodynamic organisation'.[25] Deacon's concept of 'teleonomy' from *The
Incomplete Nature* is precious for describing the kind of action that is intentional without being intended (by some-one, least of all the fully constituted
self-identical subject):

> *Teleonomy* implies law like behavior that is oriented toward a particular target
> state in systems where there is no explicit representation of that state (much less
> an intention to achieve it), but only a regular predictable orientation toward an
> end state.[26]

In conformity with Deleuzian 'static genesis', teleonomy is propelled by teleodynamics. Static genesis is pitted against its counterpart that qualifies as dynamic by virtue of its movement from a sensation-intensive encounter to the thinking of abstract-yet-real Ideas. Conversely, static geneses move from the virtual Idea to an intensive individuation process to an actual entity.[27] The concept genesis, which is static, is meant to challenge the bad habit of privileging the mechanistic (push-pull) efficient causality over the quasi-final 'braided causality'.[28] This prematurely disqualified nonlinear causal efficacy is teleonomic or tendential (i.e., *neo*finalist),[29] rather than teleological or axiomatic. It is important to stress that in terms of coping with (the constraints and opportunities of) the environment, *inter*actions are triggered as much *kinematically*—without reference to force or mass—as they are *kinetically* or techno-deterministically. Put simply, response-able life-forms respond as much to signs as they do to causal impulses, if not more.[30] Better still, what Karen Barad refers to as *intra*action[31]—the mutual constitution of entangled agencies—depends on the flow of 'epistemic engines' as much as it does on the force of 'thermodynamic engines', where 'engine' stands for any system that supplies dynamics for another system.[32]

Due to its dependence on abstract tools (for production) and concrete social purpose (of consumption), the discipline of architecture has a unique insight into the entanglement of the pathic and ontic, the kinematic and kinetic. We argue that it is the incommensurability of the non-discursive and discursive that makes involution possible and superfolding thinkable. As Bateson emphatically argued, 'confusing information processes [pathic epistemic engines] with energetic processes [ontic thermodynamic engines] was one of the most problematic tendencies of twentieth-century science ... they are in fact warp and weft of a single causal fabric'.[33]

An example is in order. Let us once again refer to the animal *umwelt*. Not a tick or fish this time, but a cat. According to Bateson, to exist is to be engaged in a certain form of play which, as he effectively argues, has a teleonomic structure: a cat's nip 'means' a 'non-bite'.[34] This, however, is not to be confused with language. The concept of involution becomes instrumental in putting the nondiscursive intensity and its affective 'catalytic operators' before intentionality or 'aboutness' of reason. In the words of David Roden, 'if the encounter gives non-inferential knowledge of the structure of reality, then it must do so without situating this categorical insight within the "space of reasons" secured by the inferential proprieties of language'.[35] After all, the development from bacteria to Bach was achieved through 'competence without comprehension'—that is, relying on significance without signification.[36]

While meaning is traditionally defined in terms of an organism's perceptions governed by 'intentionality', James Jerome Gibson proposes an alternative approach by way of 'affordance' that is a-personal, pre-subjective, extra-propositional and sub-representative—that is, immanent. This is how he introduces the neologism in his major work *The Ecological Approach to Visual Perception*:

> The affordances of the environment are what it offers the animal, what it provides or furnishes, either for good or ill. The verb to afford is found in the dictionary, but the noun affordance is not. I have made it up. I mean by it something that refers to both the environment and the animal in a way that no existing term does. It implies the complementarity of the animal and the environment.[37]

The frequent reference to animals in both Gibson's and Deleuze's work is not accidental. It is meant to emphasise the shared continuum of humans and animals rather than the break so dear to the rationalist tradition that insists on human exceptionalism. Social implications ensue. Society is *not* an aggregate of Hobbesian rational individuals as agents who are each aiming to maximise profit by way of communication. In the words of Debaise, 'What communicates are not subjects between themselves, but regimes of [subjectivation] which meet'.[38] The always-already-collective unconscious investment of desire—where desire implies rupture with linear causality—counts for more than the individual conscious investment of interest. The annexed milieu thus becomes a potential site of resistance to the hegemony of representational and instrumental thinking. The *umwelt* is a locus of creation, rather than communication. As certified niche constructionists, what architects modulate first and foremost are ethico-aesthetical affordances.

The primacy of temporal boundedness (affect/affordances) over spatial boundedness (shelter) becomes more evident as we ascend the level of biological and mental selfhood.[39] Beth Lord identifies the moment in which Kant approaches the theory of immanent differential genesis: 'it is a matter of *producing* my being by internally differentiating it from my thinking'.[40] This kind of determination does not presuppose re-cognition, as in subsuming a given being under an external concept that would determine it as my being. Ernst Cassirer would qualify it as a move from the *generic* to the *genetic* principle of determination.[41] This 'bootstrapping' moment occurs when the 'I think' generates itself from its own differential relation to itself. Dan Smith espouses Deleuze's self-declared indebtedness to Kant.[42] When desire is no longer defined in terms of lack, but in terms of production, the already miraculous 'bootstrapping' transforms itself into an even more miraculous substantiation of sorts whereby one produces the object because one desires it.[43]

By contrast to evolution, involution is not only irreducible to mechanistic causality but also free from any parochial fatalism including that of self-preservation. After all, if effects were reducible to their causes novelty would be ruled out in advance. As Sanford Kwinter recently underscored, the essential human engagement in the environment is geared toward extraction of sensory stimulation, not nourishment.[44] In this he sides with Nietzsche, who took issue with the Darwinist emphasis on the all-too-reactive 'adaptation'. He argued for the 'will to power' that provides life with new self-overcoming directions and interpretations.[45] A contemporary version of the 'power of the false' is best exemplified by the slogan concluding the recent Xenofeminist manifesto: 'If nature is unjust, change nature!'[46]

It ought to be clear by now that the exterior milieu is equally inconceivable as noncorrelative of the interior milieu. As we have argued, both interior and exterior are exterior to the *relation* of exchange (porosity) between them. This is the crux of radical empiricism. The terms of the relation are determined only *ex post facto*. First comes the *ritornello*, minimally defined as the relation which is free of conceptual prejudices. In the words of Anne Sauvagnargues from her superb *Artmachines*:

> Neither objective, cosmological time, nor a time of consciousness 'in general', ritornellos express time less as it is lived (*vécu*) than as it is inhabited (*habité*), as bundles of sensory signs by which we extract a territory from surrounding milieus through consolidation and habit. For habit very much concerns the temporal milieu in the form of repetition, but valorises the attainment of consistency as well as the crisis by which we attain consistency when we interiorise time as a power of transformation, by stabilising it as a milieu and as a habitation.[47]

In the next two sections we will position the discipline of architecture in relation to the Affect Theory and demonstrate that the so-called perceptual illusions are not illusions at all. It is not a surprise then that Deleuze and Guattari underscored the (molecular) revolutionary capacity of op art.[48]

RECLAIMING THE AFFECT THEORY FOR ARCHITECTURAL ENUNCIATION

Incorporeal materialism knows no ultimate foundation but the immanence of powers, relations, and bodily compositions. There is no need to postulate the existence of a more fundamental realm. To embrace radical empiricism is to see cognition as belonging to the same world as that of its 'objects'.[49] In Spinozian parlance, *natura naturans* and *natura naturata*—the engendering and engendered—are inseparable.

To embrace the Affective Turn is to acknowledge that, unlike affections (feelings), affect is impersonal, preindividual and unmediated. Paradoxically, feelings are states produced by thoughts, while thoughts are actually produced by affects. 'Not a thought that is assembled individually', Guattari stresses, 'but an n-dimensional thought in which everything thinks at the same time, individuals as well as groups, the "chemical" as well as the "chromosome", and the biosphere'.[50]

Instead of focusing on the all-too-human meaning (signification), the posthuman architect ought to focus on affect (affordance). In contrast to representation, expression is singularly determined (univocal). Architecture is effective not because of its predicates, but rather for the absolutely singular event of its relationality that remains irreducible to any conclusive determination. Consequently, the built environment affects without a priori determining any meaning. It neither solicits nor precludes consensus.

In this approach we side with Jeffrey Kipnis who insists on the cleavage between engineering and architecture—that is, between the subjugating effect of the former and the liberating affect of the latter.[51] While engineering—as science—delivers the greatest good for most people by reducing difference (geodesic principle), architecture—conceived as art—offers emancipatory potential by constructing new existential niches; that is, a new set of affects/affordances. Arguably, architects produce nothing but affordances, or a way of affecting which recasts them as psychotropic practitioners. Psychotropy is Daniel Smail's version of what Daniel Stern called the modulation of 'affective tonality'.[52] It includes the mood-shaping of others (tele-tropy), things we do to ourselves (auto-tropy) and things we ingest.

> The mood-altering practices, behaviors, and institutions generated by human culture are what I refer to, collectively, as psychotropic mechanisms. Psychotropic is a strong word but not wholly inapt, for these mechanisms have neurochemical effects that are not all that dissimilar from those produced by the drugs normally called psychotropic or psychoactive.[53]

To exemplify the difference between tele- and auto-tropic practices, Smail refers to Christianity. This particular faith with its *tele*tropic practices, such as liturgy and confession, is famously hostile to a range of 'sinful' *auto*tropic practices, such as masturbation and alcohol consumption.[54] It could be argued that psychotropy is one of the fundamental posthuman conditions. Smail makes a connection with the advent of civilisation which 'brought with it an economy and a political system organised increasingly around the delivery of sets of practices, institutions, and goods that alter or subvert human body chemistry. This is what gives civilisations their color and texture'.[55]

The reference to colour and texture is not coincidental. As far as we are concerned, any attempt to undermine the so-called *qualia* would result in the fallacy of what Whitehead called the 'bifurcation of nature', or the untenable split of primary from secondary qualities. Gibson was adamant: 'It is ... a mistake to separate the cultural environment from the natural environment, as if there were a world of mental products distinct from the world of material products. There is only one world'.[56] Likewise, the privilege of 'presentational immediacy' (discretion) over 'causal efficacy' (becoming) would lead to the Whiteheadian fallacy of 'misplaced concreteness'. As Deleuze's caveat goes, the true opposite of the concrete is not the abstract, but the discrete.[57]

In contrast to the metaphysical viewpoint of Nominalism, Affect Theory embraces Realism according to which virtualities or state spaces—not just actual instances—are important in determining what happens in the world. In the concluding section we will give a concrete example of such abstract space with real efficacy, akin to Karen Barad's 'agential realism'.[58] Recasting the Realism/Nominalism debate in terms of dynamics and constraints eliminates the need to pit generalities against particulars and communalism against individualism. Deacon: 'What exist are processes of change, constraints exhibited by those processes, and the statistical smoothing and the attractors (dynamical regularities that form due to self-organising processes) that embody the options left by these constraints'.[59]

Once again, we want to carve out a third line, which diverges from both the totalising wholes and constitutive parts.[60] The all-too-structuralist mereology ought to give way to the conception of the open whole that is not *of* the parts, but alongside them.[61] We thus turn our attention to mereotopology defined in terms of progressive constraint (teleodynamics). Given the growing prestige of contemporary neurosciences it has become impossible to continue to rely on armchair theorising. As Catherine Malabou argues, the reinvigorated interest in the cerebral is not to be dismissed as neuroreductionism.[62] Quite the opposite, it is the locus of the most promising research trajectory that places biology and history—nature and culture—on the same footing.[63] Only humans are biologically compelled to modify and redesign their environment in an innovative and historical manner.[64] The (neo)Lamarckian 'accelerationist' nature of cultural involution exposes the vulnerability of purely Darwinian explanations. The mode of relating itself, rather than any adaptationist end, is arguably the dominant ontopower. We are not just evolutionary products, but also evolving causes of involution. Deacon's espousal is worth quoting at length:

> The shift from simple autogen replication to information-based reproduction, though it might be a rare evolutionary transition in a cosmic sense, is one that would make a fundamental difference wherever and whenever it occurred. The capacity to offload, store, conserve, transmit, and manipulate information about the relationship between components in a teleodynamic system and its potential environmental contexts is the ultimate ententional revolution.

By combining the prefix en- (for 'within') with the adjectival form meaning something like 'inclined toward', Deacon coins the word *entential* to define intention minus intentionality. He continues:

> It marks the beginning of [asignifying] semiosis as we normally conceive of it, and with it a vast virtual representational universe of possibilities, because it marks a fundamental decoupling of what is dynamically possible from immediately present dynamical probabilities—the point at which the merely probable becomes subordinate to representational possibility. This is the source of the explosive profligacy of biological evolution.[65]

To put it succinctly, *passive* ('evo') adaptation to the environment is complemented by *active* modulation of (and by) the annexed milieu, hence 'evo-devo'. In this light we might want to recast involution as becoming active out of constitutive passivity:

> The evolution of this "anticipatory sentience"—nested within, constituted by, and acting on behalf of the "reactive (or vegetative) sentience" of the organism—has given rise to emergent features that have no precedent. Animal sentience is one of these. As brains have evolved to become more complex, the teleodynamic processes they support have become more convoluted as well, and with this the additional distinctively higher-order mode of human symbolically mediated sentience has emerged. These symbolic abilities provide what might be described as sentience of the abstract.[66]

Geno-reductionists were wrong to privilege filiation over alliance.[67] It has now become undeniable that the phenotypical expression of genes is shaped by the *umwelt*.[68] Unsurprisingly, the rates of phenotypical change are greater in urbanising systems than in natural and nonurban anthropogenic systems.[69] The Gibsonian approach was ahead of the epigenetic curve by focusing on affordances: 'ask not what's inside your head, but what your head's inside of'.[70] A contemporary version of this motto spells 'Ask not what's inside the genes you inherited, but what your genes are inside of'.[71] Epigenesis, let us remind ourselves briefly, is the theory of development in which forms are influenced and modified by the milieu. It provides for the often overlooked link between the genotype and phenotype. The fatally missing link is the process of development itself—that is, progressive differentiation.

The developmental biologist Conrad Waddington is credited with coining the term epigenetics in 1942 for the branch of biology that studies causal interactions between genes and their products giving rise to the phenotype. While the question of the extent to which we are pre-programmed—by filiation—versus developmentally shaped—in alliance—awaits universal consensus, it is safe to suggest that the field of epigenetics has helped bridge the gap between nature and nurture.[72] No wonder that it should appeal to architects as niche constructionists who could be said to sculpt brains by way of sculpting neither the genetic, nor the epigenetic, but the epi-phylo-genetic nature-cultures. The distinction between the three mnemotechnics comes from Bernard Stiegler who urges us to rethink the relationship between ontogeny and phylogeny—that is, between development at organismic scales and branching at evolutionary scales.[73] If epigenetics is the concept of nongenetic heritability such as language acquisition, then epi-phylo-genetic means that the rhetoric of 'we build our cities and in return they build us' is to be taken literally.[74]

> Epiphylogenetics … designates the appearance of a new relation between the organism and its environment, which is also a new state of matter. If the individual is organic organized matter, then its relation to its environment (to matter in general, organic or inorganic) … is mediated by the organized but inorganic matter of the *organon*, the tool with its instructive role. … It is in this sense that the *what* invents the *who* just as much as it is invented by it.[75]

It is time for the discipline of architecture to awaken from the slumber of anthropocentrism and fully embrace the posthumanist involution. By opposing the Ecumenon to the Planomenon, Deleuze and Guattari propose that we drop anthropomorphism for 'geomorphism'. The problem with our inherited abstractions is not that they are too abstract. On the contrary, they are not abstract enough. The ecological approach to cognition must not rely on representation, which typically comes in the form of a model. The problem is not to understand how to construct a simulacrum of the world, but how to cope with it. Or better, make with it, *sympoietically*. According to Donna Haraway, we ought to learn to be truly present by 'staying with the trouble'. There is no awful or edenic past to go to. There are no apocalyptic or salvic futures either. There are only 'myriad unfinished configurations of places, times, matters, meanings'.[76]

James's fellow pragmatist Charles Sanders Peirce recognised the limit of the formal *if-then* logic (induction and deduction) and argued for the hands-on *what-if* logic of abduction.[77] This form of 'material inference' or 'speculative extrapolation' presupposes an intervention into the causal fabric of reality. Paraphrasing the famous Marxist dictum, Maria Puig de la Bellacasa writes: 'theory has only observed the world; the point is to touch it'. She elaborates:

> Awareness that knowledge-making processes are inseparably world making and materially consequential evokes the power to touch of knowledge practices, and therefore a feminist concern to keep in touch with the politics and ethics at the heart of scientific and academic conversations.[78]

As we have argued, radical empiricism takes relations to be as real as objects. Furthermore, relations as higher-order facts or invariants are not only real but also directly perceivable. Under Speculative Pragmatism, reality is subject to scrutiny—that is, indefinite differentiation. It unfolds in experience, rather than sitting behind experience.

Let us consider a simple but illustrative *what-if* example. Take three snapshots of a frame within a frame (A, B, C) defined not merely by outlines, but by two superimposed textured surfaces (patterned, as they usually are in the environment).[79]

Let us now imagine that the surfaces start looming (as a result of the beholder's forward locomotion), which comes across as continuous transformation of the pattern (self-induced optical flow) both within and without the inner frame (A', B', C'). If the rate of change of the inner and outer patterns is the same, the frames are flush (A-A'). If the rate of change of the

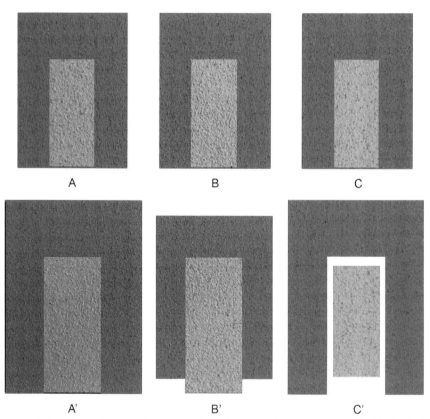

Figure 4.1:   Occlusion as a higher-order invariant. Based on 'Perception: The Ecological Approach' (Turvey 2003).

inner pattern is faster, it is a protruding obstacle (B-B'). If the rate of change of the inner pattern is slower, it is a recess which affords 'walk-through-ability' (C-C'). Curiously, even here at the level of *umwelt* (action-perceptions) we are relying on none other than the two greatest Darwinian contributions to mereotopology, namely the substitution of populations for (eternal) types, and the substitution of rates-of-change (intensity) for degrees.

In line with our previous argument, we could go as far as to suggest a reversal of the logic that rests on the substantive conception of the subject. As Leibniz knew, it is not the subject that has a point of view. Rather, the subject is second in relation to the point of view.[80] In our concrete example it would entail the following reversal: to make the optic array flow is to start moving; to cancel the flow is to stop; to make the flow reverse is to go back (and not the other way around!). By consuming these states (make/cancel/reverse flow)—the third passive synthesis of consumption—one gradually becomes aware of one's selfhood (larval subject): the experience is 'mine', hence there is also 'me'.[81]

Senses fold upon each other, intensively cross-referencing disparate planes of experience. They are neither separate nor discrete. Nor are ethics and aesthetics, action and perception, movement and image. In *Gesture and Speech*, André Leroi-Gourhan shows that encephalisation 'begins from the feet' more than from the head, since the brain 'profits' from locomotion but does not provoke it.[82] The teleodynamism of the brain that evolved to guide locomotion and the capacity to modify the *umwelt* will inevitably sculpt the brain itself. Not only does a special emergent form of self continually create its self-similarity and continuity, but it does so with respect to its alternative virtual forms.[83]

The isomorphism between the virtual space of experience (*umwelt*) and the actual experience of space (environment) does not depend on resemblance. It requires continuum-thinking attuned to transformations of states (field of rapidities and slownesses), rather than identification of transcendental objects (figure-ground). The separation between the molecular and molar is never clear-cut and that is why we resort to Guattari's concept of 'transversality', akin to Haraway's making-with (sympoiesis) rather self-making (autopoiesis). We now turn to the concluding section in order to (schizo)analyse a concrete case of the involutionary immanent relation of forces from within with forces from without.

SPECULATIONS ON COMPLEX INTERIORS
AND (SPECULATIVE) ENTENTIONALITY

In their paper 'Symmetry and Symmetry-Breaking in Thermodynamic and Epistemic Engines', the ecological psychologists Peter Kugler and Robert Shaw effectively describe an involutionary process based on nonlinear coupling of thermodynamic laws.[84] We will start this third and last section by laying out the key terms, with the exception of symmetry (breaking) that will be dealt with subsequently.

First comes the difference between the First and the Second Law. The First Law of thermodynamics is that of conservation of matter and energy, which stipulates that matter and energy cannot be created or destroyed. They can be transformed, and energy can be converted from one form into another, but the total of the equivalent amounts of both must always remain constant. The Second Law of Thermodynamics, a.k.a. *entropy*, states that energy of all sorts tends to change itself spontaneously into more dispersed, random, or less organised, forms. No wonder then that entropy is seized upon by artists such as Robert Smithson who used it to create a new kind of geophilosophical continuity between the interior and exterior, one that involved the immediate present and the most remote geological past alike.[85] The Second Law is nearly ubiquitous, yet not universal. Precisely because it is not absolutely necessary, there can be special circumstances where it does not obtain, at least locally. It is this loophole that allows the possibility of life and mind.[86]

To talk of tendency rather than law is to describe a process of falling toward regularity (contingent *nomos*), rather than being forced into it (necessary *logos*). When this 'memory of the future' is conflated with more generic notions of causality, it yields a troubling implication, especially for those with eliminativist leanings. Deacon does not shy away from the (inconvenient) truth of the involutionary effect: 'Such phenomena as life and cognition might be changing or adding to the fundamental physical laws and constants, or at least be capable of modifying them'.[87]

Traditionally, physics is taken to be the study of thermodynamic engines (movement/action), while psychology is the study of its epistemic counterparts (image/perception). By contrast to psychology and physics, biology is meant to suture the gap between the systems with and without complex interiors. By complex interiors we mean systems with entential dynamics, vital and (non-consciously) cognitive. In the wake of the Transdisciplinary Turn, it is no longer possible to place images in consciousness and movements in space, for how is one to pass from one order to another once the 'ontological iron curtain' between them is up?[88] The downfall of the disciplinary apartheid has given birth to ecology, the cross-scale science *par excellence*.

By contrast to the *ego*logical categories of time and space, *eco*logic is concerned solely with symmetry as the measure of consistency—that is, 'what on a given stratum varies and what does not'.[89] The transversal coupling (sympoiesis) remains reversible across the *same* scale (symmetry-preserving), but crucially, it is irreversible across *different* scales (symmetry-breaking). The former can be summed up in the famous mereological maxim: 'the whole is the sum of its parts'. The latter is ecological by virtue of not offering such reassurance. Simply put, the Superfold stands for irreducible complexity of the *singular-one*. Deacon: 'What we interpret as parts are in most cases the consequence of differentiation processes in which structural discontinuities and functional modularization emerged from a prior, less-differentiated state, whether in evolution or development'.[90] In contrast to agglomerations—that can be dissected into their synchronic parts and reconstructed without loss— Superfolds suffer the Humpty-Dumpty problem when taken apart. In dia-chronic superfolding, synthesis is *not* analysis in reverse.

Whereas the Second Law has traditionally been seen as a destructive agency, a new view has emerged that considers it an active participant in constructive processes. Systems open to the replenishing and dissipative processes can develop new symmetries that lead to new ententions manifested as fitness landscapes. As Waddington discovered, 'we will find that the system resists some types of changes more than others, or restores itself more quickly after changes in some directions than in others'.[91] The new attractors (*ritornellos*) that emerge out of the competition between import of high-grade energy and export of low-grade energy are invariant solutions (symmetries) that relate the molecular and molar states of a system. Kwinter elucidates:

> The relentless cleaving and changing of the universe's 'matter-flow' establishes *the rule of the differential* in nature, and following from it the irrepressible, some might even say divine reality of the gradient without which nothing would ever happen, and thanks to which so many wonderful things not yet imagined, easily could.[92]

Therein lies the most profound (negentropic) lesson for posthuman architects. There is no such thing as simple part-to-whole relationship. This is what Spinoza expressed in his oft-quoted maxim 'we don't know what a body can do'.[93] However, if we substituted mereotopology for mereology, it would become possible to find a subset of solutions for multiple interacting systems in spite of their *dynamical* relationship. The Gibsonian affordance, which is akin to the Deleuzian affect, is such a 'critical set', which specifies the symmetries shared by the systems of acting-perceiving organisms and their associated milieus. Affect always cuts both ways. The affordance of 'sit-on-ability' depends as much on the quasi-objective layout (structure formerly known as a chair) as it does on the quasi-subjective entention (agency wrongly attributed to intention).

Affordance is best described as a higher-order invariant (invariant of invariants). Deacon describes invariants with reference to constraints, as something 'less' than varying without limit. If there is a bias in the probability of the occurrence of states, not all of them are realised.[94] Any long-term tendency of a system (attractor) is but a Peircean 'habit'. In this sense, gravity is the habit of the Earth. Even things could be said to have propensities, or sympathies.[95] So do situations. The presence of constraints entails the absence of certain potential states. The nature of the constraint determines 'which differences can and cannot make a difference in any interaction'.[96] Consequently, an increase in entropy is a decrease in constraint, and vice versa, or, as Stuart Kauffman put it, 'constraints are information and information is constraint'.[97] Most importantly for our thesis, constraint *propagation*—which can be translated as habits-begetting-habits—is the ultimate locus of vicarious causality or what Deleuze calls becoming (*devenir*).

Where does it all leave us in terms of niche construction? To adopt a mereotopological approach to posthuman architecture and urbanism is to think in terms of intensive capacities rather than mere extensive properties. This understanding of response-able life is tied with Deleuze's analysis of sensation that exceeds the bounds of the organic body because it is registered at an antecedent level. Sensation is not representational. It is not *like* something, explains the champion of the Corporeal Turn, Maxine Sheets-Johnstone.[98] However, to claim that it-is-what-it-is is not a tautology, since things are powers, not forms. As we have argued, agency cannot be segregated from structure nor can it be possessed; it can only be produced *ad hoc*, as implied in the concept of assemblage (*agencement*). By the same token, the so-called perceptual illusions are not illusions, but locally generated geometro-dynamical real effects. Crucially, these curvature-based effects are forceless. They are kinematic.

We will conclude by considering a well-known but wrongly qualified 'optical illusion'. We shall argue that it is not a self-induced effect on the part of the observer, but an *effect* yielded by the observer's state space which literally gets warped by what it detects. Kugler and Shaw explain:

> By tracking the equidistant, parallel lines depicted by the trivial gradient sets of a flat space (B) to the left (A) and to the right (C), we see what failure of our nervous systems to solve the cohomology problem means perceptually.

What cohomology actually measures, at its most elementary, is failure of *local* solutions to glue together to form a *global* (cross-scale) solution. As in the process of tessellation (*planification*), the problem is how modular

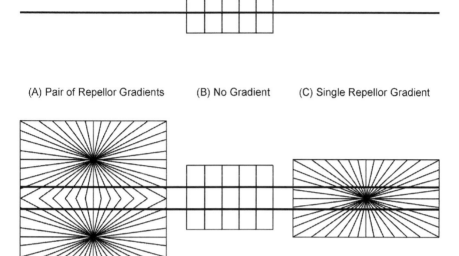

(A) Pair of Repellor Gradients   (B) No Gradient   (C) Single Repellor Gradient

Figure 4.2: Kinematic effect manifested as warping of manifolds. Based on 'Symmetry and Symmetry-Breaking in Thermodynamic and Epistemic Engines' (Kugler and Shaw 1990).

quantities (tiles), when distributed under local constraints only, fit together globally over the manifold that they attempt to cover (floor). Cohomology reveals the impossibility of patching locally consistent data into a consistent whole. Simpler still, it demonstrates the *impossibility of totalisation*. Transversal onto-hetero-genesis, or what we referred to as the Superfold, provides a frame-free means for explaining discrepancies between local and nonlocal constraints. Kugler and Shaw continue:

> The information for change in curvature of the lines is due to the failure of gradient sets (A), (B), and (C) to share a common homological solution. Hence the pair of lines conforms locally to the direction and distance metrics of the manifold to which they are most proximal. Our state space as observers is being warped by what it detects rather than causing the effect itself. The critical set properties [affordances/affects] have as much reality status as any other physical property, and more than most. Hence the lines are indeed curved, and they are not illusions![99]

It was the Stoics who first proposed that things themselves are bearers of 'ideal events' that do not exactly coincide with their properties. Any *actual* incarnation may in fact be seen as a provisional 'solution' to the *virtual* problem posed by the state space, the same way that lightning is the solution to the problem of electrical potential differences between the cloud and the ground.[100] It is why the virtual is qualified as 'problematic', real yet incorporeal. However, by no means are we proposing the Manichean opposition between the *quantitative* actual and *qualitative* virtual. Likewise, a paralogism of psycho-physical commensurability of *extensive* magnitudes and *intensive* differences must be debunked, a generalised economy of equivalences refused. The difference between the difference in degree and in kind is *not* reducible to either: 'between the two are all the degrees of difference—beneath the two lies the entire nature of difference, in other words, the intensive'.[101] And indeed, for Deleuze it is the *intensive* nature of difference that binds the virtual and actual and provides the catalyst for subjectivation.

The geometro-dynamical warping is the Stoic incorporeal effect of the kinetic corporeal cause, which in turn operates as an onto-powerful formal and kinematic quasi-cause.[102] Our conjecture is that there could be no teleonomy without mereotopology (against mereology), which in turn is a problem of sympoiesis (against autopoiesis), the hallmark of ethico-aesthetics. The concept of quasi-cause ('dark precursor') prevents regression into simple reductionism. It designates the pure agency of vicarious causality, the difference in itself that relates heterogeneities. Deacon too is unambiguous about the fact that 'all efficient causes ultimately depend on the juxtaposition of formal [quasi] causes!'[103] The warped state space of the observer from the earlier example is of the same ilk as the process by which mass singularities curve space-time. 'It is, crucially, not a matter of curves in a flat space but of the curvature of the space itself'.[104] The major difference is that such effects may be induced through neuro-perceptual fields into the abstract machines of thought and experience. In Andy Clark's terms, these are 'optimal illusions' quasi-caused by predictions.[105] These pockets of inconsistency, Kugler and Shaw insist, are like local inertial frames. They show up as nonlinearities (not 'perceptual errors') at the more exacting level of systems integration.[106] They are wrongly assumed to be self-induced alterations in the mind that distort the perception of the world. Quite the contrary, the imperceptible is virtually perceived, albeit as actually inconsistent over local frames. The failure of homologies to mesh across scales is unsurprising since the molar has fewer degrees of freedom (i.e. less symmetry) than the molecular.

In contrast to Rationalists who believe that nature has solved the cohomology problem, Speculative Pragmatists see reality more like a Harlequin's coat, 'an infinite patchwork with multiple joinings'.[107] The joinings stand for entanglements of Epi- and Para-Strata. The ontological question of what-there-is cannot be separated from its ethical counterpart of how-to-live, nor from the aesthetic imperative of constructing a new sensorium. The question of interior, interiority and interiorisation is ultimately a matter of sensibility, not of judgement.[108] It is a matter of radical auto-affectivity sustained by an ongoing artistic, conceptual and historical involution; not of pleasure, but of self-enjoyment defined as immediacy without objectification. If we can accept as really real only that which is cohomologically systematic across our experience (*partes extra partes*), perhaps the fault lies more with our all-too-phenomenological conception of *possible* experience than with the *real* unlimited finity.

NOTES

1. Spinoza 1764.
2. Bateson 1977, 245.
3. Deleuze 1988 [1986], 131.
4. Deleuze and Guattari 2004 [1980], 238–39.
5. Deacon 2012, 426.
6. Debaise 2017, 66.
7. Guattari 1995 [1992].
8. James 1979 [1897], 198.
9. Haraway 2016, 29.
10. Gibson 1986 [1979], 137–40.
11. Deleuze 1988 [1970], 17–29.
12. Speaks, 1995, xviii.
13. Deleuze and Guattari 2004 [1980], 57–60.
14. Raunig 2016.
15. Pál Pelbart 2015 [2013], 18.
16. Deleuze and Guattari 2004 [1980], 53.
17. Foucault and Deleuze 1977, 205–7.
18. Bonta and Protevi 2004, 81.
19. Deleuze and Guattari 2004 [1980], 51.
20. von Uexküll 1957.
21. Bateson 1977, 241.
22. Meillassoux 2007.
23. Radman 2017.
24. Deleuze and Guattari 2004 [1980], 54–55.
25. Deacon 2012, 462.
26. Deacon 2012, 116.
27. Deleuze 1994 [1968], 183.
28. Massumi 2017, 353–54.
29. Ruyer 2016 [1952].
30. Bains 2006, 61.
31. Barad 2007, 33.
32. Kugler and Shaw 1990, 312.

33. Bateson 1977, 241.
34. Bateson 1972, 141–46.
35. Roden 2016.
36. Dennett 2017.
37. Gibson 1986, 127.
38. Debaise 2012, 7.
39. Deacon 2012, 470.
40. Lord 2012, 92.
41. Cassirer 1970 [1945], 69, 93.
42. Smith 2012, 117.
43. Ibid., 187.
44. Kwinter 2014, 331.
45. Ansell-Pearson 2000, 26.
46. Laboria Cuboniks 2015.
47. Sauvagnargues 2016, 126.
48. Deleuze and Guattari 2004 [1980], 478.
49. Heft 2001, 73.
50. Guattari 2015, 205.
51. Kipnis et al. 2015.
52. Smail 2008. Cf., Stern 1985.
53. Smail 2008, 161.
54. Smail 2008, 177–78.
55. Smail 2008, 162.
56. Gibson 1986 [1979], 130.
57. Deleuze 1978.
58. Barad 2007, 132–85.
59. Deacon 2012, 197.
60. Bateson 1977, 244.
61. Deleuze and Guattari 2004 [1980], 266.
62. Malabou 2008, 72.
63. Deleuze and Guattari 1994, 208.
64. Kwinter 2014, 313–33.
65. Deacon 2012, 458.
66. Deacon 2012, 504–5.
67. Deleuze and Guattari 2004, 238.
68. Wexler 2013, 185–217.
69. Alberti et al. 2016.
70. Mace 1977.
71. Stotz 2017.
72. Kwinter 2008, 40.
73. Stiegler 1998.
74. Stiegler 1998, 134–79.
75. Stiegler 1998, 177.
76. Haraway 2016, 1.
77. Peirce 1955 [1903], 302–5.

78. Puig de la Bellacasa 2009, 298–99.
79. Turvey 2003, 340.
80. Deleuze 1980.
81. Deleuze 1994 [1968], 78–79.
82. Leroi-Gourhan 1993 [1964], 229.
83. Deacon 2012, 484.
84. Kugler and Shaw 1990, 296–331.
85. Smithson 1996, 23.
86. Deacon 2012, 237.
87. Deacon 2012, 368.
88. Guattari 1995, 108.
89. Deleuze and Guattari 2004 [1980], 45.
90. Deacon 2012, 135.
91. Waddington 1977, 113.
92. Kwinter 2016.
93. Deleuze and Guattari 2004 [1980], 283.
94. Deacon 2012, 202.
95. Jullien 1995. Cf. Spuybroek 2011.
96. Deacon 2012, 198.
97. Deacon 2012, 228, 392.
98. Sheets-Johnstone 1999, 139, 146–50.
99. Kugler and Shaw 1990, 328.
100. Gilles Deleuze 1994, 119.
101. Ibid., 239.
102. Deleuze and Guattari 2004 [1980], 86.
103. Deacon 2012, 232.
104. Plotinsky 2003, 101–2.
105. Clark 2016.
106. Kugler and Shaw 1990, 329–30.
107. Deleuze 1997, 86.
108. Deleuze 1983 [1962], 94.

REFERENCES

Alberti, M., et al. (2016). 'Global Urban Signatures of Phenotypic Change in Animal and Plant Populations' In *Proceedings of the National Academy of Sciences of The USA*, ed. Jay S. Golden. Durham, NC: Duke University Press. http://www.pnas.org/content/early/2017/01/01/1606034114.full.pdf. Accessed November 26, 2017.

Ansell-Pearson, K. (2000). 'Nietzsche's Brave New World of Force: Thoughts on Nietzsche's 1873 "Time Atom Theory" Fragment and on the Influence of Boscovich on Nietzsche,' *Pli* 9: 6–35.

Bains, P. (2006). *The Primacy of Semiosis: An Ontology of Relations*. Toronto: University of Toronto Press.

Barad, K. (2007). *Meeting the Universe Halfway: Quantum Physics and the Entanglement of Matter and Meaning*. Durham, NC: Duke University Press.

Bateson, G. (1972). 'A Theory of Play and Fantasy'. In *Steps to an Ecology of Mind; Collected Essays in Anthropology, Psychiatry, Evolution, and Epistemology.* New York: Ballantine, 138–48.

Bateson, G. (1977). 'Afterword'. In *About Bateson*, John Brockman, ed. New York: E.P. Dutton, 233–47.

Bonta, M., and Protevi, J. (2004). *Deleuze and Geophilosophy: A Guide and Glossary.* Edinburgh: Edinburgh University Press.

Cassirer, E. (1970) [1945]. *Rousseau, Kant, Goethe: Two Essays*. Translated by J. Gutmann, P. O. Kristeller, and J. H. Randall Jr. Princeton, NJ: Princeton University Press.

Clark, A. (2016). *Surfing Uncertainty: Prediction, Action, and the Embodied Mind.* Oxford: Oxford University Press.

Deacon, T. (2012). *Incomplete Nature: How Mind Emerged from Matter.* New York: W.W. Norton.

Debaise, D. (2012). 'What Is Relational Thinking?'. In *INFLeXions* 5: *Milieus, Techniques, Aesthetics*, M. Boucher and P. Harrop, ied. Translated by Thomas Jellis: 1–11.

Debaise, D. (2017). *Nature as Event: The Lure of the Possible*. Translated by M. Halewood Durham, NC: Duke University Press.

Deleuze, G. (1978). 'Kant, Synthesis and Time,' *Cours Vincennes*, March 14, https://www.webdeleuze.com/textes/66. Accessed November 26, 2017.

Deleuze, G. (1980). 'Leibniz,' *Cours Vincennes*, April 4, https://www.webdeleuze.com/textes/50. Accessed November 26, 2017.

Deleuze, G. (1983) [1962]. *Nietzsche and Philosophy*. Translated by Hugh Tomlinson. New York: Columbia University Press.

Deleuze, G. (1988) [1970]. *Spinoza, Practical Philosophy*. Translated by Robert Hurley. San Francisco: City Lights Books.

Deleuze, G. (1988) [1986]. *Foucault*. Translated by Seán Hand. Minneapolis: University of Minnesota.

Deleuze, G. (1994) [1968]. *Difference and Repetition*. Translated by Paul Patton. New York: Columbia University Press.

Deleuze, G. (1997). 'Bartleby: or, The Formula'. In *Essays Critical and Clinical*, Translated by D. W. Smith and M. A. Greco. Minneapolis: University of Minnesota Press, 68–90.

Deleuze, G., and Guattari, F. (2004) [1980]. *A Thousand Plateaus*. Translated by B. Massumi. London: Continuum.

Dennett, D. C. (2017). *From Bacteria to Bach and Back: The Evolution of Minds.* London: Allen Lane.

Foucault, M., and Deleuze, G. (1977). 'Intellectuals and Power'. In *Language, Counter-Memory and Practice*, D. F. Bouchard, ed. Translated by D. F. Bouchard and S. Simon. Ithaca, NY: Cornell University Press, 205–7.

Gibson, J. J. (1986) [1979]. *The Ecological Approach to Visual Perception*. Mahwah, NJ: Lawrence Erlbaum Associates.

Guattari, F. (1995) [1992]. *Chaosmosis: An Ethico-aesthetic Paradigm*. Translated by P. Bains and J. Pefanis. Bloomington: Indiana University Press.

Guattari, F. (2015). *Lines of Flight: For Another World of Possibilities*. Translated by A. Goffey London: Bloomsbury Academic.

Haraway, D. J. (2016). *Staying with the Trouble: Making Kin with the Chthulucene*. Durham, NC: Duke University Press.

Heft, H. (2001). *Ecological Psychology in Context: James Gibson, Roger Barker, and the Legacy of William James's Radical Empiricism*. Mahwah, NJ: Lawrence Erlbaum.

James, W. (1979) [1897]. *The Will to Believe and Other Essays in Popular Philosophy*. Cambridge, MA: Harvard University Press.

Jullien, F. (1995). *The Propensity of Things: Toward a History of Efficacy in China*. Translated by J. Lloyd. New York: Zone Books.

Kipnis, J., et al. (2015). '2015 Grad Thesis Prep Symposium,' http://sma.sciarc.edu/video/2015-grad-thesis-prep-symposium/ Accessed May 4, 2015.

Kugler, P. N., and Shaw. R. (1990). 'Symmetry and Symmetry-Breaking in Thermodynamic and Epistemic Engines: A Coupling of First and Second Laws'. In *Synergetics of Cognition*, H. Haken and M. Stadler, eds. Heidelberg: Springer-Verlag Berlin, 296–331.

Kwinter, S. (2008). 'A Discourse on Method'. In *Explorations in Architecture*, Reto Geiser, ed. Basel: Birkhäuser, 34–47.

Kwinter, S. (2014). 'Neuroecology: Notes Toward a Synthesis'. In *The Psychopathologies of Cognitive Capitalism: Part Two*, Warren Neidich, ed. Berlin: Archive Books, 313–33.

Kwinter, S. (2016). 'Sensing the Aerocene' http://sanfordkwinter.com/Sensing-the-Aerocene Accessed November 26, 2017.

Laboria Cuboniks. (2015). 'Xenofeminism: A Politics for Alienation', http://www.laboriacuboniks.net. Accessed November 26, 2017.

Leroi-Gourhan, A. (1993) [1964]. *Gesture and Speech*. Translated by A. B. Berger. Cambridge, MA: MIT Press.

Lord, B. (2012). 'Deleuze and Kant'. In *The Cambridge Companion to Deleuze*, D. Smith and H. Somers-Hall, eds. Cambridge: Cambridge University Press, 82–102.

Mace, W. (1977). 'James J. Gibson's Strategy for Perceiving: Ask Not What's Inside Your Head, but What Your Head's Inside Of'. In *Perceiving, Acting and Knowing: Toward an Ecological Psychology*, R. Shaw and J. Bransford, eds. Hillsdale, NJ: Lawrence Erlbaum Associates, 43–65.

Malabou, C. (2008). *What Should We Do with Our Brain?* Translated by Sebastian Rand. New York: Fordham University Press.

Massumi, B. (2017). 'Virtual Ecology and the Question of Value'. In *General Ecology: The New Ecological Paradigm*, E. Hörl, ed. London: Bloomsbury Academic, 345–73.

Meillassoux, Q. (2007). 'Subtraction and Contraction: Deleuze, Immanence, and *Matter and Memory*,' *Collapse: Unknown Deleuze* III, 63–107.

Pál Pelbart, P. (2015) [2013]. *Cartography of Exhaustion: Nihilism Inside Out*. Translated by J. Laudenberger and F. R. Palazuclos. Minneapolis: Univocity Publishing.

Peirce, C. S. (1955) [1903]. 'Abduction and Induction'. In *Philosophical Writings of Peirce*, J. Buchler, ed. New York: Dover, 302–5.

Plotinsky, A. (2003). 'Algebras, Geometries and Topologies of the Fold: Deleuze, Derrida and Quasi-Mathematical Thinking (with Leibniz and Mallarmé)'. In *Between Deleuze and Derrida*, P. Patton and J. Protevi, eds. New York: Continuum, 98–119.

Puig de la Bellacasa, M. (2009). 'Touching Technologies, Touching Visions: The Reclaiming of Sensorial Experience and the Politics of Speculative Thinking,' *Subjectivity* 28, 297–315.

Radman, A. (2017). 'Space Always Comes After: It Is Good When It Comes After; It Is Good Only When It Comes After'. In *Speculative Art Histories: Analysis at the Limits*, ed. S. van Tuinen. Edinburgh: Edinburgh University Press, 185 201.

Raunig G. (2016). *Dividuum: Machinic Capitalism and Molecular Revolution*, Vol. 1. Translated by A. Derieg. Los Angeles: Semiotext(e).

Roden, D (2016). 'A Post-Sellarsian Encounter,' https://enemyindustry.wordpress.com/2016/11/25/a-post-sellarsian-encounter/. Accessed November 26, 2017.

Ruyer, R. (2016) [1952]. *Neofinalism*. Translated by A. Edlebi. Minneapolis: Minnesota University Press.

Sauvagnargues, A. (2016). *Artmachines: Deleuze, Guattari, Simondon*. Translated by S. Verderber with E. W. Holland. Edinburgh: Edinburgh University Press.

Sheets-Johnstone, M. (1999). *The Primacy of Movement*. Aarhus: Aarhus University.

Smail, D. (2008). *On Deep History and the Brain*. Berkeley: University of California Press.

Smith, D. W. (2012). *Essays on Deleuze*. Edinburgh: Edinburgh University Press.

Smithson, R. (1996). *Robert Smithson: The Collected Writings*, J. Flam, ed. Los Angeles: University of California Press.

Speaks, M. (1995). 'Folding toward a New Architecture'. In *Earth Moves: The Furnishing of Territories*, B. Cache, ed. Cambridge, MA: MIT Press, xviii–xx.

Spinoza, B. (1764). 'Letter 62 (P03) to G. H. Schuller or Schaller (The Hague, October 1764)', http://www.faculty.umb.edu/gary_zabel/Courses/Spinoza/Texts/Spinoza/let6258.htm. Accessed November 26, 2017.

Spuybroek, L. (2011). *The Sympathy of Things; Ruskin and the Ecology of Design*. Rotterdam: V2 Pub./Nai.

Stern, D. N. (1985). *The Interpersonal World of the Infant: A View from Psychoanalysis and Developmental Psychology*. New York: H. Karnac.

Stiegler, B. (1998). *Technics and Time 1: The Fault of Epimetheus*. Translated by G. Collins and R. Beardsworth. Stanford, CA: Stanford University Press.

Stotz, K. (2017). 'Why Developmental Niche Construction Is Not Selective Niche Construction: and Why It Matters'. *Interface Focus* 7. DOI: 10.1098/rsfs.2016.0157. Accessed March 24, 2018.

Turvey, M. T. (2003). 'Perception: The Ecological Approach'. In *Encyclopedia of Cognitive Science*, Lynn Nadel, ed. New York: Nature Publishing Group, 538–41.

von Uexküll, J. (1957). 'A Stroll through the Worlds of Animals and Men: A Picture Book of Invisible Worlds'. In *Instinctive Behavior: The Development of a Modern Concept*, ed. and trans. C. H. Schiller. New York: International Universities Press, 5–80.

Waddington, C. H. (1977). *Tools for Thought*. New York: Basic Books.

Wexler, B. (2013). 'Neuroplasticity, Culture and Society'. In *The Psychopathologies of Cognitive Capitalism: Part One*, A. De Boever and W. Neidich, eds. Berlin: Archive Books, 185–217.

Chapter 5

Love of Learning

Amorous and Fatal

Elizabeth de Freitas

Here, the technical mentality successfully completes itself and rejoins nature by turning itself into a thought-network, into the material and conceptual synthesis of particularity and concentration, individuality and collectivity—because the entire force of the network is available in each of its points, and its mazes are woven together with those of the world, in the concrete and the particular. —Gilbert Simondon[1]

THOUGHT NETWORKS

New theories of learning are formulated amidst the contemporary proliferation of inexpensive micro-sensing technology, allowing researchers to track bodily activity below the bandwidth of human consciousness. Neuro-imaging, eye-tracking, electro-dermal activity mapping, 3-D accelerometers and various other sensor technologies attend to the 'precognitive' activity of the body. These accelerated computational plug-ins are used to track engagement and learning potential. Data is then fed back into live data structures so as to furnish continuous evaluations of competency and achievement, bracketing the conscious subject as the active agent of learning. This kind of *dividuation* and rupture of the organism may well be what we moderns have always feared. Learning in posthuman ecologies seems to circumvent the individual, and perhaps finally mark the moment when the organism has no future, when a digital and viral life thrives, a life that is not intent on sustaining its embodied boundaries through autopoiesis. This would be a post-traumatic life, a life that learns without the fear of failure, a life that dies everywhere and whenever there is the passage through zero intensity.[2] We might then revise the model of 'learning trajectory', as education policy conventionally names it, into 'learning de/coherence', and study the inhuman terrain of mobile little implosions where intensity bottoms out or breaks through a threshold. Given our track record—as bounded organic human bodies of malevolence and milieu destruction—maybe this other life will *learn* the earth in more inclusive and sympathetic ways.

Deleuze offers the oft-cited example of learning to swim where he suggests that learning is not a mimicry or response to a command 'do as I do', but must involve a learning 'with' whereby 'a body combines some of its own distinctive points with those of a wave'; this aspect of learning means that 'there is something amorous—but also something fatal—about all education'.[3] The suggestion that learning entails the amorous and fatal dissolving of the body as it re-articulates and re-forms with the sea, when swimming, is at once a beautiful image of learning, and an all too accurate description of the breaking apart of the organism in today's digital data deluge.[4] If posthuman ecologies thrive by means of such distributed learning, it is because of their distinctive re-assembling of technics, sense, and naturecultures.[5] We witness here how the concept of ecology has become increasingly 'denaturalized' in our current diffuse *technosphere* where 'power is environmentalized by media technologies' allowing for new forms of governmentality and control.[6] The turn to posthuman ecologies is part of a turn to a generalised ecological paradigm, a geologic technoecology, a total technical milieu. And thus there is a need for an onto-ethics adequate to current socio-technical attachments to the body, as learning and dis/ability become increasingly environmentalised through datafication.

In this chapter, I explore the Stoic concept of *sympathy* and its potential relevance to current posthuman ecologies. The word sympathy comes from ancient Greek (sumpátheia) and refers to the state of *feeling together*, derived from a composite of *fellow* and *feeling*.[7] Over the centuries, the notion of sympathy has been used to describe all sorts of activity—everything from contagious yawn catching to cosmological harmony to empathic and even telepathic association. My aim in this chapter is to explore the force of sympathy in posthuman ecologies where learning occurs somewhat indifferently to the survival of the bounded organism. I see this as an attempt to rethink the refrain 'love of learning'—this would be a love of learning that was not autopoetic or self-maintaining in the organicist image we've inherited from systems theory. This would be a love that seeks the inorganic potentialities and nonhuman forces by which a body becomes transindividual and learns to 'branch out into territories beyond its own self-maintenance'.[8]

I first explore the role of sympathy in learning, as 'something to be reckoned with, a bodily struggle'.[9] Sympathy is not a matter of identification or 'putting oneself in the other's shoes' but a matter of assembling with an independent other—a process of *becoming other that does not erase the other*.

Such a process involves a 'making with' that Haraway calls 'sympoiesis'.[10] A sympathetic coordination is not a bland alignment, nor an identification among parts, nor the creation of a unified homogeneous assemblage, but rather describes the coordinated assembling of heterogeneous agencies. Such activity entails a *sympathetic* agreement between two very different movements without erasing their distinctness (i.e., the orchid and the wasp). In the first half of the chapter, I explore Massumi's ideas about a power that is sourced at the infra-scale of intra-activity (that being beneath the time-scale of the human) in coordinating a more-than-human achievement at the transindividual scale.[11] Massumi argues that such coordination underscores the more-than-human sympathy at work through affect.

Such an approach, I suggest, helps us track the flow of affect, but doesn't adequately attend to the nonorganic life of concepts, and their role in sympathetic relations. How does thought itself (as distinct from affect) participate in a cosmic sympathy? The remaining parts of the chapter focus on Deleuze's reading of Spinoza, and in particular his suggestion that Spinoza affirms thought while bracketing consciousness. I argue that a worldly and sympathetic relationality between thought and matter requires a reconsideration of concept and form. I turn to Deleuze's Spinoza to reckon with the dangers of posthuman sympathies that are no more than linked-in liking societies and personalised learning platforms. I argue that the refrain 'love of learning' be thought of in two Spinozan ways, first in terms of a *conatus* (whereby a body strives to sustain and increase itself through connectivity), and second, in terms of a theory of *emendation of the intellect* (whereby intellect learns to love the failures and imperfections and porosity of a body, pursuing a secular 'belief in the body' that depersonalises and further disorganises it, while seeking a more generalised perfection).

Although Spinoza, like Descartes, was suspicious of occult references to sympathy, I follow Hübner,[12] and argue that sympathy helps make sense of Spinoza's parallelism between mind and body, and is precisely how we might understand the linkages between coordinated affects and Simondon's notion of the thought-network.[13] This linkage is crucial if our current posthuman ecologies are to create conditions for a kind of learning that entails more than pattern recognition, a learning that involves sympathy, defined by Spuybroek as a 'felt experience of form' or a 'felt abstraction'.[14]

TRANSINDIVIDUAL SYMPATHY

Sympathy is a complex concept with a complex history, but always seems to reference a collective or transindividual experience, whereby we are 'moved by' the other, and learn to 'move with' the other. As Deleuze suggests, sympathy involves affect and the power to be affected.[15] Indeed, sympathy often refers to the communicability of affect, and the ability of affect to circulate across *bodily* relations.

Sympathy was an important part of Stoic natural philosophy and was used to explain natural phenomena like magnetism and the molecular bonding of certain materials, but also the joining of mind and body. Sympathy in this early form of materialism and vitalism explained the forces of attraction that operated in the physical world, but also the coaffection of mind and body.[16] Sympathy was a feature of the world and an 'active principle'. The social implications of this cosmic sympathy included a kind of cosmopolitanism—a citizenship of the world—achieved through enhanced rationality and common feeling.[17] As Western science emerged, the concept of sympathy also mutated, dismissed by some, like Descartes, as being an occult concept based on a magical image of causation.[18]

Sympathy returned full-force in the eighteenth century, building on the ethical ontologies of Spinoza and Leibniz, and becoming once again a means to explain physical and cognitive convergence of feeling. It was in the eighteenth century that the term was used to capture both the corporeal 'mechanical communication of passions and feelings' as well as processes of identification (with others) using the imagination and reason.[19] One can identify three pivotal ideas at work here—a *contagion* of feeling, a *common sense* or shared sensibility, and a *compassion* for the other. Sympathy was not simply used to describe interpersonal relations, but was also deployed by chemists, physicists, astronomers and physicians to describe principles of affinity and coordinated relations among material and corporeal 'parts and functions'.[20] Whether we look to Newton or other eighteenth century scholars focused on the nature of attraction and action at a distance, or to the Medieval toxicologist Paracelsus for affinity links between headaches and acorn cures, sympathy appears as a compelling if enigmatic explanatory concept. Within physiology, a concerted effort to understand *sensation* led to studies of sympathy as an 'extension of sensibility'. Early physiologists studied the 'action of sensation, the coordination of organs in the body, and the "social principle" that allows "fellow-feeling" to emerge in a society'.[21]

The emergent metaphysical doctrine of sympathy during this period can be characterised in terms of: 'its foundations in epistemic associationism, its role as an action-motivating sentiment, and its relationship to self-interest and self-love'.[22] Sympathy thus involves a kind of amorous action to modify one's own actions so as to *feel with* the other. Here I stress the ways that sympathy is distinguished from uni-directional acts of identification that erase the other. It's not a gift (and not pity). Sympathy is a kind of *agreement* between bodies when they are mutually affected by each other in a coordinated and collective achievement. Lost to later interpretations was the crucial reciprocal tension and co-affectivity that was mobilised through agreements by which affect was shared without erasing distinctive powers.[23]

Again, such agreement is not erasure of distinctive manner nor equalising of power. Attempts to distinguish sympathy from empathy are frequent, and many claim that the latter concept—empathy was first named by the American psychologist Edward Titchener in 1909—performs that kind of erasure.[24] Theories of interpersonal empathy that emerged in the early twentieth century targeted the problem of 'other minds' and the question of how we can feel what others feel. This kind of approach first assumes a set of isolated individuated minds, and then pursues explanations for how they might connect—for instance, the work of Vittorio Gallese on mirror neurons and embodied simulations is within this area of research. In other words, empathy always comes too late, an appropriating gesture reaching out across the given distance. In contrast, sympathy operates very differently, since the charged somatic field of sympathetic intra-action comes first, and individuation comes after. In other words, the interiority of individuated organisms is a kind of topological fold in the primary dynamic affective system. This approach allows researchers to track the circulation of pre-conscious affect in complex environments where learning assemblages are 'coming together' in fellow-feeling. In other words, sympathetic bonds are the bedrock of learning and the condition for the individuation of what Deleuze calls the untimely thoughts of 'the private thinker' in an onto-ethical thought-network.

LEARNING COLLABORATIVELY

Massumi suggests that one must prime or condition the environment in order to create opportunities for transindividual sympathy to emerge. A learning environment then becomes conducive to collaborative efforts. Sympathetic relations form across bodies often unconsciously, whereby students 'feel' for each other and follow each other often without explicit or rational choice, but in ways that involve mutual tension. In such an endeavour, one can begin to imagine a sympathetic collaborative learning environment, where the micro-scale actions of the infra-individual (affect) percolate out and resonate with larger scale transindividual endeavours, circumventing the individual organism. This approach begins to track the highly *contagious* nature of affect across a learning assemblage and brackets the individual human organism in enigmatic ways. Affects are contagious because they traverse the individual somewhat indifferently; in other words, the flow of affect contracts and expands across an event, recruiting our bodies and participation to varying degrees. Of course there are different ways of partaking in this flow of affect, and different degrees of conscious involvement and refusal.

Consider, for instance, a pedagogical task that demands some kind of coordination. The relational movement that characterises this task—along with the other forces and agencies that sustain the milieu —form a generative problem. Different bodies feel each other's movements during highly collaborative efforts.[25] Sympathies proliferate in these everyday minute interactions, lived in and as affective bonds, and assemble into larger overt emotional responses. Minute sympathetic movements contribute to passionate attachments, so that the emotional investment in such shared activities becomes pronounced.

Learning becomes *a doing done through the individuals (rather than by the individuals)*.[26] When different agencies and bodies begin to work together in this way, the achievement is strangely indifferent to intent of individuals, and rests fundamentally on somatic and unconscious ways of moving together, as well as the immediate communication of affections. This kind of affective sympathy is the seed of collaborative learning, engendering new action-paths across the event, and thereby furnishing opportunities for inventive practices. But for Massumi, there is no 'reason' at work in this process:

> There is no mediation by the faculty of reason involved in the thinking-feeling process of sympathy. No subject of interest steps in. There is just the inventive complexity of the perceptual event, passing through me on the way to further transitions.[27]

Here it seems that reason is nothing more than a regulator of interests. Moreover, we can track the rippling effect across classrooms and groups, as the emotion fans out. The flow of affect recruits other bodies, as the students shift in their seats, lean in and squint, and perhaps unconsciously wiggle their toes as evidence of a sympathetic investment in the collective endeavour. As Massumi claims, sympathy 'can reverberate across a relational field, faster than the field of conscious calculation'.[28] He goes on to suggest that this is how the micro ethnographic scale reverberates out to other scales. The small gestures that occur at the infra-individual level, as well as the specificity of the tasks that are explored at the level of the individual, fan out and percolate across the transindividual classroom.

> It is a defining characteristic of complex environments that the extremes of scale are sensitive to each other, attuned to each other's modulations. This is what makes them oscillatory. They can perturb each other.[29]

Scales are interleaved in unexpected ways, so that a shared social bond can be fed by the affective forces that circulate through coordinated movement. Rather than treat individual human bodies as conventional mediators of meaning, we might see them as amplifiers of affect. The individual human body amplifies so that sympathy can scale up to the transindividual. These 'self-organising effects' at the infra-individual scale can 'channel' through the individual body, reverberating out to the larger scales. In other words, the micro-ethnographic scale plugs into the trans-individual scale of the collective endeavour so that the task is 'a doing done through us'.[30] The infra-scale of affect can be studied for how it fuels an enveloping social space.

This theoretical approach can be used to track affect across micro and macro scales, so that the heterogeneous temporalities of any learning event might be studied:[31]

> Every little act exerts a quantum of creative power, globally and locally, in accordion-playing fashion. Every little choice exerts, to some degree, a power of local-global becoming: an ontopower.[32]

Massumi stresses how affect at the micro-scale reverberates across the transindividual event; even small everyday events in classrooms can fan out and engender transindividual sympathy. In such classrooms the teacher becomes an activist of a very powerful kind—the teacher becomes someone who seeks to catalyse affective nonconscious communication, to condition and modulate the affective tonality of perception, and to trigger a coordinated endeavour whereby students enter into the dynamic intensity of an idea.

And yet, in the context of today's data industries, and personalised learning platforms, this image of affective learning raises many concerns. At the Affective Computing Lab at MIT, for instance, *Empatica* bracelets track temperature, movement, blood-volume pulse, and electro-dermal activity in experiments focused on the sympathetic nervous system.[33] Many of these experiments explore the nature of learning and individual achievement, drawing correlations between sensory data, cognition and the unconscious body. Most of this work is uncritically industry-oriented, as the researchers claim that 'by using skin conductance sensors, we can help companies better understand the unique perspective of children and build experiences fit for them'. This research aims to maximise the individual child's affective engagement, as well as their accurate evaluation of their embodied actions. These aims together reveal the dystopic desire to correlate and also control the degree of intensity in any learning experience, and to cultivate self-regulation of affect in children.

The challenge is then how to recognise the affective modalities entailed in learning without simply serving the control society.[34] Rather than conceive affective biodata as that which belongs to the individuated bounded body, and likely pathologises it, we need to conceive this sensory data as post-phenomenological, as part of a sensory milieu, circumventing consciousness and plugging into the vibrational intensity of a *more-than-human thought*. Indeed, it is this expansive thought-network that must be pursued, alongside the connectivity of affect, if there is to be an onto-ethics adequate to posthuman ecologies. The ethical dimension of learning is based on the degree of care/tension and co-affectability between participating agencies. In coordinated movement there is a moment when the shared affective bond becomes a shared obligation. What we take to be learning about and with curriculum and text is actually a dynamic field of movement and differential relations of speeds and directions, but these must 'correlate' with a dynamic thought-network as well. The conceptual plane operates through sympathy as well, without a master who legislates the nature of the sense-making. As part of the pedagogical design, one needs to engage with the virtual dynamism of curriculum and pursue emendation through the ever-modulating body.

WHAT CAN A BODY DO?

Cutler and Mackenzie understand Deleuze's commitment to learning (rather than knowledge) as part of his critique of the dogmatic image of thought. They argue that Deleuze conceives of learning as partly 'an involuntary adventure' entailing preconscious activity and bodily coordination.[35] In other words, learning to swim commences as a passive synthesis, as though the swimmer were unaware of how she learned to swim, or as though the learning occurred unconsciously, in the intensification of differential relations between human body and body of water. They suggest that Deleuze and Guattari's 'pedagogy of the concept' makes this proposal more than a behaviourist reductivism, because it puts knowledge into the mixture. Thus concepts have bodies that are in dynamic relation to other bodies (human, ocean, number, etc.). All bodies are relatively closed systems of differential relations, closed off from chaos by degree. They point to the tension between the impersonal learning of passive synthesis and the feeling a 'body' experiences when learning—that is, the feeling of 'active learning' that accompanies a process of bodying. Consequently, they end their discussion of Deleuze and learning by asking, somewhat skeptically: 'can the creative dimension of learning be expressed in a form that does not subvert Deleuze's account of the passive synthesis of the sensible?'[36] Although Massumi pursues this creative dimension through affect and sympathetic relationality, Deleuze's Spinoza helps us understand how this also entails a thought-network.

Deleuze draws attention to a powerful insight from Spinoza regarding bodies, characterising it as follows: 'We do not even know of what a body is capable. … We do not even know of what affections we are capable, nor the extent of our power'. This claim is so significant, says Deleuze, that we must describe it as 'practically a war cry'.[37] According to Deleuze's reading,

Spinoza offers a naturalism that radically centres the material power of bodies. For Spinoza, bodies are not the mere analogies of thought, nor does thought or some even higher being (God) emanate in the material world in the form of bodies. As Deleuze indicates, emanation and analogy are the terms used by a negative theology that always demotes the body as the abject duplication of spirit or intellect, as that which carries or transports or communicates an abstract meaning that ultimately transcends the natural world. Deleuze argues that Spinoza uses the body as a model, that is, looks to the body (and nature) for how it lives and operates, so as to develop a practical philosophy and onto-ethics or ethology.

Spinoza's actual words (in Curley translation), regarding this war cry, are: 'They do not know what the body can do, or what can be deduced from the consideration of its nature alone'.[38] This comment appears in a section of the *Ethics* where Spinoza is criticising scholars and clerics who overemphasise the power of the mind to dictate and determine the actions of the body. The statement occurs in the scholium following proposition 2, book III: 'The body cannot determine the mind to thinking, and the mind cannot determine the body to motion, to rest, or to anything else (if there is anything else)'.[39] In this particular scholium, Spinoza's focus is on how foolish men think that the mind has dominion over the body, and as well that the body is inactive if the mind fails to think. And he goes on in the same scholium to critique these people for believing that they freely choose what their bodies shall do. Instead, says Spinoza, it is evident that 'the decisions of the mind are nothing but the appetite themselves, which therefore vary as the disposition of the body varies'. This claim, Spinoza explains, is more clearly understood by stating that the mind and the body are 'one and the same thing, which is conceived now under the attribute of thought, now under the attribute of extension'.[40] This affirms the ontological identity of concept and matter, which rests on the fundamental infinite relationality of nature (God), and points to a kind of *necessary* cosmic sympathy between thought and extension, with the important caveat, unpacked below, that sympathy may entail an *amor fati* and harsh reality.[41]

Spinoza's monist substance is folded into an infinity of *formally* distinct attributes, two of these being thought and extension. The notion of a 'formal' distinction between attributes is crucial for Spinoza's ontology because it allows for the plurality and diversity in the one substance—it allows for the many in the one. In other words, formal distinction, as well as the fact that substance is 'absolutely infinite', is why Deleuze will offer the formula that monism = pluralism. Deleuze argues that Spinoza cannot have mind and matter as ontologically distinct substances, for such a distinction always leads to a moral trap for the body. Mind and body must partake of the same substance, to ensure that the world is ethical—that is, to ensure that there is equality among the attributes.[42]

The difference between specific bodies, however, is not formal but rather *modal*. A modal distinction is 'numerical' in the sense that bodies express different degrees of the one 'intensive spatium'.[43] Each body, be it a human, dog or rock, is of the same quality of the one substance, and is directly rather than indirectly an expression of that substance. But each plugs into the intensity of that substance to a different degree. Each body expresses a degree of that power. Thus individuation for Spinoza, at the level of bodies, involves a quantitative process of differentiation, a particular ratio or rapport or relation of speed and rest. His ethics rests on the fact that everything in the world— plants, molecules, stones and goblets—is an *immanent expression* of that one substance in varying degrees.

The fact that bodies partake in 'varying degrees' is precisely what makes the question of learning central to this ontology. How does the world become more perfect (or more adequate) if not through learning? How to convert passive affections into joyous encounters if not through intensifying the sympathetic links? Spinoza's onto-ethics pivots on a theory of learning captured in his account of how humans move towards intuitive knowledge. This process of learning must, according to Spinoza, attend sympathetically to the imperfection of bodies, and the need to emend the intellect so as to understand the nature of embodiment, that is, the nature of our imperfection or sensory hallucination. Bodies correct their misunderstanding through empirical experiment, through encounters. As O'Donnell states:

> A properly Spinozist understanding of education would require it to be understood as the practice of experimentation. … This entails developing practices of composing relations in such a way that one develops a growing awareness of oneself as finite, dependent, vulnerable and as a part of nature. Seemingly paradoxically then, having understood how and that one is determined, and which bodies agree or disagree with one, one becomes more capable of agency. Composing joyous relations becomes the first aim of education, just as it is the aim of politics.[44]

Composing relations in which 'bodies agree or disagree' is clearly necessary but not sufficient for ethically attuned collectives. As Dennis (2018) suggests, conatus is the appetite or desire for learning and 'is the way in which an individual responds and adapts, as cause and effect, through the rhythms of activity and passivity in the universe'.[45]

LOOP-AFFECTION AND *EMENDATION*

In his *Treatise on the Emendation of the Intellect* (*Tractatus de Intellectus Emendatione*) Spinoza briefly proposes a 'Doctrine of Children's Education', suggesting that such a pursuit be considered alongside medicine and mechanics. Emendation of the intellect is not an ascetic process of denying the flesh, but instead demands that we incorporate and admit the non-knowing body into our learning process, the way a mechanic or a doctor by necessity must treat a body. And although Spinoza speaks of emendation as healing the intellect, this healing is not a response to disease, but a form of cultivation that grows ideas through the 'vulgar' body. Rezende nicely summarises:

> Thus, healing and purifying the intellect would be, then, like cultivating the intellect's intelligence by the full practice of its own nature. In this sense, Spinoza emphasizes that the intellect does not need to acquire anything new that is not already there. ... And we also know that rendering *intellectus* capable of *intelligere*—i.e. rendering understanding capable of understanding—is not an acquisition of new predicates, but a matter of letting the intellect become what it is, and, liberating men's minds of the ill-fated pursuit of ideals of perfection that are external to it.[46]

Spinoza affirms the role of passive affections in our learning and development into ethical beings; we try to maximise these passions, often with misguided hedonism, but in so doing, we arrive at the stage when we can begin to form *common notions*. We form a common notion when we find other bodies that agree with ours, other bodies that affirm our body's existence and perspective. The first common notions are formed at this simple level, when we find food that agrees with us, or feel warmth from a fire on a cold night, or find in someone else a shared sense of humor, or find that we can move our body with the movements of water. The common notions are the germinal seeds of conceptual activity: 'There is a whole learning process involved in common notions, in our becoming active: we should not overlook in Spinozism this formative process; we have to start from the least universal common notions, from the first we have a chance to form'.[47]

We see here again how the common notions, which are crucial to Spinoza's epistemology and his proposal for a way of doing rationalism differently from Descartes, are strongly linked to Spinoza's naturalism, and indeed to a theory of learning. There is a kind of sympathy that 'associates' bodies, be they conceptual or organic—a sympathetic relation that brings bodies together into a common notion. This is a learning that involves sharing in each other without passing through a transcendent ideal. But how does the intellect assist in refining these common notions, and in seeking out the nuances of their expanded significance? How do we strive beyond online liking-societies that affirm a common affinity across vast modulating networks, in populist movements that often seem bereft of thought? The act of *following* a common notion is a primary mode of digital life, as seen in swarming sweeps of online dis/agreement. In fact, such spectres are precisely why Spinozan monism and sympathy are so relevant to current theorising of posthuman ecologies. How does learning become conceptual and plug into thought-networks that further advance transversal sympathetic links?

A posthuman ecology must reckon with the kind of convulsions that occur in a system that nears saturation without adequate intellect, a control society in which self-touching fails to imagine the virtual inhuman forces for which touch is not corporeal.[48] Compulsive connectivity in our current computational publics, and the turn to affective computing in the learning sciences, is a bleeding-out of the sensory milieu without the necessary power of thought. We need to reclaim affective-activity below the timescale of the human and relink with the power of thought and intensive matter. What role for reason and thought in an ever-shrinking earth populated with terrans who chase their own tail through linked-in affiliations? If this is a materialism without 'ideals', as Grosz suggests,[49] or perhaps a worlding without intensive concepts, it seems likely to spiral into organic destruction. Humans seeking sustainability or even survival in the anthropocene will need to reconsider the power of thought in action.

Spinoza's parallelism—an awkward word that he never actually used—captures a sympathy between the two powers of action and thought as expressions of the same substance. The laws of thought point to the 'spiritual automaton' that 'parallels' the mechanical material chains of causality and affective contagion. It's crucial to grasp how this parallelism is not a correspondence of truth and object, nor a mirroring of logic with mechanics, but a direct linkage—thought and matter thread together as one substance. Only through an entirely immanent ontology do we get the fusion of the two powers of action and thought that is needed for an ethics responsive to posthuman naturecultures (where technics, nature and sense are re-assembled into a posthumous life). Why? Because, suggests Deleuze, ethics is always about power and capacity, and laws of nature are never about a transcendental moral duty, but rather a 'norm of power'.[50] A generalised ecology or environmentality demands an ethics, not a morality. For Deleuze, Spinoza's project turns to Nature to show us how to live, it shows us tyranny and it shows us love.

And yet the joys of nature are haphazard and chance-driven, and we must 'strive to organise our encounters'.[51] We must maximise our joy through the coordination of that which agrees with our nature. Spinoza is concerned with the infinite intellect of God (Nature) expressed in finite being, by which passions and affections are organised into joyous encounters.[52] The power of thinking to form *the idea of the idea* ad infinitum is what furnishes us with a method to become more wise. Thought indeed has a special privilege and much wider extension because of this infinite participation.[53] Spinoza is as much interested in a deductive method as Descartes is, but for Spinoza there is an empiricism that is necessary for a proper deduction to proceed. Descartes' 'clear and distinct' ideas don't guarantee any purchase on the material world, while Spinoza's materialism and his image of cognition as a 'spiritual automation' is a way of bringing thought together with matter, a way of reconceiving learning. The state of reason that Spinoza aims for should not be considered as artificial and outside of nature. Reason's calculations are as much a part of nature as anything else: In Deleuze's words: 'This striving of reason' to coordinate multiple bodies is 'to reproduce and express the effort of nature as a whole'.[54]

If for Deleuze thought has the power to be indifferent to the body, in that it pursues lines of flight and aleatory points that escape the 'regime of localizable relations, actual linkages, legal, causal and logical connections', it must nonetheless achieve this escape *through the body*.[55] The passive body becomes active as thought reverberates or perhaps percolates, enabling the body to 'attain to active affections'. The body's confusion must be turned to action, for the 'power of action is the sole expression of our essence'.[56] Hughes argues that for Deleuze this is a 'reclaimed passivity' achieved through a kind of dramatisation—a style, manner or gestural form of activity.[57] Learning entails this dramatisation—not a repetition or mimicry, but an active experimentation with the familiar habits of the body. And thus what is achieved in learning is a new mode of existence, a new modal being. Hughes states, 'If the different kinds of knowledge are also different ways of living or different modes of existing, it is because in each kind of knowledge I become capable of organising the parts of my body in different ways'.[58] In this manner, through experimentation, the 'what' of being is expressed through the modal 'how' of being; and this modal 'how' of being is the problem space of learning.

The 'I' cited here pursues a more-than-human thought (indifferent to organic capture), entering into an amorous and fatal transindividual sympathy. Spinoza's concept of 'immanent cause' is crucial for a theory of learning that resists external idealisms and reductive realisms, staying within the affective loop or the parallelism of mind-body. An immanent cause doesn't emanate or emerge but is operative through directionless loops and meshworks. In a modal ontology 'being uses-itself, that is to say, it constitutes, expresses, and loves itself in the affection that it receives from its own modifications'.[59] It is through modality that Spinoza can bring *effectuation* together with *affect*, where the effecting power of modal existence is essentially a new kind of reflexivity, a recursive loop-relation that intensifies and clarifies a thought-network. This is why Deleuze will focus on how immanent cause always expresses itself in substance as an *active principle*, but does not emanate or escape the loop. This is also why love of learning must refuse the compulsive auto-reflection and become the painful *disparation* entailed in a branching out endeavour.[60] The transindividual plugs into the preindividual affective sympathic relation, but precisely in order to sunder the individual and pursue an '*amor dei intellectualis*'.[61]

CONCLUDING COMMENTS

Love of learning must involve sympathy for the body's confusion and disorder, for it is only through modal imperfection that the intellect can pursue emendation. If learning and emendation are typically deemed a correction of errors, Deleuze, through Spinoza, instead conceives learning as a branching out and away from the confines of the bounded body, towards a sensitivity of the fine texture of the encompassing ecological mixture. Learning seeks out the causal links that chain the body to its modal being, deforming the plane of immanence with each new conceptual mutation. What seems to be at stake in learning is a belief in the body, a belief in the body's capacities or capabilities, but for Deleuze this is a secular belief that drives a new kind of empirical experimentation with the body.

Such experimentation, fuelled by an expanding ecological and transindividual thought-network, would need to include philosophy as method.[62] Learning in posthuman ecologies would then entail the creation of new (minor) *forms* of existence, bringing them to bear on the body-concept relation, literally deforming and re-articulating our in/corporeal dis-organisation. In related fashion, Braidotti makes a plea for a *becoming minor* for the human, according to a 'monistic affirmative politics grounded in immanent interconnections'.[63] In the context of today's computational cultures, Deleuze's Spinoza helps us theorise bio-sensor data in new ways, as part of a posthuman ecology (an intensive spatium) striving to learn through transindividual sympathetic coordination. The challenge we face, in a super saturated digital milieu, quivering with affect, is the systemic tendency for abstract pan-human stupidity to emerge and dominate. In some small measure, sympathy becomes the means of pursuing a different kind of transindividual, where love of learning is absolute. This would be a collaborative achievement that sustains the preindividual intensities of the affective plane, and makes the current membranes tremble with inventive thought.

NOTES

1. Simondon 2012, 9.
2. Colebrook 2014.
3. Deleuze 1994, 23.
4. de Freitas 2016.
5. Braidotti 2013.
6. Hörl 2018, 173.
7. Schliesser 2015.
8. Colebrook 2014, 138.
9. Deleuze and Parnet 2007, 53.
10. Haraway 2016.
11. Massumi 2015.
12. Hübner 2015.
13. Simondon 2012.
14. Spuybroek 2016, 144.
15. Deleuze and Parnet 2007, 53.
16. Brouwer 2015.
17. Emilsson 2015.
18. Schliesser 2015.
19. Hanley 2015, 172.
20. Ibid., 173.
21. Forget 2003, 291–92.
22. Hanley 2015, 174.
23. See Bignall 2010 for related work.
24. Debes 2015.
25. de Freitas 2017a.
26. Massumi 2015.
27. Ibid., 62.
28. Ibid., 84.
29. Ibid., 10.
30. Ibid., 20.
31. de Freitas 2017b.
32. Massumi 2015, 15.
33. Banaee, Ahmed and Loutfi 2013.
34. de Freitas 2018.
35. Cutler and Mackenzie 2011; Deleuze 1994, 165.
36. Cutler and Mackenzie 2011, 70.
37. Deleuze 1990, 226 and 255.
38. Spinoza 1994, E III.3s, 156.
39. Spinoza 1994, 155.
40. Spinoza 1994, 157.
41. In his discussion of the sympathy of things, Spuybroek 2016 discusses wasps and torturers as well.
42. Deleuze 1990; see Gatens 1996.

43. Deleuze 1994.
44. O'Donnell 2018, 820.
45. Dennis 2018, 852.
46. Rezende 2018, xxxx.
47. Deleuze 1990, 288.
48. Barad 2017.
49. Grosz 2017.
50. Deleuze 1990, 259.
51. Deleuze 1990, 261.
52. Grosz 2017.
53. Deleuze 1990, 124.
54. Ibid., 265.
55. Deleuze 1989, 126–27.
56. Deleuze 1990, 219, 226.
57. Hughes 2011, 82.
58. Ibid., 85.
59. Agamben 2016, 165.
60. Simondon 2012.
61. Melamed 2014.
62. Simondon 2012, 2017.
63. Braidotti 2017, 93.

REFERENCES

Agamben, G. (2016). *The Use of Bodies, Homo Sacer IV*, 2. Translated by A. Kotsko. Stanford, CA: Stanford University Press.

Banaee, H., Ahmed, M. U., and Loutfi, A. (2013). 'Data Mining for Wearable Sensors in Health Monitoring Systems: A Review of Recent Trends and Challenges'. *Sensors*, 13(12), 17472–500.

Barad, K. (2017). 'When Two Hands Touch, How Close Are They? On Touching the Inhuman That Therefore I Am'. In *Power of material/politics of materiality* K. Stakemeier and S. Witzgall, eds., 153–65. Zurich: Diaphanes. Retrieved from http://www.diaphanes.de/titel/ontouching-the-inhumanthattherefore-i-am-v1-1-3075. Originally published in *Differences: A Journal of Feminist Cultural Studies*, 23(3), 206–23.

Bignall, S. (2010). *Postcolonial Agency*. Edinburgh: Edinburgh University Press.

Braidotti, R. (2013). *The Posthuman*. Cambridge: Polity Press.

Braidotti, R. (2017). 'Critical Posthuman Knowledges'. *South Atlantic Quarterly*, 116(1), 83–96.

Brouwer, R. (2015). 'Stoic Sympathy'. In *Sympathy: A History*, Eric Schliesser, ed. Oxford: Oxford University Press, 15–35.

Colebrook, C. (2014). *The Death of the Posthuman: Essays on Extinction, Volume I*. Ann Arbor, MI: Open Humanities Press.

Cutler, A., and MacKenzie, I. (2011). 'Bodies of Learning'. In *Deleuze and the Body*, Guillame, L. and Hughes, J., eds. Edinburgh: Edinburgh University Press, 53–72.

Debes, R. (2015). 'From Einfühling to Empathy: Sympathy in Early Phenomenology and Psychology'. In *Sympathy: A History*, Eric Schliesser, ed. Oxford: Oxford University Press, 286–322.

de Freitas, E. (2016). 'The New Empiricism of the Fractal Fold: Rethinking Monadology in Digital Times'. *Cultural Studies—Critical Methodologies*, 16(2), 224–34.

de Freitas, E. (2017a). 'Karen Barad's Quantum Ontology and Posthuman Ethics: Rethinking the Concept of Relationality'. *Qualitative Inquiry* 23(9), 741–48.

de Freitas, E. (2018). 'The Biosocial Subject: Sensor Technology and Worldly Sensibility'. *Discourse: Studies in the Cultural Politics of Education*, 39(2), 292–308.

de Freitas, E. (2017b). 'The Temporal Fabric of Research Method: Posthuman Social Science and the Digital Data Deluge'. *Research in Education*, 98(1), 27–43.

Deleuze, G. (1989). *Cinema 2: The Time Image*. Translated by Hugh Tomlinson and Robert Galeta. Minneapolis: University of Minnesota Press.

Deleuze, G. (1990). *Expressionism in Philosophy: Spinoza*. Translated by Martin Joughin. Brooklyn, NY: Zone Books.

Deleuze, G. (1994). *Difference and Repetition*. Translated by Paul Patton. New York: Columbia University Press.

Deleuze, G. (2001). *Spinoza: A Practical Philosophy*. Translated by Robert Hurley. New York: City Lights Publishers.

Deleuze, G., and Parnet, C. (2007). *Dialogues 2*. New York: Columbia University Press.

Dennis, J. (2018). 'Imagining Powerful Cooperative Schools: Theorizing Dynamic Cooperation with Spinoza'. *Educational Philosophy and Theory*, 50(9), 849–57.

Emilsson, E. K. (2015). 'Plotinus on Sympatheia'. In *Sympathy: A History*, E. Schliesser, ed. Oxford: Oxford University Press, 36–60.

Forget, E. L. (2003). 'Evocations of Sympathy: Sympathetic Imagery in Eighteenth Century Social Theory and Physiology'. *History of Political Economy*, 35(1), 282–308.

Gatens, M. (1996). *Imaginary Bodies: Ethics, Power, and Corporeality*. London: Routledge.

Grosz, E. (2017). *The Incorporeal: Ontology, Ethics and the Limits of Materialism*. New York: Columbia University Press.

Hanley, R. P. (2015). 'The Eighteenth-Century Context of Sympathy from Spinoza to Kant'. In *Sympathy: A History*, E. Schliesser, ed. Oxford University Press, 171–98.

Haraway, D. (2016). *Staying with the Trouble: Making Kin in the Chthulucene*. Durham, NC: Duke University Press.

Hörl, E. (2018). *General Ecology. Posthuman Glossary*. London: Bloomsbury, 172–74.

Hübner, K. (2015). 'Spinoza's Parallelism Doctrine and Metaphysical Sympathy'. In *Sympathy: A History*, E. Schliesser, ed. Oxford: Oxford University Press, 146–70.

Hughes, J. (2011). 'Believing in the World: Towards an Ethics of Form'. In *Deleuze and the Body*, L. Guillaume and J. Hughes, eds. Edinburgh: Edinburgh University Press, 73–95.

Massumi, B. (2015). *The Power at the End of the Economy*. Durham, NC: Duke University Press.

Melamed, Y. Y. (2014). *Spinoza's amor dei intellectualis*. Accessed February 2018. https://www.academia.edu/6791070/Spinozas_Amor_Dei_Intellectualis.

O'Donnell, A. (2018). 'Spinoza, Experimentation and Education: How Things Teach Us'. *Educational Philosophy and Theory*, 50 (9), 819–29.

Rezende, C. N. (2018). Spinoza's Proposal for a Doctrine of Children's Education. *Educational Philosophy and Theory*, 50 (9), 830–38.

Schliesser, E. (2015). 'Introduction: On Sympathy'. In *Sympathy: A History*, E. Schliesser, ed. Oxford University Press, 3–14.

Simondon, G. (2012). 'Technical Mentality' (Translated by A. de Boever). In *Gilbert Simondon: Being and technology*, A. de Boever, A. Murray,J. Roffe and A. Woodward, eds. Edinburgh University Press.

Simondon, G. (2017). *On the Mode of Existence of Technical Objects*. Translated by C. Malaspina and J. Rogove. Minneapolis, MN: Univocal.

Spinoza, B. (1994). *A Spinoza Reader: The Ethics and Other Works*. Translated by E. Curley. Princeton, NJ: Princeton University Press.

Spuybroek, L. (2016). *The Sympathy of Things: Ruskin and the Ecology of Design*, 2nd edition. New York: Bloomsbury Academic Press.

Chapter 6

Time and the Posthuman

Rosi Braidotti and A. W. Moore on the Posthuman and Anthropocentrism after Deleuze's Philosophy of Time

James Williams

The aim of this chapter is to bring Gilles Deleuze's philosophy of time to bear on an opposition between two recent ways of taking up his philosophy over the question of posthumanism.[1] One way, defined by Rosi Braidotti, adopts Deleuze's philosophy as a starting point for an exploration of a posthuman future which leads to posthumanism in the humanities. The other way, presented by A. W. Moore, develops a sympathetic interpretation of Deleuze's work, but then departs from it around Moore's claim that philosophy needs to be anthropocentric. I want to show how Deleuze's philosophy of time supports the posthuman approach and sheds light on the forms it might take. Thereby, this philosophy of time also provides rejoinders to Moore and to his defence of anthropocentric necessity.

The following passage from Braidotti's *The Posthuman* illustrates her argument and its connection to work by Deleuze and Guattari. I should stress that they are not the only source for her position and she draws on a wide set of philosophical, social, political, artistic and science-based examples and ideas. It could therefore be claimed that the connection to Deleuze and Guattari can be discarded or needs to be viewed as working alongside others. I accept both these possibilities. My point is about different ways of following on from Deleuze and Guattari, rather than a challenge to Braidotti's wider philosophy. In her reading of Deleuze and Guattari, Braidotti comments that:

> Art, not unlike critical philosophy, is for Deleuze an intensive practice that aims at creating new ways of thinking, perceiving and sensing Life's infinite possibilities. By transposing us beyond the confines of bound identities, art becomes necessarily inhuman in the sense of non-human in that it connects to the animal, the vegetable, earthy and planetary forces that surround us. Art is also, moreover, cosmic in its resonance and hence posthuman by structure, as it carries us

to the limits of what our embodied selves can do and endure. In so far as art stretches the boundaries of representation to the utmost, it reaches the limits of life itself and thus confronts the horizon of death.[2]

Deleuze's philosophy of time can explain the following ideas from this argument for the posthuman: 'intensive practice', the 'new', 'transposition beyond confines' and the 'passage to or beyond limits'.

An intensive practice is driven by the intensity of its affects, that is, the drives and emotions giving power and direction to more conscious acts. For instance, an art-form drawing on animal and human connections can be driven by the intensity of empathy. The way intensities function within practices is not bound by the idea that acts are strictly performed by humans, under any common definition of humanism. So to continue with the example, the affect of empathy transforms the human artist beyond the boundaries of human existence and into the animal realm, while also drawing the animal towards the human.

New ways of responding creatively to contemporary problems and challenges can be explained by referring to Deleuze's ideas about the connection between revolutionary breaks and continuities in time. These continuities go beyond a location in any specifically human phenomenology; for example, actions in the present are passive contractions of past events which extend the human to animals, plants, and natural and technological spaces, because those actions are formed by joint evolution. As such, creativity involves transformations beyond categorical confines, such as predicates defining the human (e.g., animal *capable of reflection*). It also involves transpositions beyond limits ascribed to members of such categories; for instance, around ideas of limited capacities, powers or functions. In the animal-human conjunction, humans and animals are given new powers which neither have when taken as a member of either the human or animal category; for example, when a Harris Hawk works with a human to control pigeon infestation, this work should be understood as forming a hawk-human assemblage. Or, to take a more technological assemblage, contemporary humans form assemblages with networked communication systems, such that human identity and affects should be seen as distributed through such systems, while the systems move into the human body and brain.[3]

Art, science, technology and philosophy take us beyond the limits of identity, body and representations of the human defined according to humanism. Thereby, they take us into a posthuman future, but this future should not be seen as a clean break with the positive and negative forces that came to shape humanism. This future is characterised as an extension of the human, and sometimes as a threat to it, but this does not imply that it is inhumane in terms of values and qualities. It is nonhuman in location; that is, in terms of limits and boundaries. It is not necessarily inhumane ethically or in terms of violence against other beings and life forms. Values will not be justified according to the priority of humanism, but they can be seen as extensions of values once seen as confined to humans, both as subjects of such actions and as drawing benefits from them. A simple human ethical responsibility is thereby replaced by a joint ethical task in a shared ecosphere; we move from questions of what is right for us humans to questions of how to care for an ecology as a complex series of interdependencies. For example, though some human values can be accused of leading to the exploitation of animals and ecologies, this does not mean that all humane values are to be abandoned. It is rather that they need to be transformed and distributed more widely beyond human actors and claimants.

For instance, there still needs to be an ethics about pest control using hawks, but this ethics must extend to include birds of prey and so-called pests as having ethical import alongside humans and in complex assemblages with them. Similarly, with the extension and distribution of the human through technological systems new ethical challenges arise such as the shift from direct responsibility, assigned to well-located identity, to more loosely defined and harder to control proxies, such as those found in internet defamation and flaming. It is therefore human supremacy, simple location and exceptionalism that are called into question here. This is important in relation to Moore's argument, since we must take account of the ethical dimension of Braidotti's position. The posthuman must not be equated with an unethical stance. For Braidotti the implication is quite the reverse. In order to be ethical in the age of the Anthropocene we need to move to a posthuman ethics.

It is helpful to consider some of the more standard philosophical objections to Braidotti's arguments; these point to why Deleuze's philosophy of time should be taken into consideration. Broadly, the objections concede that art and philosophy, and indeed modern technologies and modern scientific discoveries, place the human beyond boundaries defined by the body or brain. Technical extensions to human limbs and minds, through a wide range of machines and artificial intelligence, have taken humans beyond physical flesh and brain-bound thinking. However, this does not necessarily imply that body and mind in restricted senses aren't essential conditions for human existence. Neither, therefore, does it necessarily imply that the values we might associate with human limits do not apply to extensions beyond the human. The human might well be extended and placed beyond traditional limits, but this does not discount a role for those limits.

Human-centred narratives demonstrate how such traditional forms continue to be influential and perhaps even essential in a changed world. They describe and evaluate the ways in which extensions have enhanced human capacities *by humans and for humans*, for better or worse, in relation to their environment. This is Moore's central point. Narratives—including the posthuman one—are narratives by humans and aimed at humans. This argument can be split into the aims of the narrative and its form. It is by and for humans seeking to give a narrative line to their concerns. That's the aim. The narrative also takes linguistic and rhetorical forms that are humanist historically and in terms of their flavour and character. That's the form. It is therefore possible that the identities, bodies and representations that Braidotti seeks to move beyond are still present in contemporary narratives on the posthuman, including hers. In fact, Moore's claim is stronger than this. His view is that it is *necessarily* the case that narratives remain anthropocentric. This can be put very simply: our narratives are narratives for and about us. It is not a matter of choice, but analytical necessity that the subjects, aims and forms of narratives are human.

To begin to grasp Braidotti's response, we should consider her book as offering a distinctively posthuman narrative in both style and content. It is an account of a development towards a philosophy where the human is neither the sole audience, nor central character, nor source of value, nor foundation for the narrative. This might seem strange, since a book is aimed to be read by humans. That reaction is countered by the idea that humans do not exist as free-standing entities. Any book is taken up by, depends upon, and has effects across nonhuman and posthuman assemblages. We can focus on the human reader, but the book is addressed to and enabled by much wider connections and transformations. On one level, there is the wide technology of printing and dissemination, reading aids and linguistic evolution. On another level, there are the ways books take their place in extended networks of influences and effects, such as the consequences of written recommendations on ecologies and the scene changes brought about by new affects and ideas (indeed humanism was one such technological and bookish idea; we are still wrestling with its effects across many wider human, plant and physical environments).

The Posthuman invites us to move out into an ecosphere where the human no longer exists as a secure reference point and where ethical relations not only cannot rely on human values but must realise that many of the immoral and nonethical events that have taken place over recent history demonstrate that human-centred actions have led to terrible violence not only towards humans but also towards animals, plants and the world. Ethical responses shouldn't be seen as dependent on maintaining anthropocentrism at the core or various kinds of enhancement and extensions. It is exactly the opposite, as humans are transformed they become hybrids and members of assemblages with dispersed ethical problems. This means that the idea of a human core and control becomes obsolete in relation to new forms of existence and narratives about the development and future of those new forms.

This leads to a strong context for the opposition between Braidotti's posthumanism and Moore's anthropocentrism around different requirements for a narrative adequate to our times. Following Moore, we could agree that our bodies and minds are inserted in complex external networks, but still insist that the reason we can say it, is that they are *our* bodies and minds. Similarly, we could accept that we live in coordination with wider natural and social processes, but also say that the reasons why we care and why we should care about them are that they are vehicles for necessarily human aims, values and intentions. Following Braidotti, we would accept that there are still recognisably humane ethical and narrative traits to our posthuman condition, but insist that ideas of human exceptionalism and existential priority fail to understand an essentially distributed and interdependent nonhuman reality.

For Moore, the step into the posthuman might be helpful as a way of describing our situation, but unhelpful in deciding about the deep reality of our identities and about how we should act in accordance with them. For example, in contemporary science fiction, though there are many examples of cyborgs in Cyberpunk literature by William Gibson, Pat Cadigan and Philip K. Dick, it could be claimed their fiction is still recognisably traditional in human ethical concerns and human-like actors. Indeed, famously in the case of *Blade Runner*'s Voight-Kampff test, one of the most important narrative lines is around how to keep a human core and evaluate humaneness with the rapid increase in the number and powers of cyborgs.[4] Similar points could be made around plot lines involving the Borg and Seven of Nine in *Star Trek*, or much more humourously, the android Kryten ('I serve, therefore I am') in *Red Dwarf*.

For Braidotti, our bodies and minds, and our wider relations to animals and to other forms of existence, depend on connections which undo human identities and lead them into the posthuman, whereas Moore relies upon narratives around those identities to argue for his humanism and anthropocentrism. It must be stressed that this reliance is not tied to permanent definitions of the human. His argument rests on changing and changeable accounts. The idea of the human can go through successive and impermanent human narratives rather than conform to a transcendent and eternal definition. Moore even allows for the possibility that we might become posthuman. His argument, though, is that we are a long way from that now.

Against this argument for anthropocentrism, Braidotti seeks to show that we are already in a posthuman condition because the wider connections that the human has plugged into, or been forced into, have eroded and replaced anthropocentric forms of existence and narrative. She also argues that this is a good thing. The connections and their displacement of a centralising human identity lead to the following manifesto for a 'nomadic' and 'posthuman' philosophy:

Very much a philosophy of the outside, of open spaces and embodied enactments, nomadic posthuman thought yearns for a qualitative leap out of the familiar, trusting the untapped possibilities opened up by our historical location in the technologically mediated world of today. It is a way of being worthy of our times, to increase our freedom and understanding of the complexities we inhabit in a world that is neither anthropocentric nor anthropomorphic, but rather geo-political, eco-sophical and proudly *zoe*-centred.[5]

The argument set out in *The Posthuman* depends on an inversion where a human inside and identity is projected outwards. It is driven towards and transformed by forms of life commonly defined as external to and different from the human, such as animals and plants, but also technological systems and machines.[6] Braidotti demonstrates the strong interdependencies of human, animal and plant life. She shows how technological and geophysical factors determine and participate in posthuman existence. Any separation of the human from them must therefore be seen as an arbitrary and misleading claim to well-defined centrality.

An image for understanding the opposition between Moore and Braidotti would contrast a series of concentric circles, with a changing yet recognisably human core at their centre (Moore) and a constellation of shifting relations which form many different assemblages (Braidotti). She gives us a philosophy of multiple movements: towards the outside, across new open spaces, towards new possibilities and potentialities, in new assemblages and alliances with technologies, ecologies and animal and plant life. It is ethical through a principle of a search for worthiness, understood as the demand to act ethically within the new connections redefining our identities. When the performative contradiction of this position is drawn to our attention—Who acts ethically, if not humans?—Braidotti's response is to appeal to a 'qualitative leap'. It means that the actor can no longer be found in any human characteristic, or power, or faculty, since each of these has been taken beyond its boundaries by forces bringing them into new assemblages which cannot be severed in order to reestablish some kind of secure human actor. An analogy could be drawn to the question 'Who proves?' for computer-based proofs in mathematics. The answer is an assemblage of human and artificial intelligence does the proof. Neither human nor machine, but both: a posthuman intelligence.

When the image of circles with a relatively stable core is replaced by constellations and assemblages, the change goes right down to the idea of a stable human actor and of stable human values the actor is to be guided by. This means the difficult ethical problem is not how to ensure a human actor is worthy of encounters with others that demand a shift in perspective towards them, but rather whether these new assemblages can entertain ideas of worthiness or care when they are shorn of human actors. This problem connects to ethical challenges brought about by powerful, self-producing and evolving artificial intelligences. Why should such intelligences act in ways that are recognisably ethical? How can it be made so they do, when their evolution and self-production seem to make versions of Asimov's ethical Three Laws of Robotics redundant, because of the difficulty in programming them into autopoietic systems which can then reject them?[7]

Braidotti's claims and high energy style could lead to the conclusion that this new nomadic philosophy is one of extremes and of some kind of 'end-of-the-human' destructiveness, despite her claims to ethical worthiness. To understand why this is not the case, it is instructive to follow the stages and rhythms of those nomadic movements. The key here is in the expression 'embodied enactments'. Strong bodily and act-based relations provide a frame and scale for this posthuman philosophy, such that it is in no way empty of specific content and value. We need to be worthy of the new possibilities afforded by connections and potentialities for our bodies; for the way in which, for instance, we think about gender beyond the gendered legacies of Man in humanism, or think about animals beyond the hierarchies of Man, then beast. However, all this presupposes that the 'we' is no longer humanity but assemblages that include human elements but do not carry them at their core. The centre has shifted, and this explains Braidotti's emphasis on *zoe*-centredness, the centre becomes a constellation out in the ecosphere.

Here, Moore's point about narratives returns with greater strength because, even if we can suppose that these assemblages are capable of ethical reflection and action, it is hard to envisage that they will have collective and effective narratives to support that action. What would the coherent 'story' be for such assemblages? Might it not founder on destructive tensions, such as different interests for different parts of the assemblage: animal, human and ecological? Moore's claims for the necessity of an anthropocentric sense-making are starkly at odds with Braidotti's account of a posthuman condition and arguments for a posthuman ethics. The opposition, though, is not principally about whether Deleuze and Guattari lead to a posthuman philosophy. He is in agreement with Braidotti about that conclusion. It is rather about whether philosophy can be posthuman given the current state of evolution of our metaphysical ideas, arguments and narratives.

Moore makes the claim for anthropocentric philosophy as metaphysics in *The Evolution of Modern Metaphysics: Making Sense of Things*. The argument can be summed up briefly as following from two premises: first, that the evolution of modern metaphysics can be understood as an effort to make sense of things; second, that to make sense of things metaphysics must do so 'for us' where 'us' stands for we humans. Following from these premises, Moore concludes that metaphysics must have a humanistic aspect, understood as a need to be anthropocentric:

[Metaphysics] does nonetheless have a humanistic aspect; and it needs to be true to that aspect. Metaphysics may not be anthropological; but it does need to be anthropocentric. That is, it needs to be from a human point of view. It needs to be an attempt to make the sort of general sense of things that we its practitioners can appropriate as distinctively ours. Only then can it involve the kind of self-consciousness that it should. Only then can it enjoy the kind of importance that it should. Importance, where human beings are concerned, is importance to human beings.[8]

The Evolution of Modern Metaphysics: Making Sense of Things takes Deleuze as the accomplishment of a long line of philosophical sense-making, because of the emphasis Deleuze puts on the creation of concepts and because of the specific concepts Deleuze creates. However, this position is ambiguous because Moore is concerned that Deleuze takes metaphysics too far away from a necessary humanistic aspect.

To grasp fully the differences and stakes at play in Braidotti's posthuman and Moore's humanistic aspect, it is useful to see if the two positions can be brought close to one another. It is uncontroversial to note that Braidotti is in agreement with Moore where he lays stress on creation in metaphysics. It is less obvious, but equally important, to note how Moore has no problem with pushing the boundaries of what it is to be human. His humanistic aspect is open to evolution and to evolution through extension of boundaries alongside making sense of the human in sometimes radically different ways: 'In particular we should be open to the possibility that our metaphysics will one day no longer need to be anthropocentric'.[9]

The first way of understanding the depth of opposition between Braidotti and Moore is through their contrasting appeals to philosophical necessity. There is a necessity to the human point of view in Moore. There is a necessity for an overcoming of that view for Braidotti. It is interesting to note that, for both, necessity follows from a state of evolution, but for Moore this evolution involves the slow and lengthy development of metaphysical sense-making, whereas for Braidotti it appears to be the rapid evolution towards a posthuman condition. I say 'appears to be' because although it might seem that the posthuman is a recent and fast development, this is itself an illusion if we suppose that the human has always been involved in posthuman assemblages.

For instance, in our dependence on and exploitation of animals and in our status as part of the animal world and as dependent on a wider ecosphere, we have always been posthuman. In that sense, we might have thought that the Anthropocene was a relatively rapid development. In fact, it has been through a very long gestation that implicates and transforms the metaphysical narratives that Moore wants to appeal to. A similar point can be made in relation to technology. Scientific and technological extensions and assemblages of the human are not at all new. Take, for example, the assemblage of a seventeenth-century ship with its dependence on new technologies in ship building, diet and food storage, exploitation of natural resources, farming and mapping. Any human on such a ship was completely dependent on those technologies and exploitations of plants and animals; without them there would only be death. A similar argument could be made for early technologies such as writing, mathematics, the printing press or the domestication of animals. Technological and animal assemblages with the human are longstanding, not recent.

According to Moore, even though the meaning of the human changes over time, we maintain a human focus for our sense-making as this meaning evolves. Metaphysics should therefore remain anthropocentric, if it is to be true to its vocation of sense-making: '… we cannot oversee its becoming non-anthropocentric except by overseeing its evolution from something anthropocentric'.[10] Metaphysics needs to be anthropocentric because it can only make sense for humans if it evolves in a manner consistent with current ways of understanding humanity. For Braidotti, art and philosophy demonstrate how there can be no human centre for us to return to, not only because 'we' no longer exist as such a centre, but also because 'we' never existed as such. We are dependent upon distributed assemblages and we have always been 'out there' such that any effort to return to a human centre is a false representation of our place in a world. This place has always been posthuman but it now appears so all the stronger given the prominence of technological and ecological change.

Philosophy therefore needs to be posthuman, if we are to be true to our posthuman condition. For example, over time, the human has been defined in opposition to that which it is not (animals, barbarians, women, nature, technology) but this opposition introduces the nonhuman into the human core through this very effort at expulsion (rational as opposed to merely instinctive, civilised as opposed to savage, male reason as opposed to feminine passion, human dwelling and freedom as opposed to natural being and determination, human wisdom as opposed to mechanical calculation). The human was dependent on these false representations of nonhuman others from the very beginning, not only as that which had to be rejected as the foe that defined us, but also as sources of desire, drift, transformation and dependency for the human.

When Moore claims that our narratives must necessarily be anthropocentric he misses the way in which anthropocentric narratives have always been shaped by the nonhuman. They are not stories of anthropocentrism but accounts of joint struggles and co-evolution around the human, the nonhuman and the posthuman. In that sense, our narratives have always been posthuman,

but have always been driven by an interest in hiding that fact in order to celebrate human exceptionalism and purity. The human is not a narrative necessity but rather a political product and choice.[11]

This difference in accounts of necessity in metaphysics defines the stakes
of the opposition. For Moore, though our place in the world demands creative
responses, these must be considered according to a humanistic narrative about
making sense of things and an account of what new conditions imply for what
it means to be human: 'To substantiate that claim, some story needs to be
told about how understanding the place of humanity in the larger scheme of
things could in turn help humanity to live in that place'.[12] So if we return to
the passage on the posthuman by Braidotti, according to Moore human identity, the human, embodiment and representational narratives must be returned
to, even in posthuman moments. For Braidotti, the right movement is away
from the human and towards the posthuman. This is an ethical direction, in
the sense of seeking to be worthy of new conditions.[13]

DELEUZE'S PHILOSOPHY OF TIME AS A
CRITIQUE OF ANTHROPOCENTRISM

Deleuze's work on time appears in different forms across many books over
the full length of his career. There is work on time in his early studies of other
thinkers, such as Kant, Bergson and Nietzsche. There are two related versions
of a philosophy of time in *Difference and Repetition* and *The Logic of Sense*.
There is work on time in the cinema books, in particular around Bergson. In
this short study, I will concentrate on *Difference and Repetition* and Deleuze's
description of time as three syntheses of time which include one another as
dimensions. For example, the present is defined as a passive contraction of
the past and the future which in turn are to be thought of as passive syntheses
in their own right.

The task for this study is restricted. It is to show that Deleuze's philosophy
of time, as developed in *Difference and Repetition*, can help us adjudicate
between different takes on anthropocentrism in philosophy. The aim is to
decide between appeals to necessity: to the necessity of an anthropocentric narrative and to the necessity of a posthuman future. This means that
Deleuze's philosophy of time must help decide between the idea that the
human is still a necessary and plausible foundation for metaphysics, and the
idea that the human needs to be replaced by the posthuman. It could be argued
that it would have been better, here, to refer to Deleuze's work with Guattari,
since *Anti-Oedipus* and *A Thousand Plateaus* are more directly about anthropology and ideas of the human and posthuman. I do not deny that claim, but
my purpose is different. I want to show that even at the most metaphysical

level of the philosophy of time, Moore's claim for anthropocentrism fails, if we follow Deleuze's ideas on time and ontology.

Braidotti's and Moore's arguments have a historical frame: the evolution of metaphysics and the necessity for a human core to the narration of this evolution, for Moore; the contemporary posthuman condition and its effects on the transfer beyond the human and into the nonhuman, for Braidotti. In *Difference and Repetition*, Deleuze's relation to history is complicated because his work combines transcendental philosophy, with its nonhistorical elements, and empirical philosophy, with its historical immersion. This means that although history has a role to play, it is as vehicle for contingent facts rather than a formal role. Any given historical epoch or trend plays a role within a transcendental formal frame, but this role is not fully determining because transcendental arguments add formal determination to contingent historical information. This means that though history provides evidence for philosophy it must also be taken in accordance with a prior transcendentally deduced frame. For example, for Deleuze, the future is defined as a passive synthesis that introduces a cut into the present independent of any empirical historical observation. Every historical epoch is open to such cuts. We are always amidst the new, independent of the particular historical state we are in.[14]

This implies that arguments from history are incomplete and open to revision on nonhistorical grounds. For example, Deleuze's work on philosophical ideas pays very little heed to the history of ideas as chronological and historically grounded practice. Instead, his arguments take place in a metaphysical realm where ideas jump across historical times and periods. Philosophy, while historical, is also outside history and determines it. The strongest sign of this is in Deleuze's work on ideal problems; for instance, in *The Logic of Sense*, where the actual historical side of events is conditioned by a virtual problem outside historical time. This is the reciprocal determination of ideal virtual time and actual physical time that is central to Deleuze's model for reality in *Difference and Repetition* and *The Logic of Sense*. In the language of *The Logic of Sense*, the reciprocal determination is between Aîon or the time where every event plays out in eternity across the past and the future, and Chronos or the time where the past and future are concentrated in a physical event such as a wound or mixture of incompatibles.

For example, the event of humans living with artificial organs, like mechanical hearts and kidneys, is not only a concentration of past efforts in medicine and the opening up of new possibilities for the human. Past research and failures lead to and come to fruition with *actual* successes in the present. Future research is directed and opened up by new breakthroughs. However, this event is also a transformation back in time, of *ideas* about the human such as the values assigned to organs and their specifically human 'humours', and forward in time, with the *idea* of a nonhuman cyborg taking on human functions and attributes. So there is a reciprocal determination of the actual and the ideal, of the virtual and actual, since the virtual gives value to the actual and the actual determines those virtual ideas. Ideas inform the intensities of attraction and repulsion, of fear and hope, around a scientific breakthrough. Whereas the actual sets off new lines of changing intensities in the virtual; for instance, an actual invention and the shock accompanying it force a reassessment of past and future ideas.

Reciprocal determination is important in relation to the question of the posthuman for two reasons. First, Deleuze gives us a process account of time. It means that we have to think of the human as a process and one that goes much wider than even flexible definitions following from a given narrative. This can be seen in the description of times as passive syntheses. The present as synthesis is made by contractions. For example, a sense of urgency in the present depends on relative speeds of contraction of the past, because urgency is relative to the habits and speeds we have become used to and acquired. If repeated past actions are overcome by an unexpected acceleration in the present, then this process changes the nature of present time; it gives a sense of time as pressing. We experience this very directly when we master a difficult task. At first it seems clunky and demanding, but then becomes fluid and automatic. However, this is only one strand of time among many others. Time is a manifold of such processes and each one extends humanity and each individual human forward and back across many times. Narratives giving us a sense of human identity allow us to make some sense of this manifold, but only by reducing a more complex and extended reality. *In time, we are always prehuman and posthuman, even if we tell ourselves stories to render those facts more manageable.*

Time is not a representation of a space on which processes occur, a line of time, for instance. Time is not a container for actual or virtual processes, such that they could be said to happen in time. It is the opposite, time happens through actual and virtual processes. There is no independence of time from constitutive processes which could legitimate a free-standing representation or realm which could stand as the place where events happen. So, second, it is not only that time is made by processes but also that all things are determined by this making of time. All things are actual and ideal passive syntheses of time. So in the same way as we cannot decide to live outside time, nothing exists independently of time as manifold process. If the present is a process of contraction of the past and the future, so are all things. For example, a new technology such as a heart pacemaker must be understood as a contraction of past research on pacemakers and a change to the future of heart technologies.

For Deleuze, there is no limit to these contractions, to their past as passive synthesis of all the past, or to the future as cut, seriation and reassembly for all times as expressed by the thing. By seriation and assembly he means that the new alters the way time is ordered in competing series; for example, in the way a new discovery changes the importance given to a discredited line of research. He also means that *all* processes are assembled in a different way; for instance, when a new way of thinking about gender not only changes our views of sex and gender, but also family, marriage, ideas of masculinity, femininity, strength, weakness, passion, abilities, fashion and so on. This means each thing must be seen as a process that transforms all the past and all the future in an individual mode, and this mode is multiple according to the different ways it involves syntheses of time. In short, and in support of the idea of the posthuman, time is much more revolutionary, complex and multiple than humanist narratives allow. We are constantly being remade as posthuman individuals and groupings.

If we combine these points, we get a fairly simple proposition for our work on the posthuman: *humans are made by the manifold processes that make times and these processes are necessarily pre- and posthuman.* Once we describe processes on the basis of Deleuze's philosophy of time in *Difference and Repetition*, we are in a position to reflect critically on the opposition between Braidotti and Moore. However, before going into the detail of the philosophy of time it is important to add a rider to the notion of 'made'. Deleuze's philosophy gives us a set of formal conditions for how humans must be made with times defined as processes. It does not provide the specific ways this can occur. We are given a frame, but not its specific content for individual situations. This is a weak transcendental and formal type of determinism, rather than a strongly causal one. It provides a necessary frame but no necessary individual content.

The proposition about human and times is important because it means that each human is not a well-located individual belonging to a species, or even an individual identified loosely within a broad definition or narrative about the human. Instead, each human is an individuation or a series of processes over all events and times. In that sense, each human is always posthuman in participating in many nonhuman processes—past, present and future.[15] For Deleuze, when something becomes habitual in the present it involves a passive selection of all past movements to greater and lesser degrees. A throwing action in the present involves sometimes slight, sometimes quite large variations which take past repetitions and set them in a new line, a new contraction of the past. So the past series is passively selected in a process. There can be an activity in the present; for instance, a decision to emphasise some part of the throw, the follow-through, say. However, beyond that activity the overall effect through time is a synthesis outside the control of past and present activity, because action is also habit—a passive synthesis. Thus, if we say that a given sport has shaped a throwing action, we should also say that technologies and human-animal interactions have done so too. Like human affects, human actions and ideas are distributed because they are syntheses. They are pre- and posthuman.

For Deleuze, there are three syntheses of times which can take themselves and each other as dimensions. This leads to nine different processes as syntheses of time. We have a combination of each time with the others and with itself: present by present, past by present, future by present, past by past, present by past, future by past, future by future, past by future, and present by future. The definition of processes of time as passive syntheses places human activity in a secondary relation to passive syntheses that condition it. According to this philosophy of time, an anthropocentric philosophy based around the priority of human activity and decision making, or on its independence and freedom, cannot be valid. The human will always presuppose passive syntheses that go beyond human activity and cognitive representation. There will always be more to humans than the accounts they can give of their decisions and the knowledge on which they are based. There is a posthuman background to such decisions and to such knowledge. This background is a condition for them, even when they seek to deny it.

Free will or an independent act presupposes passive syntheses. Where Moore claims that we narrate and make sense of things for us, Deleuze's philosophy of time gives the rejoinder that when we make sense we are conditioned by other passive syntheses, such as past repetitions leading into habits of thought. This implies that it is false to claim a necessity for that narration as anthropocentric. The expression that when we write we are also written captures this passivity and extension beyond our actions. Braidotti is right to emphasise that we need to narrate the real processes that go beyond and undermine accounts of human identity or exceptionalism. We do not simply narrate for us. When we make sense, we are also being made sense of. When we think the narration is for us, it is also directly by and for others, for all the series synthesised in and around us. Once again, this confirms the projection of the human out into a world such that the priority of the human as some kind of centre for judgement and value is reversed.

In Deleuze's philosophy of time, the nine processes of time are interrelated such that everything presupposes each of the syntheses. This is significant for the argument because it extends the number of ways in which the human can be taken to presuppose processes connecting it to the nonhuman; for instance, as a synthesis of the past and future in the present, or as a synthesis of the present and the past through the cut made by the future. This supports Braidotti's position more than Moore's because his claim for an anthropocentric metaphysics depends on some kind of limited definition of Man, even if this changes over time, whereas Braidotti's argument stresses the extent and depth of the connection of humans to the nonhuman across a much wider and more eclectic set of beings, times and locations. According to Deleuze's philosophy of time this extension is very large indeed, as can be shown through a closer study of each of the passive syntheses.

We can see the limits imposed by Moore's position in his appeal to human self-consciousness as a remedy for catastrophic errors in metaphysics: 'The failure in some of these cases is a failure of due self-consciousness'.[16] The counter-argument is that this self-consciousness is not there to be able to fail. There is no free-standing self-consciousness in the present that can consider its past and narrate it and take account of that for its future. Instead, the present is conditioned by the past and by the future such that consciousness is always taken beyond its boundaries and cannot take on the role of reliable form of reflection and barrier against error. That's not to say that we should not reflect or be self-conscious. It is to say that the fact that we do so—and that this can be beneficial for us—does not support the conclusion that metaphysics needs to be anthropocentric. This is because we also need to take account of how consciousness is nonhuman and beholden to the nonhuman.

Towards the end of her book, Braidotti criticises the over-privileging of consciousness in a series of questions which follow from her situation of the human in relation to environment, technology and animals:

> What if consciousness were, in fact, just another cognitive mode of relating to one's environment and to others? What if, by comparison with the immanent know-how of animals, conscious representation were blighted by narcissistic delusions of transcendence and consequently blinded by its own aspirations to self-transparency? What if consciousness were ultimately incapable of finding a remedy to its obscure disease, this life, this *zoe*, an impersonal force that moves us without asking for our permission to do so?[17]

Two linked moves take place in these questions. First, the priority assigned to human consciousness is criticised given its situation within and interdependence to other modes of relation. Second, human consciousness is seen as incapable of resolving its deepest problems, its finitude and being-towards-death. Unless it is extended into the posthuman, human consciousness cannot correctly address its own relation to death or its relation to the death of others.

Deleuze's account of time is a deep critique of the privilege given to any human present and not only the present of consciousness. He stresses the interconnectedness of times and their chaotic and nonlinear relations:

> Between successive presents, it implies non-localisable links, action at a distance, systems of replay, of resonances and of echoes, objective chance, signals and signs, roles transcending spatial situations and temporal successions.[18]

The manifold nature of time and the way in which it connects successive presents is such that a series of disparate relations between times is constantly altering them. This ongoing determination and transformation undermines claims to priority for any given present—for instance, of human consciousness—exactly because its spatial and temporal location is conditioned by kinds of events that reflective consciousness is supposed to avoid: 'action at a distance', 'nonlocation', 'resonances and echoes', 'chance', 'signals' and 'signs'.

It is because time is a manifold of processes transforming all things in wide and multiple ways that it makes no sense to appeal to some kind of anthropocentric necessity. The centre does not exist except as an illusory way of telling a humanist story. The story is false and damaging, even if it is sometimes reassuring. In time, we have always been posthuman.

NOTES

1. For a fuller critique of Moore's reading of Deleuze, see Williams 2015. For a full account of Deleuze's philosophy of time, see Williams 2011.

2. Braidotti 2013, 107.

3. The concept of assemblage, taken from Deleuze and Guattari's work in the two volumes of *Capitalism and Schizophrenia* among other sources, has been widely influential in new theoretical models. For a study of the concept, see De Landa 2006, especially chapters 1 and 2.

4. As N. Kathryn Hayles points out in her work on the posthuman, in Philip K. Dick's original book version for *Blade Runner*, *Do Androids Dream of Electric Sheep?*, android simulacra of humans are not allowed into the human realm but are rather legally classified as objects. See Hayles 1999, 169.

5. Braidotti 2013, 193.

6. Donna J. Haraway's work is among the strongest in investigating the joint transformation of human and animal into new assemblages. See, for instance, Haraway 2008. In earlier work Haraway has also investigated posthuman cyborgs in an ethical vein that connects to Braidotti's ethical concerns around the posthuman. See Haraway's iconic and ironic manifesto in 1991, 149ff.

7. For many cautions about the dangers and challenges of artificial intelligence and its surpassing of human intelligence, as well as a strong defense of the potential benefits of artificial intelligence, see Bostrom 2014.

8. Moore 2012, 603.

9. Moore 2012, 604.

10. Moore 2012, 604.

11. The thinker who has done most to demonstrate this historical and political construction of the human as contingent rather than necessary is Michel Foucault, most notably in his *The Order of Things: Archeology of the Human Sciences* (Foucault 2011).

12. Moore 2012, 343.

13. Patricia MacCormack has argued for such a posthuman ethics based on readings of Spinoza and Deleuze and Guattari: 'Ethical encounters with liminal bodies (of which our own is always one) are good for [expanding the body and allowing the other to be]. It is an act of love between things based on their difference.' (MacCormack 2016, 4).

14. The transcendental interpretation of Deleuze's work, in particular in *Difference and Repetition*, has been developed by Anne Sauvagnargues (2009), Dan Smith (2012) and Henry Somers-Hall (2013), among others. I discuss these recent interpretations of Deleuze in the second edition of my Gilles Deleuze's *Difference and Repetition: a Critical Introduction and Guide* (Williams 2013, esp. chapter 8).

15. It is important to distinguish the holistic posthuman of one posthuman system and Braidotti's pluralist posthuman related to the pluralism of Deleuze's philosophy of time. We should think of many times and many posthumans, rather than of one interconnected posthuman system. Claire Colebrook (2014, 166) makes this point forcefully in relation to the critical role played by Braidotti, Deleuze and Guattari against monistic humanism and posthumanism: 'The posthumanism of which Braidotti is critical is of a single-system where all observations can be grounded on a single self-expressive living whole'.

16. Moore 2012, 602.

17. Braidotti 2013, 193.

18. Deleuze 1968, 113; my translation.

REFERENCES

Bostrom, N. (2014). *Superintelligence: Paths, Dangers, Strategies*. Oxford: Oxford University Press.

Braidotti, R. (2013). *The Posthuman*. Cambridge, MA: Polity.

Colebrook, C. (2014). *Death of the Posthuman: Essays on Extinction, Vol. 1*. Ann Arbor, MI: Open Humanities Press.

Deleuze, G. (1968). *Différence et repetition*. Paris: Presses Universitaires de France.

De Landa, M. (2006). *A New Philosophy of Society: Assemblage Theory and Social Complexity*. London: Continuum.

Foucault, M. (2011). *The Order of Things: Archaeology of the Human Sciences*. London: Routledge.

Haraway, D. (2008). *When Species Meet*. Minneapolis: University of Minnesota Press.

Haraway, D. (1991). 'Cyborg Manifesto'. In *Simians, Cyborgs and Women: The Reinvention of Nature*. New York: Routledge.

Hayles, N. K. (1999). *How We Became Posthuman: Virtual Bodies in Cybernetics, Literature and Informatics*. Chicago: University of Chicago Press.

MacCormack, P. (2016). *Posthuman Ethics*. London: Routledge.

Moore, A. W. (2012). *The Evolution of Modern Metaphysics: Making Sense of Things*. Cambridge: Cambridge University Press.

Sauvagnargues, A. (2009). *Deleuze: l'empirisme transcendental.* Paris: Presses Universitaires de France.

Smith, D. W. (2012). *Essays on Deleuze.* Edinburgh: Edinburgh University Press.

Somers-Hall, H. (2013). Deleuze's *Difference and Repetition: An Edinburgh Philosophical Guide.* Edinburgh: Edinburgh University Press.

Williams, J. (2011). *Gilles Deleuze's Philosophy of Time: A Critical Introduction and Guide.* Edinburgh: Edinburgh University Press.

Williams, J. (2013). *Gilles Deleuze's Difference and Repetition: A Critical Introduction and Guide.* Edinburgh: Edinburgh University Press.

Williams, J. (2015). 'Deleuze, Moore and Anthropocentrism in Metaphysics', *Philosophical Topics*, 'The Evolution of Modern Metaphysics: Responses to A. W. Moore with His Replies', 43, 1–2, 301–18.

Chapter 7

'Becoming-Equal to the Act'

The Temporality of Action and Agential Responsibility

Sean Bowden

What does it mean to be the agent of an action if that action, in its very temporal structure, outstrips what its agent initially intends and foresees? Is agential responsibility thereby denied? This chapter attempts to address these questions in three steps. First, it will develop an account of the temporality of action and agency with reference to Deleuze's account of the three syntheses of time in *Difference and Repetition*. Second, it will apply this account of temporality to two kinds of action: ordinary actions whose 'success conditions' can be specified in advance of that action; and actions aimed at something whose success conditions cannot be specified in advance but only within the situated and temporally unfolding action itself. Finally, with reference to the latter type of action, it will draw on some of Deleuze's references to Hölderlin in the exposition of the third synthesis of time in order to sketch an account of thought and agency that does not depend on the ideal or achievement of an agent's full self-understanding of what is expressed in their activity, and that is capable of bearing what is 'incomplete' in thought and action without denying the very notion of agential responsibility. By way of conclusion, it will then be suggested that such an account of agency and agential responsibility is called for by our contemporary situation, insofar as this is characterised by the demand for actions that are currently 'too big' for us.

THREE SYNTHESES OF TIME

In chapter 2 of *Difference and Repetition*, Deleuze is concerned to show how various forms of repetition in everyday experience presuppose more profound repetitions which are themselves constitutive of, and hence prior to, everyday experience: those of habit, memory and difference.[1] These three repetitions are elaborated by Deleuze in the context of an exposition of three syntheses of time—the present, the past and the future, respectively—and it is these three syntheses that are of concern here, insofar as they tell us something important about the temporality of action and agency.

The First Synthesis of Habit or the Present

As is well-known, Deleuze argues that the time of the present is constituted in a synthesis which contracts successive independent instants into one another.[2] This synthesis does not, however, depend upon the activity of a subject; rather, the synthesis is 'passive'. It takes place insofar as otherwise indifferent moments of sensation come to be related to one another through the contraction of a habit, where this latter is defined as the formation of a horizon of anticipations on the basis of the qualitative impressions generated by received sensations. The contraction of a habit is, in this way, a synthesis of time—the establishment of a lived, or living, present which embraces a relative past and future: 'the past in so far as the preceding instants are retained in the contraction; the future because its expectation is anticipated in this same contraction'.[3]

This synthesis of the present, Deleuze argues, is not brought about by a subject, because this contraction or temporal organisation of the flux of experience in habits is itself the constitution of a subject or self. And not only the psychological self. Indeed, for Deleuze,

> [e]very organism, in its receptive and perceptual elements, but also in its viscera, is a sum of contractions, of retentions and expectations. ... [Habit] concerns not only the sensory-motor habits that we have (psychologically), but also, before these, the primary habits that we are; the thousands of passive syntheses of which we are organically composed. ... What organism is not made of elements and cases of repetition, of contemplated and contracted water, nitrogen, carbon, chlorides and sulphates, thereby intertwining all the habits of which it is composed?[4]

Every 'thing'—every organism and every part of an organism—is thus a contracted habit and hence, in a sense, 'a maker of time'.[5] The existing world is thereby constituted as a field of co-existing 'living presents', each with its own particular rhythm, and we ourselves are nothing but systems of passive syntheses, composed of relations between numerous habits at different levels.[6]

Deleuze also argues that the passive synthesis of habit makes possible active syntheses of memory and judgement. As he puts it, on the basis of the qualitative impressions contracted in habit memory reconstitutes the particular cases as distinct, conserving them in its own 'temporal space'. The past is then no longer the immediate past of retention but the reflexive past of representation, of reflected and reproduced particularity. Correlatively, the future also ceases to be the immediate future of anticipation in order to become the reflexive future of prediction, the reflected generality of the understanding (the understanding weights the expectation ... in proportion to the number of distinct similar cases observed and recalled).[7]

Being concerned here with action and agency, we can note that insofar as action involves active syntheses of memory and judgement—the reflection upon particular past experiences to make predictions of a general nature about the future to which activity is directed—action is made possible and supported by passive syntheses of habit. Moreover, as Williams rightly notes, in the context of action, the past particulars reflected upon by the agent, as well as the future generalities that are predicted on their basis, both presuppose and are 'cut out' from 'wider sets' of retentions and anticipations. This means that, even throughout the performance of an action, the contemplative self or selves which underlie the agent of action will continue to be passively absorbed in and transformed by contractions of habit 'beyond the set considered in the action'.[8] In other words, even if action depends upon the active syntheses carried out by the agent of that action, the agent is not 'master of their own house', even throughout the performance of their actions.

The Second Synthesis of Memory or the Past

The time of the present is 'originary', but there is more to the story of time. Indeed, there is something paradoxical about the present. Contractions of habits constitute time as a living present with a relative past and future, but the present also appears to pass in the time thus constituted, which is to say that the present appears to pass into one of its own dimensions. Deleuze's response to this 'paradox of the passing present' is to argue that the first synthesis must already be 'intratemporal'. There must be another time in which the first synthesis of time operates. More specifically, Deleuze will argue that the passing present or passage of time depends upon a synthesis of the past or of 'Memory', which is understood as the *a priori*, transcendental ground of the passing present—a ground that was never itself present and that does not itself pass.[9] It should immediately be said, however, that the synthesis of the past is not the active synthesis of a thinking subject. As with the synthesis of habit, the synthesis of the past is passive. Moreover, it is also a condition for the subject's active 'use' of the past in the present: in recollection, perception and agential action. In other words, Deleuze will argue that the subject's capacity to represent former and present presents to itself in an action situation depends upon the *a priori* synthesis of the past.[10]

Deleuze 'deduces' the features of the *a priori* past that was never present by working through a series of four temporal paradoxes, which he draws from Bergson's *Matter and Memory*. The first such paradox, as Deleuze formulates it, is that the past is contemporaneous with the present that it *was*.[11] Indeed, it is the 'contemporaneity' of the past and the present which, for Deleuze, accounts for the passing of the present, and so dissolves the paradox of the passing present mentioned earlier. As he puts it, '[n]o present would ever pass were it not past "at the same time" as it is present; no past would ever be constituted unless it were first constituted "at the same time" as it was present'.[12] Indeed, we cannot start with the present and hope to explain its passing, for the present has no *internal* reason or means to pass.[13] We must rather begin with the past and say that the present is able to pass because it is *already* a dimension of the past. By the same token, then, we must say that no past present is constituted *after* having first been present; it is rather formed at the same time as the present that it was.[14]

But now, Deleuze proceeds to argue that the first paradox of contemporaneity implies a second paradox: that of 'coexistence'. As he puts it, '[i]f each past is contemporaneous with the present that it was, then *all* of the past coexists with the new present in relation to which it is now past'.[15] In other words, the present present is not only contemporaneous with its correlative past present, the present present coexists with the past 'in general'—the pure past through which *all* presents pass, but which itself does not pass. As Lapoujade summarises it, the pure past 'gathers in itself each present, but as past, such that the past coexists entirely with itself and with every passing present'.[16]

Deleuze now argues that a third paradox 'completes' the first two: the so-called paradox of 'pre-existence'. As he puts it,

> when we say that it is contemporaneous with the present that it *was*, we necessarily speak of a past which never *was* present, since it was not formed 'after'. Its manner of being contemporaneous with itself as present is that of being posed as already-there, presupposed by the passing present and causing it to pass. Its manner of coexisting with the new present is one of being posed in itself, conserving itself in itself and being presupposed by the new present. ... The paradox of pre-existence thus completes the other two: each past is contemporaneous with the present it was, the whole past coexists with the present in relation to which it is past, but the pure element of the past in general pre-exists the passing present.[17]

If the first three paradoxes oblige us to recognise the existence of a pure past in general as the *a priori* transcendental ground of the passing present, the fourth paradox of the past arguably tells us something about the *manner* in which this pure past exists, both in itself and in the passing present, insofar as this latter is understood as one of the past's dimensions. Deleuze here speaks of the past by drawing on the Bergsonian metaphor of the virtual 'cone' of memory and claims that the past is constituted by relations of virtual coexistence between diverse 'levels', which are themselves different degrees of 'contraction' (generality) and 'relaxation' (specificity) with respect to the events making up the entire past.[18] At the apex of the cone—the moment of the passing present—the past exists in a maximally contracted way: summed up, as it were, into a point of 'practical generality' comprised of bodily motor habits and sets of useful general concepts that integrate past experiences.[19] But the further we get from the demands of the present—which is to say as we approach the base of the cone—the past exists in an increasingly relaxed manner, and events increasingly appear in their distinctness and specificity. Taken as a whole, then, the pure past is thus comprised of an infinity of coexisting 'repetitions' of the entire past, contracted and relaxed in various aspects, all of which coexist virtually with the passing present.

To give plausibility to this idea that each passing present is a contraction of the entire past that pre-exists it and coexists with itself at an infinity of levels, Deleuze asks us to consider what is meant by the notion of 'destiny'. He writes:

> Presents succeed, encroaching upon one another. Nevertheless, however strong the incoherence or possible opposition between successive presents, we have the impression that each of them plays out 'the same life' at different levels. This is what we call destiny. Destiny never consists in step-by-step deterministic relations between presents which succeed one another. ... Rather, it implies between successive presents non-localisable connections, actions at a distance, systems of replay, resonance and echoes, objective chances, signs, signals and roles which transcend spatial locations and temporal successions. We say of successive presents which express a destiny that they always play out the same thing, the same story, but at different levels: here more or less relaxed, there more or less contracted. ... The succession of present presents is only the manifestation of something more profound—namely, the manner in which each continues the whole life, but at a different level or degree to the preceding, since all levels and degrees coexist and present themselves for our choice on the basis of a past which was never present ... In short, what we live empirically as a succession of different presents from the point of view of active synthesis is also *the ever increasing coexistence of levels of the past within passive synthesis.*[20]

For Deleuze, in short, a present passes and is replaced with a new present to the extent that the new present comes to 'contract' or 'sum up' in a novel way the entire past at once, including the immediate former present. But this is only possible insofar as the past is 'already there', contemporaneous with the present: an *a priori* synthesis of the totality of time which 'telescopes' together successive presents understood as coexisting levels of varying degrees of contraction/generality and relaxation/specificity with respect to the events comprising the entirety of the past. Moreover, the active synthesis of memory—understood as the representation of the present under the dual aspect of the reproduction of former presents and the reflection of the new present—also presupposes the pure past or the past 'in general'. As was argued earlier, the active synthesis of memory is *founded* upon the passive synthesis of habit insofar as this constitutes the thinking subject along with its lived present of retentions and anticipations. However, the capacity of this constituted subject to *transcend* its particular lived present of retentions and anticipations, and to actively reproduce *former* presents in the act of representing to itself its present present, requires the lived present to be *grounded* upon, and to be 'operating' within, a passive synthesis of the *a priori* past which 'makes the former and the present present … two asymmetrical elements of the past as such'.[21]

The Third Synthesis of Difference or the Future

In accounting for the passing present and the active synthesis of memory, it has been argued *that* the past contracts. However, it still has not been explained *how* or *why* the past contracts. This explanation only comes with Deleuze's discussion of the third synthesis of time.[22]

Deleuze's presentation of the third synthesis of time is notorious for its difficulty. We will here focus upon three of its most general features. First, Deleuze claims that the third synthesis is a 'static synthesis' in which time appears as 'a pure *order*', comprising a formal distribution of a before and an after on either side of a 'caesura'.[23] The caesura is to be understood as inseparable from a 'present of metamorphosis' which both *distinguishes* the past from a radically new future, and *relates* the past and future to each other as the before and the after of the metamorphosis.

Second, time in the third synthesis is defined by a *totality*. As Deleuze puts it, 'the caesura, of whatever kind, must be determined in the image of a unique and tremendous event, an act which is adequate to time as a whole'. And insofar as this image draws together—distinguishes and relates—the past and the future, it can be said to be 'adequate to the totality of time', torn between the unequal or incommensurable dimensions of past and future.[24]

Third, insofar as it carries out a distribution of the incommensurable dimensions of past, present and future, the image of the act from which the caesura is inseparable creates the possibility of a temporal *series*. Serially speaking, the past or the before is defined as the time in which the subject of the imagined action is not capable of it. In other words, the past is that which is lived by the habitual subject of the present as the 'problem of the internal conditions of the action in relation to the redoubtable image',[25] and the subject effectively exists *in* the mode of the past insofar as he or she fails to relate the past to the action that is projected to bring about something new. In other words, the subject remains 'stuck' in the pure past insofar as he or she fails to bring about a novel 'contraction' of the co-existing levels of the past in the act of bringing about the new.

The next time in the series—the present, which relates to the caesura—is defined as the time of metamorphosis or of the actor's 'becoming-equal to the act' that was previously 'too big' for it. In the caesura, we thus find the subject constrained by the demands of their situation to experimentally establish new 'pathways' in the past, forcing different events at different levels of the past to communicate and thereby 'contracting' a past that has never been present as the condition of the production of the new.[26]

The final time in the series—the time of the future—is defined as the time in which the actor will have become equal to the imagined act, but *only* insofar as it becomes something *other* than it was.[27] In other words, the future appears as a product that exceeds the initial conditions of its production, and that outstrips what its author, enmeshed in its habits and co-existing past presents, could have intended or foreseen. Or again, the future is the time in which the actor will have become equal to its action by becoming open to, and transformed by, the future-directed unfolding of its action. As Deleuze puts it, the actor becomes equal to its action only by becoming equal to 'the unequal in itself', the difference that draws together and distinguishes the before from the radically new in the formal order of time.[28] In short, while the advent of the future demands an agent of change, this agent must be one that is 'open' to difference, bringing about the different only to the extent that it is brought about by it.

We can now more clearly grasp the relation between the contraction of the past, the passing of the present, the synthesis of memory in the representation of the new present, and the dimension of the future. It was argued previously that a given present could never pass if it were not already past, but we now see that the present could never pass (with a novel contraction of the past) if it were not already past *and also* yet to come, at the same time as being present.[29] More precisely, what we now see is that it is the third synthesis of time—understood from the point of view of its formal order, totality and seriality—that causes the present to pass. For in the third synthesis of time, the past and the present appear as dimensions of the future (the past as condition, the present as agent), and are made use of as 'stages' that will be left behind in the production of change.[30]

To return to the problem with which this section began, we have outlined Deleuze's account of *how* the past contracts: by means of an agent whom the future will transform. However, we have yet to fully understand *why* the past contracts, which is to say, why an agent would aim to bring about the radically new by making novel use of the past in the present. Although Deleuze does not discuss this explicitly in chapter 2 of *Difference and Repetition*, over several pages of the following chapter he makes it clear that it is an encounter with something that disrupts settled habits that forces a creative act from the subject. In other words, when it is confronted with something it has no ready-made sensory-motor or conceptual schema to deal with, the subject is constrained to embark upon a future-oriented process of reconstituting the habits that it has, developing new ways of being in its world and new modes of thinking, which is to say, new ways of living (contracting, generalising, integrating, etc.) the different levels of its past.[31] Or again, as Deleuze puts it, in order to make sense of and resolve the encountered problem, the subject is forced to 'remember ... that which can only be recalled'[32] insofar as it differs from every empirical memory, being rather constituted by 'the dissimilar in the pure form of time'[33] or the demands of the new.

THE EXPRESSION OF AGENCY AND AGENTIAL RESPONSIBILITY

Two Types of Action and Several Definitions

Deleuze's account of the three syntheses of time raises a number of issues for our understanding of action and agency. First and foremost, it appears that we must distinguish between two types of action. On the one hand, some actions simply draw upon existing sensory-motor and conceptual schema. In such cases, the action can be said to take place within the bounds of a living present of settled habits and untroubled expectations. On the other hand, some actions demand the transformation of such schema, and hence of the agent and its various capacities, in the very performance of that action. In these latter cases, the temporality of the action is that of the third synthesis of time.

But now, another issue follows from this. In cases where an action outstrips what its agent initially intends and foresees, or what the agent is initially capable of, what can be said about agential responsibility?[34] If the product of an action exceeds its initial conditions, or if the agent that emerges from the action is other than the agent who initiated it, does the very notion of agential responsibility even make sense? I will argue here that it does. Before coming to the argument, however, we will need to explicate several of the key terms and claims on which the argument depends.[35]

First, what is meant by an 'action'? We will stipulate that actions are distinguished from other kinds of 'happenings' insofar as they are directed by an 'intention' of some kind. My raising my arm is an action that is directed by, for example, an intention to ask a question. On the other hand, if my arm simply 'goes up', perhaps due to a muscular spasm, this is an unintended 'happening'.[36] This way of distinguishing actions and happenings with reference to intentions clearly differentiates my account of action and agency from that of 'new materialists' such as Bennett, who views action in general as the product of human-nonhuman assemblages that owe their agentic capacities to the vital materialities constituting them.[37] While I agree with Bennett that we must dispense with overly simplistic conceptions of autonomous human agency that overlook the complexity of situations in which human action is produced, I am unable to follow her in altogether dispensing with the notion of intentions. As I have argued in more detail elsewhere, without a notion of this kind we are unable to distinguish between actions and happenings—and hence agents and patients—in ways that are relevant to an adequate causal analysis of the production of events. Such a notion, moreover, is not only key to the analysis of causal responsibility for what happens, it is also presupposed by Bennett's own discussion of ethical and political responsibility.[38] These critical remarks should not, however, be construed as a call to return to the all-too-human conception of an independent and self-determining human agent. Rather, it is a call to reconsider the nature of intentions and their specification *within* the situated and temporally unfolding actions that express them, and in a way that is commensurate with the posthuman critique of human mastery and autonomy.

I argue, then, that actions are directed by intentions. But what is an intention? I claim that an agent's intention directs their action by setting the conditions that an agent must bring about in the world in order for their action to be deemed successful.[39] The 'success conditions' that make up the content of an intention can, however, be specified in different ways. On the one hand, they may be specified in advance of the action to be performed. This is what tends to happen in action cases of the first type, within the bounds of the habitual present. For example, the intention I form tonight to get to work tomorrow by means of the 6.11 train specifies in advance what will count as the successful execution of that intention. On the other hand, an intention's success conditions may be specified throughout the very situated and temporally extended performance of the action which the evolving intention nevertheless animates. This is characteristic of action cases of the second type, unfolding in the pure order of time. Here, we can perhaps think of an author who, in the very act of writing, only gradually discovers what the successful realisation of an intention to give literary expression to the complex history of her oppressed nation would look like, and what this demands of her.[40] Or again, consider what it means to intend a response to potentially catastrophic climate change. Given the complexity of the Earth's climate system—as well as the complex imbrication of this system with our social, political, economic and legal systems—our actions will inevitably produce unintended and unforeseeable effects which themselves progressively reveal what it *actually* means to intend a response to climate change.[41]

The content of an intention is made up of success conditions that are specifiable either in advance of the corresponding action or in the very performance of that action. But what is the relation between an intention and an action? I claim that intentions and actions are not related to one another as prior, free-standing causes and subsequent effects, but rather that intentions are ontologically inseparable from their corresponding actions.[42] In other words, intentions effectively exist in the intrinsic direction of their corresponding actions. Intentions are thus internal causes of action, but they are not *prior* causes. This is to say that to have an intention—even a so-called prior intention whose particular content is specifiable in advance of its eventual instantiation—is to already be acting on it, be this only in the very minimal sense of purposefully avoiding situations which will frustrate the eventual execution of the intention.

Another way to put this point is to say that intentions are *expressed* or manifested in their corresponding actions, as long as we understand the relation of expression from the three interrelated points of view Deleuze identifies in his work on the concept of expression in Spinoza: being, knowing and acting.[43] The first point of view, then, is an *ontological* one, and relates to the inseparability of intentions and actions just mentioned. It holds that an intention (the expressed) is an internal or immanent cause that, while not reducible to its expression in an action, does not have actual existence apart from the action it animates. Indeed, a professed intention which is never acted upon, especially when there exist the means and opportunity to do so, is no intention at all. The second point of view is an *epistemological* or *noetic* one. It holds that the action expresses or manifests the 'sense' of its internal or immanent cause. In other words, insofar as the actual existence of the intention is inseparable from the situated action it animates, the content of the intention cannot be grasped without reference to that action. The third point of view concerns the *production* of the expressed. What is claimed here is that the expression (the action) not only expresses the sense of its immanent cause (the intention), the action also dynamically actualises its immanent cause as it unfolds over time in a concrete situation and responds to encountered problems.

The overarching idea, in short, is that it is in the temporal unfolding of an action that its agent is able to grasp what is really demanded by that action, and so what is demanded of the agent him- or herself to keep the evolving action on track. Even in action cases of the first type it can still be said that actions express intentions in this way. It may be the case that the manner in which the action unfolds demands nothing more of the agent than what was initially anticipated. Nevertheless, the action must still be performed in order to 'confirm' the concrete actuality of the prior intention. In actions of the second type, of course, things are more complex. Recalling some of the vocabulary in which Deleuze's third synthesis of time is articulated, we must say that in the activity of 'becoming-equal' to the initial image of his or her action the agent is forced to creatively respond to problems that arise, contract its past in novel ways, and discover or invent the 'success conditions' which comprise the real content of his or her intention to produce the new. In line with the posthuman critique of human independence and mastery, then, action is not so much the product of an autonomous agent as the agent's actualised intentions are the product of their situated and temporally extended actions.

Agential Responsibility on the Straight Line of Time

We must now return to the question posed at the start of the previous section: does it make sense to talk about agential responsibility in action cases of the second type? If an unfolding action outstrips what an agent initially intends, foresees and is capable of—if, in other words, the unfolding action itself demands the transformation of the agent's thoughts and capacities as the very condition for the agent's direction of that action—in what sense is that action *theirs*? In what sense is the agent the *author* of such an action, as opposed to what is authored *by* the action? I argue that an answer to this question can be approached by coming to grips with Deleuze's discussion of Hölderlin in his presentation of the third synthesis of time.

Deleuze claims that it is Hölderlin who first formulates the idea of a pure and empty order of time, fractured by a 'caesura' that distinguishes a past and future that fail to 'rhyme' or coincide.[44] Moreover, for Deleuze, it is also Hölderlin 'who discovers, in this emptiness, simultaneously the continued diversion of the divine, the prolonged fracture of the I and the constitutive passion of the self'.[45] The works he cites to support these claims are Hölderlin's 'Remarques sur Oedipe/Remarques sur Antigone'[46] and Jean Beaufret's 'Hölderlin et Sophocle'.[47] The former text contains Hölderlin's accompanying theoretical notes to his highly idiosyncratic translations of Sophocles's *Oedipus the King* and *Antigone*. The latter is an extended commentary on Hölderlin's notes.

The claim that Deleuze focuses upon in Hölderlin and Beaufret is that there was a rather profound shift between the works of earlier Greek tragedians such as Aeschylus and those of Sophocles. This change is described in terms of an uncoupling of the human being and God, as well as the introduction of a new conception of time. Moreover, these last two claims are related.

Older tragedies, according to this argument, are framed by a type of divine law which goes hand in hand with a circular or 'curved' conception of time. More particularly, these tragedies are populated by characters who violate in various ways the 'limits' imposed by divine law, but to that extent also have to 'atone' for these violations, often through their demise, so that justice is done and order restored. In this way, the end of such a tragedy returns us to the prior order of things: time bends back on itself, as it were, such that beginning and end 'rhyme' or coincide with each other.

With Sophocles, however, we have something rather different. Violations of a supposed natural order are met only with silence from the heavens. The gods fail to mete out punishments that would restore order to the world, and the author of the criminal deed is thrown back upon themselves. In such tragedies, the beginning and end are said to no longer rhyme or coincide: the circle of time is broken and unfolded, becoming a straight line, with the tragic hero occupying a present which both separates out and draws together the already past and a radically open future. As Deleuze put it, 'before Sophocles ... it is man who eludes the limit' that has been pre-established; with Sophocles, 'it is the limit which is elusive'. Or again, with Sophocles, the God who had previously set everything within their proper limits turns away and 'is no longer anything but empty time', and the human being who must now assume responsibility for those limits is lodged in a 'caesura' from which a past and future will be continuously produced on this straight line of time, symbolised by Oedipus's long wandering and the perpetual suspension of a final judgement with respect to his deeds.[48]

Beaufret argues that, for Hölderlin, insofar as human beings are abandoned by God and thrown back on themselves, left with nothing other than the pure forms of time and space, they must assume responsibility for the law by determining it for themselves through the use of reason, in the manner of Kant. In Hölderlin's notion of the 'categorical turning' of God and humankind from one another, Beaufret claims, we are to hear echoes of the Kantian notion of the 'categorical imperative'.[49] But as Voss rightly points out, Deleuze will not, and cannot, pursue the Kantian solution to the problem.[50] In the third synthesis of time, and in line with the posthuman critique of the sovereign human subject, the agent eludes not only the judgement of the gods, but also of human reason. Indeed, as we have seen, the thinking subject, along with the categories of thought that are deployed in judgement, belong to the future and are only progressively produced on the straight line of time.

The Kantian conception of the thinking and acting subject, in short, is not compatible with the pure and empty form of time identified by Hölderlin. Indeed, no conception that posits the agent as a free-standing entity that exists independently of and prior to the actions it performs is compatible with the third synthesis of time, for actions whose temporality is that of the third synthesis demand that this agent become *other* than it was in the very performance of their action. But now, to put this in terms of the question of agential responsibility, if we conceive of an agent as an independently existing entity, and if agent A of unfolding action X at T_1 is not the same as agent B of unfolding action X at T_2, then it cannot be said that agent A is responsible for what agent B is doing. In other words, on this conception of agency, it does not make sense to talk of agential responsibility for actions that outstrip what the agent who initiates it intends, foresees and is capable of.

There are, however, other conceptions of agency. As has been argued, on an expressive account, what an agent 'is about' does not exist independently of and prior to its actions. What an agent is about is expressed in—which is to say, inseparable from, grasped through and produced by—his or her situated action as it unfolds over time in response to encountered problems. Does such a conception of agency allow us to talk about agential responsibility in action cases that involve a synthesis of the future or of difference?

Hegel, as is known, developed a post-Kantian expressive account of agency in which an agent 'learns from its deed the developed nature of what it *actually* did',[51] and without denying the possibility of responsibility. He claimed that the determination of agential responsibility for an action is the product of a process of mediation between the agent's first-person point of view on their action, wherein they take themselves to be responsible only for what they initially intended, and a third-person or public understanding of what the action turned out to be, which takes the agent to be responsible for whatever effectively took place, regardless of their initial intentions. In other words, the determination of agential responsibility is a product of a process of reciprocal recognition wherein what the agent comes to acknowledge as his or her deed is also that which comes to be attributed to him or her from the third-person, public point of view.[52]

Deleuze, clearly, will not follow the Hegelian solution which, through the mechanism of reciprocal recognition, ties intentional agency and authorial responsibility to the ideal or achievement of an agent's full self-understanding of what is expressed in their activity. Such a position attempts to subordinate the play of difference in the pure and empty form of time to a form of identity. However, the pure and empty form of time disallows such a form of identity. Deleuze, then, must tread another post-Kantian path. Indeed, I claim that he follows Hölderlin who, as Eldridge rightly argues, understands the agent to be capable of bearing what is 'incomplete' in the thought and action that express his or her agency, and without denying the very notion of agential responsibility.[53] In other words, for Deleuze and Hölderlin, the agent assumes responsibility for their actions that outstrip what they intend, foresee and are capable of insofar as they open themselves up to and allow themselves to be transformed by the demands of their action as it unfolds into the future.

CONCLUSION

There is no doubt that many major problems confronting us today—catastrophic climate change prime among them—demand a response whose contours we cannot currently envisage. Moreover, as recent posthuman and new materialist approaches have emphasised, any response to such problems demands that we ourselves are transformed in ways we cannot currently anticipate.[54] The impotence or paralysis many feel in the face of such monumental problems is tied to this uncertainty. But arguably, it is also tied to a certain understanding of what is needed to act, to be the agent of change. As I hope to have established earlier in relation to Deleuze's presentation of the third synthesis of time and his references therein to Hölderlin, we do not need to be in possession of a clear and fully specified plan in order to begin to act and take responsibility for the future. We do not have to know in advance exactly what 'success' will look like, or what we will need to become to realise it. What we need to do, rather, is project ourselves in the image of an action we are not currently capable of, and learn how to become equal to it.

The demand for actions that are currently 'too big' for us appears to call, not only for a new conception of agency, but also for a new ethics commensurate with this conception of agency. The elaboration of such an ethics is beyond the scope of the present work. Nevertheless, it can be said that this ethics must involve, in part, what Schmidt calls (following Latour, Coole and Frost, Connolly, Bennett and others), an ethics of 'self-reorientation' that aims to overcome the illusion of human independence, autonomy and sovereignty by coming to grips with the myriad ways in which agency is enmeshed in, and inseparable from, a world of multiple interacting systems.[55] On the other hand, this ethics must involve what Neimanis and Walker call (drawing on Barad, Grosz and others) an ethics of 'responsivity', which is attuned and responsive to the multiple, unintended and unforeseeable effects of our situated and temporally extended actions.[56] Such a 'posthuman' ethics clearly supports the account of agency and agential responsibility presented here. But at the same time, the 'expressive' account of intentional agency offered here supports such an ethics (and despite new materialist reservations about the conceptual baggage attached to the very notion of intentional agency), insofar as it clarifies what it means to employ such an ethics in the active pursuit of a future whose shape remains to be specified.

NOTES

1. Deleuze 1994, 70–128.
2. Deleuze 1994, 70.

3. Deleuze 1994, 70–71.
4. Deleuze 1994, 73–75.
5. Williams 2011, 37.
6. Deleuze 1994, 78. See also the discussion in Somers-Hall 2013, 65.
7. Deleuze 1994, 71.
8. Williams 2011, 27.
9. Deleuze 1994, 79–82. See also on this Ansell-Pearson 2002, 187.
10. Deleuze 1994, 80–82.
11. Deleuze 1994, 81.
12. Deleuze 1994, 81.
13. Al-Saji 2004, 209–10.
14. See also Deleuze 1991, 58; and Lapoujade 2017, 87.
15. Deleuze 1994, 81–82.
16. Lapoujade 2017, 87.
17. Deleuze 1994, 82.
18. Deleuze 1994, 82–83. Deleuze 1991, 59–60.
19. See Somers-Hall 2013, 71.
20. Deleuze 1994, 83.
21. Deleuze 1994, 81. See also Rölli 2016, 232.
22. A point rightly emphasised by Jay Lampert in his *Deleuze and Guattari's Philosophy of History* (2011, 51). See also Williams 2011, 78: Deleuze 'detects the need for another synthesis, because though the pure past shows us *what* we must create with, it does not show us *how*: the echo of the two presents only forms a persistent question, developed in representation as the field of a problem, with the rigorous imperative of searching, answering and resolving'.
23. Deleuze 1994, 88–89.
24. Deleuze 1994, 89.
25. Deleuze 1994, 295.
26. See on this, Lampert 2011, 54–55. As he puts it, the pasts that will be put to use in the production of the new are 'virtual events that have insisted without necessarily having been represented in empirical fact, and that hence belong to innovation'.
27. Deleuze 1994, 89–90. Somers-Hall provides an especially illuminating reading of Deleuze's reference to Hamlet in the presentation of the third synthesis of time. See Somers-Hall 2013, 78–81; 2011, 56–76.
28. Deleuze 1994, 90.
29. See also on this, Deleuze 1992, 48; and Deleuze 1990b, 165, 176.
30. Deleuze 1994, 93–94. As Roffe rightly notes, what the third synthesis of time imposes is 'an impassive and inflexible NEXT', which breaks open the self-contained or circular nature of the past and arrays it in the form of a before and an after. See Roffe 2014, 95.
31. See Deleuze, 1994, 139–41 and 143–45. See also Bowden 2018, 55–60.
32. Deleuze 1994, 141. See also Bryant 2008, 102–8.
33. Deleuze 1994, 144.
34. It should be emphasised here that the question of responsibility here is not one of 'moral' responsibility, but only of authorship. In other words, in the sense of

responsibility being used here, an agent is responsible for an action if that action can be said to be *theirs*.

35. I have treated these points elsewhere at greater length. See, especially, Bowden 2014.

36. 'An intention' is the answer typically given to Wittgenstein's question, 'what is left over if I subtract the fact that my arm goes up from the fact that I raise my arm?' See Wittgenstein 1953, §621.

37. See Bennett 2010, 34. See also Marchand 2018, 292–95.

38. See Bowden 2015a, 63–68.

39. The claim is broadly Anscombian and Searlean. See Anscombe 2000, §32; and Searle 1983, especially chapter 3.

40. On this distinction between two ways of specifying the content of an intention, see Ridley 2009, 187–89.

41. I thus agree with Neimanis and Walker that 'discourses that hinge on what we humans can do *now* to fix the *future* may require tempering. An ethic of fixing, making-up-for, and even sustaining cannot recognize that all actions are forever contracted in lines-of-flight whose effects will continue to be made and unmade in many futures to come'. That said, however, I do not believe that their new materialist conception of human agency can underpin the kind of 'responsivity' to climate change they envisage. What is needed, rather, is a revised conception of intentions and their situated and progressive specification. See Neimanis and Walker 2014, 572–73.

42. A view which effectively distinguishes my view from Searle's. See also on this Bowden 2015b.

43. See Deleuze 1990a. It should be noted here that we are primarily concerned with the *relation* of expression, and not with the particular *relata* examined in Deleuze's Spinoza book: substance–attributes–essence of substance, and attributes–modes–modifications of substance. On what follows, see Bowden 2017, 219–26.

44. Deleuze 1994, 89. See also Deleuze 1978.

45. Deleuze 1994, 87.

46. Hölderlin 1965. An English translation of Hölderlin's 'notes' can be found in Hölderlin 2001.

47. Beaufret 1965.

48. Deleuze 1978. See also Voss 2013, 231–36; Bogue 2001, 14–19.

49. See Beaufret 1965, 13–14.

50. See Voss 2013, 233–34.

51. Hegel 1977, §469. See also Taylor 1983.

52. For the detail of this argument, see Bowden 2015c, 213–21.

53. See Eldridge 2006.

54. See, for example, Neimanis and Walker 2014; Alaimo 2012, 558–64; Schmidt 2013.

55. See Schmidt 2013, 178–81.

56. See Neimanis and Walker 2014, 571–73.

REFERENCES

Alaimo, S. (2012). 'Sustainable This, Sustainable That: New Materialisms, Posthumanism, and Unknown Futures'. *PMLA* 127, no. 3, 558–64.

Al-Saji, A. (2004). 'The Memory of Another Past: Bergson, Deleuze and a New Theory of Time'. *Continental Philosophy Review* 37, 203–39.

Anscombe, G. E. M. (2000). *Intention*. Cambridge, MA: Harvard University Press.

Ansell-Pearson, K. (2002). *Philosophy and the Adventure of the Virtual: Bergson and the Time of Life*. London: Routledge.

Beaufret, J. (1965). 'Hölderlin et Sophocle'. In *Remarques sur Oedipe/Remarques sur Antigone*, Friedrich Hölderlin, ed., François Fédier, trans. Paris: Union Générale d'Editions, 7–42.

Bennett, J. (2010). *Vibrant Matter: A Political Ecology of Things*. Durham, NC: Duke University Press.

Bogue, R. (2001). 'The Betrayal of God'. In *Deleuze and Religion*, M. Bryden, ed. London: Routledge, 9–29.

Bowden, S. (2014). ' "Willing the Event": Expressive Agency in Deleuze's *Logic of Sense*'. *Critical Horizons* 15(3), 231–48.

Bowden, S. (2015a). 'Human and Nonhuman Agency in Deleuze'. In *Deleuze and the Non/Human*, J. Roffe and H. Stark, eds. Basingstoke: Palgrave Macmillan, 60–80.

Bowden, S. (2015b). 'Normativity and Expressive Agency in Hegel, Nietzsche and Deleuze'. *Journal of Speculative Philosophy* 29(2), 236–59.

Bowden, S. (2015c). 'Tragedy and Agency in Hegel and Deleuze'. In *At the Edges of Thought: Deleuze and Post-Kantian Philosophy*, C. Lundy and D. Voss, eds. Edinburgh: Edinburgh University Press, 212–28.

Bowden, S. (2017). 'The Intensive Expression of the Virtual: Revisiting the Relation of Expression in *Difference and Repetition*'. *Deleuze Studies* 11(2), 216–39.

Bowden, S. (2018). 'An Anti-Positivist Conception of Problems: Deleuze, Bergson and the French Epistemological Tradition'. *Angelaki* 23(2), 45–63.

Bryant, L. R. (2008). *Difference and Givenness: Deleuze's Transcendental Empiricism and the Ontology of Immanence*. Evanston, IL: Northwestern University Press.

Deleuze, G. (1978). 'Cours Vincennes 21/03/1978'. Melissa McMahon, trans. Accessed May 21, 2018. https://www.webdeleuze.com/textes/67.

Deleuze, G. (1990a). *Expressionism in Philosophy: Spinoza*. Martin Joughin, trans. New York: Zone Books.

Deleuze, G. (1990b). *The Logic of Sense*. Constantin V. Boundas, ed., Mark Lester with Charles Stivale, trans. London: The Athlone Press.

Deleuze, G. (1991). *Bergsonism*, Hugh Tomlinson and Barbara Habberjam, trans. New York: Zone Books.

Deleuze, G. (1992). *Nietzsche and Philosophy*, Hugh Tomlinson, trans. London and New York: Continuum.

Deleuze, G. (1994). *Difference and Repetition*, Paul Patton, trans. London: Athlone.

Eldridge, R. (2006). ' "To Bear the Momentarily Incomplete": Subject Development and Expression in Hegel and Hölderlin'. *Graduate Faculty Philosophy Journal* 27(2), 141–58.

Hegel, G. W. F. (1977). *Phenomenology of Spirit*, A. V. Miller, trans. Oxford: Oxford University Press.

Hölderlin, F. (1965). *Remarques sur Oedipe/Remarques sur Antigone*, François Fédier, trans. Paris: Union Générale d'Editions.

Hölderlin, F. (2001). *Hölderlin's Sophocles: Oedipus and Antigone*, David Constantine, trans. Highgreen, Tarset, Northumberland: Bloodaxe.

Lampert, J. (2011). *Deleuze and Guattari's Philosophy of History*. London: Bloomsbury.

Lapoujade, D. (2017). *Aberrant Movements: The Philosophy of Gilles Deleuze*, Joshua David Jordan, trans. South Pasadena: Semiotext(e).

Marchand, J. S. (2018). 'Non-Human Agency'. In *Posthuman Glossary*, Rosi Braidotti and Marai Hlavajova, eds. London: Bloomsbury, 292–95.

Neimanis, A., and R. L. Walker. (2014). '*Weathering*: Climate Change and the "Thick Time" of Transcorporeality'. *Hypatia* 29(3), 558–75.

Ridley, A. (2009). 'Nietzsche's Intentions: What the Sovereign Individual Promises'. In *Nietzsche on Freedom and Autonomy*, Ken Gemes and Simon May, eds. Oxford: Oxford University Press, 187–89.

Rölli, M. (2016). *Gilles Deleuze's Transcendental Empiricism*, Peter Hertz-Ohmes, trans. Edinburgh: Edinburgh University Press.

Roffe, J. (2014). *Badiou's Deleuze*. London: Routledge.

Schmidt, J. (2013). 'The Empirical Falsity of the Human Subject: New Materialism, Climate Change and the Shared Critique of Artifice'. *Resilience: International Policies, Practices and Discourses* 1(3), 174–92.

Searle, J. R. (1983). *Intentionality: An Essay in the Philosophy of Mind*. Cambridge: Cambridge University Press.

Somers-Hall, H. (2011). 'Time out of Joint: Hamlet and the Pure Form of Time' *Deleuze Studies* 5(4), 56–76.

Somers-Hall, H. (2013). *Deleuze's* Difference and Repetition. Edinburgh: Edinburgh University Press.

Taylor, C. (1983). 'Hegel and the Philosophy of Action'. In *Hegel's Philosophy of Action*, Lawrence S. Stepelevich and David Lamb, eds. Atlantic Highlands, N.J.: Humanities Press.

Voss, D. (2013). *Conditions of Thought: Deleuze and Transcendental Ideas*. Edinburgh: Edinburgh University Press.

Williams, J. (2011). *Gilles Deleuze's* Philosophy of Time: *A Critical Introduction and Guide*. Edinburgh: Edinburgh University Press.

Wittgenstein, L. (1953). *Philosophical Investigations*, G.EM. Anscombe and R. Rhees, eds., G.E.M. Anscombe, trans. Oxford, Blackwell.

Chapter 8

Heterogeneous Collectivity and the Capacity to Act

Conceptualising Nonhumans in Political Space

Suzanne McCullagh

This chapter develops the concept of heterogeneous political space as an alternative to the exclusively human political sphere which dominates Western political thinking about collective action and justice. The aim is to make evident that capacities for action are constituted in heterogeneous milieus and to argue that insofar as political thought does not register this it is inadequate to thinking justice and flourishing in a world where ecological change renders human and nonhuman modes of life increasingly precarious. Heterogeneous political spaces are constituted by compositions of material, affect and desire which are occluded by humanist and individualist theories of action that theorise collective action at the register of a macro-political order made up of unified rational subjects with clear intentions and commitments. Gilles Deleuze and Félix Guattari's concepts of following and assembling enable accounts of a molecular or micro-political register composed of heterogeneous collectivities in processes of composition. In their insistence that human action cannot be separated from the productions of nature, we find that heterogeneity, rather than human plurality, is given as a condition of action. Conceiving of political action in terms of heterogeneity brings into view the processes by which capacities for political action are constituted by nonhuman forces, entities and elements. It focuses attention on that in virtue of which political action occurs, rather than on the intentional aspect of actions which aim to achieve an individualised interest (whether it be the interests of a human individual or individuated group). Heterogeneous political space complexifies our thinking about political action and diffuses the agency of political subjects so as to render our thinking more adequate in several significant regards. It provides a conceptual resource that brings the diverse human-nonhuman entanglements to the fore and thus acknowledges the differing ways that capacities for political action are constituted in different assemblages that always comprise nonhumans. This disrupts the liberal, humanist view of politics where nonhumans are excluded from the domain of action and appear only as passive resources to be exploited for human plans and actions. Further, by challenging the view of the more-than-human world as passively 'standing-reserve'[1] for the purposes of human agents, the concept of heterogeneous political space invites a critical questioning whether the conception of political space as exclusively human is capable of attending to issues of ecological justice where the well-being of humans and ecosystems is inextricable. In short, when the more-than-human world is excluded from conceptions of political space neither the needs of nonhumans (plants, animals, ecosystems, waterways) nor the constitution of human capacities in relation with nonhumans (co-habitation, dependence, care) register as politically significant. This, in effect, obscures the ways that different human-nonhuman assemblages increase and diminish capacities for action.

Heterogeneous political space considers human-nonhuman assemblages as a genetic condition for the emergence of capacities to act. All action can thus be seen as emerging from constellations where humans are assembled with material and incorporeal elements (plant, animal, mineral, technological bodies and statements, utterances, expressions, affects, moods, gestures, etc.). The breakdown of human exclusivity not only places humans within a system of nature but can also bring nonhumans into our understanding of ethics and politics, and this is evidenced by the care that political theorists take in justifying the exclusion of the nonhuman from political space, or the sphere of political action.

Two major obstacles to figuring nonhumans within the sphere of the political are liberal individualism and humanism. Liberal individualism focuses on the sovereignty of the individual subject over their actions; action and freedom are conceived along individualist lines. The humanism of Western political theory focuses on the uniquely human attributes of the political subject in terms of autonomous rationality. Together, these two features work to exclude nonhumans from the space of politics. Hannah Arendt's political thought provides important resources for thinking political action beyond the confines of the narrow individualism of liberal conceptions of action. Her concept of the public sphere as the political space of action foregrounds the power of collectivity as constitutive of action. The collective nature of all action is attested to in her thought, as is the significance of thinking actions as resonating outside the confines of goals and intentions. In these respects, then, her conception of political space goes some way towards thinking action collectively rather than individualistically. It stops short, however, of supporting a conception of action that involves nonhumans. Thus, for Arendt, political space is constituted by a plurality of actors who are all human.

Nonhumans, as will become clear in what follows, are resolutely excluded from the domain of the political on her account.

Thinking political space by way of heterogeneity facilitates an ecological conception of political action; the nonhuman world is moved from the position of passive resource for human ends to active participant in political action. This shift in perspective can enable increased ethical and political consideration of the ways that human actions, decisions, policies and modes of living affect the nonhuman world for better and for worse, as well as increasing attention to different ways of 'acting with' the nonhuman world. In what ways might we 'follow' heterogeneous materials rather than imposing forms that shape nonhuman materials for human ends? Such 'following' has the potential to increase ethical modes of engagement with nonhumans rather than enacting a violence towards the world. This shift in perspective has important consequences for human beings and social justice as it renders more visible heterogeneous entanglements between humans and nonhumans, entanglements that are invisible from the instrumentalist view of the nonhuman world practiced within liberal, pluralist political discourse. In other words, by excluding nonhumans from political thought human-nonhuman assemblages are also thereby excluded, assemblages which are necessary for human capacities for action. For instance, humanist conceptions of the political are unable to adequately account for the social and ecological implications of extractivist development practices. Humanism elides and depoliticises human-nonhuman entanglements thus occluding from view the ecopolitical reconfigurations enacted by these development practices that adversely affect human communities. The concluding section of this chapter will engage the concept of heterogeneous political space in thinking about a specific case of Indigenous resistance to extractivism, the *Mi'kmaq* protest actions against the development of hydraulic fracturing in *Elsipogtog* (Mi'kmaq territory in eastern Canada).

Heterogeneous political space is a posthuman ecopolitical concept that overcomes the limitations of humanist political concepts and thus increases the adequacy of political thought to attend to the real implications of material interventions for human and nonhuman life. It accords with the strand of posthumanism that aims to overcome the 'binary logic of identity and otherness' at the core of humanism that has lethal consequences for those deemed as other and thereby inferior. 'These are the sexualised, racialised, and naturalised others, who are reduced to the less than human status of disposable bodies'.[2] This strand of posthuman thought, developed by thinkers such as Rosi Braidotti, Patricia MacCormack and Claire Colebrook, calls for ethical and political attention to the ways that life and subjectivity are constituted in multiple and complex relations with differing others. The posthuman political subject is nonunitary and in continual processes of differentiation,[3] in contrast with the stability of the fully constituted liberal, humanist political subject. In this vein, heterogeneous political space foregrounds the processes through which capacities for action are constituted and from which individuals and groups emerge. The focus is on the complex, ecological constitution of action rather than on already constituted individuals and groups with varying interests that are the focus of liberal, humanist political thought.

COLLECTIVITY AND POLITICAL SPACE

In certain important respects, Hannah Arendt as well as Deleuze and Guattari (together and separately) are interested in political philosophical problems related to the human condition. They share an approach to action which shifts the focus from the individual to the contexts that enable action, or which constitute the capacity to act. In their own ways, they are interested in the emergence of change and newness in the natural, social and political processes through which individuals are constituted. For Arendt, this context is an exclusively human political space where individuality and capacities for action emerge. For Deleuze and Guattari the context consists in human-nonhuman assemblages that increase or diminish capacities for action. Arendt posits a murky moment in the constitution of the capacity for action, opening it up to the question of the collective production of power. Unlike Deleuze and Guattari, however, she does not give an account of nonhuman elements as contributing to this production. Instead she separates the realm of action or political space, what she calls the space of appearance or public space, from natural processes and nonhuman entities. So, although the collective production of the power that constitutes the capacity to act is very significant for Arendt, her analysis is built upon a strict divide between humans and nonhumans. In this way she remains within the tradition of humanist political philosophy in its exclusion of the nonhuman from the political. Deleuze and Guattari do not maintain this exclusion, and this is one reason why some might claim that there is no significant theory of agency in their work; they are read as philosophers of machinic processes who exclude human individuals.[4] This, however, is to miss their move which posits assemblages as a genetic condition of the emergence of capacities for action. In Deleuzian philosophy, humans are not reduced to mere cogs in the machine; rather, the analysis of action becomes more complex and difficult to think, but arguably provides a more adequate construal of the real conditions for action.

It is clear that Deleuze and Guattari move their analyses of capacities for action beyond Arendt's humanist concerns with the traditional political sphere. What is less apparent, however, is the degree to which their works in this area contribute to political philosophy; for what reasons should we take seriously their expanded approach to the fields in which capacities for action are constituted? Their work can be read as pointing to significant ways in which human individuals and groups can manifest change and bring about newness. However, the path to this is not in opposing the processes by which we are constituted as concrete individuals. We act, and thus bring about variation and newness, only in conjunction with the elements of the heterogeneous assemblages of which we are a part, and by taking into account those processes from which we emerge and which enable us to act. This capacity for action is thus always heterogeneous and collective, the capacity to act arises in virtue of a host of other entities and elements, human and nonhuman.

The capacity to act, for Arendt, (likewise) has the power of collectivity as a condition; it is constituted by a power that can only be conceived in nonindividualistic terms.[5] For her, the power of an actor only ever arises from a collective. This is because she understands that action is political only ever with or in the midst of the actions of others. Collective power enables people to act together and is produced by their acting together.[6] In other words, collectivity is both a source of the capacity to act and a product of action. It is by virtue of our relations with others that we are endowed with the capacity to act, or capacities for action. In beginning something new, the actor *enables* the actions of others, and in this sense also, action is engaged with collectivity; in acting, one is both capacitated by others and capacitating the actions of others. Rather than locating power in the actor as sovereign, Arendt locates it in the potentiality for action that is a part of the being together of people.[7] 'Action, as distinguished from fabrication, is never possible in isolation; to be isolated is to be deprived of the capacity to act'.[8] A key feature of Arendt's argument for the distinction between acting and fabricating stems from her analysis of power as different from strength.

> Power is always, as we would say, a power potential and not an unchangeable, measureable, and reliable entity like force or strength. While strength is the natural quality of an individual seen in isolation, power springs up between men when they act together and vanishes the moment they disperse.[9]

Action for both Arendt and Deleuze and Guattari is nonsovereign, the actor is not in control of the outcome. Nonsovereign action for these thinkers is both unpredictable and relational: unpredictable because the effects of action are boundless,[10] and relational because actors always act into a web of relationships.[11] Actors do not seek to instil or maintain stable powers, but instead favour 'a fabric of immanent relations'.[12] Actions are open-ended[13] as the consequences reverberate endlessly and thus can never be predicted from the beginning.

> Because the actor always moves among and in relation to other acting beings, he is never merely a 'doer' but always and at the same time a sufferer. To do and to suffer are like opposite sides of the same coin, and the story that an act starts is composed of its consequent deeds and sufferings. These consequences are boundless, because action, though it may proceed from nowhere, so to speak, acts into a medium where every reaction becomes a chain reaction and where every process is the cause of a new process.[14]

By reserving for action openness and unpredictability, Arendt's thought gives us a view of action as highly complex and diffuse. It is complex because actions intervene in webs of relations where effects cannot be foreseen, and diffuse because actions are taken up by other actors by way of response or reaction. Therefore the one who acts is never the sole author or producer of their acts, but rather simultaneously actor and sufferer.[15] To act is to begin a process that has no end.

However, in elucidating a conception of nonsovereign action, Arendt invokes the concept of plurality as the necessary condition of the capacity to act.[16] In this move she limits action to an entirely human sphere wherein actors have the human condition of natality[17] (capacity for new beginning) in common, and are also distinguished (pluralised) by this condition. Plurality is a necessary condition of political space for Arendt where actors are all the same, because they are human, and they are different in that each has a capacity for new action. 'Action, the only activity that goes on directly between men without the intermediary of things or matter, corresponds to the human condition of plurality … this plurality is specifically the condition … of all political life'.[18] For Arendt, fabrication is in contact with the world, and action is in contact with webs of human actions and relations. She cautions that we should not see action as analogous with fabrication because, unlike fabrication, action is not *upon* the web of human acts and deeds in the way that fabrication works *upon* material.[19] Humans are not mere material with which to make something.[20] It is with *strength* that individuals work *upon* the world,[21] but it is *power* rather than strength that is the motor of action, as power rises up between people when they act.[22]

Arendt sees an attitude of sovereignty in the figure of *homo faber* who violently opposes nature by forcing natural materials into the forms that pre-exist the production process as ideas. 'The implements and tools of *homo faber*, from which the most fundamental experience of instrumentality arises, determine all work and fabrication. … The end justifies the violence done to nature to win the material, as the wood justifies killing the tree and the table justifies destroying the wood'.[23] The main relationship involved is between the maker and their material, which they shape to match their mental designs. In this way, making is structured by a division between knowing and doing.

This corresponds with the respective stages of a fabrication process that begins with an image or an idea of an end-product, and is followed by a stage of execution.[24] For Arendt, action is only immanent to the sphere of action insofar as the latter is founded on the transcendence from nature achieved by *homo faber*. In creating a truly human world which transcends nature, *homo faber* is thus, in her view, able to provide the foundation *upon* which political space emerges and political action is possible.

It is not the case, then, that the nonhuman world doesn't appear in Arendt's political thought. The nonhuman material world is shaped by the human activity of fabrication into a common human world from which political space can emerge. The common human world, the world built by humans, is a condition of human plurality. Each individual actor is the same, insofar as they are human, and yet different because each is individuated by having a different spatial location in and perspective on the common world. For Arendt, it is the common built world which is the ground of human difference. This individuating capacity of the common human world is what leads Arendt to disavow the political significance of those activities done in intimate relation with the nonhuman world. Insofar as one's activities are entangled with the rhythms and flows of nature they are not political because they are done with the nonhuman world rather than differentiated from it. What are these activities that humans do with the world that are designated as nonpolitical on an Arendtian account? Eating, growing and gleaning food, working with waste, bearing children, caring for the sick are all activities done with the nonhuman world and which as such are excluded from Arendt's conception of political space. Judith Butler and Gayatri Chakravorty Spivak claim that Arendt fails to provide a theory of power and politics by which economic injustice and political disenfranchisement could be analysed and critiqued. In separating the public sphere from the sphere of labour, she depoliticises activities done with the material world (labouring) while at the same time making the public depend upon it.[25] In her marginalisation of labour Arendt seems to silently endorse material conditions that detract from the capacities of certain people to participate in politics, those people who provide the conditions that enable others to act. This problem, however, is not unique to Arendt; it is a perennial component of humanist conceptions of the political that exclude from political space, not just the nonhuman material world, but those peoples who are seen to be in most intimate contact with it (women, migrant workers, indigenous peoples, racialised 'others').[26]

HETEROGENEITY AND THE CAPACITY TO ACT

Posthuman politics, insofar as it thinks political space and action beyond the exclusivity of humanist political thought, offers a way to overcome the exclusion of both humans and animals from political space by reconceiving political action as 'fully immersed in and immanent to a network of non-human (animal, vegetable, viral) relations'.[27] By invoking the concept of heterogeneity rather than plurality Deleuze and Guattari facilitate a conception of collective action that does not rest on a primary and constitutive distinction between human and nonhuman because it does not locate action in an exclusively human domain and does not conceive of collective action in terms of the identity of actors but in terms of constitutive processes of differentiation. The political problem shifts away from questions of constituted individuals and groups (with varying interests and perspectives) towards the collective processes within which individuals and groups are constituted with varying capacities for action. An important feature of this shift away from conventional humanist political thought is achieved by Deleuze and Guattari when they eschew a distinction between humans and nature. In *Anti-Oedipus*, they theorise nature as interconnected machines; not machines rationally designed to serve a purpose, but productive processes that encompass both producer and product.

> There is no such thing as either man or nature now, only a process that produces the one within the other and couples the machines together. Producing-machines, desiring machines everywhere, schizophrenic machines, all of species life: the self and the non-self, outside and inside, no longer have any meaning whatsoever.

On their account, nature can be understood 'machinically', as a process of production;[28] as a result, the distinction between humans and nature is broken down. They outline three aspects of their use of the term 'process'. First, production processes include recording, consumption and reproduction as aspects of a single process. Second, production as process overcomes any dichotomy between man and nature, cause and effect, subject and object by entwining these terms in one reality as producer-product. Last, processes are not goals or ends.[29] If machines are understood as processes of production, then our standard understanding of humans as tool makers and machine designers does not work and technology cannot be used to get humans beyond or outside of nature. Humans do not introduce the technological into nature, as they are already technological themselves. 'The "human" is now understood solely and strictly in terms of being a component in a machinic assemblage'.[30] To consider tool-use as the primary feature that sets humans apart from other animals (or as that which constructs a world of artifice upon which exclusively human political space is made possible) is to use technology to see the human as transcending nature. 'Machinic thought', which places the human within the machine, asserts that there is no discontinuity between humans and the natural world. Clearly this is in stark contrast to Arendt's conceptual attempts to establish clear distinctions between humans, artifice and nature.

Their proposal that we see humans as a part of nature as processes of production dismantles the realm of artifice (the realm constructed by *homo faber*) which Arendt posits as the necessary condition for action. They suggest that there is a constitutive power to the activity of making when it is not done according to a hylomorphic model where form is seen as actively imposed on passive matter. By contrast, Arendt holds that it is strength and violence that exist in making, and that power arises solely in the realm of human affairs. In refusing to separate the activity of making from the productions of nature, Deleuze and Guattari deny that actions ever occur outside and separate from nature, materials and artifice. Rather than being confined to human-to-human intercourse, Deleuze and Guattari expose human action as occurring *with* heterogeneous others (books, weather, humans, animals, plants, affects, desires, gestures, moods, etc). In their insistence that action cannot be accounted for in exclusively human terms, we find that it is heterogeneity, rather than (human) plurality, that is given as the collective condition of action. When action is conceived outside of nature, taking place between *human* agents, human life is distinguished from the rest of nature in a way that preserves a view of nonhuman nature (animal, plant and mineral) as an exploitable resource for human ends. Given the increasing vulnerability of human and nonhuman life resulting from anthropogenic environmental change, such a view is simply no longer ethically and politically appropriate.

The idea that actions occur in virtue of a heterogeneous host of elements is unacceptable to Arendt because her theorisation of action—which relies on distinctions between action, work and labouring—sharply and effectively separates action from all nonhuman elements. In her theorisation of the figure of *animal laborans*, the human considered in terms of the activity of labouring, she argues that *animal laborans* is incapable of true plurality[31]—and consequently action—because her activities are driven by and occur in conjunction with natural processes. In other words, one's capacities for action are disabled when one's activities are *mixed* with nature and the nonhuman. Deleuze and Guattari's work, by contrast, implies a way of conceiving of action as occurring on the 'plane of composition' that consists in *mixing with* the nonhuman. Their concepts of becoming, assemblage and symbiosis enable us to conceive of this mixed kind of action as arising from heterogeneous collectives composed of both human and nonhuman elements. So, Deleuze and Guattari are in agreement with Arendt that '[a]ction ... is never possible in isolation; to be isolated is to be deprived of the capacity to act',[32] but they reject her view that action only 'goes on directly between men without the intermediary of things or matter'.[33] As a capacity, action cannot be stripped of its heterogeneous, collective nature. It is always dependent on much more than just the human realm of affairs, and thoroughly mixed and entangled with other material entities and nonmaterial elements (affects, words, space, etc.).

A capacity can be thought of as a kind of power, specifically a constitutive rather than a constituted power. Let's explore this through the example of swimming: what does it mean to think of swimming as a constitutive rather than a constituted power? One important feature we pointed to was that constitutive powers are not possessed by individuals but rather circulate in webs within which, or by virtue of which, individuals are constituted. Normally, we would think that the capacity to swim is possessed by an individual; I *have* the capacity to swim. What is the significance of thinking the capacity to swim free from possession by an individual? And how is this even possible? First, if we think of capacities as powers which are in processes of constitution, then we look to the elements at play in that constituting process. The capacity to swim is a power which is in an open process of constitution by such elements as: water, a particular kind of body, experience and skill, culture, geography (river or lake) or architecture (swimming pool), physical strength, desire. At the very least, the capacity to swim is constituted by a body of water capable of sustaining a swimmer, and a body with the minimal structure and strength capable of swimming. In other words, the capacity to swim is constituted at the intersection of, or through the relationship to, sets of other capacities; it can be adequately understood as constituted through dynamic processes whereby other capacities inform or give rise to the capacity to swim. Although we might say that one has a capacity to swim, focusing on capacity as a power which can be possessed (a property of an individual), we will illuminate a more complex dynamic if we consider capacities as constituted in virtue of other capacities. In other words, when we think capacity, we should be prompted to consider the elements in virtue of which the capacity is activated and exercised.

In what way is political space revealed as heterogeneous when we consider how capacities for action are constituted in conjunction with nonhuman elements? When we consider something in terms of capacity we are prompted to acknowledge its heterogeneous, rather than plural, collective constitution. Plants have capacities for osmosis and photosynthesis, and these are connected with the ways in which it is able to compose its body with other bodies: sun, water, nutrients in the soil, etc. In a similar vein we can consider that capacities for political action are enabled by complex compositions; it is by combining with others that affects are produced in ways that will either increase or decrease a given body's capacity to act. Indignation may give rise to powerful collective actions capable of overthrowing a given political order. But, militancy and *ressentiment*, as sad or reactive passions, may lead to a general decrease in capacities for action. Further, the fluctuation in the capacities of bodies for action (human and nonhuman) are dependent upon combinations formed with heterogeneous others.

In contrast with Arendt's depiction of fabrication as the forced submission of nature and material to human violence, Deleuze and Guattari propose that the relation between a maker and their material consists in the maker 'surrendering' and 'following' the material.

> On the other hand, to the essential properties of the matter deriving from the formal essence we must add variable intensive affects, now resulting from the operation, now on the contrary making it possible: for example, wood that is more or less porous, more or less elastic and resistant. At any rate, it is a question of surrendering to the wood, then following where it leads by connecting operations to a materiality, instead of imposing a form upon a matter: what one addresses is less a matter submitted to laws than a materiality possessing a *nomos*. One addresses less a form capable of imposing properties upon a matter than material traits of expression constituting affects.[34]

The material takes on an active dimension; it has the capacity to *inform* and *guide* the actions of the maker. As a result, we get a view of action as a kind of co-action comprising humans and materials. This account of productive activity makes room for the conceptualisation of human activities with nonhumans to be rendered in political terms; it creates an opening for the conceptualisation of collective political space as heterogeneous rather than exclusively human. Rather than disparaging bodily activity as less than fully human, as Arendt does when she claims that *animal laborens* whose activities are entwined with nature cannot act, Deleuze and Guattari celebrate the diverse capacities of bodies for being affected. Capacities for being affected do not render bodies passive and incapable of action, but active and capable. The notion that one could 'follow matter' rests on a consideration of bodies in terms of their affects, as complex and heterogeneous entities. In contrast with Arendt's individualistic view of the body (which she derives from John Locke) as absolutely private, incommunicable, and unshareable,[35] Deleuze and Guattari advance a nonindividualistic conception of bodily life. On their account, the body is shot through with elements shared with heterogeneous others; *the body* is never separable from the milieus and assemblages with which it is connected as part or element. This conception of bodily life enables us to think about political actors as having, what Rosi Braidotti calls, 'multiple ecologies of belonging',[36] and this opens conceptions of political space and community as involving the more-than-human world. Developing the conceptual resources to think nonhumans within the sphere of politics can aid in countering the exploitation of the nonhuman world which, if not explicitly supported, is silently condoned by political theory that registers the exploitation of the nonhuman world as apolitical.

As part of a complex and nuanced depiction of bodily composition, Deleuze and Guattari offer the concept of assemblage, a term that points to the heterogeneous multiplicities that generate capacities for action. Assemblages are multiplicities composed of bodies, desires and enunciations. The concept of assemblage takes the place of the subject and reveals actors as heterogeneous composites and action as co-action or symbiosis. Deleuze declares, with specific reference to speaking and writing, that one writes *with*: 'With the world, with a part of the world, with people. … There is no judgement in sympathy, but agreements of convenience between bodies of all kinds'.[37] Assembling is a kind of *acting with*; whether the action be teaching, protesting or making art it is to be done *with* the world and *with* others. Where a plural conception of political space and action only registers human participants, heterogeneous political space points towards the complex human-nonhuman entanglements that constitute actions. Pluralist political space fails to register the real conditions of action because it disavows the role of heterogeneous assemblages in constituting capacities for action.

The tendency in political philosophy to overemphasise the human ability to shape and order materials, de-emphasises the capacities of the materials to certain kinds of shaping and arrangement. Nonhuman materials play significant roles in political action which are not adequately registered by conceptualising political space as exclusively human. Consider the role of materials (the metal coltan in the Democratic Republic of Congo for instance, which is used in the manufacture of mobile technology and is mined using child labour), constellations of desires (for cheap mobile technology, political power, freedom), global political and economic systems (liberalism and capitalism), regimes of enunciation (speeches and the popular press) and a host of other material and nonmaterial entities with which actions occur. Just as an ecological perspective of plant life would take into consideration the larger processes in which a given plant is immersed, Deleuze and Guattari, in their providing resources for thinking through a nonindividualistic conception of any body (from humans to words to insects), could be said to facilitate an ecological conception of action. Guattari argues that mental, social and environmental ecologies are radically intertwined and that the partitioning of the real contributes to deterioration of psyche, society and environment.[38] To see the human as one component in an assemblage (and not necessarily the most important component) brings into view the complex, heterogeneous constitution of capacities for action. Thus, when we analyse political space, the space of action, we will consider the nonhuman components of the assemblage with which actions are capacitated. 'Each multiplicity is symbiotic; its becoming ties together animals, plants, microorganisms, mad particles, a whole galaxy'.[39] Multiplicities 'with heterogeneous terms, confunctioning by contagion, enter certain assemblages';[40] the 'assemblage is co-functioning, it is "sympathy", symbiosis'.[41]

HETEROGENEOUS POLITICAL SPACE

In the fall of 2013 Mi'kmaq peoples and non-Indigenous residents of New Brunswick, Canada, engaged in a series of protest actions to oppose the development of the shale gas industry which would employ hydraulic fracturing ('fracking') on lands (which were never ceded) in *Elsipogtog* (a community located near Rexton, New Brunswick). The government of New Brunswick (NB) had contracted a US company, Southwestern Energy Company (SWN), to conduct seismic testing for the exploratory phase of extracting gas from the Frederick Brook shale deposit. Hydraulic fracturing, an unconventional gas extraction process, is considered by many to be excessively invasive, resource intensive, and a potential contaminator of ground water.[42] The protestors' actions were supported by a diversity of Indigenous and non-Indigenous groups (Council of Canadians, students, NB residents and labour groups) across Canada.

The SWN-NB-shale-fracking assemblage had the potential to significantly impact Mi'kmaq and settler assemblages with the land (altering capacities for fishing, hunting, farming), but also, importantly, activated new political assemblages that resisted the realisation of the potential assemblage that the SWN-NB alliance was attempting to actualise. In fact, it was the potential assemblage itself which became a component in the resistance assemblage. The assemblage that emerged in resistance to the plan to extract oil from the Frederick Brook shale was not only a Mi'kmaq–settler assemblage in defense of Indigenous rights, justice for the land, and ways of life that depend on the land (fishing, hunting, farming), but was arguably a collective action constituted by existing heterogeneous assemblages (entanglements of humans, soil, waterways, animals, history, colonial politics, ancestral and traditional practices) that gave rise to the capacity for resistance in the form of a collective political assemblage of Mi'kmaq, settlers and land. The activation of this assemblage produced a heterogeneous political space that involved a becoming and reassembling of previous forms of relations and capacities for action. Unlike previous Mi'kmaq political resistance in Atlantic Canada, the Elsipogtog protestors were joined by non-Indigenous residents; potentials for new alliances emerged with transformative potentials for settler-Indigenous relations. Collective becomings continued beyond the end of the protest and the halt of SWN exploratory testing, as is evidenced by the recent claim to Aboriginal title over one-third of the province of New Brunswick made by the Mi'kmaq. Recognition of Aboriginal title would give Mi'kmaq the legal right to decide what happens to the land. Kenneth Francis, a member of Elsipogtog First Nation, says of the recent title claim: 'We never really used to take ourselves seriously. ... After the blockade—the feeling of empowerment that we got from it, the co-operation we were getting from our allies, is that this can be done, that we can do this. You say, "Oh my goodness we can do this"'.[43] Mi'kmaq capacities for action have been amplified through the emergence of a heterogeneous space of action. Insofar as our manner of conceptualising human space and action adamantly refuses to attend to the active power of nonhuman entities and elements in capacitating human political action, we fail to recognise degrees of complexity requisite for registering potentials for transformation. Thus, liberal political thought, though it may oppose social and ecological injustices resulting from neoliberalism and globalisation, reinforces the depoliticisation of heterogeneous assemblages wherein injustices are actualised, suffered and resisted.

The alliance forged between the NB provincial government in Canada and SWN is a political alliance constituted by the material capacity of the Frederick Brook shale deposit, an Atlantic economy characterised by high unemployment, a general lack of recognition for Indigenous land rights nationally and for Mi'kmaq land rights locally, the widespread desire for cheap oil and the corollary material, ethical and political habits through which humans and nonhumans are assembled in such a way that the more-than-human world appears simply as a resource for human ends. We are our habits and it is through habit that we contract elements of the world. 'Every contraction is a presumption, a claim—that is to say, it gives rise to an expectation or a right in regard to what it contracts, and comes undone once its object escapes'.[44] As such, the human habits and ways of living that depend upon a steady flow of petroleum point us towards human-nonhuman assemblages that humanist political theory casts as nonpolitical, thus obscuring the very real implications for human lives that certain modes of assembling actualise.

Kathryn Yusoff argues for the importance of developing a philosophy of the geologic that attends to the agency of fossil fuels in shaping what human bodies can do. 'The work of fossil fuels is everywhere evident, and yet there is a strange absence in the conceptualization of the agency and historicity of fossil fuels within corporeality and an overreliance on the study of the effects of fossil fuels on the Earth in political geology. ... At present, accounts of the work of fossil fuels are centred on human subjects and their practices, rather than on developing a philosophy of the geologic that grapples with what fossil fuels allow and what they might say to the work of inhuman forces'.[45]

Such conceptual work is a necessary component of our becoming less reliant on fossil fuels, developing new geologic subjectivities, and activating new potential futures. 'All this entails understanding and experimenting with the active forces of the geologic—both as inheritance and future force. Refusing the reproduction of this inheritance requires ... unlearning forms of geologic corporeality as far as we are able, and fostering new geologic subjectivities'.[46] The shift from thinking about nonhumans as mute and passive recipients of human active practices to active and differentiating forces with capacities to shape human actions echoes Deleuze and Guattari's account of following the material traits of matter. This shift in conceptualising moves us from seeing humans as being in control of material practices and towards being collaborators with material agencies, and it reveals political space as heterogeneous rather than homogeneously human. Humanist political theory provides accounts of the macro-political order made up of molar subjects. Deleuze and Guattari's concept of becoming describes a micro-political register composed of multiplicities, collectivities and assemblages in processes of composition. In contrast to political philosophies that view political agency as human and individual, the concept of heterogeneous political space considers action as a capacity constituted by heterogeneous collectives of both humans and nonhumans. The starting point, then, for thinking about political action along these lines is to understand the capacities and conditions from which collective actions emerge.

NOTES

1. Heidegger 1977, 17.
2. Braidotti 2013, 15.
3. MacCormack 2012, 12; Braidotti 2013, 49.
4. Hayles 2001, 147.
5. The concept 'nonindividualistic' is here being transported from work in the philosophy of mind: Preston 1998; Burge 1986. Preston argues for a nonindividualistic understanding of tools and artefacts and Burge argues for a nonindividualistic individuation of mental content, sometimes understood as wide content or social externalism. In each case, they are interested in the supra-individual elements that bear on individuating the entity under consideration.
6. Arendt 1958, 200.
7. Arendt 1958, 202.
8. Arendt 1958, 188.
9. Arendt 1958, 200.
10. Arendt 1958, 190.
11. Arendt 1958, 184.
12. Deleuze and Guattari 1987, 358.

13. Arendt 1958, 233.
14. Arendt 1958, 190.
15. Arendt 1958, 184.
16. Arendt 1958, 7.
17. Arendt 1958, 9.
18. Arendt 1958, 7.
19. Arendt 1958, 136–41.
20. For a critical discussion of the ways of thinking that support a social engineering approach to politics see Mead 1942; and Bateson 2000, 159–76.
21. Arendt 1958, 140 and 188.
22. Arendt 1958, 200.
23. Arendt 1958, 153.
24. Arendt 1958, 225.
25. Butler and Spivak 2007, 16.
26. Plumwood 1993, 118.
27. Braidotti 2013, 193.
28. Deleuze and Guattari 1983, 3.
29. Deleuze and Guattari 1983, 4.
30. Ansell-Pearson 1999, 140.
31. Arendt 1958, 212.
32. Arendt 1958, 188.
33. Arendt 1958, 7.
34. Deleuze and Guattari 1987, 408.
35. Arendt 1958, 111.
36. Braidotti 2009, 105–6.
37. Deleuze and Parnet 1987, 52.
38. Guattari 1989, 134.
39. Deleuze and Guattari 1987, 250.
40. Deleuze and Guattari 1987, 242.
41. Deleuze and Parnet, *Dialogues*, 52.
42. Moore, Shaw and Castleden 2018, 150.
43. Baker 2017.
44. Deleuze 2001, 74–79.
45. Yusoff 2013, 789.
46. Yusoff 2013, 791.

REFERENCES

Arendt, H. (1958). *The Human Condition*. Chicago: University of Chicago Press.
Ansell-Pearson, K. (1999). *Germinal Life: The Difference and Repetition of Gilles Deleuze*. London: Routledge.
Baker, O. (2017). 'A Mi'kmaq Seat at the Table'. November 20, 2017: http://www.cbc.ca/news2/interactives/a-mikmaq-seat-at-the-table/

Bateson, G. (2000). 'Social Planning and the Concept of Deutero-Learning'. In Steps to an Ecology of Mind. Chicago: University of Chicago Press, 159–76.

Braidotti, R. (2009). 'Locating Deleuze's Eco-Philosophy between *Bio/Zoe*-Power and Necro-Politics.' In *Deleuze and Law: Forensic Futures*, Rosi Braidotti, Claire Colebrook, and Patrick Hanafin, eds. New York: Palgrave Macmillan.

Braidotti, R. (2013). *The Posthuman*. Cambridge, MA: Polity Press.

Burge, T. (1986). 'Individualism and Psychology.' *Philosophical Review* 95, 3–45.

Butler, J., and Spivak, G. C. (2007). *Who Sings the Nation-state? Language, politics, belonging*. New York: Seagull Books.

Deleuze, G. (2001). *Difference and Repetition*. Translated by Paul Patton. London: Continuum.

Deleuze, G., and Guattari, F. (1983). *Anti-Oedipus: Capitalism and Schizophrenia*. Translated by Robert Hurley, Mark Seem, and Helen R. Lane. Minneapolis: University of Minnesota Press.

Deleuze, G., and Guattari, F. (1987). *A Thousand Plateaus: Capitalism and Schizophrenia*. Translated by Brian Massumi. Minneapolis: University of Minnesota Press.

Deleuze, G., and Parnet, C. (1987). *Dialogues*. Translated by Hugh Tomlinson and Barbara Habberjam. New York: Columbia University Press.

Guattari, F. (1989). 'The Three Ecologies'. Translated by Chris Turner. *New Formations* 8, 131–47.

Hayles, N. K. (2001). 'Desiring Agency: Limiting Metaphors and Enabling Constraints in Dawkins and Deleuze/Guattari', *SubStance* 94/95, 144–59.

Heidegger, M. (1977). *The Question Concerning Technology and Other Essays*. Translated by William Lovitt. New York: Harper and Row.

MacCormack, P. (2012). *Posthuman Ethics*. Farnham: Ashgate Publishing Limited.

Mead, M. (1942). 'The Comparative Study of Culture and Purposive Cultivation of Democratic Values', Science, Philosophy and Religion, Second Symposium, ed. Lyman Bryson and Louis Finkelstein. New York: Conference on Science, Philosophy and Religion in Their Relation to the Democratic Way of Life, 56–69.

Moore, M., Shaw, K., and Castleden, H. (2018). '"We Need More Data!" The Politics of scientific Information for Water Governance in the Context of Hydraulic Fracturing', *Water Alternatives* 11(1), 142–62.

Plumwood, V. (1993). *Feminism and the Mastery of Nature*. London: Routledge.

Preston, B. (1998). 'Cognition and Tool Use', *Mind & Language* 14, 513–47.

Yusoff, K. (2013). 'Geologic Life: Prehistory, Climate, Futures in the Anthropocene', *Environmental Planning D: Society and Space* 31, 779–95.

Chapter 9

Indigeneity, Posthumanism and Nomad Thought

Transforming Colonial Ecologies

Simone Bignall and Daryle Rigney

The Autochthon can hardly be distinguished from the stranger because the stranger becomes Autochthonous in the country of the other who is not, at the same time that the Autochthon becomes stranger to himself, his class, his nation, and his language. —Gilles Deleuze and Félix Guattari[1]

Are the 'new Humanities' inclusive of Indigenous perspectives, and do they acknowledge the specificity of Indigenous experiences of human being? On the one hand, posthumanism describes features also at the heart of internationally shared Indigenous conceptualisations of their humanity as being constituted in inextricable relations with the nonhuman world. Such philosophies include a refusal of anthropocentrism and human exceptionalism; a genealogical and constructivist account of identity; and an acknowledgement of species interdependence and consubstantial intersubjectivity in interactive ecologies shared by human and nonhuman beings. They convey an expressive and process-oriented ontology accompanied by an ecological understanding of the interconnected forces, including nonhuman agencies, operating formatively within a complex system; and an associated materialist and vitalist ethics of human responsibility, which registers an intimate and ontological connection of humanity with the ecological health of the environment that sustains life-forms and diversifies creative potential through rich networks of interconnectivity. These 'more-than-human' ways of knowing, being and acting have characterised Indigenous ontology, epistemology, axiology and ethology since time immemorial, and today they constitute a significant site of shared identification across the Indigenous world. And yet on the other hand, according to the terms of its emergence in the Western academy 'after humanism', Continental posthumanism appears to ignore the prior existence of Indigenous knowledge of this kind. In a solipsistic gesture

159

long typical of Western imperialism, posthumanist theory at times risks the elision of Indigenous cultural and intellectual authority by remaining blind to the ancient presence and contemporary force of Indigenous concepts of human being. This exclusion allows Western philosophy to claim the 'new Humanities' as its current 'discovery' after modern humanism, but this apparently 'new' intellectual frontier in fact traces an ancient philosophical terrain already occupied by Indigenous epistemologies and associated modes of human experience.

By working together across our respective knowledge traditions as an Indigenous and a non-Indigenous scholar, we bring an Indigenous conceptualisation of 'more-than-human' being into alliance with notions of 'posthumanity' arising in Continental philosophy. Our aim in this chapter is to contribute to the ongoing task of intellectual decolonisation in postcolonial contexts.[2] This is a crucial global duty, including in our home country Australia where Indigenous and settler peoples continue to struggle with and against the complex legacies of European cultural and territorial imperialism. Insofar as Western posthumanism has emerged strongly influenced by the philosophy of Deleuze and Guattari, we enquire about the role of their philosophy in the continuing elision of Indigenous ontologies in the disciplines comprising the new Humanities. While we value the emphasis they place upon Indigenous conceptual frameworks, experiences and examples, we remain troubled by the expression indigeneity receives as a consequence of the cluster of associations Deleuze and Guattari create, as well as by the structuring or constructive role indigeneity plays in this assemblage. If, as Deleuze and Guattari insist, concepts should be evaluated pragmatically in light of the new possibilities they create, then our intention in this paper is to scrutinise, through a postcolonial and Indigenous lens, Deleuzian thought as 'nomad'; especially because this concept informs the 'new Humanities' in an emerging paradigm of 'posthumanism'. We ask: what is at stake politically when Indigenous ways are conceived erroneously as unstructured and deterritorialising, when (Western) subjectivities are constructed as 'nomad' but nomadism is no longer marked as a mode of existence special to Indigenous humanity, and when (Western) subjective transformation is construed as a process of 'becoming-autochthonous'[3] that erases the specificity of 'the Autochthon' and results in her self-alienation? Who benefits from this construction, and how?

We ultimately seek to explore how contemporary renditions of Deleuze's philosophical nomadology, notably by Rosi Braidotti, are engaged in advancing a nonimperial posthumanism. We argue that posthumanism as the thought of a 'nomad' being (or becoming) is a valuable resistance to Eurocentric, modern (and imperial) formations of power, knowledge and subjectivity; but it can threaten to elide Indigenous realities or rewrite Indigenous ontologies even while Deleuze and Guattari appear to embrace them. The potential usefulness of 'nomadic thought' is, then, by no means unambiguous when viewed from a postcolonial perspective. It may indeed have multiple potentialities: some appear colonialist in effect, others decolonising or 'excolonial' in outcome; for this reason it is necessary to look again with critical postcolonial eyes at the intersection that Deleuzian philosophy forges between indigeneity, nomadology and the creative exercise of thought. This enables us to discern better how the idea of nomad thought might serve—or alternatively, obstruct—an alliance between Continental posthumanism and Indigenous thinking about colonialism and its contemporary transformation.

INDIGENOUS BEING-MORE-THAN-HUMAN

The world's Indigenous peoples are diverse and cannot be identified homogenously; however, many Indigenous Nations find they share significant commonalities associated with a philosophy of 'being-more-than-human' and a science based upon 'natural laws of interdependence'.[4] The first principle of the Treaty binding the United League of Indigenous Nations asserts:

> The Creator has made us part of and inseparable from the natural world around us. This truth binds us together and gives rise to a shared commitment to care for, conserve and protect the land, air, water and animal life within our usual, customary and traditional territories.

This premise expresses general principles common in Indigenous worldviews and self-understandings: relationality, reciprocal generosity and respectful care. These key ontological-ethical concepts are articulated in various ways by Indigenous philosophies, which range from pantheism, to genealogical constructivism, to expressivism. For example, the Huuy-ay-aht people of Vancouver Island consider themselves governed by three core principles: *Hishuk Tsa'walk* (Everything is One, denoting the interconnected, interdependent and reciprocal relationship between the people, the land and the wider world(s) in a physical, spiritual and social sense); *Uu-a-thluk* (taking care of present and future generations and of the resources provided by the land and the natural world); and *Iisaak* (relational respect, entailing both personal and collective respect for the community and its people, traditional knowledge, the natural world, the metaphysical world and other peoples and communities).[5] In the southern hemisphere, the Maori experience of existence as vibrant and affective matter is similarly a relational view of the world, where we are called into being through our relationships, through the interaction with kin, genealogies, and events. Rocks, rivers, birds, plants, mountains, animals and oceans, all possess a genealogy, and the divine genealogical order of *whakapapa* extends through aeons to a common genealogical origin which is Io, the Creator of the Cosmos.[6]

Whakapapa means that everything is connected through shared networks and processes of creative becoming. *Mauri*, or striving to persevere in being, is the animating force of all being and becoming. This vitality continually grows and unfolds as reciprocal relationships become increasingly complex and rich in *mana* or dignity. However, 'the *mauri* of a being can be affected by the way in which it is engaged with or treated. For example, the level of *mauri* contained by a river can be determined by its capacity to maintain and support life. Through ill-treatment (e.g., pollution), the *mauri* of the river can decline, which will in turn mean that its capacity to support life will decline'.[7] Accordingly, Maori ethics involves the practice of *mauri*-enhancing positive relationships within human communities, and between humans and non-human entities:

> For example, a positive relationship between humans and a river would be evidenced by human land management practices that enable a river to maintain and enhance its *mauri*, which would result in its life-generating capacities being maintained. In this way, the *mauri* of the river is grown or maintained through ensuring that its life-generating vibrancy is not diminished. Simultaneously, the *mauri* of people is maintained through the provision of food and other resources to the humans from the river.[8]

When key Maori values of kinship, reciprocity, hospitality and respect for life guide human behaviour, the *mauri* of both human and nonhuman life is more likely to be maintained and, in turn, the life-generating capacity and sustainability of these entities is enhanced.[9] However, *tino rangatiratanga* is additionally required to put values into practice: 'having the power to give effect to these values within a place—for example, having the power to guide land management practices according to relational values that maintain or enhance the *mauri* of the land, rivers, and coastal areas affected by those practices'.[10] This power to materialise positive relational values for ecological benefit is how Aboriginal people typically understand their sovereignty. Writing from an Australian Indigenous perspective, Aileen Moreton-Robinson explains: 'Our sovereignty is embodied ... grounded within complex relations derived from the intersubstantiation of ancestral beings, humans and land'.[11]

In Southern Australia, this understanding of sovereignty lies at the heart of the Ngarrindjeri peoples' program of 'Speaking as Country', through which they manage contemporary political negotiations with settler-colonial powers. In the context of severe drought at the start of the new millennium, Ngarrindjeri leaders and Elders began a programme of Indigenous Nation rebuilding in order to better advocate for Country and protect their lands and waters and all associated life-forms from further injury. In 2007, they reconsolidated their political authority in a governing body, the Ngarrindjeri Regional Authority. Identifying, organising and acting as an Indigenous Nation under a unified political authority enabled Ngarrindjeri to engage more effectively and consistently with federal Sea-Country planning processes, and so to express in an amplified voice their expectations for the protection of their Country and its well-being.[12] The Ngarrindjeri *Yarluwar-Ruwe* (Sea-Country) Plan produced in 2007 explains to non-Indigenous policy-makers how the Ngarrindjeri Nation's vision for its future is based upon a traditional philosophy of interconnectedness, *Ruwe/Ruwar*: 'The land and waters is a living body. We the Ngarrindjeri people are a part of its existence'.[13] In December 2014, Ngarrindjeri further developed their statement of position in a Ngarrindjeri *Yannarumi* (Speaking as Country) Deed. This explains in a more explicit fashion the deep interconnectedness between health of Country and health of people and cultural life: Ngarrindjeri *Ruwe/Ruwar* (lands, waters, body spirit and all living things) needs to be healthy for Ngarrindjeri to be healthy, and for this reason Ngarrindjeri care for, speak for and exercise cultural responsibility *as* Ngarrindjeri *Ruwe/Ruwar*. This ontological statement of an ecological character description is attended by axiological concepts for the evaluation of activities affecting the health of Country and its interconnected lifeforms.

The Ngarrindjeri ontology of Being as 'more-than-human' vital matter is now included in formal legal agreements, and its associated ecological principles for guiding the art of living well—through relations that strive for *kartjeri* (the beauty of universal health)—are beginning to shape environmental practice and policy. Political negotiation and agreement-making based on Ngarrindjeri *Yannarumi* is an initiative that prioritises an Indigenous understanding of the intrinsically connected agencies defining complex ecologies. Employing principles of contract law, the negotiation regime initiated by Ngarrindjeri is geared towards the creation of legally binding accords, through which all parties agree to *Kungun Ngarrindjeri Yunnan*, 'listen to Ngarrindjeri people speaking as Country'.[14] This allows Ngarrindjeri to speak with cultural specificity and authority *as their Country*; and at the same time provides a basis for building positive intercultural partnerships that recognise Indigenous rights, are mutually respectful, and enable common and ecological benefits through ongoing and comprehensive negotiation of the practical terms of coexistence. The agreements allow all parties to recognise how Ngarrindjeri are rightfully entitled to a practical exercise of governance over all matters affecting the Country and its life-forms in their Nation's jurisdiction, even where these matters now register coexisting interests as a consequence of colonial settlement. Ngarrindjeri have negotiated a number of such contracts. For example, in 2009 the State Department of Environment, Water and Natural Resources entered into an agreement with Ngarrindjeri regarding a comprehensive program of co-management of Country. The common aim of the partnership is to work together towards the future health of the regions of Southern Australia comprising wetlands recognised as internationally significant and protected under an international Ramsar Treaty; however the respectful and 'listening' terms of the agreement necessarily also require partners to pay new attention to social and cultural elements capable of realigning actor networks by transforming colonial habits and relations of power.[15]

One of these elements concerns processes of responsible knowledge-formation on Ngarrindjeri Country. When research is conducted under the auspices of a *Kungun Ngarrindjeri Yunnan* agreement, it no longer simply extracts 'expert' knowledge from research 'on the environment' and 'on people'. It takes place instead according to an Indigenous epistemological and methodological paradigm of connected interdependence, organised by

> the fundamental belief that knowledge is relational. Knowledge is shared with all creation. ... It is with the cosmos; it is with the animals, with the plants, with the earth that we share this knowledge ... you are answerable to all your relations when you are doing research.[16]

Although the few Indigenous perspectives we have presented here in no way reflect the rich diversity evident across native philosophies, we consider these examples are indicative of how core ontologies, epistemologies, method-ologies and ethical understandings are shared across Indigenous ecological worldviews. Aboriginal philosophies typically include a refusal of human exceptionalism; a constructivist and relational view of natural and cultural network creativity; an expressive process ontology based upon an ecological understanding of the interconnected forces that combine to produce emergent forms; and an associated materialist and vitalist ethics of human responsibility towards all life-forms, which diversifies creative potential and shapes environmental outcomes by directing engagements in complex networks through methods of positive reciprocity. We think these notions share much in common with the Continental posthumanism that similarly conceives of humanity as being constituted in inextricable relations with the nonhuman world. In particular, they resonate strongly with Deleuze and Guattari's 'eccentric' model 'of becoming and heterogeneity', in which 'flux is reality itself, or consistency' and the model is 'problematic, rather than theoremic: figures are considered from the viewpoint of the *affections* that befall them'. This kind of system 'operates in an open space throughout which things-flows are distributed, rather than plotting out a closed space for linear and solid things'.[17] For us, these congruencies evidence the contemporary contribution that Indigenous philosophies can make to global efforts currently underway to imagine a 'new Humanities'.

CONTINENTAL POSTHUMANISM

Meditating on the academic profession defining the progressive work of the university as the free expression of truth, Jacques Derrida portends a new direction for the 'Humanities of tomorrow'. He asserts:

> this immense question of truth and of light, of the Enlightenment—*Aufklarung, Lumieres, Illuminismo*—has always been linked to the question of man, to a concept of that which is proper to man, on which concept were founded both Humanism and the historical idea of the Humanities. ... The concept of man, of what is proper to man, of human rights, of crimes against the humanity of man, we know organizes ... a *mondialisation* or worldwide-ization. This worldwide-ization wishes to be a humanization. If this concept of man seems both indispensable and always problematic, well ... it can be discussed or reelaborated, as such and without conditions, without presuppositions, only within the space of the new Humanities.[18]

The 'new Humanities' to which Derrida refers, and for which he provides some framing content, have since begun to consolidate around an emerging paradigm of 'posthumanism'. In fact, however, the 'new Humanities' are best considered less as a current break with European modernism and its humanist tradition of progressive Enlightenment; and more as a continuation and elaboration of an alternative contemporaneous thread evident *within* the modern period of Western philosophical thinking about the nature of humanity and of human knowledge. This alternative strand within Western philosophy has been expressed momentarily, debated over time, and rearticulated variously by figures including Spinoza, Godwin, Nietzsche, Feuerbach, Tolstoy, Althusser, Foucault, Irigaray, Cixous, Deleuze and Latour, among others. Though diverse in philosophical and political intent, their thinking about the question of humanity and about the justice and injustices associated with historical understandings of 'what is proper to man', shares certain features that set it apart from—and sometimes set it against—humanist modernism.

The definition and elaboration of these features has been a task assumed in recent years by 'posthuman' philosophy, developed notably (though not exclusively) in important and original works by Donna Haraway, Rosi Braidotti, Karen Barad and Cary Wolfe. In various ways, they explain how philosophy in the 'postmodern' condition involves a 'posthumanist' commitment to a process-oriented ontology of constructivist naturalism. Instead of defining humanity in modern terms, as definitively separated from object matter and animality, posthumanism connects human being creatively with the natural world; but at the same time it resists dogmatic accounts of the 'givenness' or 'naturalness' of worldly affairs.

Posthumanism is an important intellectual and political response (or alternative) to Eurocentric modernism. It promises an antidote to the worst excesses of this tradition, which are today evident in a worrying cluster of symptoms of deepening global malaise including, for example, the erosion of diversity as a consequence of Western cultural imperialism; the socio-economic catastrophe, for the majority of the world's poor, of late capitalism; and anthropocentrism as the genetic condition of environmental collapse and climate change tipping world society into the age of the Anthropocene. In various ways, posthumanism intends a certain reversal of the agentic priority and privilege that have attended Western anthropocentric modes of thinking and acting: when it is considered as enmeshed in ecological networks, human endeavour is no longer valued for its exceptional capacity to tran-scend existing limits or natural conditions. Instead, posthumanism recognises the rightfully limited powers of human agency: the ways in which human action is, or should be, subject to other agencies operating—often recipro-cally—in complex networks of existence. Attending this reconceptualisation of 'the posthuman' is a new acknowledgement within Western philosophy that 'nature' itself is a cultural construct. Indeed, posthumanist philosophy following Nietzsche is deeply critical of the ways in which 'nature' has been construed in modern European frameworks of thought that demarcate it as an ontological negativity conditioning human presence and power: human being is here defined as exceptional only through an original exclusion and deni-gration of animal nature. As a consequence of this ontological separation of humanity from animality, modern European political theories of social con-tract have conceived 'nature' as a pre-social baseline from which human cul-ture advances through increments of 'civilisation' and 'Enlightenment'. And accordingly, human achievement has typically been measured in the modern era by the advancing technologies through which nature can be subjugated as an inert substance freely available for human appropriation and exploit-ation. As a corollary, those 'native' human societies perceived to be 'closer to nature' have historically been understood by modern European agents of empire as being open to manipulation and development ('civilisation') by apparently 'superior' human social forces that demonstrate a greater control over natural circumstance.

As a form of self-correction that originates predominantly *within* Western philosophy, posthumanism is critical of each of these tendencies. In part, this self-transformation stems from a postcolonial concern for cultural difference. Indeed, Europe's intimacy with its colonised Others was experienced personally by a generation of European intellectuals, including Sartre, Fanon, Guattari, Derrida and Cixous, who spent time in French colonies including Algeria and Martinique and witnessed with sympathy their peoples' struggles for independence. Their intimate encounters with colonisation influenced the formation of poststructuralism as a 'philosophy of difference'.[19] The postcolonial context of this new emphasis of French thought at the same time spawned the new Humanities as a struggle to 'reelaborate' the 'concept of man, of what is proper to man', beyond Eurocentric whiteness and androcentrism. Posthumanism is heir to these influences: Braidotti, for example, is careful to reference and address criticisms of Eurocentric humanism made by postcolonial theory and by feminism.[20] However, posthumanism is predominantly a Western philosophical phenomenon, emerging as a critical strain *within* the Western academy. This is true also of much postcolonial theory, even when it is articulated by intellectuals such as Said, Chakrabarty or Spivak who hail originally from colonised societies or who identify with colonised peoples, but whose work is situated within the Western academy. For this reason, posthumanism has tended to criticise and reconceive 'humanity' and 'nature' mainly as these appear as cultural constructs of the West, with the (unintended) consequence that alternative, non-Western concepts of human being are frequently eclipsed.

Continental philosophy has begun to seek out perspectives beyond its own Western horizons as it becomes outwardly engaged in helping to forge the new Humanities as a genuine 'mondialization', receptive to non-European conceptualisations of self and world.[21] We believe this resetting of previously imperial modes of relationship responds to new understandings about an ethical and political imperative of global hospitality, conceived in the wake of the decolonisation of many of Europe's (and Britain's) former overseas imperial territories in Asia and Africa. However, not all of Europe's colonies have undergone decolonisation: Indigenous peoples in Canada, the Americas, Australia, New Zealand and elsewhere remain subject to the foreign occupation of their territories by settler-colonial populations, who now dominate in these regions. Lorenzo Veracini (2010) has explained how the internalised settler-colonial paradigm differs in important respects from the external model typically considered by postcolonial theory.[22] European colonies in Asia and Africa were governed externally from the 'Mother Country', with local colonised populations employed as an indentured labour force used for fattening the imperial coffers until independence was achieved. While external colonisation has naturally left the postcolony troubled by a legacy of poverty and strife, to some extent the colonial trauma has been resolved by the postcolonial achievement of independence from Empire; consequently the damaged relationship between France or Britain and many of their former colonies has recovered significantly. By contrast, settler-colonial polities established new self-governing societies and made themselves a far-flung home on Indigenous peoples' lands, which they seized for possession either by treating the land erroneously as '*terra nullius*' (as vacant, unowned and nonsovereign), or by imposing dispossessing terms of Treaty in conditions of conflict, ambiguous consent, and forced surrender. Independence, when it happens, involves severing the governmental ties between the Imperial Crown and the settler society, which thus becomes self-governing; but Indigenous peoples in these situations remain colonised by the structures of settler government imposed upon them. Settler colonial nations characteristically remain traumatised by their violent founding through the expurgation of a sovereign Indigenous presence: this erasure of indigeneity is a symptom of colonial fantasy (when settlers imagined the land as vacant and free for taking); but often also took place literally, in colonial acts of biological and cultural genocide sanctioned covertly by government policy. The trauma remains unresolved, because it is *formative*: settler nations were constituted as such only through the negation of Indigenous presence and sovereignty. Accordingly, Indigenous Australian Geonpul theorist Aileen Moreton-Robinson argues that postcolonial settler identity *depends* upon a possessive and patriarchal whiteness, inextricably connected to dispossessing Indigenous peoples of country, sovereignty and collective identity.[23] Settler societies today appear to repeat compulsively this condition of their determination even while repressing the harrowing collective memory of colonial violence aimed at the elimination of Indigenous peoples from the land. This unresolved trauma tears at the social fabric and manifests in various unhealthy ways, typically involving the continuing disavowal by settlers of a significant contemporary Indigenous presence, as well as the disinclination of settler society to acknowledge the ways in which Indigenous disadvantage stems from a legacy of original and ongoing colonial injustice, and not from supposed deficiencies inherent to Indigenous humanity or Indigenous sociality; imagined deficits which historically served as an imperial justification for colonisation and 'civilisation'.

The practical erasure, through settler-colonial policy and governance, of Indigenous power and presence is doubled in the domain of theory, where 'epistemic ignorance' of Indigenous traditions of thought continues to shape the contemporary academy. Sami philosopher Rauna Kuokkanen notes: 'Having participated historically in the displacement of indigenous peoples, today's universities reflect and reproduce epistemic and intellectual traditions and practices of the West through discursive forms of colonialism', so that in the 'contemporary university, it is no longer [indigenous] people, but rather their systems of knowledge and their perceptions of the world, that are labelled inferior' and dismissed as irrelevant and unworthy of academic hospitality.[24] We suggest that contemporary Western institutions of knowledge retain vestiges of an imperial attitude of negation towards Indigenous philosophies, because this attitude is not incidental but rather is *constitutive* of Western epistemology and subjectivity: as posthumanism has shown, the subjectivity of Western thought is defined by its departure from 'primitive' or 'animal' nature, which typically has been cathected onto Indigenous peoples by agents of imperialism. Decolonisation in Asia and Africa has allowed the imperial West to begin reconceiving its systems for knowing self and other, apart from Orientalist frameworks of understanding including European modernism and humanism. However, it seems clear to us that the ongoing situation of settler-colonisation prohibits a similar transformation in the relationship between Western philosophy (including nascent Western philosophies such as posthumanism) and the Indigenous knowledges it denied, displaced, and attempted to destroy during genocidal moments of European imperialism. These acts of negation cannot be reversed with ease by thinkers whose subjective coherence as Western philosophers relies upon a structural refusal of Indigenous authority, insofar as Western philosophy remains implicated in global world histories of European settler colonialism and the ongoing (widely unacknowledged) dispossession of Indigenous peoples. Western philosophy, and the academy more generally, remains subconsciously, compulsively blind to Indigenous expertise. One effect of this scotoma, according to Chickasaw critical theorist Jodi Byrd, is that the Western 'philosophies of difference' we see in poststructuralism, deconstruction, postcolonialism and posthumanism continue to 'demonstrate a colonialist trace that continues to prevent indigenous peoples from having agency to transform the assumptions within postcolonial and poststructuralist conversations, despite the best work of postcolonial scholars to make room'.[25]

Their elision of Indigenous philosophies threatens to render the new Humanities parochial in unwitting Eurocentrism. Cary Wolfe has been criticised for his silence,

> about the fact that Enlightenment humanist dogmas represent a particular, indeed provincial, body of thought on the question of the human. Thus, he does not mention that such dogmas originated in European societies involved in colonization, were globalized in and through colonial practices, and are currently given life in white supremacist settler societies. Along these lines, Wolfe makes no mention of past and present knowledge systems founded in non-dualist thinking. Consequently, Wolfe universalizes Enlightenment humanist dogmas and participates in on-going colonial practices that eliminate or erase other ontological frameworks in other knowledge systems.[26]

Viewed from an Indigenous perspective, the ideas expressed in posthumanism do not constitute a 'new paradigm', and there is nothing especially new about the vibrant 'new materialism' presently gaining traction in the philosophical academy.[27] Such claims of innovation can appear reasonable only because Indigenous knowledges are not widely referenced in the indexes of the scholarly works currently creating the 'new Humanities'. A notable exception to this tendency lies in the work of Deleuze and Guattari, whose 'philosophical nomadism' is rich with reference to studies of Indigenous ways of knowing the world and experiencing their humanity. This exception seems especially surprising, when we consider that Deleuze and Guattari are frequently cited as a shaping influence for posthumanism.[28] What role does their philosophy, or the reception of it, play in the continuing elision of Indigenous knowledges by the new Humanities?

NOMADIC THOUGHT

Significant critical attention has been directed towards the association made by Deleuze and Guattari between nomad experiences and the creative process of philosophy conceived as a dynamic constructivism. Relatively early interrogations by Christopher Miller and by Caren Kaplan of the colonialist underpinnings apparent in Deleuze and Guattari's nomadology prompted swift responses from Eugene Holland and Paul Patton, both in the main defending Deleuze and Guattari against the charge of colonialist referentiality towards figures of indigeneity.[29] While we agree with the assessment made by Patton that Miller's and Kaplan's arguments are misguided with respect to key aspects of Deleuze and Guattari's methodology, we remain troubled by their use of indigeneity as an element in the idea of 'nomad thought'. This is not a representational or metaphorical use, as Miller and Kaplan charge, and which Patton notes would sit contrary to Deleuze's strict antirepresentationalism and his frequent warnings against a metaphorical interpretation of his concepts. Instead, Deleuze and Guattari make a *constructivist* use of indigeneity as an element in their assemblage of the idea of 'philosophical nomadology' and in their associated account of the deterritorialising operation of the nomadic war-machine.

In answer to the question *What Is Philosophy?* Deleuze and Guattari answer that it is 'the art of forming, inventing and fabricating concepts'.[30] For them, this is a nonfrivolous and indeed *disciplined* art of creation, requiring sober techniques of evaluation immanent to the constructive process:

> The philosopher is expert in concepts and in the lack of them. He knows which
> of them are not viable, which are arbitrary or inconsistent, which ones do not

hold up for an instant. On the other hand he knows which are well formed and attest to a creation, however disturbing or dangerous it might be.[31]

Deleuzian concepts are created through a method of assemblage: conceptual elements are combined to produce the concept as a complex formation, which 'solves' a problematic Idea or sense-event. The concept is defined by the elemental parts it contains and unites, and also by the consistency of the relations binding these elements. Furthermore, because its constituting elements can be shared with other conceptual structures, each concept not only is characterised by its internal consistency, but also by the set of external relations it has with neighbouring concepts. This network of connections renders the concept mobile and infinitely open to alternative possible configurations of sense, since the significance granted to an elemental idea by virtue of its inclusion in a concept can affect the sense of other concepts also containing that element. All concepts and complex conceptual systems are assemblages; however Deleuze and Guattari distinguish between two different kinds of assemblage on the basis of the disposition of the multiplicity they form. One is rigid in its structure: it aims to consolidate an established meaning, by disciplining and institutionalising an interiorised system of sense that conforms to regular channels of knowledge, and by closing off relations to exterior concepts and conceptual elements that potentially challenge this order. The other kind of assemblage is open to transformation because it prioritises the external relations it enjoys with a range of neighbouring concepts. It is characteristically fluid, since it is 'traversed by a movement which comes from the outside'.[32] Its constitutive connections to the 'outside' cause the permanent metamorphosis of the assemblage as it takes up new elements of sense and discards others, according to the shifting compatibilities it forges through various environmental associations.

For Deleuze and Guattari, the critical and creative vocation of philosophy aligns best with this second kind of conceptual assemblage, which they characterise as 'nomadic' because of its mobility. This is not at all a metaphorical identification: according to them, thought is not 'like' a style of thinking exercised by nomadic peoples, but *is itself nomadic*. Knowledge, by contrast, is 'sedentary' or 'royal' in the nature of its assemblage of sense: it disciplines orders of 'truth' on the basis of property regimes and property relations; and once a 'truth' is established it can be staunchly resistant to transformation. In the service of knowledge, 'philosophical discourse has always maintained an essential relation to the law, the institution, and the contract, all of which are the Sovereign's problem, traversing the ages of sedentary history from despotic formations to democracy'.[33] In comparison with this operation of disciplinary regulation, nomadic thought is a 'counter-philosophy' that liberates sense for a new use; a new creation. Nomadic movement is valorised by

Deleuze and Guattari as something for thought to aspire towards, and is a mode of thinking not connected essentially with itinerant peoples. At their best, Europeans can be nomad thinkers, and indeed Nietzsche is described by Deleuze as a nomad thinker *par excellence*. And yet at the same time, throughout their *oeuvre*, nomad thought *is* clearly associated with figures of indigeneity, such as Indians 'without ancestry' or 'with subtlety of perception'; or the 'primitive rural communities' upon which 'the despot sets up his imperial machine'.[34]

We suggest that a particular construction of indigeneity as primitive and preconceptual appears in Deleuze and Guattari's philosophy, because it plays a necessary structural role in their assemblage of the concept of 'nomad thought'. This becomes clear once we understand how the two different kinds of assemblage they describe in various ways—as nomad and state-form; as smooth and striated; open and captured; fluid and fixed; and so forth—compare not only in independent contrast to one another, but also are joined inextricably in a reciprocal relationship of hostility or opposition: they coexist and are definitively, constitutively, at war with one another. In this respect, Deleuze and Guattari's treatise on nomadology and the war machine is influenced by the work of Pierre Clastres, who posits that nomadic society always-already anticipates the state-form, which it deliberately and strategically wards off by disbanding concentrations of power that may result in the emergence of a state.[35] At the same time, the state-form is constitutionally opposed to those loose elements that escape its purview and challenge its control; it seeks to capture them and assimilate them within its order, and thereby to consolidate its sovereign reach and power. This imposition of an imperial order of logic upon a nomadic process of life or of sense-making is violently constraining, and Deleuze writes: 'we know all too well that nomads are unhappy in our regimes: we use any means necessary to pin them down, so they lead a troubled life'. However, this capture is never complete, since 'at the periphery, the communities [integrated tenuously into the state-form] display another kind of unity, a nomadic unity, and engage a nomadic war-machine, and they tend to come uncoded rather than being coded over. … [This adventure] is the call of the outside, it is movement'.[36]

Nomadic thought answers this call: its art is to 'find, assign, join those external forces which give … [an expression] its liberating meaning, its sense of exteriority'.[37] Conceiving of thinking as a process of conceptual assemblage gives an image of thought as constructive, but also as critical. If a conceptual system is an assemblage of elements interconnected in a complex network or relationships, then elements participate in the structure as 'piecemeal insertions';[38] conceptual elements join a structure of thought according to the ways in which they are affected (attracted or repelled) by other elements in the arrangement. Some of these affective bonds will be strongly compatible and consistent, and in their continuity of association they will form the core structure of the assemblage. Other elemental relations, though, will be fragile and shifting: some ideas may be associated in part, only until they are challenged by alternative ideas that come into contact with the conceptual system and contradict its previous order of sense. This image of thought is therefore rhizomatic: the core structure, being a consistent order or a relatively stable interiority, constantly sends out creative offshoots that may combine productively with fresh ideational material encountered by the thinker affected by the changing situations in which she is embedded. But it is also deterritorialising: at the periphery of a conceptual order, where its composing elements are least stable in their participation, the structural organisation may shift as new ideas combine with old ones. Sometimes new encounters can radically challenge an existing order, when its elemental configuration becomes entirely destabilised within the structure as a consequence of a new incompatibility of some of its composing parts. Such sites of partial disjunction can cause the interior order of a previously fixed conceptual arrangement to escape its confines, to trace a creative line of escape. Conversely, sites of partial disjunction in thought-relations combining at the edges of a conceptual order can destabilise the structure so that it becomes flooded with a potentiality for radical change, as conceptual connections that were previously unthinkable suddenly become possible. In such cases, the established territory of the conceptual structure is eroded as it encounters a foreign alterity, an 'outside' force of affection that claws and gnaws at its borders, breaches its boundaries and rushes in to overwhelm and transform it. For Deleuze and Guattari, this deterritorialising activity is necessary to free up stymied thought for its proper creative vocation. The liberating task involves the operation of a nomadic war-machine that comes from without to challenge the state-form and resist its order:

> It is necessary to reach the point of conceiving the war machine as itself a pure form of exteriority, whereas the State apparatus constitutes the form of interiority we habitually take as a model, or according to which we are in the habit of thinking.[39]

We value Deleuze and Guattari's constructivist emphasis on the creativity of thought, and also the ways in which they prioritise a nomadic force of resistance against the imperial state-form. Similarly, we value efforts by thinkers after Deleuze, notably Rosi Braidotti, to theorise the importance of philosophical nomadology for political perspectives including feminism and postcolonialism that affirm a positive role for difference in constitutive relation to identity and processes of identification. However, there are aspects of Deleuze and Guattari's 'treatise on nomadology' that we find disconcerting when viewed from an Indigenous and anticolonial perspective. First, historically speaking, 'deterritorialisation' is far less an Indigenous strategy of resistance against the formation of a state, than it is an imperial technique used in the dispossession of Indigenous peoples by claiming that their homelands are 'terra nullius', owned by nobody and free for the taking. It is not clear to us what a valorisation of deterritorialisation implies for an ethical response to actual colonial histories of Indigenous dispossession and forced transit. And second, the radical exteriority of the nomad war-machine in relation to the state apparatus concerns us, insofar as it implies that the 'smooth space' home to the Indigenous nomad is without sovereignty, without law, without governing institutions. This closely mirrors a colonial ideology that Indigenous peoples strongly contest.

In fact, Deleuze and Guattari are careful to note that *actual* Indigenous societies are not always or essentially nomadic or without law and order: they describe the Native American Hopi, for example, as a 'sedentary people', and they understand that 'bands and clans are no less organised than empire-kingdoms'.[40] However, as Paul Patton has explained, Deleuze and Guattari are engaged in concept creation and not in social science or the anthropological study of actual nomadic societies: 'Deleuzian nomads are *virtual* or conceptual objects whose features are *settled not by observation but by definition*'.[41] As 'conceptual objects' in the assemblage that nomad thought forms in its conflictual relationship with 'sedentary knowledge' or 'royal science', Indigenous figures are defined as radically external to the imperial state-form that captures them and against which their war-machines are aimed; they occupy (and define by the mode of their occupation) the deterritorialised smooth space of the steppes or the desert, constituting the open exterior that the creative thinker must hook into. The problem that concerns us here is that, in constructivist philosophy, a concept receives its determination through the affections it receives from proximal concepts. When Deleuze and Guattari link a concept of nomadic subjectivity to a concept of indigeneity without law or land and as radically exterior to a sovereign space, to notions of existential imperceptibility as qualitative being 'without number', and to a preconceptual (primitive) or nonconceptual (disordered or irrational) state of flux that resists, contests and disrupts organised thought, then we end up with a 'definition' of indigeneity that connotes nonsovereignty void of territory and law, invisibility and marginality, irrationality, and a permanent situation of oppositionality within the system. These are *conceptual* linkages that Indigenous peoples have long resisted in their struggles against settler colonialism and its ideologies. And yet, for Deleuze and Guattari, indigeneity conceived as a pure exteriority, an imperceptibility, a placelessness or formlessness, operates as a crucial element within their conceptual assemblage of nomadic thought: it is something the sedentary, despotic, imperial (European) thinker relies upon in the creative process of becoming-nomad: '[The thinker] becomes Indian and never stops becoming—perhaps so that the Indian who is himself Indian becomes something else'.[42]

Indigenous critical theorist Jodi Byrd is deeply critical of the ways in which indigeneity is figured in Deleuzian nomadology as a placeholder of alterity available for the Western thinker: it is a conceptual site of access to potentiality, traversed by the non-Indigenous philosopher engaging in a creative process of subjective revision, via the transcendence or dissolution of his sovereign limits. This schema mirrors Europe's developmental movement through colonialism, where the native colonies are the necessary economic and epistemological supports for the expansion of the imperial centres. According to Byrd, this kind of thinking entails the Indigenous presence is 'not a fully realised one'; it is a 'latency' that others must 'learn to access, to channel and to recognise in order to fully grapple with modernity. That native presence has no agency of its own, in its own right'.[43] Byrd is also critical of the ways in which Indianness or indigeneity in Deleuzian nomadology is something 'beyond' thought: it escapes representation and its unruliness destabilises the sovereignty of the concept itself; it disrupts 'the known' and operates as the limit of the Western subjective reach. Indigeneity cannot be captured, but neither can it be known. It is imperceptible, inexpressible, a radical exteriority beyond knowledge. Byrd points out that this is a parochial conceptualisation, which is alien (and alienating) when considered from the perspective of Indigenous philosophers whose intellectual authority as such relies upon the accessibility of their cultural knowledge and subjectivity, their 'Indianness' as it is known to them. For Byrd, these tendencies in contemporary European philosophy are markers of an ongoing imperial violence waged by Western minds against the knowledge systems of the Indigenous peoples on whose traditional lands European settlers now live. Relegated to a nonconceptual, preconceptual space in relation to organised knowledge, Indigenous thought is rendered 'imperceptible'; no wonder, then, that Continental philosophy today seems to think it unnecessary to engage with Indigenous philosophies as organised systems of thought in their own right.

What, then, should we conclude regarding the de-colonial potential of Deleuze and Guattari's nomad thought, and of the contemporary strains of posthumanist philosophy they have influenced? It is important to attend critically and strategically to how concepts in constructivist philosophies are ambivalent, 'improper' in their essence: their properties come to them in the context in which they are formed and used. Noting that Indigenous peoples globally have suffered the 'transit of Empire', Byrd points out that, for colonised Indigenous peoples, being in nomadic movement has often meant 'to be made to move by force', or 'having one's movement policed'; though it also can mean 'to exist relationally in process, to be human by being multiply moved by others, to transition creatively through the affective input of others, active in a world of relational movements and counter-movements'.[44] Employing posthumanist philosophy in a way that is sensitive to differential experiences arising from colonial legacies of imperial humanism and contributes to the ongoing task of decolonisation, can require 'joyful acts of disobedience and gentle but resolute betrayal' to conceptual assemblages originating in the (imperial) West.[45] One such assemblage is the 'treatise on nomadology' presented originally by Deleuze and Guattari in *A Thousand Plateaus*, which we have indicated retains problematic elements associated with an imperial mindset. And yet, as a complex assemblage of elemental ideas, the concept of nomadic thought is in any case multiple and shifting: this is evidenced, for example, by Rosi Braidotti's significant elaboration of 'nomad subjectivity' as a nonhumanist, feminist framework for conceiving processual embodiment and ethical processes of co-relational becoming. Another 'improper' (reconsidered or transformed) use of Deleuzian nomadology is made in an Indigenous Australian context by Bentarrak, Muecke and Roe, who use it as a framework for 'Reading the Country' in a way that brings to light the consubstantial intersubjectivity of human becomings, conceived in complex interactions with nonhuman modes of existence.[46] Indeed, 'nomad thought' is given various expressions by Deleuze and Guattari themselves, who on occasion prefer to understand the nomadic exterior of the plane of consistency, not simply as a 'smooth space' that is formless and radically exterior to the organisation of the state-form, but rather as 'the intersection of all concrete forms' in a zone of proximity.[47] 'Becoming-nomad' in this particular configuration of their philosophical framework does not dissolve the subject or the concept in virtual deterritorialisation, but rather opens it to the complex actuality of existence, as a relational multiplicity that intersects potentially with diverse others in an affective neighbourhood.

Through a strategically 'improper' use of its defining concepts—such as 'philosophical nomadology'—posthumanism may become less collusive with past tendencies to exclusion within the Humanities and more adept at bridging the 'missing links' characteristic of such exclusions, including those between 'postcolonial theories, the environmental humanities and indigenous epistemologies'.[48] If Aboriginal philosophies can assume their rightful place in the affective neighbourhood of the new Humanities, postimperial humanity will be better equipped to undertake the work of 'excolonisation',[49] which requires nonimperial styles of thought and cross-cultural conceptual communication as much as it needs collaborative practices of social reconstruction. The value of an ethos of cross-cultural philosophical engagement lies partly in shared contributions to the work of critique, revealing through a disjunctive awareness which concepts are 'not viable, which are arbitrary or inconsistent, which ones do not hold up for an instant'.[50] However, we agree especially with Rosi Braidotti when she argues for a 'cartographic move, which aligns theoretically diverse positions along the same axis to facilitate the transposition of the respective political affects that activate them ... like a musical variation that leaps across scales and compositions to find a pitch or a shared level of intensity'.[51] Jodi Byrd expresses a similar view when she suggests 'indigenous critical theory could be said to exist *in its best form* when it centers itself within indigenous epistemologies and in the specificities of the communities and cultures from which it emerges and then looks outward to engage European philosophical, legal and cultural traditions in order to build upon all the *allied* tools available'.[52] Such alliances generate expansive concepts for a new earth and a people to come, bringing new conceptual understandings about the play of difference in complex ecologies, and how human values (including values related to the nonhuman world) can sometimes be shared across cultures. For us, just as for Deleuze and Guattari, these forms of alliance 'attest to a creation, however disturbing or dangerous that might be'[53] to Western humanism and its insular modes of thought and being.

ACKNOWLEDGEMENTS

We are grateful to Steve Hemming and the Ngarrindjeri Regional Authority, whose work on 'Speaking as Country' has inspired our argument. This article was produced with the support of the Australia Research Council for projects, Negotiating a Space in the Nation: The Case of Ngarrindjeri (DP1094869) and Indigenous Nationhood in the Absence of Recognition: Self-Governance Insights and Strategies from Three Aboriginal Communities (LP140100376).

NOTES

1. Deleuze and Guattari 1994, 110.
2. See also Bignall, Rigney and Hemming 2016.
3. Deleuze and Guattari 1994, 110.
4. See, for example, Cajete 2016; Panelli 2010; Rice 2005.
5. Wesley 2013.
6. Reid et al., 2013, 5; see also Marsden 2003.
7. Reid et al., 2013, 5.
8. Ibid.
9. Henare 2001.
10. Reid et al., 2013, 6.
11. Moreton-Robinson 2007, 2.
12. Cornell 2015; Hemming and Rigney 2008; Hemming, Rigney and Berg 2011.
13. Ngarrindjeri Nation 2007, 5.

14. Hemming, Rigney and Berg 2011; Rigney, Hemming and Berg 2008. See Hemming et al. 2015.

15. See Bignall 2018.

16. Wilson 2001, 177; see also Smith 2012; Cajete 2016; Berkes 2012.

17. Deleuze and Guattari 1987, 361–62.

18. Derrida 2001, 25.

19. Ahluwalia 2010.

20. Braidotti 2006b; Braidotti 2011; Braidotti 2002.

21. For example, Braidotti et al. 2017.

22. Deleuze's appreciation of this distinction is clearly evident in his interview with Elias Sanbar, published in *Two Regimes of Madness*. See Deleuze 2007.

23. Moreton-Robinson 2015.

24. Kuokannen 2007, 14–16; see also Nakata 2008.

25. Byrd 2011, xxxiii; see also Watson and Huntington 2014.

26. Sundberg 2014.

27. Bennett 2010; Coole and Frost 2010.

28. See, for example, Roffe and Stark 2015.

29. Miller 1998; Kaplan 1996; Holland 2003; Patton 2010.

30. Deleuze and Guattari 1994, 2.

31. Deleuze and Guattari 1994, 3.

32. Deleuze 2004, 256.

33. Ibid., 259.

34. Deleuze and Guattari 1987, 283; Deleuze 2004, 258.

35. Deleuze and Guattari 1987, 357–61.

36. Deleuze 2004, 259.

37. Ibid., 256.

38. Deleuze and Guattari 1987, 504.

39. Ibid., 354.

40. Ibid., 359.

41. Patton 2000, 118 emphasis added.

42. Deleuze and Guattari 1994, 109

43. Byrd 2011, 88; 112; chapter 1.

44. Ibid.

45. Braidotti 2006b, 203.

46. Bentarrak, Muecke and Roe 2014.

47. Deleuze and Guattari 1987, 251.

48. Braidotti 2016, 27.

49. Bignall 2014.

50. Deleuze and Guattari 1994, 3.

51. Braidotti 2006a, 56. See also Braidotti 2009.

52. Byrd 2011, xxx.

53. Deleuze and Guattari 1994, 3.

REFERENCES

Ahluwalia, P. (2010). *Out of Africa: Post-structuralism's Colonial Roots.* London: Routledge.

Barad, K. (2007). *Meeting the Universe Halfway: Quantum Physics and the Entanglement of Matter and Meaning.* Durham, NC: Duke University Press.

Bennett, J. (2010). *Vibrant Matter.* Durham, NC: Duke University Press.

Benterrak, K. Muecke, S., and Roe, P. (2014). *Reading the Country: Introduction to Nomadology.* Melbourne: Re.Press.

Berkes, F. (2012). *Sacred Ecology.* London: Routledge.

Bignall, S. (2018). 'The Obscure Drama of the Political Idea: Postcolonial Negotiations, Deleuzian Structures and the Idea of Cooperation', *New Formations*, 101–21.

Bignall, S., Rigney, D., and Hemming, S. (2016). 'Three Ecosophies for the Anthropocene: Environmental Governance, Indigenous Expressivism and Continental Posthumanism', *Deleuze Studies*, 10(4), 455–78.

Bignall, S. (2014). 'The Collaborative Struggle for Excolonialism', *J. Settler Colonial Studies*, 4(4), 340–56.

Braidotti, R. (2002). *Metamorphoses: Towards a Materialist Theory of Becoming.* Cambridge, MA: Polity Press.

Braidotti, R. (2006a). 'Posthuman, All Too Human: Towards a New Process Ontology', *Theory, Culture & Society*, 23(7–8), 197–208.

Braidotti, R. (2006b). *Transpositions: On Nomad Ethics.* London: Polity Press.

Braidotti, R. (2009). *The Posthuman.* London: Polity Press.

Braidotti, R. (2011). *Nomadic Subjects: Embodiment and Sexual Difference in Contemporary Feminist Theory*, 2nd ed. New York: Columbia University.

Braidotti, R. (2016). 'The Contested Humanities'. In *Conflicting Humanities*, R. Braidotti and P. Gilroy, eds. London: Bloomsbury, 9–46.

Braidotti, R., et al. (eds). (2017). *Deleuze and the Cultural Humanities—East and West.* London: Rowman and Littlefield International.

Byrd, J. (2011). *The Transit of Empire: Indigenous Critiques of Colonialism.* Minneapolis: University of Minnesota Press.

Cajete, G. (2016). *Native Science: Natural Laws of Interdependence.* Santa Fe, NM: Clear Light.

Coole, D., and Frost, S. (2010). *New Materialisms: Ontology, Agency, and Politics.* Durham, NC: Duke University Press.

Cornell, S. (2015). 'Processes of Native Nationhood: The Indigenous Politics of Self-Government', *The International Indigenous Policy Journal*, 6(4). Retrieved from http://ir.lib.uwo.ca/iipj/vol6/iss4/4.

Deleuze, G. (2004). 'Nomadic Thought'. In *Desert Islands and Other Texts 1953–1974*, D. Lapoujade, ed., M. Taormina, trans. New York: Semiotext(e), 252–61.

Deleuze, G. (2007). 'The Indians of Palestine: Interview with Elias Sanbar'. In *Two Regimes of Madness: Texts and Interviews 1975–1995*. D. Lapoujade (Ed); A. Hodges and M. Taormina (Trans). New York: Semiotext(e), 194–200.

Deleuze, G., and Guattari, F. (1987). *A Thousand Plateaus*. Translated by B. Massumi. Minneapolis: Minnesota University Press.

Deleuze, G., and Guattari, F. (1994). *What Is Philosophy?* Translated by G. Burchell and H. Tomlinson. London: Verso.

Derrida, J. (2001). 'The Future of the Profession or the University without Condition'. In *Jacques Derrida and the Humanities*, T. Cohen, ed. Cambridge: Cambridge University Press, 24–57.

Haraway, D. (1997). *Simians, Cyborgs and Women: The Reinvention of Nature.* London: Free Association.

Henare, M. (2001). 'Tapu, Mana, Mauri, Hau, Wairua. A Maori Philosophy of Vitalism and Cosmos'. In *Indigenous Traditions and Ecology*, G. Grim, ed. Cambridge, MA: Harvard Divinity School.

Hemming, S., and Rigney, D. (2008). Unsettling Sustainability: Ngarrindjeri political Literacies, Strategies of Engagement and Transformation. *Continuum: Journal of Media and Cultural Studies, 22*(6), 757–75.

Hemming, S., Rigney, D., and Berg, S. (2011). 'Ngarrindjeri Futures: Negotiation, Governance and Environmental Management'. In S. Maddison and M. Briggs (Eds.), *Unsettling the settler state: Creativity and resistance in Indigenous settler-state governance* (pp. 98–113). Sydney, Australia: Federation Press.

Hemming, S., Hartman, T., Rigney, C., Rigney, D. Trevorrow, L., Rigney, G., and Sutherland, L. (2015). 'Murrundi (Murray River): Ngarrindjeri Yarluwar-Ruwe (Caring as Country) Program', *18th International River Symposium*, Brisbane, Australia, September 21–23, 2015.

Holland, E. (2003). 'Representation and Misrepresentation in Postcolonial Literature and Theory', *Research in African Literatures* 34(1), 159–72.

Kaplan, C. (1996). *Questions of Travel: Postmodern Discourses of Displacement.* Durham, NC: Duke University Press.

Kuokkanen, R. (2007). *Reshaping the University: Responsibility, Indigenous Epistemes and the Logic of the Gift.* Vancouver: UBC Press.

Marsden, M. (2003). *The Woven Universe.* (Ed. C. Royal). Otaki: Estate of Rev. Maori Marsden.

McCormack, P. (2012). *Posthuman Ethics: Embodiment and Cultural Theory.* Abingdon: Ashgate.

Miller, C. (1998). 'Beyond Identity: The Postidentitarian Predicament in a Thousand Plateaus', in *Nationalists and Nomads: Essays on Francophone African Literature and Culture.* Chicago: Chicago University Press, 171–244.

Moreton-Robinson, A. (2007). *Sovereign Subjects: Indigenous Sovereignty Matters.* Sydney: Allen & Unwin.

Moreton-Robinson, A. (2015). *The White Possessive: Property, Power, and Indigenous Sovereignty.* Minneapolis: Minnesota University Press.

Nakata, M. (2008). *Disciplining the Savages, Savaging the Disciplines.* Canberra: Aboriginal Studies Press.

Ngarrindjeri Nation. (2007). *Yarluwar-Ruwe (Sea Country) Plan.* Ngarrindjeri Country: Ngarrindjeri Regional Authority. Retrieved from http://www.environ-ment.gov.au/indigenous/publications/pubs/ngarrindjeri-scp-2006-1.pdf

Panelli, R. (2010). 'More-Than-Human Social Geographies: Posthuman and Other Possibilities', *Progress in Human Geography* 34(1), 79–87.

Patton, P. (2000). *Deleuze and the Political*. London: Routledge.

Patton, P. (2010). *Deleuzian Concepts: Philosophy, Colonisation, Politics*. Stanford, CA: Stanford University Press

Reid, J. Barr, T., and Lambert, S. (2013). *Indigenous Sustainability Indicators for Maori Farming and Fishing Enterprises: A Theoretical Framework*. Ngai Tahu Research Centre: University of Canterbury.

Rice, B. (2005). *Seeing the World with Aboriginal Eyes*. Winnipeg: University of Manitoba.

Rigney, D., Hemming, S., and Berg, S. (2008). 'Letters Patent, Native Title and the Crown in South Australia'. In *Indigenous Australians and the Law*, M. Hinton, D. Rigney and E. Johnston, eds. New York: Routledge, 161–78.

Roffe, J., and Stark, H. (2015). *Deleuze and the Non/Human*. New York: Palgrave Macmillan.

Smith, L. (2012). *Decolonizing Methodologies*. New York: Zed Books.

Sundberg, J. (2014). 'Decolonising Posthuman Geographies', *Cultural Geographies* 21(1), 33–47.

Watson, A., and Huntington, O. (2014). 'Transgressions of the Man on the Moon: Climate Change, Indigenous Expertise, and the Posthumanist Ethics of Place and Space', *Geojournal 79*, 721–36.

Wilson, S. (2001). 'What Is Indigenous Research Methodology?' *Canadian Journal of Native Education* 25(1), 175–79.

Wolfe, C. (2010). *What Is Posthumanism?* Minneapolis: University of Minnesota Press.

Veracini, L. (2010). *Settler Colonialism*. Basingstoke: Palgrave Macmillan.

Wesley, A. (2013). 'A "Made in Huu-ay-aht" Constitution', Tribal Constitutions seminar. Native Nations Institute for Leadership, Management, and Policy, University of Arizona. Tucson, Arizona. April 4, 2013. Presentation, https://nnidatabase.org/video/angela-wesley-made-huu-ay-aht-constitution.

Chapter 10

Kinopolitics

Borders in Motion

Thomas Nail

We live in an age of movement. More than at any other time in history, people and things move longer distances, more frequently, and faster than ever before. We live in an age of world historical global migration, increasingly rapid climatic changes, of high-speed digital images, of accelerating universes and accelerated particles. All that was solid melted into air long ago and is now in full circulation around the world like dandelion seeds adrift on turbulent winds. We find ourselves, at the turn of the twenty-first century, in a world where every major domain of activity, from nature and society to the arts and sciences, has become increasingly defined by patterns of motion that precede and exceed human agency.[1]

We can no longer continue on with the same old theoretical tools under these circumstances. We need a new theoretical humanities that no longer starts and ends with humans and human systems (language, society, culture, the unconscious, and so on). Today, more than ever before, it is apparent that humans and their systems are not the only agents on this planet. Humans and their social structures are shot through and exceeded by more primary and constitutive material-kinetic processes and patterns. Humans are thus caught up in much larger meta-stable patterns of motion with their own kind of logic, yet to be systematically studied across the disciplines. Matters both living and nonliving (geological, geographical, climatological, microbiological, technological, and so on) are not merely passive objects of human construction. Humans and nonhuman beings are two dimensions or regions of the same systems of collective interactional agency or patterns of motion.

Studying these patterns does not mean, however, that we should abandon the study of human agency and structures. Far from it. The challenge of what is now being called 'posthumanism' or 'new materialism', of which I see my work as a part, is to provide a new theoretical framework to help us think through the entangled continuity of human and nonhuman agencies that now confront us. The natural sciences, typically charged with the study of non-human structures, have largely treated these structures as independent objects of subjective knowledge, without attending to the active role their objects of study have played in the shaping of scientific knowledge itself.[2] The sciences, just as much as the humanities, therefore require a new theoretical foundation that takes seriously the collective agency of humans and nonhuman systems as dimensions of something else—of what I call 'kinetic systems'. The anthropocentric project has come to an end.[3] We have crossed the threshold of a new Copernican revolution. Now is the time to put forward new ideas, such as a theory of kinetic systems.

The contribution of my chapter to this larger project is to show some of the political consequences of posthumanist kinetic systems with the aim of avoiding 'inhumanism'.[4] In the hopes of bringing the theoretical human-ities closer to a more posthuman and movement-oriented perspective this chapter proceeds in three parts. Part one motivates and contextualises the shift in the theoretical humanities away from thinking about anthropocen-tric systems—starting with Deleuze and Guattari's theory of assemblages. Part Two then provides a definition of and argument for a shift towards a movement-oriented perspective for thinking about politics in particular. Part three provides a concrete example of how this new perspective helps us to think about the contemporary border politics.

FROM HUMAN TO POSTHUMAN SYSTEMS

My aim in focusing on patterns of circulation or systems of motion is to con-tribute to the theory of 'systems' or 'structures', which takes seriously the agency and mobility of nonhuman matters. In politics, for example, the focus of this chapter, I show that humans are only some of the agents involved in the patterns or regimes of circulation. All kinds of geographical, geological, biophysical, technological and architectural matters play an active and con-stitutive role in the expansion of bordered societies and the expulsion of the migrant bodies that sustain them. In the case of climate change, both historical and contemporary, this is obvious. Climate change is expected to nearly double global migration in the next twenty-five years. Human social movement both shapes and is shaped by changes in climate and geology. Together they comprise an interactional system. In architecture, too, geology plays an active role shaping humans in places with minerals, who in turn reshape the mineral sources through buildings, which in turn structure human and animal regimes of social motion in ways not entirely under their control.

In short, instead of looking strictly at human agency or human structures we should look at the whole kinetic pattern or regime of motion within which human and nonhuman agencies *both* circulate together. The aim of this kind of kinetic new materialism is not to strip agency from humans but rather to locate it within larger structures of collective kinetic agency in which humans are part. Movement is something that all matters do. So instead of beginning our studies with language, consciousness, power or even life, starting with motion provides us with a shared and materialist basis for posthuman systems analysis.

The Assemblage

Perhaps one of the most important precursors to the study of posthuman systems and agencies is the concept of *agencement*, developed by the French philosophers Gilles Deleuze and Félix Guattari and translated into English as 'assemblage'. The French word *agencement* comes from the verb *agencer*, 'to arrange, to lay out, to piece together'. The noun *agencement* thus means 'a construction, an arrangement, or a layout', in contrast to the English word 'assemblage' meaning 'the joining or union of two things'. This difference being noted, I will continue to use the English word assemblage but in reference to the original French meaning. Deleuze and Guattari's concept of the assemblage makes three major contributions to any future posthuman system theories.

Heterogenesis. The first major contribution is that it provides an alternative to the theory of unities. The concept of organic unity is the linchpin of anthropocentrism and 'closed systems'. Without the organic unity of the *anthropos* distinct from nature, anthropocentrism never gets off the ground. A unity is defined by the intrinsic relations that various parts have to one another in a whole. A unity is an organic whole whose parts all work together like the organs of the human body. Each organ performs a function in the service of reproducing its relations with the other parts and ultimately the harmony of the whole organism. A heart separated from a body does not survive as a 'heart', since the function of a heart is to circulate blood through a body. Similarly, the organism does not survive without a heart, since it is the nature of the organism to have a heart.

The unity of an organic system is given in advance of the emergence of the parts and subordinates the parts to an organising principle or spirit. Unities can develop themselves, but they never change the whole of what they are. Thus unities do not allow for the possible emancipation or recombination of their parts without destroying themselves in the process. On the other hand, when component parts subsist independently from their internal relations within a unity they cease to be unities and become mechanisms: defined only by their external relations. As Hegel writes, 'This is what constitutes the character of mechanism, namely, that whatever relation obtains between the things combined, this relation is extraneous to them that does not concern their nature at all, and even if it is accompanied by a semblance of unity it remains nothing more than composition, mixture, aggregation, and the like'.[5]

In contrast to organically unified systems, assemblages are more like machines, defined solely by their external relations of composition, mixture and aggregation. In other words, an assemblage is a multiplicity, neither a part nor a whole. If the elements of an assemblage are defined only by their external relations, then it is possible that they can be added, subtracted and recombined with one another *ad infinitum* without ever creating or destroying an organic unity. This is what Deleuze and Guattari paradoxically call a 'fragmentary whole'.[6] The elements of the assemblage are 'not pieces of a jigsaw puzzle', they say, but like a 'dry-stone wall, and everything holds together only along diverging lines'.[7] Each new mixture produces a new kind of assemblage, always free to recombine again and change its nature. Thus, as Deleuze says, 'in a multiplicity, what counts are not the terms or the elements, but what is "between" them, the in-between, a set of relations that are inseparable from each other'.[8] The assemblage constructs or lays out a set of relations between self-subsisting fragments—what Deleuze calls 'singularities'. 'The system', Deleuze says, 'must not only be in perpetual heterogeneity, it must also be a heterogenesis'.[9] Humans and human systems, for Deleuze, are not discrete unities cut off from the influence and agencies of the material world.

Event. The assemblage's second major contribution to posthuman systems is that it provides an alternative to the logic of essences. The essence of a thing is what uniquely and necessarily defines it; in other words, what it is about a thing that makes it what it is such that it is not something else, that endures despite all its unessential aspects. This is the second great bastion of anthropocentrism insofar as it provides the basis of a hierarchy between fixed classes or species of beings. The problem with this sort of question is that the answer requires us to already assume the finished product of what we are inquiring into. Assuming the thing to be the complete product or closed system, we simply identify the enduring features of its history and retroactively posit them as those unchanging and eternal features that by necessity must have pre-existed the thing.

In contrast to this, Deleuze and Guattari do not ask 'What is . . .?' But rather how? Where? When? From what viewpoint? And so on. These are not questions of essence, but questions of events. An assemblage does not have an essence because it has no eternally necessary defining features, only contingent and singular features. In other words, if we want to know what something is, we cannot presume that what we see is the final product or that this product is somehow independent from the network of social and historical processes to which it is connected. Systems are relational.

For example, we cannot extract the being of a book from the vast historical conditions of the invention of an alphabetic language, distribution of paper, the printing press, literacy, and all the social contingencies that made possible the specific book of our inquiry with all of its singular features (colour, lighting, time of day and so on) and all the conditions under which someone is inquiring into the book. A vast network of processes continues to shape the book, and thus there is no final product. We do not know what the book might possibly become or what relations it may enter into, so we do not yet know its universal or essential features. We know only its collection of contingent features at a certain point in its incomplete process. As Deleuze says, 'If one insists, the word "essence" might be preserved, but only on condition of saying that the essence is precisely accident, the event'.[10]

Collective Agency. The assemblage's third major contribution to posthuman systems is that it provides an alternative to anthropocentric theories of agency in which only the human acts. The idea that only humans have genuinely free action is very old, but lies at the heart of humanism. Human agency is linked not only to the unity of the human subject but also the essence of the human being, distinct from others, to have free, conscious action in the world. Agency is tied to freedom, and freedom is tied to consciousness, which is something possessed only by humans. Anthropocentrism has used this theory as a weapon to subordinate the actions of all beings without consciousness. Humans act freely, but animals, plants and minerals act by necessity. Nonhumans move, but this movement is not a genuinely free or agential movement. A contemporary version of this still persists in various structuralisms and poststructuralisms grounded in collective human agency.

In contrast, Deleuze and Guattari's theory of the assemblage offers us a truly posthuman theory of collective agency. There are geological, biological and technological assemblages just as there are political, literary and musical ones. They all mix together freely, collectively transforming one another. Metal, for example, has a geological and material agency all its own that humans follow into the earth and that transforms them collectively: metallurgy. Deleuze and Guattari thus describe 'the immanent power of corporeality in all matter' as 'a material vitalism'. 'Because metal is the pure productivity of matter, those who follow metal are producers of objects par excellence'. Metallurgists, they say, have relations with 'the others, those of the soil, land, and sky'.[11] Metal liberates itself from the mines using humans and in turn is transformed by metal's particular agencies to take on many hardened forms: weapons, armour, horse-mounted weapon assemblages and so on. Humans and their social structures are the way they are in part because of their particular location near metal mines, relations with metallurgists, and whether the metal ore is wealthy or poor, powerful or weak. The human-metal assemblage is a collective one in which humans act through metal and metal acts through humans.

These are the three major contributions of Deleuze and Guattari's concept of assemblage to posthuman systems theories. They are the beginnings from which posthumanism emerged from poststructuralist theories grounded in strictly human systems of language, power, economy, the unconscious and so on. There is, however, much work yet to be done and new moves still to make beyond Deleuze and Guattari's theory of assemblages.[12] For example, more recent contributions to posthumanism have developed and expanded this systems approach to important areas in feminist, decolonial, disability, critical race, and queer theories, as well as critical science studies, previously underdeveloped in Deleuze and Guattari's work.[13]

My own unique contribution to this growing tradition is to focus on systems or patterns of *motion* and *mobility*. In particular, I would like to argue in this chapter that such a movement-oriented approach allows us to see something extremely counter-intuitive about political borders: that they are in motion and circulation.

KINETIC SYSTEMS

Within the thriving posthuman systems tradition, one way of thinking about systems is by looking at their motion—what I call 'kinetic systems' or 'kinetic structures': A kinetic system is different than the 'structures' found in both structuralism and poststructuralism. A kinetic system is, first of all, not a reductively anthropocentric structure that explains all the others (power, language, economics, the unconscious and so on), nor is it a single total structure with no 'outside' to it, or even some combination of such structures like various Freudo-Marxist (post)structuralist positions. Kinetic structures are not anthropocentric because what is in motion are matters both human and nonhuman, with their own kinetic agency. Since all matter is in motion the study of kinetic systems or structures allows us to look at both at once. Kinetic structures are not reductive, or total either, because what is primary is not the kinetic structure itself but the flows of matter that compose, decompose and recompose the emergent patterns.

Kinetic systems theory is thus both inspired by but distinct from new materialist vitalism and from Deleuzean nomadism.[14] Kinetic systems are distinct from 'vitalist new materialisms' in which the motion and activity of matter is explained by recourse to something else: ontologically 'vital powers' or 'forces' of the Spinozist or Deleuzian variety.[15] Kinetic systems are also distinct from the Deleuzean theory of nomadism, defined by the 'immobility' of *speed* and the 'motionless voyage' of the nomad.[16] Kinetic systems theory is not a theory of powers, forces or immobile speeds, but empirically and historically emergent patterns of motion.

The study of kinetic systems is thus not an ontology of becoming. It is a practical and historical study situated in the present. Like the owl of Minerva, theoretical practice flies at dusk after the day is done, and looks back on its immanent conditions. However, once it has seen the practical and historical conditions of its own appearance, it then descriptively transforms them, not from nowhere, but precisely from the very point from which it is at: the present. Theoretical description is thus always backwards-looking, like Walter Benjamin's kinetic reading of Paul Klee's *Angel of History*. The angel of history theoretically faces the past but is continually and blindly propelled forward into the future. As Marx writes of his method in the 'Postface' to the second edition of *Capital*:

> Of course the method of presentation must differ in form from that of inquiry. The latter has to appropriate the material in detail, to analyse its different forms of development and to track down their inner connection. Only after this work has been done can the real movement be appropriately presented. If this is done successfully, if the life of the subject-matter is now reflected back in the ideas, then it may appear as if we have before us an a priori construction.[17]

Kinetic systems are therefore historical; that is, immanently extracted from the past, from the perspective of the present. This practical approach is different from the more 'conceptual' approaches found in certain ahistorical versions of structuralism and poststructuralism.[18]

Systems-in-Motion

Movement is a common feature of all posthuman systems. In contrast to essences, forms and structures, which are defined by stasis, immutability, fixity and anthropocentrism, kinetic systems are defined by their flux, mobility and circulation. Kinetic systems are not just 'open' or 'closed' at their limits but the whole system is in continual meta-stable motion. Every aspect of the system is a continuously reproduced flow in a mixture of centripetal, centrifugal, tensional, elastic and pedetic motions. A kinetic system, like Deleuze and Guattari's assemblage, is heterogeneous, nonessentialist, nonteleological, and is defined by collective agency.

However, a kinetic system is not the same as an assemblage of *heterogeneous* or even heterogenetic *elements*. A kinetic system is instead composed of *continuities*: flows, folds, and fields of kinetic *patterns* or regimes of circulation through which flows of matter are continuously reproduced and transformed. Assemblages, Deleuze and Guattari say, are 'fragmentary wholes' where 'everything holds together only along diverging lines'[19] and are composed of 'singularities'. Kinetic systems, however, are not defined by their fragments or wholes but by their continuities and folds. They hold together not by divergence but by knotting and knotworks. Their collections are not defined by singularities but by confluences, conjunctions and circulations.[20]

The goal of what follows next is to provide an elaboration of kinetic systems theory and its consequences in the domain of border politics, or what I have called elsewhere 'kinopolitics'. Instead of adopting the typical anthropocentric categories of political analysis (citizens, rights, states, laws and so on), I believe that there are numerous important implications for shifting our perspective on politics from anthropocentric systems and cultural structures to one of material kinetic systems. For example, if we define political systems not by their anthropocentric and ideological content (authoritarianism, liberalism, Marxism and so on) but more fundamentally by their patterns of motion, then political theory can provide a much closer analysis of the material and kinetic systems within which humans and nonhumans share collective agency and responsibility.[21]

Kinopolitics

Kinopolitics is the theory and analysis of social motion: the politics of movement. Instead of analysing societies as primarily static, spatial or temporal, kinopolitics or social kinetics understands them primarily as 'regimes of motion'. Societies are always in motion: directing people and objects, reproducing their social conditions (periodicity), and striving to expand their territorial, political, juridical and economic power through diverse forms of expulsion. In this sense, it is possible to identify something like a political theory of movement.

However, a political theory of social motion based on movement, not derived from stasis, time, or space, will also require the definition of some conceptual terms important for this analysis. The core concepts in the definition of social motion are 'flow', 'fold', and 'field of circulation', from which an entire logic of social motion can be defined. After we lay out these concepts in Part Two, we can look more closely in Part Three at the concrete consequences this theory has for our understanding of how social borders work.

Flow. The conceptual basis of kinopolitical systems is the analysis of social flows. The key characteristic of flows is that they are defined according to their continuous movement. In this sense, the philosophical concept of flow parallels the historical development of the fluid sciences, aerodynamics and hydrodynamics.[22] In fluid dynamics, a flow is not the movement of fixed solids analysed as discrete particles, as it is in solid mechanics; the presupposition of the fluid sciences is continuum.[23]

However, measuring 'a' flow is difficult because a flow, like a river, is indivisible and continually moving. Thus there is never only one flow or any total of flows, but a continuous process. A flow is by definition a nonunity and nontotality whose study can never be completed because it keeps moving along to infinity like a curved line. However, regional stabilities composed of a certain confluence or flowing-together of two or more moving streams do exist.[24] One flow does not totalise or control the other, but the two remain mixed like different regions in the same fluid. Confluent flows are diverse but also continuous and thus overlap in a kind of open collection of knots or tangles. In this sense, flows are not only physical, metabolic or statistical but also social. Kinopolitics is precisely the analysis of social flows.

A flow is not a probability; it is a process. A political philosophy of flows is an analysis of their bifurcations, redirections, vectors, or tendencies—not their unities or totalities. The science of probability assumes that a flow is a percentage of 100 (i.e., a totality): $x / 100$. A *percent*age presumes a knowledge of the whole such that the *per-* is a part of the known *cent-*, or whole. But a flow is not a part in a whole (even a fragmented whole) it is a percentage of infinity: x / ∞. For this reason flows include chance, uncertainty and events. Every point or node in a network already presupposes a more primary process that made it. A point, node or singularity is simply something passed through and traversed by flows. This also explains why social flows, and borders in particular, are so poorly understood in terms of inclusion and exclusion. Nothing is done once and for all: a flow is only on its way to something else. One is never completely included or excluded but always inclusively excluded or exclusively included: hybrid.[25] Movement, as a continuous flow, is always both/and: it is an inclusive disjunction.

Finally, flows are just as difficult to study as they are to control. They are not controlled by blocking or stopping them, but rather by redirecting or slowing them down. Every systemic aim for totality is confronted with the continuity and nontotality of flows that leak from its periphery. The control of flows is a question of flexible adaptation and the modulation of limits. Accordingly, the politics of movement is first and foremost defined by the analysis of continuous movement, changes in speed and the redirection of flows.

Fold. The second basic conceptual term of kinopolitics is the fold. If all of social reality comprises continuous flows, folds explains the phenomenon of relative or perceived stasis. However, this relative stasis is always secondary to the primacy of the social flows that compose it. A fold is not something other than a flow; it is the redirection of a flow back onto itself in a loop or junction. In this way, the fold is distinct from a confluence. A confluence is an open whole of overlapping flows, but a fold occurs when a single flow loops back over itself. A fold remains a process but a vortical process that continues to repeat in approximately the same looping pattern—creating a kind of mobile stability or homeorhesis.[26] A fold is the joining together of a flow with itself. The point at which the flow returns to itself is an arbitrary one, but also one that constitutes a point of self-reference or haptic circularity that yokes the flow to itself (see figure 10.1).

The fold then acts like a filter or sieve that allows some flows to pass through or around the circle and other flows to be caught in the repeating fold of the circle. The movement of the captured flow can then be connected to the movement of another captured flow and made into all manner of mobile technologies: a vehicle for travel, a tool for moving the ground or a weapon of war. But the yoking of the flows also augments them, not necessarily by moving them faster or slower but by putting them under the control of something else: a driver. The driver is not necessarily a person but the given point at which the flow intersects with itself. Although the flow is continually changing and moving around the loop, the driver appears to remain in the same place. In this sense, the driver absorbs the mobility of the yoked flow while remaining relatively immobile itself: a mobile immobility, a relative immobility that moves by the movements of others.

The concept of the fold stands in contrast to the concept of node, developed in spatial location theory and the geography of movement. For example, Lowe and Moryadas define movement as the routes between prior discrete nodes. Movement is purposive, and 'each bit of movement has a specific

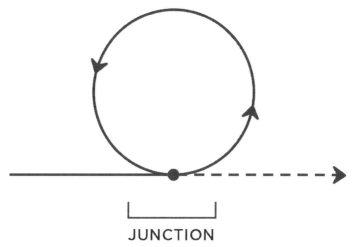

JUNCTION

Figure 10.1:   Fold. Constructed by author.

origin and destination. ... Our schema is predicated on the existence of nodes prior to the development of networks and movement. ... Without nodes, why is there movement, and where is it consigned?'[27] Kinopolitics offers an alternative to this sort of static and spatialised theory, which has been thoroughly critiqued elsewhere.[28] In fact, one could easily invert Lowe and Moryadas's question and ask, 'Without movement, how did nodes or stable points emerge in the first place?' Placing the fixed nodes first means that movement is always already yoked to an origin and destination, so there is no fold. Bergson argues that we will never understand movement beginning with immobility. My argument is that movement cannot be understood as a route between presupposed origins and destinations, and that junctions are not fixed nodes given in advance of movement.[29] Folds, as the joining of flows, are secondary to the continuous movement of those flows.

Field. The third basic term of kinopolitics is the field of circulation, which connects a series of folds into a larger curved path. This curved path continually folds back onto itself, wrapping up all the folds together. Circulation is the regulation of flows into an ordered knotwork of folds, but flows are indivisible, so circulation does not divide them but rather bifurcates and folds them back onto themselves in a series of complex knots. Since flows are continuously variable and the junctions are vortical, circulation is dynamic. It acts less like a single ring than like an origami object that brings together multiple folds, changing the neighbourhoods each time it folds. Even to remain the same, circulation has to keep changing at a relatively stable rate. Since flows have no absolute origin or destination, neither does circulation; it always begins in the middle of things (Figure 10.2).

Circulation, just like flows, is not well understood by using the concepts of exclusion and inclusion. The conceptual basis of circulation is that something goes out and then comes back in, again and again. It is a continuum. In this sense, circulation is both inside and outside at once. It is a multifolded structure creating a complex system of relative insides and outsides without absolute inclusions and exclusions, but the insides and outsides are all folds

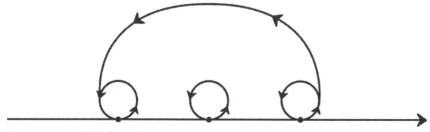

Figure 10.2:   Field of circulation. Constructed by author.

of the same continuous process or flow. Each time circulation creates a fold or pleat, both a new inclusion and new exclusion are created.

However, circulation itself is not reducible to just these two categories. The aim of circulation is not only to redirect flows through a network of multiple folds but also to expand them. Just as flows are yoked into folds, so are folds conjoined together through circulation. The folds remain distinct, but flows tie them together. Through circulation, some folds act together (by connecting flows) and become larger; others separate and become weaker. Circulation turns some folds away and merges other folds together in an expanding network. As a circulatory system increases the power and range of its folds, it increases its capacity to act in more and more ways. It becomes more powerful. Circulation is more complex than movement in general or even harnessed movement (fold); it is the controlled reproduction and redirection of movement.

With the basic terms of kinopolitics in hand—flows, folds, and fields of circulations—we are now in a position to see two examples of how this changes the typical political theory of borders based on stasis and blockage.

KINOPOLITICS OF THE BORDER

A kinopolitical and posthuman systems theory of the border allows us to overturn two commonly held but false beliefs about how borders work. First, we tend to think of borders as static structures under the control of human agents. On the contrary, what I would like to show next is that borders are in constant motion and have a material nonhuman political agency of their own. Second, we tend to think that the primary function of borders is to keep people out or let them in. Again, this only appears to be true from the perspective of human agency and human structures. In fact, on the contrary, the main function of the border is not to stop movement but to *circulate it*.[30]

Thesis One: The Border Is in Motion

Borders are always and everywhere in motion. It is precisely the mobility of borders themselves as nonhuman agents that continuously modulates and multiplies social flows.

This is at first glance a highly counter-intuitive thesis. What I am saying is that the problem is not so much that the border is too fixed and impassable, *but precisely the opposite.* It is because the border is so malleable and fluctuating—continuously moving between the two sides it separates—that it ends up changing the topology of the two sides and thus the figures defined by them. Borders are not static. They are open kinetic systems. They are always made and remade according to a host of shifting material variables. In this sense, the border should not be analysed according to motion simply because people and objects *move across it*, or because it is 'permeable'. The border is not simply a static membrane or space through which flows of people move. In contrast to the vast anthropocentric literature on the movement of people and things across borders, there is, unfortunately, relatively little analysis of *the motion of the border itself*. Even many so-called theorists of flows, fluidity and mobility such as Manuel Castells and Zigmunt Bauman continue to describe the border in primarily extensive and spatial terms: as 'borderscapes … shaped by global flows of people', or as 'the material form of support for flows',[31] whose mobility or fluidity is purely 'metaphorical'.[32]

The movement of the border is not a metaphor; the border is literally and actually in motion in several ways.[33] First, the border moves itself. This is especially apparent in the case of geomorphology: the movement of river borders, the shifting sands and tides along coastlines, and so on. The border also moves itself in not-obvious ways, such as the constant state of erosion, decay, and decomposition to which every physical object on earth is subject. This includes the crumbling of mortar that holds walls together, rains and floods that rot wooden fences, fires that burn down buildings and towers, rust that eats holes through fences and gates, erosion that removes dirt from underneath a building, and so on. Every physical border is subject to the movement of constant self-decomposition, which has consequences for migrants who, for example, use these weak spots for crossing. Or authorities may take advantage of this nonhuman political agency and leave these spots weak in order to force migrants into fatal situations such as the Devil's Highway on the US-Mexico border, boat passage across the Mediterranean or dangerously cold mountain passages in the Alps. Human and nonhuman political agencies are thus two sides of the same pattern of motion that 'funnels' migrants to their death. From a naively anthropocentric perspective, these migrant-border deaths look like unfortunate accidents of the nature of those borders. In fact, however, the material agency of the sea, mountains and desert are part of the agency of the border itself in a certain pattern of funnelled motion.

Second, the border is also moved by others. This is especially apparent in the case of territorial conflicts in which two or more social parties negotiate or struggle over land divisions; political and military conflicts over control of people, land and resources; juridical partitions of legal domains or police municipalities; and economic reforms that directly change trade barriers, tariffs, labour restrictions and production zones. Borders with large zonelike areas may persist as sites of continual negotiation, slived differences, and movement, like the settlements on the West Bank. The status of the migrant as enemy combatant, or settler, fluctuates alongside the fluctuations of the border.

But the border is also moved in not so obvious ways, such as the continual process of management required to maintain the border. Without regular intervention and reproduction (or even legal or economic deployments), borders decay, are forgotten, are taken over by others, weaken and so on. Borders are neither static nor given, but kinetically and materially reproduced. Humans intra-act with borders and their environments, each reproducing the conditions for the other. As Nick Vaughan-Williams writes, 'None of these borders is in any sense given but (re)produced through modes of affirmation and contestation and is, above all, lived. In other words borders are not natural, neutral nor static but historically contingent, politically charged, dynamic phenomena that first and foremost involve people and their everyday lives'.[34] However this same fact also makes possible the arbitrary use of police power, the profiling of migrants, micro-economies of bribery and so on. Even in US sanctuary cities anyone can still report suspected migrants to federal immigration enforcement. In this sense anyone can *become a border*, even migrants themselves.

The common idea many people have of borders as static walls is therefore neither conceptually nor practically accurate. If anything, borders are more like motors, folds or bifurcation points. Just like any other motor, border technologies must be maintained, reproduced, refuelled, defended, started up, paid for, repaired and so on. In short, a vast nonhuman knotwork of agencies is involved in reproducing and transforming border systems. This is not a new phenomenon that applies only or largely to contemporary life;[35] borders have always been mobile and multiple. Humans and nonhumans have always managed borders in some form or another throughout history.

Therefore, the distinction between natural and artificial human borders posed by early border theorists[36] cannot be maintained. This is the case not because borders today are radically different than they used to be, but because throughout history 'natural' borders were always delimited, disputed, and maintained by 'artificial' human societies. A river only functions as a border if there is some social impact of it being such (i.e., a tax, a bridge, a socially disputed or accepted division). Additionally, so-called artificial borders always function by cutting or dividing some 'natural' flow of the earth or people (who are themselves 'natural' beings). A dramatic example of this is the US government's attempt to change the naturally 'insecure' topology of the border outside San Diego by moving two million cubic yards of earth (enough dirt to fill the Empire State Building) from a nearby mountaintop, only to have it erode within months, destroying the new roads and the whole ecology. Borders are in constant motion and intra-action with humans, each one continually supporting and undermining the other at the same time.

Thesis Two: The Border Is a Process of Circulation

The second counter-intuitive idea rendered visible by our kinopolitical framework is that borders function not to keep in or keep out but rather to circulate social motion. Borders, like migrants, are not well understood only in terms of inclusion and exclusion, but rather by *circulation*. In part this follows from the first thesis about the mobility of the border. Since the border is always in motion, it is a continually changing process. Borders are never done 'including', someone or something. This is the case not only because empirically borders are at the outskirts of society *and* within it and regularly change their selection process of inclusion, as we said before, but also because exclusion is not synonymous with stasis. The exclusion is always mobilised or circulated.

In practice, borders, both internal and external, have never succeeded in keeping everyone in or out. Given the constant failure of borders in this regard, the binary and abstract categories of inclusion and exclusion have almost no explanatory power. The failure of borders to fully include or exclude is not just an effect of the contemporary waning sovereignty of postnational states;[37] borders have always leaked. The so-called greatest examples of historical wall power—Hadrian's Wall and the Great Wall of China—were not meant to keep people out. Rather, their most successful and intended function was the social circulation of labour, taxes and nonhuman provisions.[38] Humans thus circulated as the bearers of nonhuman agents. Or nonhuman agents (food, building materials, weapons, etc.) circulated as bearers of human agents. The two function as sides of the same form of motion.

This continues today with the US-Mexico border wall.[39] The success rate of illegally crossing is around 90 percent, according to several studies. Most of the traffic across the border is related to economic regulation. Thus one of the main effects of borders is not keeping out but circulating bodies, both human and nonhuman, in a particular pattern: by criminalising them, killing them, extracting a tax from them, and so on. Contrary to most critiques of the US-Mexico border, this is poorly understood as a 'failure' of the wall—rather it simply succeeds in other ways that may not be directly 'keeping people out'. Here again, anthropocentric politics misses the whole pattern of motion because it looks only at humans and passive objects. If we look at the agency of nonhuman matters we see a much more complex picture in which animals, insects, water, weather, wind, dirt, trash and rivers are constantly crossing the border, circulating back again, often transforming the border each time.[40] Such material agencies circulate and thus cooperate with and against various humans, sometimes making the border more or less dangerous, more or less stable, more or less effective, and so on.

But border circulation is not just the ongoing process of dividing; its tech-nologies of division also have a direct effect on what is divided. What is divided by the border is also recirculated, defended, maintained, and even expanded, but also expelled and pushed away. The whole system, not just part of it, is continually reproduced by continuous flows and bifurcations. Division is not simple blockage—it is a redirection. What is circulated does not stop after the division—it often comes back again and again. Thus 'it is the process of bordering', as border theorist David Newman writes, 'rather than the border line per se, that has universal significance in the ordering of society'.[41] The border is the social technique of reproducing the limit points, after which that which returns may return again and under certain conditions (worker, criminal, commuter, etc).

The border does not logically 'decide', as Agamben says. Rather, it prac-tically redistributes. Undocumented migrants, for example, are, for the most part, not blocked out but rather redistributed as functionally 'criminalised' persons into underground economies. Or an economic surplus is extracted from their incarcerated bodies as they pass through the private detention-industrial complex. They are released just on the other side so they may go through the process again, creating a whole regime of social circulation.

However, since the border is not a logical, binary or sovereign cut, its processes often break down, function partially, multiply or relocate the div-ision altogether. Instead of dividing into two according to the static logic of sovereign binarism, the border bifurcates by circulation and multiplication. The border adds to the first bifurcation another one, and another, and so on, moving further along. Instead of 'the sovereign who decides on the excep-tion', as Carl Schmitt writes,[42] we should say instead that it is 'the border that circulates by division'.

CONCLUSION

The age of the human, as the sole origin and end of the theoretical human-ities and sciences, is over. The twenty-first century marks a Copernican turn toward the emergence of new posthuman systems. Motion is at least one major defining characteristic of these systems with relevance for every kind of material agency.[43] Political theory, in particular, cannot go on as if humans and human social structures were not entangled in much larger regimes of motion and material agencies: climate change, mass migration, landscape and environmental transformations, and the agencies of the matters and critters that populate and suffuse all political events.[44]

In this short chapter, I have tried to briefly introduce some key methodo-logical concepts and practical consequences I have developed for thinking about border politics in terms of entangled material kinetic agencies, beyond merely human agents or human systems. Future work is needed not only to develop other posthuman system theories but also to apply those currently available to new domains. I look forward to seeing and participating in this invention of a 'new humanities'.

NOTES

1. This is an ambitious claim and requires more than the few paragraphs I have offered to prove. In fact, each area (politics, science, and art) requires its own book-length argument showing the historical and contemporary importance of motion. I have tried to do this in Nail 2015; 2016; forthcoming 2018c; forthcoming 2018d.

2. For a full critique see Barad 2007.

3. See Braidotti 2013.

4. This is a much larger project. See Nail forthcoming 2018d.

5. Hegel 1999, 71.

6. Deleuze and Guattari 1994, 16.

7. Deleuze and Guattari 1994, 23.

8. Deleuze and Parnet 1987, viii.

9. Deleuze 1994, 365.

10. Deleuze 1994, 91.

11. Deleuze and Guattari 2007, 411–12.

12. For example, much important work has been done by Rosi Braidotti (2012) and Patricia MacCormack (2012).

13. See Braidotti 2012; Buchanan and Colebrook 2005; Bignall and Patton 2012; Roets and Braidotti 2012; Saldanha and Adams 2013; Nigianni and Storr 2012; Haraway 1991; and De Landa 2013.

14. I am in agreement with Rosi Braidotti (2012, 256) when she writes that 'From Aristotle to Freud woman has been described as immobile, that is to say passive, or quite inactive'. I see much to praise in Deleuze's theory of nomadism, but for the same reason Braidotti cites, I must part company with Deleuze on the existence of the immobility or 'immobile journey' that Deleuze and Guattari explicitly attribute to the nomad.

15. See Bennett 2010; Connolly 2013; Coole and Frost 2013.

16. 'It is thus necessary to make a distinction between *speed* and *movement*: a movement may be very fast, but that does not give it speed; a speed may be very slow, or even immobile, yet it is still speed.' Hence the nomad's 'motionless voyage.' Deleuze and Guattari 2007, 381, 159, 197, 199.

17. Marx *Capital*, 102.

18. For a full discussion of the three differences between 'kinetic systems' and Deleuze's assemblages (history, becoming, and vitalism) see Nail 2018d, chapter 3; and Thomas Nail 2018a.

19. Deleuze and Guattari 1994, 16, 23.

20. For a complete account of this theory see Nail 2018d, book one.

21. Theories of collective agency have so far been largely captured by liberal political theory and grounded in the colonial statism. This has restricted collective agency to citizens (against migrants) Western colonial states (against the colonised), and humans (against the devalorisation of nature, women, animals, and the colonies). On the further critique of this restricted notion of agency see Bignall 2012.

22. Fluid dynamics also has its conceptual origin in the work of Lucretius, as Michel Serres (2000) argues. See also Nail 2018a.

23. In fluid dynamics the density, pressure and velocity of fluids are assumed to be well defined at infinitesimally small points, which vary continuously.

24. Serres 2000, 141.

25. Papastergiadis (2000), Gloria Anzaldúa (1987), Homi Bhabha (1994), and others argue that we should understand the migrant in terms of hybridity.

26. Michel Serres develops a similar theory of vortices: 'The vortex conjoins the atoms, in the same way as the spiral links the points; the turning movement brings together atoms and points alike' (Serres 2000, 16). Deleuze and Guattari then further develop this under the name of 'minor science' (2007, 361–62).

27. Lowe and Moryadas 1975, 54.

28. Lowe and Moryadas have been thoroughly critiqued in Cresswell 2012, 27–29.

29. Peter Haggett (1966, 31) puts movement first, but only arbitrarily: 'It is just as logical to begin with the study of settlements as with the study of routes. We choose to make that cut with movement'.

30. For much more detailed treatment, defense, and history of these thesis and others see Nail 2015; 2016.

31. Castells 1996, 376.

32. For examples of the metaphorical usage of concepts of mobility and fluidity see: Urry, 2000, 2 'to deploy "fluidity" as the leading metaphor for the present stage of the modern era.'; Bauman, 2013, 2.

33. By saying the border is not a metaphor I mean that the mobility of the border is not 'like' something else that actually moves—implying that the border has no actual movement, but only a metaphorical, ideal, or representational one. This does not mean that there is no such thing as metaphor—only that linguistic metaphor presupposes matter that moves. This is directly attested to in the original Greek meaning of the word metaphor as 'transport'. Metaphor is a kinetic process by which the features of one material thing are literally or affectively transported to another. The danger is that the original kinetic definition has been lost in favor of an idealist and representational model that simply compares essences by analogy. If a soldier is the human brick stacked into the military wall, it is not because the soldier is like a brick or the brick is like the soldier, but that both actually move according to the same border regime. They share the same affective capacity without being modeled on one another. For more on this idea of affect vs. metaphor see 'Becoming Intense, Becoming Animal' in Deleuze and Guattari 1987.

34. Vaughan-Williams 2009, 1.

35. Borders have always been mobile. Their management has always been crucial. This is not a new phenomenon—as some have argued. 'If the major focus of past

research into borders was concerned with the way in which they were demarcated and delimited, it is the management of the border regime which is of greater importance today.' Newman 2003, 16. See also: Johnson et al. 2011, 61–69.

36. For a summary of historical positions affirming a difference between natural and artificial borders see Prescott 1987, 51. See also: Ancel 1936, 51 on 'frontiére naturelle'.

37. Brown 2010.

38. See Nail 2015, chapter 3.

39. This argument is fully defended in Part III of Nail 2015.

40. Squire 2015.

41. Newman 2003, 15.

42. See Agamben 1998.

43. This is not strictly unique to the twenty-first century. Only now because of its predominance do we realise that the processes have been at work the whole time.

44. For several interesting examples of such interspecies politics see Haraway 2016, chapter 1.

REFERENCES

Agamben, G. (1998). *Homo Sacer*. Translated by Daniel Heller-Roazen. Stanford, CA: Stanford University Press.

Ancel, J. (1936). *Les Frontières, Étude De Géographie Politique.* Recueil des cours, I(55), 203–97.

Anzaldúa, G. (1987). *Borderlands: The New Mestiza = La Frontera.* San Francisco: Spinsters /Aunt Lute.

Bauman, Z. (2013). *Liquid Modernity*. Hoboken, NJ: Wiley.

Bhabha, H. (1994). *The Location of Culture.* London: Routledge.

Barad, K. (2007). *Meeting the Universe Halfway: Quantum Physics and the Entanglement of Matter and Meaning.* Durham, NC: Duke University Press.

Bennett, J. (2010). *Vibrant Matter: A Political Ecology of Things*. Durham, NC: Duke University Press.

Bignall, S. (2012). *Postcolonial Agency: Critique and Constructivism.* Edinburgh: Edinburgh University Press.

Bignall, S., and P. Patton (2012). *Deleuze and the Postcolonial*. Cambridge: Cambridge University Press.

Braidotti, R. (2012). *Nomadic Subjects: Embodiment and Sexual Difference in Contemporary Feminist Theory*. New York: Columbia University Press.

Braidotti, R. (2013). *The Posthuman.* Oxford: Polity Press.

Brown, W. (2010). *Walled States, Waning Sovereignty*. New York: Zone Books.

Buchanan, I., and C. Colebrook (2005). *Deleuze and Feminist Theory.* Edinburgh: Edinburgh University Press.

Castells, M. (1996). *The Rise of the Network Society*. Malden: Blackwell.

Connolly, W. E. (2013). *The Fragility of Things: Self-organizing Processes, Neoliberal Fantasies, and Democratic Activism.* Durham, NC: Duke University Press.

Coole, D. H., and Frost, S. (2013). *New Materialisms: Ontology, Agency, and Politics.* Durham, NC: Duke University Press.

Cresswell, T. (2012). *On the Move: Mobility in the Modern Western World.* Hoboken, NJ: Taylor & Francis.

Deleuze, G. (1994). *Difference and Repetition.* Translated by Paul Patton. New York: Columbia University Press.

Deleuze, G., and Guattari, F. (1994). *What Is Philosophy?* Translated by Hugh Tomlinson, and Graham Burchell. New York: Columbia University Press

Deleuze, G., and Guattari, F. (2007). *A Thousand Plateaus.* Translated by Brian Massumi. Minneapolis: University of Minnesota Press.

Deleuze, G., and Parnet, C. (1987). *Dialogues.* New York: Columbia University Press.

De Landa, M. (2013). *Intensive Science and Virtual Philosophy.* New York: Bloomsbury.

Haggett, P. (1966). *Locational Analysis in Human Geography.* New York: St. Martin's Press.

Haraway, D. J. (1991). *Simians, Cyborgs, and Women: The Reinvention of Nature.* New York: Routledge.

Haraway, D. J. (2016). *Staying with the Trouble: Making Kin in the Chthulucene.* Durham, NC: Duke University Press.

Hegel, G. W. F. (1999). *The Science of Logic.* Amherst: Humanity Books.

Johnson, C., Jones, R., Paasi, A., Amoore, L., Mountz, A., Salter, M., and Rumford, C. (2011). 'Interventions on Rethinking "the Border" in Border Studies', *Political Geography*, 30(2), 61–69.

Lowe, J., and Moryadas, S. (1975). *The Geography of Movement.* Boston: Houghton Mifflin.

MacCormack, P. (2012). *Posthuman Ethics: Embodiment and Cultural Theory.* New York: Routledge.

Marx, K. (1976). *Capital, Volume 1.* New York: Penguin.

Nail, T. (2015). *The Figure of the Migrant.* Stanford, CA: Stanford University Press.

Nail, T. (2016). *Theory of the Border.* Oxford: Oxford University Press.

Nail, T. (2018a). 'The Ontology of Motion', *Qui Parle: Critical Humanities and Social Sciences*, 27(1).

Nail, T. (2018b). *Lucretius I: An Ontology of Motion.* Edinburgh: Edinburgh University Press.

Nail, T. (forthcoming 2018c). *Theory of the Image.* Oxford: Oxford University Press.

Nail, T. (forthcoming 2018d). *Being and Motion.* Oxford: Oxford University Press.

Newman, D. (2003). 'On Borders and Power: a Theoretical Framework', *Journal of Borderlands Studies*, 18(1), 13–25.

Nigianni, C., and Storr, M. (2012). *Deleuze and Queer Theory.* Cambridge: Cambridge University Press.

Papastergiadis, N. (2000). *The Turbulence of Migration.* Oxford: Polity Press.

Prescott, V. (1987). *Political Frontiers and Boundaries.* London: Allen & Unwin.

Roets G., and Braidotti, R. (2012). 'Nomadology and Subjectivity: Deleuze, Guattari and Critical Disability Studies'. In *Disability and Social Theory*, Goodley D., Hughes B., Davis L., eds. London: Palgrave Macmillan.

Saldanha, A., and Adams, J. M. (2013). *Deleuze and Race*. Edinburgh: Edinburgh University Press.

Serres, M. (2000). *The Birth of Physics*. Translated by Jack Hawkes, ed. David Webb. Manchester: Clinamen Press.

Squire, V. (2015). *Post/humanitarian Border Politics between Mexico and the US: People, Places, Things.* New York: Palgrave Macmillan.

Urry, J. (2000). *Sociology beyond Societies: Mobilities for the Twenty-First Century.* London: Routledge.

Vaughan-Williams, N. (2009). *Border Politics: The Limits of Sovereign Power.* Edinburgh: Edinburgh University Press.

Chapter 11

Out of Control

From Political Economy to Political Ecology

Gregory Flaxman

POLITICAL ECOLOGY AND POLITICAL ECONOMY

In recent years, Gilles Deleuze's philosophy has become a critical touchstone for new materialisms, new ontologies and (now) new ecologies.[1] Though Deleuze almost never uses this word, not even in his collaborations with Félix Guattari,[2] the intimations of ecology can be found at a great many points in his thought—in the insistence on the externality of all relations, in the expression of rhizomatic assemblages, and especially in the concept of 'a life' that exceeds the organic bodies. When it comes to devising a posthuman ecology and formulating a new eco-philosophy, one could do a lot worse than to consult Deleuze—but for all that, his work poses a genuine problem. The recourse to ecologism obligates us, I'd argue, to reckon with Deleuze's misgivings about what we are becoming, about our collective existence and about the prospects for life.

In later years, when a note of pessimism crept into his writing, Deleuze sought to analyse, in admittedly broad strokes, the emergence of a new regime of power. With control, the collective assemblage of forces undergoes a radical—or, as Deleuze would say, *diagrammatic*—transformation. Catalysed by structural transformations of capitalism and operationalised by rapid advances in digital technology, control designates the social machine, at once subtle and vast, meticulous and overarching, within which we move, think, and live today. We constantly confront new techniques of social organisation and behavioural modification, though these are often sold to us (figuratively or literally) under the guise of convenience, security or 'connectedness'. In any event, control societies subject us to surveillance, analysis, calculation, integration, prediction, valuation, engineering, and extraction. My point, then, is that if we're to draw on Deleuze to develop something like the concept of a socioecology, we cannot ignore the political economy, or biopolitics, he diagnoses. This is especially important to remember if, following a number of recent thinkers (e.g., Jane Bennett, Rosi Braidotti, Erin Manning, Brian Massumi),[3] we regard ecology in expressly political terms.

In 'Postscript on Control Societies', a brief essay later collected in *Negotiations (Pourparlers)*,[4] Deleuze analyses the gestation of this new sociopolitical regime against the backdrop of an earlier episteme. The text is set amidst the crumbling and the dismantling of the welfare state. The great institutions of modernity—the school, the military, the factory, the hospital, the prison—are beleaguered; 'everyone knows these institutions are in more or less terminal decline'.[5] What's at stake for Deleuze is nothing less than the slow collapse of 'disciplinary society', the regime of power, per Michel Foucault, that dominated the eighteenth, nineteenth, and much of the twentieth century. Having divested power from the centralising pretence of sovereignty, discipline describes the distribution and refraction of forces among new discourses, new species of knowledge, and new (or renewed) institutions. Foucault's studies of discipline trace the features—the architectures of confinement, structures of segregation, and techniques of individuation—of a *dispositif* that traverses the school, the barracks, the factory, the hospital and the prison.[6]

Nevertheless, Deleuze insists that 'Foucault knew how short-lived discipline was'[7] and the 'Postscript' duly takes up the question—what's next? Doubtless, discipline began to break down in the first half of the twentieth century, but only after the Second World War, when new forces, machines, and techniques 'made rapid advances', did control society take shape: 'we were no longer in disciplinary societies, we were leaving them behind'.[8] By the time the 'Postscript' was published, the new regime of power was discernible if not entirely comprehensible. Of course, the disintegration of disciplinary institutions, particularly those intended to promote the general welfare, has provoked understandable alarm and justified outrage. Having said that, Deleuze suggests that by 'nursing' these institutions 'through their death throes' we risk ignoring 'the new forces knocking at the door'[9]—or, worse, embracing them under mistaken pretences. Hence, while some mourn the passing of discipline, others welcome control as if it promised emancipation, and this liberatory sentiment lies at the heart of my analysis. Unlike the segmentary 'sites of confinement'[10] concretised by disciplinary institutions, control societies are characterised by dispersive relations, modular designs, open floor plans, endless options, and almost unceasing movement—that is to say, by a world in which power becomes both imperceptible and ubiquitous.

Ostensibly, control societies offer the pretence of infinite individual autonomy: unfolding networks of communication and information extended along a 'continuous range of different orbits',[11] control induces a sense of frictionless mobility—whether in space or cyberspace. '*Surfing* has taken over from all the old *sports*', Deleuze writes in 'Postscript', and it's worth noting that within two years of its publication, 'surfing the internet' was coined. Nevertheless, the great theme of control, its abiding conceit, consists in making the smooth space of this regime, and the ostensible promise of freedom, the basis for a 'new system of domination'.[12] With control we leave behind the institutional architectures and normative categories of discipline for an increasingly insidious and illegible power. Control societies 'no longer operate by confining people', Deleuze says, 'but through continuous control and instant communication'.[13] We are no longer herded so much as we are *tracked*: virtually every transaction, decision, movement and choice is recorded, harvested, analysed and instrumentalised. 'Compared with the approaching forms of ceaseless control in open sites', Deleuze says, 'we may come to see the harshest confinement as part of a wonderful happy past'.[14] What can ecology mean under the auspices of control? How can we understand (much less affirm) Deleuze's concept of 'a life'? Control society constitutes the crucible and condition with which political ecology is faced.

For this reason, I'll begin by returning to the 'Postscript' in order to develop the 'varying geometry'[15] of control and to indicate the collective and altogether technical assemblage that it comprises. Precisely because it's so brief and so provocative, critics have often imagined themselves 'resuming' Deleuze's analysis. The discussion to follow is by no means immune to this tendency, but if we are to look forward, and to consider the transformation of biopolitics and the challenge to political ecology, we ought to look (ex-postscript) backwards insofar as Deleuze explicitly casts his essay as the resumption of Foucault's historical analyses (or, better still, as the resumption of Deleuze's monograph, *Foucault*). My intervention, however, consists in arguing that the full scope of control ought to be understood by reading the 'Postscript' in relation to Foucault's *The Birth of Biopolitics*. More to the point, I'd suggest that this is the very challenge which confronts us today, for only on this basis can we begin to articulate the objective of political ecology—namely, to grasp the society of control in view of an 'other' system to which the organic as well as the inorganic belongs.

THE GEOMETRY OF CONTROL

Far from concentrating power (in a sovereign) or distributing it (among institutions), control corresponds to a profound transformation of power-relations. Above all, control dispenses with institutional 'moulds' in order to precipitate what Deleuze, following Gilbert Simondon, calls 'modulation'.[16] In control societies, then, we move through the endless 'modulations of a finely woven and infinitely flexible "sieve [*tamis*]"'.[17] Ubiquitous, intimate and yet elusive, the 'mesh [*les mailles*]' of control 'varies at each moment from one point to another'.[18] Thus, as Deleuze observes, control is a 'system of varying geometry', and we might begin here by redefining its basic elements—points and lines. We can imagine these elements of geometry as if they were different dimensions of control or, better still, different styles: the first is pointillist, pixilated, and molecular; the other is expressionist, delineated, and bifurcating. Thus, power is increasingly disseminated into swaths of ceaselessly varying singularities and splintered into a filigree of countless, constantly varying vectors.

The varying geometry of control has profoundly altered our sense of space and spatialisation. In the first place, and as a matter of biopolitics, control concerns the modern management of populations and the corresponding deployment of statistics. Take, for instance, a paradigmatic instrument of this new regime—the census. The nomenclature of the census derives from the Romans, who used it to record names of men of military age, and while the practice was revived in the Middle Ages and thereafter became common practice (for townships, cities, and of course colonial territories, and eventually for nation-states), it wasn't until the nineteenth century that the census fully became an instrument of governmental reason. The great age of demography, which underwrote the administrative state, has not waned—far from it. Rather, with new communications and computational technologies, the demographic instinct has been appropriated to other fields and other enterprises (actuarial tables, liability indexes, market research, advertising placements, target audiences). Despite the global scope of 'big data', we'd have to admit that the reach of control society—the capacity to swallow ever greater swaths of population and digest ever greater data sets—is complemented by a second faculty, the capacity to tailor control to individual tastes, fears, addictions, etc. for which there can be no other name than 'micropolitics'.[19] Thus, the collection and selling of one's data (now openly condoned with abolishment of 'net neutrality') fuels the analytic machinery whereby our patterns, habits, predilections and desires are analysed. Each profile will be aggregated into the larger data set, but by the same token, that data set will be brought to bear on each profile so as to refine the endless series of carefully calibrated alerts, advertisements, sales, appeals, recommendations and reminders to which we are subject. The massification of control proceeds through the 'nichification' of power—once more, a dispersive regime.

The third and final aspect of control further distorts the particularity of the site or milieu. We've effectively described control as both macrological and micrological, but the relation between the two cannot be brokered on the basis of the local, locality, or locus which would otherwise lead, *partes extra partes*, to the whole. More than ever before, control is characterised by *delocalisation*. This concept claims a critical, if underappreciated, place in twentieth-century continental philosophy, conjured as it by the German phenomenological tradition (a consequence of Heidegger's Being-in-the-world [*In-der-Welt-Sein*]) and then cashed out in a French tradition that includes (among others) Gaston Bachelard, Raymond Ruyer, Paul Virilio, as well as Deleuze and Guattari.[20] Admittedly, the latter rarely deploy delocalisation as such, usually assimilating its sense to the nomenclature of 'deterritorialisation'. But in their famous 'Treatise on Nomadology', later included in *A Thousand Plateaus*, Deleuze and Guattari acknowledge the significance of delocalisation by proxy. In the course of elaborating the 'war-machine', the authors refer to Paul Virilio's analysis of modern sea power—'the fleet in being'.[21] In essence, Virilio argues that not only maritime strategy but our sense of space itself has been transformed by new, military technology. To wit: far from making a show of military strength, the modern navy deploys nuclear submarines, which are 'content, while controlling the sea, to remain invisible'. Because it can launch its warheads from any navigable point on the globe, the submarine lacks a destination. As Deleuze and Guattari explain: 'one no longer goes from one point to another, but rather holds space beginning from any point: instead of striating space, one occupies it with a vector of deterritorialization in perpetual motion'.[22]

Notably, in a critical footnote, the authors substantiate this contention with a series of passages from Virilio's *Speed and Politics*. The montage of quotations concludes:

> If, as Lenin claimed, 'strategy means choosing which points we apply force to', we must admit that these 'points', today, are no longer geostrategic strongpoints, since from any given spot we can now reach any other, no matter where it might be … *geographic localization seems to have definitively lost its strategic value, and, inversely, that this same value is attributed to the delocalization of the vector, of a vector in permanent movement.*[23]

The privileged 'geostrategic' point, on the basis of which force was stereotypically applied, has been dissolved into a smooth space within which the telemetry of a missile can precisely connect any given location to any other. Inasmuch as no point (of localisation) is more intrinsic than the rest, Virilio proposes to speak, instead, of the 'delocalisation of the vector', which is to say, the metamorphic modulations of the line.

If the traditional coordinates of space, to which the 'geometric' or 'spatial' vector first applied, was effectively delocalised by military technology, control concerns the commercialisation and dissemination of this technology (above all, the availability of accurate GPS for civilian use, which began in 2000). The advancements that made it possible to strike a site from 'any point whatever' (*queleque point quleconque*) have enabled the global communications and information networks with which one can appear in a classroom, trade a derivative, view a drone strike, or corrupt another computer from thousands of miles away. Delocalisation means action at a distance. Whereas sovereign power had been violently direct, and disciplinary power was oblique, one might say that, with control, power is increasingly *remote*. In the 'Postscript', Deleuze explains that control society 'functions with a third generation of machines'.[24] The first generation, corresponding to sovereign power, refers to simple machines (levers, pulleys, etc.). The second generation, corresponding to disciplinary society, was mechanical, thermodynamic. But the emergence of control is inseparable from the roughly contemporaneous development of 'cybernetic machines': above all, 'information technology and computers'.[25]

THE BUSINESS OF CONTROL

Despite his acknowledgement of technological transformations, Deleuze insists that 'machines don't explain anything' about control.[26] In other words, machines cannot explain control society but, rather, stand in need of explanation. In this context, Deleuze writes, the revolution of digital technology is 'more deeply rooted in a mutation of capitalism'.[27] What is this mutation? Consider the preceding stage of industrial capitalism. The latter was 'concentrative, directed toward production, and proprietorial'; it typically succeeded by means of 'specialisation', 'colonisation', or 'reducing the costs of production'.[28] By contrast, the 'Postscript' sketches three aspects of a transformed capitalism—(1) metaproduction, (2) business (marketing), and (3) debt—with which the emergence of control is immanent.

In the first place, Deleuze says, we have reached a phase of capitalism in which production is outsourced, such that a business seeks to purchase activity (labour power) and sell 'products'.[29] Needless to say, 'metaproduction' is driven by sales and markets. As Deleuze writes, rather loosely, 'Markets are won by asserting control rather than by establishing discipline, by fixing rates rather than by reducing costs, by transforming products rather than by specializing production'.[30] In this respect, Deleuze broadly describes a kind of post-fordist economy, one driven by marketing ethos and a managerial culture. 'The sales department becomes a business center or "soul"', Deleuze writes, and where this was once 'terrifying news', we are now habituated to a world in which the rhetoric of corporate personhood is ubiquitous.[31] Thus, in control societies, the factory gives way to the business (or, simply, to 'business'). 'Factories formed individuals into a body of men' which management could monitor as a mass and unions could mobilise *en masse*.

But with the shift to metaproduction, to markets and marketing, a different organism takes shape. When Deleuze says that 'a business is a soul, a gas',[32] he underscores that it is also a *dispersive enterprise*. In contrast to the factory model, which was capable of conditioning camaraderie, 'businesses are constantly introducing an inexorable rivalry presented as healthy competition, a wonderful motivation that sets individuals against one another and sets itself up in each of them, dividing each within himself'.[33] The objective and result is that businesses introduce a principle of 'modulation into all wages, bringing them into a state of constant metastability punctuated by ludicrous challenges, competitions, and seminars'.[34]

The third aspect of the 'mutation of capitalism' concerns debt. Needless to say, the question of debt is hardly new, and elsewhere Deleuze imagines the 'adventure of debt' as a kind of *longue durée*, the 'prejudicative' beginnings of which elude us.[35] At any rate, the point here is that, from early on, debt and judgement are imbricated: 'Man does not appeal to judgment, he judges and is judgable only to the extent that his existence is subject to an infinite debt: the infinity of the debt and the immortality of existence each depend on the other'.[36] Inasmuch as existence never ceases to accrue debt, no amount of time will be sufficient to repay the debt. Pace Nietzsche, Deleuze follows debt from the domain of the gods to the triumph of Christianity, but in the 'Postscript' the concept of debt is squarely cast in terms of the aforementioned 'mutation in capitalism', which is to say, as a matter of control. Once we assume a debt, our freedoms are circumscribed by obligations that effectively territorialise us in relation to institutions, interest rates, finance laws and the like, not to mention all the collateral administrative expectations. Judgement today is delivered and emblematised by a credit score, the product of calculations that reflect the way we, in turn, manage our debts. As Deleuze writes in the 'Postscript': 'A man is no longer a man confined but a man in debt'.[37]

However provocative, Deleuze's meditation on capitalism strikes me as a kind of compromise formation, at once gesturing to a future transformation and beholden to a number of older conceits. In the first place, although Deleuze's concern with sales and advertising augurs a new age of market research and behaviour modification, his 'business model' retains vestiges of an older conception of capitalism. The 'Postscript' arguably preceded the apotheosis of finance capital, when the process of production was decidedly subordinated to the accumulation of profit. Ours is an age of investment banks, hedge funds, and derivatives, but for that reason, it is also an age in which stock markets are computerised and we pass, irrevocably, into a digital economy. In this respect, once more, Deleuze's account of control needs to be updated: while digital technology ought to be grasped in view of a 'mutation of capitalism', we cannot fail to note that this 'third generation of machines' is also the condition and driving force of whatever capitalism is becoming—of market research, statistical modelling, risk analysis, cost/benefit calculation, etc. This leads to my last, and surely most provocative, point about Deleuze's remarks, which reflect a divergence between Marxist language and concepts and the terms of what we might call 'control-capitalism'. Notwithstanding the value of his conceptual instruments, Deleuze ignores the 'grid of intelligibility' (Foucault) that economists bring to bear—the insistence that well-nigh everything can be understood on the model of the marketplace.

POST-DISCIPLINARITY

As an epistolary and legal conceit, a postscript refers not only to a prior instance of writing but to the suggestion that the preceding script suffered from omission, ambiguity, even error—in short, whatever circumstance demands writing *post* script. What, then, is the script to which Deleuze's essay refers?

We can trace the 'Postscript' back to three occasions, all revolving around Foucault, that carry us from a concrete and referential case, to an implicit and evidentiary example, and finally to a pure fiction. The first and most obvious occasion is Deleuze's 1989 interview with Toni Negri, 'Control Societies', which provides the ostensible pretext for the 'Postscript'. It's difficult to say whether the forum was simply generative or whether its frustrating sense of misalignment generated the need for the subsequent essay. In relation to philosophy and 'revolutionary politics', Negri pushes a number of Marxist assumptions that Deleuze gently resists. The dynamic culminates with the introduction of the concept of control. Negri admits that, on the one hand, 'the control of "communication"' introduces 'the most perfect form of domination, extending even to speech and imagination', but on the other hand, he suggests that

> any man, any minority, any singularity, is more than ever before potentially able to speak out and thereby fully recover a greater degree of freedom. In the Marxist utopia of the *Grundrisse*, communism takes precisely the form of a transversal organization of free individuals built on a technology that makes it possible. Is communism still a viable option? Maybe in a communication society it's less utopian than it used to be?[38]

At this point, more than anywhere else in the interview, Deleuze draws a distinction between his position and Negri's (i.e., Marxism)—and he does so by recourse to Foucault. 'We're definitely moving toward "control" societies that are no longer exactly disciplinary', he responds. 'Foucault's often taken as the theorist of disciplinary societies and of their principal technology, *confinement* (not just in hospitals and prisons, but in schools, factories, and barracks). But he was actually one of the first to say that we're moving away from disciplinary societies, we've already left them behind'. Thus, whereas Negri's question tries to frame politics in the terms of a renewed 'Marxist utopia', Deleuze lays waste to this sunny version of 'communication society': 'The quest for "universals of communication" ought to make us shudder'.[39]

This interview was originally published in *Futur Antérieur* under the title 'Revolutionary Becoming and Political Creation'; only when it was republished (along with the 'Postscript' in *Negotiations* [*Pourparlers*]), was it retitled. While the new title draws an explicit link between the two pieces, 'Control and Becoming' is almost too slender to have inspired an addendum, correction or continuation (the subject of control society occupies little more than a page of text). In a sense, we'd do better to understand the 'Postscript' in reference to Deleuze's earlier book on *Foucault*. Not only does the essay immediately plunge us back into Foucault's thought as if, despite the four intervening years, we had never left it; but Deleuze returns, in a sense, to the very point at which *Foucault* left off—with the end of disciplinary power. Foucault 'knew how short-lived this model was',[40] and it's worth noting that here, as elsewhere, Deleuze credits Foucault with having anticipated the emergence of 'something new'—a new regime of power.

For this reason, Deleuze doesn't write the 'Postscript' in response to what was left unsaid by Foucault but, rather, in relation to what he'd left unsaid in *Foucault*. To wit: where one would expect the monograph to presage the age of control, *Foucault* concludes with a genealogy of the 'man-form', extended into the future, that rings with Nietzschean optimism. 'Man tends to free life, labor, and language within himself', Deleuze writes, only to ask: 'with what new forms do [humans] now risk entering into a relation, and what new form will emerge that is neither God or Man?'[41] The reference to the 'superman' (*Ubermensch*) in the next sentence underwrites a power of vital metamorphosis to which the 'Postscript' looks back with scepticism and perhaps even regret. Gone is the brave posthumanism of the earlier text: here, instead, the 'Postscript' ventures a speculative stab at the mutation of capitalism. The irony of this situation is that Deleuze's impulse—to turn to Foucault for a theory of control—never led him to Foucault's lectures on neoliberalism. Given at the Collège de France from 1978 to 1979 and collected in *The Birth of Biopolitics*, these lectures would have confirmed and transformed Deleuze's theory of control.

NEOLIBERALISM AND CONTROL

The Birth of Biopolitics is a kind of misnomer. 'I thought I could do a course on biopolitics this year', Foucault writes at the outset of these lectures, but we quickly discover that this topic (which Foucault was compelled to give a year in advance) has been recast. 'It seems to me that the analysis of biopolitics can only get under way when we have understood the general regime of this governmental reason'.[42] In other words, one cannot grasp biopolitics as such without having understood the development of what the eighteenth century came to call 'political economy'. Thus, in the opening lecture, Foucault explains that the question of biopolitics demands a prior reckoning with the way that populations came under the purview of governmental reason:

> I will try to show how the central core of all the problems that I am presently trying to identify is what is called population. Consequently, this is the basis on which something like biopolitics could be formed. But it seems to me that the analysis of biopolitics can only get under way when we have understood the general regime of this governmental reason I have talked about, this general regime that we can call the question of truth, of economic truth in the first place, within governmental reason.[43]

Notably, Foucault had developed the concept of governmental reason in his prior lectures at the Collège de France (*Society Must Be Defended* and *Security, Territory, Population* etc.). If *The Birth of Biopolitics* continues in this vein, the lectures also mark a decisive shift, both historically and epistemically, by taking up neoliberalism. In the first place, *The Birth of Biopolitics* represents its author's only extended foray into the present. While every history is, in Foucault's own words, a history of the present, nowhere else does he devote so concerted an analysis to the contemporary moment. In the second place, Foucault conceives of neoliberalism in distinctly American terms that he traces back to the peculiarity of the nation's origins. Unlike seventeenth century England or France, which appealed to liberalism—the marketplace, the sphere of competition, capitalism—as a hedge against the despotic tendencies of the state, the United States makes economic liberalism its 'founding and legitimizing principle'.[44] In other words, liberalism was not conceived of as a limit to state power, or *raison d'état*, but as the *raison d'être* of the state itself. Thus, compared to the 'ambiguity' of German ordoliberalism, which retains a moral impulse to humanise an uninhibited market economy, 'American neo-liberalism evidently appears much more radical or much more complete and exhaustive'.[45] More to the point, Foucault's elaboration of neoliberalism ought to be read as the overture to control society.

For Foucault, neoliberalism can be defined in a number of discrete, if intimately related, ways. It is 'a sort of utopian focus' that always responds to the question 'how much government?' the same way—'as little as possible'. As an expression of 'state phobia', neoliberalism consists in the endless attenuation of the state and the transfer of authority and autonomy to enterprises themselves. More concretely, then, this predilection guides a 'method of thought', such that neoliberalism comprises a faculty of 'permanent criticism' and a corresponding 'type of programming'.[46] Thus, under the eyes of efficiency experts and technocrats, even (or especially) public institutions are subject to 'market criticism', which is to say, criticism that opposes the 'cynicism of a market criticism' to the 'action of public authorities'. Above all else, though, neoliberalism represents a regime of power that, though born of economics, can be brought to bear on virtually any social questions by discovering the 'internal rationality' at the heart of 'human behavior'.[47] This rationality, often beginning with simple questions, turns to a large degree on the concept of 'human capital'. Ventriloquising neoliberalism, Foucault says that capital is whatever can be made a source of future income; but apart from material capital (property, investments, savings), the individual also claims a share of human capital—simply put, the 'physical and psychological factors' which make one able to earn a given wage.

While some portion of human capital is 'innate', neoliberal economists have devoted much of their most well-known work to 'acquired' human capital, especially as it pertains to child care and education. Far from being reducible to an abstraction, a worker 'comprises a capital' that is inalienable: 'the worker's skill really is a machine, but a machine which cannot be separated from the worker himself' and the correlative production of 'an earnings stream'.[48] The worker in possession of variable levels of skill, knowledge, training, education, pedigree or accreditation can expect a commensurate income-wage, and however simple this may seem, Foucault's point goes to a fundamental neoliberal conceit: 'the worker himself appears as a sort of enterprise for himself'. In taking on the worker's perspective, and abandoning abstract labour, neoliberalism understands the individual as both an investor and an investment. *Homo œconomicus* is no longer simply a 'partner of exchange' but, rather, 'an entrepreneur of himself, being for himself his own capital, being for himself his own producer, being for himself the source of [his] earnings'.[49]

Though human capital is one of a number of innovations belonging to neoliberalism it is, for Foucault, the one that enables its logical drive—not simply to subsume everything to the marketplace but, more profoundly, to grasp even ostensibly noneconomic questions in view of an economic 'grid of intelligibility'.[50] In other words, 'the reintroduction of labor or work into the field of economic analysis will make it possible, through a sort of acceleration or extension, to move on to the economic analysis of elements which had previously totally escaped it'.[51] American Neoliberalism undertakes the 'absolute generalization of the economic form of the market, which is henceforth extended throughout the social body and including the whole of the social system not usually conducted through or sanctioned by monetary exchanges'.[52] As a result, the market becomes a 'principle of decipherment of social relationships and individual behavior', such that questions of supply and demand can be brought to bear on virtually any domain whatever. Foucault calls this neoliberal framework a 'grid of intelligibility' inasmuch as even 'non-economic processes, relations, and behavior' can be subjected to a schema and thereby made legible.[53]

For our purposes, however, the significance of Foucault's analysis lies in having presaged control society:

> what appears on the horizon of this kind of analysis is not at all the ideal or project of an exhaustively disciplinary society in which the legal network hemming in individuals is taken over and extended internally by, let's say, normative mechanisms. Nor is it a society in which a mechanism of general normalization and the exclusion of those who cannot be normalized is needed. On the horizon of this analysis we see instead *the image, idea, or theme-program of a society in which there is an optimization of systems of difference, in which the field is left open to fluctuating processes, in which minority individuals and practices are tolerated, in which action is brought to bear on the rules of the game rather than on the players, and finally in which there is an environmental type of intervention instead of the internal subjugation of individuals.*[54]

In this description Foucault outlines the economic constituents of a society given over to neoliberalism. This society can no longer be defined by virtue of the disciplinary logic of a legal and juridical network, nor of 'scientific' discourses and standards, nor finally of normalising procedures. Rather, *The Birth of Biopolitics* lays out a vision of a society that devises and amplifies a new, postdisciplinary dispositif. In the smooth space of 'fluctuating processes', where normativity merely provides a baseline, idiosyncrasies furnish the very data points with which to optimise difference. In other words, minoritarianism and even resistance are not simply 'tolerated' but embraced, since the exercise of individuality and the expression of freedom ironically make the subject more legible.

ECOLOGY AT THE END OF CONTROL?

In the 'Postscript', Deleuze invokes a fictional city, envisioned by Félix Guattari, to describe what technology has in store for us. In this metropolis, each person possesses a card that permits entrance to certain precincts on some days, and at some times, but not on others, all depending on 'a computer that is making sure everyone is in a permissible place, and effecting a universal modulation'.[55] By the standards of what control has become, this metropolis seems vulgar, if not tame. Whereas Guattari's city relies on the premise of an overarching machine, a centralised supercomputer, to which the 'universal modulation' is entrusted, control is increasingly dispersed and disseminated among a variety of users, nodes, towers, satellites and servers. The cellphones that link us to the network and internet, the credit/debit cards which record our purchases, the entry cards and EZ-Pass systems that track our commutes and travels: rather than radiate from a centre, or even from several centres, power is delocalised by the endless skein of overlapping networks. This is not to dismiss the significance of the security state, but to insist that this state relies on the commercialisation, privatisation, consumerisation and consumption of control.

Control society has no need for the older modes of mass confinement because it consists in the offer of unimpeded movement and the unceasing exercise of free choice: our countless decisions (the route home, what we buy for dinner, stray transactions, browsing history, phone calls) produce the reservoir of data whereby, along so many different axes, we are subject to calculation. Take a long-running campaign by Progressive Insurance: the company promises to adjust automobile rates based on one's actual driving habits, and so it offers a device that, placed in a car, records one's driving data and communicates it to a server. The brilliance of the offer consists in incentivising what amounts to mobile surveillance and thereby capitalising data—and this is only one such source of the information companies harvest, analyse and subject to the algorithms of our digital economy. With each decision, each new data point, the grid of intelligibility is refined and difference is optimised. The National Security Agency locates possible threats in vast sweeps of telephone communications on the same basis that Target accurately predicts customers' pregnancies and due dates based on shopping history, or that political organisations micro-target messages for particular donors, or that Cambridge Analytica selected subjects for Russian misinformation campaigns.

In this respect, fittingly, the 'Postscript' concludes by addressing the (subject of) 'young people'—those whose lives are already shaped by the regime of control and, indeed, those future generations for whom *new and improved* versions of control await. 'Many young people have a strange craving to be "motivated," they're always asking for special courses and continuing education', Deleuze remarks, only to add, abruptly, 'it's their job to discover the ends they're made to serve'. The prospect of resistance doesn't inspire a *cri de coeur* but an acknowledgement of our complicity in the perpetuation of control and perhaps a sense of resignation. The 'Postscript' evokes 'new forms of resistance against control societies', but in reading Deleuze's essay alongside Foucault's *Birth of Biopolitics*, I've tried to suggest the constituents of this new regime of power in which we become not only trackable but, also, legible, calculable, pliable, and finally *programmable*. Under the circumstances, what do we mean by ecology? Apart from the rhetorical appropriation of ecology (e.g., the 'ecology of global capitalism'), what place can we claim today for the concept of ecology?

Perhaps we can envision ecology, with respect to control, inasmuch as both concepts actually reflect the invention of cybernetics. On the one hand, as we've seen, Deleuze refers to the cybernetic machines that underwrite control societies, and even Foucault's notion of neoliberal (or control) capitalism proposes a regulative and effectively homeostatic model of pain management as the basis for the entrepreneurial 'subject of interest'.[56] On the other hand, the concept of ecology was, historically, recast along the lines of cybernetics by (among others) Gregory Bateson; in *Steps Toward an Ecology of Mind* and elsewhere, Bateson argues that systems theory qua cybernetics represents a significant contribution to the 'ecology of ideas'[57] inasmuch as it provided the means to think about ecosystems—communal milieus comprised of interdependent components, both organic and inorganic, networked and communicating though a complex web of feedback loops. Given the ambit that Bateson gives the term, then, is control a political ecology? He suggests that we're forced to concede the point: 'There is an ecology of bad ideas, just as there is an ecology of weeds, and it is characteristic of the system that basic error propagates itself', Bateson writes.[58] The problem with this conceptual system, he adds, is that when you 'narrow down your epistemology'—when you determine everything on the basis of interest or, let us say, enterprise—'you chop off consideration of other loops of the loop structure'. Indeed, the singular sense of ecology is always based on an arbitrary cut, beyond which ecologies proliferate, often at different scales or according to different temporalities, but nevertheless linked and looped back into the self-deluded ecology, that is, the ecology that imagines itself as a closed system. If it is to mount a real resistance, ecology can mean nothing less than an open system—a politics formulated on the basis of the earth.

NOTES

1. My own sense of ecology draws in large part from my collaboration with Anne Sauvagnargues. In our current work (tentatively titled *Under Control*), the recourse to ecology represents a means of philosophical resistance to control society and neoliberalism.

2. Not incidentally, Guattari eventually published *The Three Ecologies*.

3. See, for instance, Jane Bennett 2010; Rosi Braidotti 2013; and Erin Manning and Brian Massumi 2014. Needless to say, the question of political ecology can be traced back to earlier texts, such as Latour 1998 and Escobar 1996. Still, an earlier (and more strictly social-scientific) history of political ecology can be traced back to anthropological and environmental literature of the 1970s.

4. The 'Postscript on Control Society' and its ostensible precursor, 'Control and Becoming', were both included in Deleuze 1995.

5. Deleuze 1995, 178.

6. Above all, see Foucault 1995.

7. Deleuze 1995, 177.

8. Ibid., 178.

9. Ibid.

10. Ibid., 182.

11. Ibid., 180.

12. Ibid., 182.

13. Ibid., 178.

14. Ibid., 175.

15. Ibid., 178.

16. Deleuze lifts the distinction between modulation and the mould (or moulding) from Simondon, for whom it lies at the heart of individuation and technical mentality. See Simondon 2007. Also see Sauvagnargues 2012.

17. Deleuze 1995, 178–79.

18. Ibid., 178–79.

19. This concept is most fully developed by Deleuze and Guattari in *A Thousand Plateaus*. See the book's ninth chapter (or plateau) on 'Micropolitics and Segmentarity'.

20. On delocalisation, see Bachelard 1937.

21. See Virilio 2006, 62.

22. Deleuze and Guattari 1987, 386.

23. Ibid, 559, n. 65; italics mine. See Virilio 2006, 150–51.

24. Deleuze 1995, 180.

25. Ibid., 175 and 180.

26. Ibid., 177.

27. Ibid., 180.

28. Ibid.

29. Ibid., 181.

30. Ibid.

31. Ibid.

32. Ibid., 179.

33. Ibid.

34. Ibid.

35. Deleuze 1997, 126, 127.

36. Ibid., 126.

37. Deleuze 1995, 181.

38. Deleuze 1995, 174.
39. Ibid., 175.
40. Ibid., 177.
41. Deleuze 1988, 132.
42. Foucault 2008, 21–22.
43. Ibid.
44. Ibid., 217.
45. Ibid., 243.
46. Ibid., 219.
47. Ibid., 233.
48. The conjunction of machine and earnings stream 'is not a conception of labor power; it is a conception of capital-ability' (Foucault 2008, 225). Foucault adds: 'An earnings stream and not an income, precisely because the machine constituted by the worker's ability is not, as it were, sold from time to time on the labor market against a certain wage' (224). This transformation has only grown more profound in subsequent decades (we rarely speak of wages except to indicate a minimum wage).
49. Ibid., 226.
50. Ibid., 243.
51. Ibid., 226.
52. Ibid., 243.
53. Ibid. Of course, the examples on which Foucault dwells—the penal system, the school system—are increasingly privatized and run for-profit today, but Foucault's point is that, even when this isn't the case, the logic brought to bear upon questions of criminality and education are no less submitted to cost/benefit analyses.
54. Ibid., 259, italics mine.
55. Deleuze 1995, 182.
56. Foucault 2008, 272.
57. Bateson 2000, 467.
58. Ibid., 492.

REFERENCES

Bachelard, G. (1937). *L'expérience de l'espace dans la physique contemporaine.* F. Alcan.
Bateson, G. (2000). *Steps to an Ecology of Mind.* Chicago: University of Chicago Press.
Bennett, J. (2010). *Vibrant Matter: A Political Ecology of Things.* Durham, NC: Duke University Press.
Braidotti, R. (2013). *The Posthuman.* Cambridge: Polity Press.
Deleuze, G. (1988). *Foucault.* Translated by Séan Hand. Minneapolis: University of Minnesota Press.
Deleuze, G. (1997). *Essays Critical and Clinical.* Translated by A. Gerco and D. W. Smith. Minneapolis: University of Minnesota Press.
Deleuze, G. (1995). *Negotiations, 1972–1990.* Translated by Martin Joughin. New York: Columbia University Press.

Deleuze, G., and Guattari, F. (1987). *A Thousand Plateaus: Capitalism and Schizophrenia.* Translated by B. Massumi. Minneapolis: University of Minnesota Press.

Escobar, A. (1996). 'Construction Nature: Elements for a Post-Structuralist Political Ecology'. *Futures* 28 (4): 325–43.

Foucault, M. (1995). *Discipline and Punish: The Birth of the Prison.* Translated by A. Sheridan. New York: Vintage Books.

Foucault, M. (2008). *The Birth of Biopolitics: Lectures at the Collège de France, 1978–1979.* Translated by G, Burchell. New York: Palgrave Macmillan.

Guattari, F. (2008). *The Three Ecologies.* London: Continuum.

Latour, B. (1998). 'To Modernize or to Ecologize? That's the Question'. In *Remaking Reality: Nature at the Millenium,* ed. N. Castree and B. Willems-Braun. London: Routledge.

Manning, E., and B. Massumi. (2014). *Thought in the Act: Passages in the Ecology of Experience.* Minneapolis: University of Minnesota Press.

Sauvagnargues, A. (2012). 'Crystals and Membranes: Individuation and Mentality'. In *Gilbert Simondon: Being and Technology,* eds. A. de Boever, A. Murrayr, J. Roffe and A. Woodward. Edinburgh: Edinburgh University Press.

Simondon, G. (2007). *L'individuation psychique et collective.* Paris: Flammarion.

Virilio, P. (2006). *Speed and Politics.* Translated by Marc Polizzotti. Los Angeles, CA: Semiotext(e).

Chapter 12

Economic Systems and the Problematic Character of Price

Jon Roffe

Economic activity is not easy to isolate. —Georges Bataille[1]

Georges Bataille's celebrated analysis of economics would appear to completely undermine any attempt to isolate a discrete economic system. The central thesis of this analysis is well-known: that a fundamental character of reality is its production of an overabundance, a surplus, of energy. This excess, unable to be consumed entirely within the sphere of utility, must be used up in some other way: through wilful destruction and violence, the excesses of eroticism, unhinged laughter, 'ritual dilapidation',[2] sacrifice— spent without fundamental goal. This general economy of existence, whose paradigmatic example is the expenditure of energy by the sun, is at once sub-human and posthuman, thrumming beneath the apparently stable systems that support the existence of *Anthropos*; and always already pushing beyond them. This excess not only in fact exceeds our capacity to subordinate it to discrete ends, it stands at the threshold of rational thought.

Bataille's analysis presents a challenge that is at once ontological and definitional to any theory of an economic system. The ontological problem consists in the fact cosmic expenditure is not and could never be a closed system. Consequently, every system—and for Bataille every system is finally an economic system, such that no thought will ever be 'considered free of this primary question of economy'[3]—undermines its own unity and self-sufficiency, up to and including the notion of a total system of being itself.

The definitional problem follows; as Bataille laconically remarks, 'Economic activity is not easy to isolate'.[4] On the one hand, even should we be aware of the ontological framework of what we normally call 'the economy', any attempt to enclose this network within a grounded, self-enclosed theory will reproduce the error of the most naïve economism. Even the most perspicuous approach would be an attempt to systematise what is by its very nature unsystematisable, and thereby return it to the restricted economy of the concept, whose supreme instance or animating spirit is, for Bataille, Hegel. If we are not willing to endorse an absolute economy of spirit in which everything is recuperable and will ultimately be recuperated—and Bataille certainly is not—all rational discourse would seem to be reduced to silence, there at the threshold where philosophy would seem to have something decisive to say. In Derrida's fine description, 'It cannot be inscribed in discourse, except by crossing out predicates or by practicing a contradictory superimpression that then exceeds the logic of philosophy'.[5] In sum, any science of the general economy would appear to be impossible.[6]

On the other hand, we must recognise just how far mainstream economic thought falls short of even possessing the terminology to frame Bataille's claim. This is fundamentally because this thought—including Marx's critique of political economy—is governed in its entirety by the notion of use.[7]

> Economic activity, considered as a whole, is conceived in terms of particular operations with limited ends. The mind generalizes by composing the aggregate of these operations. Economic science merely generalizes the isolated situation; it restricts its object to operations carried out with a view to a limited end, that of economic man.[8]

The notion of utility—and the distinction between the useful and useless expenditure that it presupposes, which this analysis illicitly affirms—allows for a definition of the economy solely on this basis. But the object of this theory is as a result a *restricted economy*, an illegitimate selection.

So the question is finally the one framed by Jean Baudrillard: 'Is political economy at bottom only a frustrated avatar of the single great cosmic law of expenditure?'[9] It is this question that I would like to respond to in what follows, from the point of view offered by the philosophy of Gilles Deleuze. To be more precise, I would like to show that Deleuze gives not one but two answers to the question 'what is an economic system?' that appear to evade the force of Bataille's thought. The first of these is furnished by Deleuze in *Difference and Repetition*, and the near-contemporary piece 'How can we recognise structuralism?'[10] The second answer is presented in what is perhaps the locus of Deleuze's thought regarding economics, *Anti-Oedipus*.[11] Both accounts allow for a positive delimitation of economic systems, albeit in quite different terms. Consequently, the third and final part of this chapter will consider one approach to unifying these two sets of insights around the concept of *price*.

FIRST DEFINITION: THE ECONOMIC IS THE SET OF VIRTUAL PROBLEMS TO WHICH THE SOCIAL IS THE CONTINGENT SOLUTION

What is a system? *Difference and Repetition* will tell us that three registers or elements are in play, answering respectively to the names of the *virtual*, *intensity*, and the *actual*. Correlatively, the guiding question is: 'For each type of system, we must ask what pertains to Ideas and what pertains to implication-individuation and explication-differenciation respectively'.[12] That is: for a given system, what are its intensive traits? What are the virtual problems expressed by these traits? And in which extended and qualified elements of reality are these problematic traits actualised?

The Embryonic System

We can begin by considering a paradigmatic example for Deleuze, in *Difference and Repetition* as elsewhere: the embryo, or egg. The embryo is paradigmatic for Deleuze—it 'provides us with a model',[13] he says—because it presents the level of intensive individuation so clearly: it is a dynamic field in which processes move not step by step and from one established part to another, but through differences in kind, constituting dramatic torsions which would not be able to be sustained by the actual living animal. As Deleuze puts it, 'there are "things" that only an embryo can do, movements that it alone can undertake or even withstand'.[14]

Intensive individuation is not, however, lacking in structure. Every individual clearly expresses a certain portion of the virtual, qua differential, problematic register of the Idea. In the case of the embryo, these structural relations are expressed through genes, which—despite what Deleuze sometimes seems to indicate—are not material components, the 'building blocks of life', but differential structures in relation to which certain intensive embryogenetic processes turn around: 'The nucleus and the genes designate only the differentiated matter—in other words, the differential relations which constitute the pre-individual field to be actualised'.[15]

If we look at what the virtual contributes to intensive processes, and even more to the realm of actual things (anatomical parts in the case of the biological system of the embryo), we see that it constitutes a series of relationships between *unoccupied positions*—genetic structure subsists without necessarily coming to bear on a particular biological system. Levi-Strauss' analysis of the structure of kinship systems makes this element particularly clear. He identifies, according to Deleuze, '*kin-emes*, positional units which do not exist independently of the differential relations into which they enter and that determine each other reciprocally. It is in this way that the four relations—brother/sister, husband/wife, father/son, maternal uncle/sister's son—form the simplest structure'.[16] This structure is entirely differential, since no one position persists without all of the others, but it is equally a structure that is prior to any occupancy. Actual people both come to occupy these positions but, more significantly, are constituted by the differential relations that hold between them. Consequently, 'Structuralism cannot be separated from a new transcendental philosophy, in which the sites prevail over whatever occupies them'. Here, as he does throughout the 'How do we recognise structuralism?' essay, Deleuze is describing his own position.[17]

In sum, then: 'Intensities presuppose and express only differential relations; individuals presuppose only Ideas'.[18] Actual, extended and qualified reality is, in turn, the result of the way in which the dynamic expression of differential relations in intensive processes play out. At this stage, Deleuze's account of the embryo can be usefully characterised as a kind of transcendental anatomy: an account of how the extended and qualified parts of the adult tortoise or cat came to be on the basis of differential relations and expressive, intensive processes.[19]

But two further details are now required, due to the fact that the virtual qua structure is not exhaustively described in terms of differential relations. On the one hand, this would be to overlook the interrelated categories of singularity and potentiality. Deleuze will insist that singularities correspond to the differential relations that constitute the virtual as structure. Whereas these relations manifest the reciprocal determination of the empty positions in the structure, the singularities manifest the *potentiality* of a given area of the virtual that completely determines that area. Put another way, the actualisation of the pair 'empty positions' and 'differential relations' would not take place unless there was also an actualisation of a potential—a positive, if neutral, structural 'gap'—in the intensive field. 'It is this, in effect, which determines or unleashes'[20] the terms and relations that otherwise constitute the virtual.

In his more structuralist moments, Deleuze will call this nonlocalised singularity that expresses the potentiality of a pre-individual system the *object = x*, a virtual object which circulates throughout the changes in a system (a developing embryo, the ongoing practice of kinship relations) as the *agent provocateur* in that system—the expression of the potentiality that the virtual structure embodies. The same point holds, as Deleuze says, for the system of sexuality, where the distribution of empty positions at the virtual level is expressed through the object = x of the phallus:

> the phallus appears not as a sexual given or as the empirical determination of one of the sexes. It appears rather as the symbolic organ that founds sexuality *in its entirety* as system or structure, and in relation to which the places occupied

variously by men and women are distributed, as also the series of images and realities.[21]

On the other hand, we need to recognise the active significance of the actual: of the extended and qualified regime of differenciated things. The kinship structures identified by Levi-Strauss do not come to bear on, problematise, or structure the ongoing morphogenesis of the human body, any more than the virtual structure of DNA does in the formation of social relations: a tortoise does not lay salamander eggs. In each case, it is the existing material circumstance that disposes it to being problematised in a determinate fashion.

In other words, the differential structural positions and the object = x that animates their distribution do not function causally. Being composed of ideal elements that polarise reality, the virtual must have an efficacy that is immanent and, as it were, inactive or neutral. Its closest analogue is arguably, and quite significantly, as we will see in a moment, the concept of absent or structural causality advanced by Althusser. According to his famous definition in *Reading Capital*:

> The structure is not an essence *outside* the economic phenomena which comes and alters their aspect, forms and relations ... *on the contrary, it is the very form of the interiority of the structure, as structure, in its effects.* This implies therefore that the effects are not outside the structure, are not a pre-existing object, element or space in which the structure arrives to *imprint its mark*; on the contrary, it implies that the structure is immanent in its effects.[22]

The Economic in Social Systems

Though this passage through embryology, and the various invocations of other systems, may seem to have been unwarranted, the detail with which Deleuze discusses it allows us to isolate the major categories that will be required to define economic systems, about which he says a good deal less. The list of relevant categories has now expanded to four: (1) differential relations, or relations without occupants, (2) potentiality, or the object = x, (3) intensity, or the local field of intensive processes, (4) the actualised or differenciated regime of real, discrete objects in determinate, extrinsic relations.[23]

In both *Difference and Repetition* and 'How do we recognise structuralism?', Deleuze draws heavily on Althusser in accounting for the nature of the economic.[24] The key passage reads as follows:

> 'the economic' is never given properly speaking, but rather designates a differential virtuality to be interpreted, always covered over by its forms of actualisation; a theme or 'problematic' always covered over by its cases of solution. In short, the economic is the social dialectic itself—in other words, the totality

of the problems posed to a given society, or the synthetic and problematising field of that society. In all rigour, there are only economic social problems, even though the solutions may be juridical, political or ideological, and the problems may be expressed in these fields of resolvability.[25]

The first upshot of this text is that there is not, strictly speaking, a theory of economic systems at this point in Deleuze: the economic is rather the *virtual* component of every social system. That is, the economic is composed of differential 'economic relations'[26] between empty structural positions. A second, correlative, point follows: the virtual economic structure is incarnated in various ways, 'in the concrete differenciated labours which characterise a determinate society, in the real relations of that society (juridical, political, ideological) and in the actual terms of those relations (for example, capitalist-wage-labourer)'.[27]

Moving now to the register of *intensive processes*, Deleuze indicates, however briefly, that we must identify this facet of social processes with *freedom*, a 'freedom, which is always hidden among the remains of an old order and the first fruits of a new'.[28] This perhaps surprising term does not refer to a state of nature in the spirit of a Rousseau, but rather to a regime of social dynamics which does not possess any exclusive disjunctions: freedom is not a possession of a liberal subject, but the exercise and activity of the swarming posthuman larval selves that subtends and composes this recognised subjectivity at the intensive level. Just as the embryonic tortoise is capable of undergoing transformations that would destroy the adult individual, so too freedom names the play of social relations 'which cannot be lived within actual societies',[29] being contradictory and mutually exclusive from the point of view of the actual: *both* male *and* female, *both* capitalist *and* wage-labourer, and so on. Or, to invoke Freud, and to anticipate certain elements of the economic analysis of *Anti-Oedipus*, freedom in social systems is akin to the primary organisation of the id, where drives do not contest one with each other despite the fact that, from the point of view of the ego and the reality principle, they cannot all be resolved at once and by the same material means.

The third element is *differenciation*, the manner in which the disposition of existing reality orients it towards certain virtual problems (certain differentially related positions). Here, Deleuze cites Marx's famous claim in the *Contribution to the Critique of Political Economy*: 'mankind always sets itself only such tasks as it can solve'.[30] He then glosses this claim in terms which are now familiar to us. On the one hand, Marx should not be taken to mean that 'problems are only apparent or that they are already solved, but, on the contrary, that the economic conditions of a problem determine or give rise to the manner in which it finds a solution within the framework of the real relations of the society'.[31] But on the other, and 'More precisely, the solution is always that which a society deserves or gives rise to as a consequence of the manner in which, given its real relations, it is able to pose the problems set within it and to it by the differential relations it incarnates'.[32]

A final question: in this account of economic systems, what plays the role of the *object* = *x*, the animating feature of the differential structure that is at play throughout actualisation but is never localisable at any one point? What is it that expresses the potentiality of the virtual structure in the system? In a word, *value*.

> Let us again consider the analyses of Althusser and his collaborators: on the one hand, they show in the economic order how the adventures of the empty square (Value as object = *x*) are marked by the goods, money, the fetish, capital, etc., that characterize the capitalist structure.[33]

On this reading, value does not have an *origin* at the level of use, exchange or labour. It is instead what is actualised in relations of use, exchange and exploitation, but without being identifiable with any of these incarnations, individually or collectively. This rather explains the significant problems that have attended the definition of value in the history of economic thought: simply, value cannot be defined in any one discrete fashion because its apparition and mode of functioning is not that of any one discrete set of criteria, whether objective (classical and Marxist accounts) or subjective (neo-classical accounts).

SECOND DEFINITION: ECONOMIC SYSTEMS ARE THE EXTENDED SOCIO-MATERIAL APPARATUSES FOR THE CIRCULATION OF DEBT

The account of the economic in *Difference and Repetition* locates the ideal register of the virtual at its heart: 'The totality of the system, the unity of the divergent series as such, corresponds to the objectivity of a "problem"'.[34] This is a particularly important criterion given our earlier encounter with Bataille. A system is unified, and therefore exists *as* a discrete system, by virtue of the problem (or problems) to which it corresponds or expresses. Notice that this way of *determining* the nature of a system does not trigger Bataille's critique, since it does not need to invoke *delimitation*.

But when we turn to *Anti-Oedipus*, the other major point of reflection on questions pertaining to economics, there is no such ideal locus to function in this way. Contrary to what Ian Buchanan has suggested, it would be a mistake to think that desiring-production in *Anti-Oedipus* takes place in the register of the virtual.[35] Indeed, the allegations of a Deleuzean materialism find in this book a substantive resource. The overall ontological project of the book is well summarised in the following phrase: 'The problem is one of passing from an intensive energetic order to an extensive system'.[36] That is, *Anti-Oedipus* is broadly interested in how and under what conditions the dynamic reality of intensity comes to be extended and qualified.

Put this way, it becomes clear that while its account of the nature of systems differs from that of *Difference and Repetition*, it is nevertheless closely related. Instead of asking 'what pertains to Ideas and what pertains to implication-individuation and explication-differenciation respectively',[37] the question becomes 'what pertains to the intensive energetic order and what pertains to extension respectively?' Or, to use Deleuze and Guattari's own terminology, the aim is 'to analyse the specific nature of the libidinal investments in the economic and political spheres',[38] where the libido is to be understood as an intensive flux, and the economic and political as registers in extension.

The references to economics in the strict sense that we are interested in here appear predominantly in the third chapter, devoted to Deleuze and Guattari's 'universal history'[39] of the three extant social formations, or kinds of societies. These, the so-called savage, barbarian and civilised formations correspond to pre-State, State and capitalist (para-State) social formations.

In presenting their tripartite history, Deleuze and Guattari make two claims about the economic that seem *prima facie* to contradict each other. The first is that all three formations are economic systems insofar as the major active social category is debt. The second claim is that capitalism alone is an economic system because it is not founded on an 'extra-economic instance that serves as a support',[40] but on money. What we will see, however, by way of a quick survey of Deleuze and Guattari's accounts of the three formations, is that the second claim about capitalism is derivative on the first.[41]

Stone Age Economics[42]

The first, savage pre-State formation is characterised by two poles: an intensive matrix that Deleuze and Guattari associate with filiation, and an extensive matrix that they associate with alliance, that is, political and economic relations.

While it is intensive rather than virtual, intensive filiation operates in a way very close indeed to the vision of kinship in Levi-Strauss' terms that Deleuze presents in his earlier work. It is peopled by what Deleuze and Guattari call 'prepersonal variations in intensity'.[43] These are dynamic, interrelated tendencies that cannot be identified with concrete identities, 'a network of intensive and inclusive disjunctions',[44] which is 'not yet extended, and does not as yet comprise any distinction of persons, nor even a distinction of sexes'.[45]

Intensive filiation provides the quasi-structural element in the formation of particular social formations, but it comes into play by being caught up in the extended, material driftwork of inter-family alliances. Consequently, it is not enough to simply affirm that 'Filiation is administrative and hierarchical, but alliance is political and economic'.[46] We must also recognise that, in the words of the anthropologist Eduardo Viveiros de Castro, the function of alliance 'is precisely to code kinship, to carry out the transition from intensive to extensive kinship'.[47] He adds: 'My sister is my sister because she is someone else's wife. Sisters are not born sisters without at the same time being born as wives; the sister exists in order that there will be a wife'.[48] It is alliance, moreover that guarantees social dynamism: 'A kinship system only appears closed to the extent that it is severed from the political and economic references that keep it open'.[49] Granted, the intensive matrix of filiation is a requisite (just as the virtual is requisite in *Difference and Repetition*), but without alliance relations, there would be no actual families, lineages.

The fundamental form of the economic system in pre-State society is therefore the kinship system itself: it includes both an intensive matrix of positions—'prepersonal variations in intensity'[50]—and an extended and qualified set of lateral alliance relations which determine the realisation of these positions. And, as in *Difference and Repetition*, it is the latter real material circumstances that function to determine which elements of the intensive register come to bear, even though the latter play the formative role in turn. As Deleuze and Guattari write: 'if kinship is dominant in primitive society, it is determined as dominant by economic and political factors. And if filiation expresses what is dominant while being itself determined, alliance expresses what is determinant'.[51]

But in what sense is alliance economic? We need to first recognise that it does not buy into the metaphysics of value that Bataille targets. Indeed, for Deleuze and Guattari, pre-State society is organised to ward off the advent of exchange and therefore value in this problematic sense:

> exchange is known, well known in the primitive socius—but as that which must be exorcised, encasted, severely restricted, so that no corresponding value can develop as an exchange value that would introduce the nightmare of a commodity economy.[52]

This is to say, to cite Pierre Clastres, that pre-State society is both 'society without economy, certainly, but, better yet, a society against economy'.[53]

But the invocation of a specifically commodity-based economy should give us pause in asserting that no economic relations exist at all in pre-State society. We have already seen that 'alliance is political and economic'.[54] This is the case not because there is already some kind of proto-economic regime in the form of primitive barter—a fiction of mainstream economics—but because *debt* is the primary operational term deployed in the play of alliances.

Debt, in this sense—'open, mobile, and finite blocks of debt',[55]—consists in a primary and ineradicable situation of inequality in social relations. One family always already owes another for a previous marriage, the resolution of a difficulty, the overlooking of a slight. The 'coarse and approximate ... statistical dream'[56] of a primary or mythic social homogeneity falsifies this basic social fact. We can see then that the work of alliance is *motivated* by finite, local debts; its practice consists in *realising* the intensive matrix of filiation as concrete new kinship structures (modifying families through marriage); it results in the *displacement* of the debt to a new social location. And so the process goes.

The State Formation and the Advent of Money

Without being able to dwell on the State formation at length here, we can say that it is characterised, in contradistinction with pre-State formation and for our purposes, by three important differential traits.

First, there is a transformation in the nature of debt. Instead of being a finite and mobile social inequality that works as a kind of motor for social change through kinship practices, the debt becomes at once *infinite* and *static*. To the State, we owe everything: 'The infinite creditor and infinite credit have replaced the blocks of mobile and finite debts ... the debt becomes a *debt of existence*, a debt of the existence of the subjects themselves'.[57] In the State formation, debt peonage is a near-pleonasm: to be is to be in debt. In sum, then, 'the blocks of debt become an infinite relation in the form of the tribute'.[58]

This transformation also, ineluctably, comes to bear on the nature of filiation and alliance: 'all the debts of alliance are converted into the infinite debt of the new alliance, and all the extended filiations are subsumed by direct filiation'.[59] But, again for our purposes here, the key point concerns the identity of the intensive matrix to which alliance and extended filiation are related. Deleuze and Guattari's well-known answer is the body of the despot himself: not the material body of the king, high priest or emperor, but the intensive precursor of all social organisation that, in the State formation, appears as its double. It is to the despot that the infinite debt is owed, and it is in the despot that every family finds its patriarch and the principle of its practical organisation. What is allowed at the level of kinship practice is always referred back to the State and its law, and 'the law is the invention of the despot himself: it is the juridical form assumed by the infinite debt'.[60]

But now (the third point) it is, for Deleuze and Guattari, with this second mode of debt that money enters into the picture: money as the material means by which this debt-relation is effected. 'In a word, money—the circulation of money—is the means for rendering the debt infinite'.[61] It does this by facilitating *taxation*. As in pre-State society, debt is the primary social fact. As Clastres puts it, 'To hold power, to impose tribute, is one and the same, and the despot's first act is to proclaim the obligation of payment'.[62] Money, as an institution of material tokens, gives to the State a form in which this debt can be extracted.

This is once more to break with the false and infantile vision of the history of economic relations that opens most textbooks in that subject: first barter between equals, and then the advent of money as a means to reduce the cost of transactions (no need to lug all of my pumpkins to market every week). In one such textbook, Paul Samuelson (continuing a long tradition that runs back to Smith and Ricardo) speaks of money as an 'obscuring layer', writing that 'even in the most advanced industrial economies, if we strip exchange down to its barest essentials and peel off the obscuring layer of money, we find that trade between individuals or nations largely boils down to barter'.[63]

This account presents socioeconomic reality back to front or upside down ('Always the candle in the bovine eye')[64] because it does not identify the common origins of the infinite debt in the form of taxation and the monetary form. As the modern monetary theorist L. Randall Wray puts it, the monetary form first appears 'in the tax levies of the palaces'; money's *raison d'être*, correlatively, is as a means for 'the state to impose a tax debt on its subjects'.[65]

Capitalist Society and the Emergence of the Economic System Properly Speaking

The third social formation is capitalism itself, and the real locus of our concern here, and as Deleuze and Guattari drolly put it, 'Things are very different in capitalism'.[66] We can begin by asking what becomes of debt in the capitalist formation. The shift from pre-State to State society rendered debt infinite and transformed it from being a matter of lateral alliance into a 'vertical' relation of unilateral dependence. In capitalism, both of these traits remain what they were, but the answer to the question 'to whom do we owe everything?' definitively shifts to capitalism as the machine for the production of surplus value, which is to say that we now owe our debt to *money itself*. A new form of debt peonage also appears: the endless extraction of surplus-value due from every 'productive member of society'.

Deleuze and Guattari identify a related change in the nature of money: money is no longer solely operative at the level of sociopolitical domination, but is doubled by a second form of money that appears as the intensive matrix of society itself. This is to say that money appears in a new position, this time on the side of the intensive socius itself—and indeed, not just on that side, but constituting it as such.[67] Formerly the sole province of alliance, money now also appears at the level of filiation: no longer is money just a part of the commodity circuits (M-C-M' and C-M-C'), it now appears in a second place as able to give rise to its own increase (M-M'). As Deleuze and Guattari put it, 'the capitalist machine begins when capital ceases to be a capital of alliance to become a filiative capital. Capital becomes filiative when money begets money, or value a surplus value'.[68] The aberrant and unnatural self-replicating capacity of money loathed by Aristotle now becomes the fundamental feature of the system.[69]

So, for our purposes, the most important feature of capitalism in contradistinction with the State is the advent of a second form of money, and the parallel and complicit operation of the two forms. And it is for this reason that Deleuze and Guattari will insist that capitalism constitutes an economic system in a way that the pre-State and State formations fundamentally do not.[70] Recall once again that in the earlier formations, the economic register is strictly concerned with the sociopolitical circulation of debt, that is, alliance. In these formations, though, the debt was always affiliated with a noneconomic instance: the intensive matrix of the Earth (pre-State society) and the body of the despot (State society). In capitalism, that to which debt is owed is now a fully economic element: money qua filiative capital. The key passage is the following:

> The socius as full body has become directly economic as capital-money; it does not tolerate any other preconditions. What is inscribed or marked is no longer the producers or nonproducers, but the forces and means of production as abstract quantities that become effectively concrete in their becoming related or their conjunction: labor capacity or capital, constant capital or variable capital, capital of filiation or capital of alliance. Capital has taken upon itself the relations of alliance and filiation.[71]

Or, as they put it later, in a more svelte fashion, 'capital itself figures as a directly economic instance, and falls back on production without interposing extraeconomic factors that would be inscribed in the form of a code'.[72]

Notice too that, like the account in *Difference and Repetition*, this theory of economic systems evades the force of Bataille's critique. In fact, it appears to do so in two ways: by defining economic systems in terms of debt—that is, inequality, and difference—and not value, which would be maintained through circulation; and by defining the capitalist economic system as necessarily monetary in character. The appearance is, however, somewhat misleading in the second case. This is because the monetary circuit (or circuits) is not self-enclosed: money must itself be produced, be paid for, and in this way its circulation opens onto the general economy of solar expenditure.[73] In keeping with its general blindness with respect to money, orthodox economic theory treats the cost of money as negligible in accounting for the economy, despite the fact that it is a real site of production and expenditure of its own. The problem is indeed more extreme than one might think—after all, as Deleuze and Guattari exclaim in *A Thousand Plateaus*, 'No one is even capable of predicting the growth in the money supply'.[74]

SUPPLEMENTARY DEFINITION: PRICES ARE
THE PROBLEMS CAPITALISM POSES

These are the two major definitions of economic systems in Deleuze's philosophy. What they share is significant: an emphasis on the centrality of intensity, the distinction between two registers, and a displacement of value relative to its orthodox acceptation in mainstream and Marxist economic thought.

Their differences are also pronounced. As we have noted already, there is an absence of anything resembling the role of the virtual Idea or problematic structure in *Anti-Oedipus*; this would seem to rule out any attempt to bring the two together. Nevertheless, I would like to briefly outline how I think an economic theory of capitalism can be extrapolated from these two sources; it would involve *in nuce* the following four points.[75]

1. We need to first appreciate the significance of price in the capitalist economic system. Unlike value, which is the result of coding—the constitution of a difference in kind—it is price as a vector of pure quantity that is the signature of capitalism. Indeed, and this is a thread running all the way through Deleuze and Guattari's social theory and which aligns them with Bataille, the category of value is not an economic category in the strict sense. Moreover, as Deleuze and Guattari write: 'the code relation is not only indirect, qualitative, and limited; because of these very characteristics, it is also extraeconomic'.

Price, on the other hand, functions as the problematic feature of the capitalist system. Prices appear as 'ambiguous signs', 'nonsigns, or rather nonsignifying signs',[76] which must in each case be 'actualised' as values. That is, lacking any native meaning, their meaning must be established from the points of view of the various parties that engage with them. That is, the essential characteristic of price is that it is a problematic rather than substantive feature of the capitalist economic system.

2. To emphasise the problematic nature of price is not here to identify it as virtual, a conclusion we would have to draw from within the framework of *Difference and Repetition*. To be more precise and in light of the analysis of

the preceding section, price constitutes the extant array of *intensive traits* in relation to which determinate socioeconomic structures come into being and are troubled.

The most useful parallel here is with Deleuze and Guattari's account of kinship systems. While there is a set of pragmatic, economic and political processes that go on at the level of extended filiation and alliances, these presuppose and play out the 'prepersonal variations in intensity'[77] that characterise the intensive matrix of kinship, the primitive socius, or body of the earth. In a word, then, prices are the intensive features of capitalist society, which various sites of political power interpret (that is, *code*) as qualities or values.

3. The immediate obstacle with this formulation is that there is no room for it within the logic of *Anti-Oedipus*. After all, the intensive matrix or socius of capitalism is, for Deleuze and Guattari, money, and specifically credit or finance capital. But can the category of finance capital play the role of a differentiated matrix of intensive traits, as they claim?

There is no question that Suzanne de Brunhoff—the Marxist economist cited by Deleuze and Guattari—is correct in asserting that two monetary circuits exist, corresponding to a general means of payment on the one hand, and the spontaneously produced credit that a bank provides to its debtors on the other. It seems equally true that a dissimulation (or at least commensuration) takes place between the two, and that the bank plays a primary role in this. But neither of these functions seem to be able to be identified with the intensive matrix of capitalism or the capitalist *socius*, as this latter is defined with respect to the other two formations.

Moreover, it would appear that the role of money itself does not substantially change between the State and capitalism. In both cases, it is the material medium for the circulation and payment of debt, even though two circuits (and two creditors, at least numerically distinct) and not just one are now in play. This is just what Marx himself had already asserted: 'Money is already a *representation* of value, and presupposes it. ... Money is merely the form in which the values of commodities appears in the process of circulation'.[78]

What is required is to identify an alternative conception of the intensive matrix of capitalism that allows it to play the role of the capitalist socius. That is, 'It is a question of knowing how, starting from this primary intensity, it will be possible to pass to a system in extension where ... the ambiguous intense signs will cease to be ambiguous and will become positive or negative'.[79] This alternative is the *market*. The market is the intensive matrix of capitalism, which is to say, it is a social surface occupied by the ambiguous, meaningless signs, or 'non-signs', of price, conceived as an intensive, preindividual quantity. It is, in short, the defining posthuman ecology of capitalist society.

4. In this final instance, it is by breaking with the hegemony of value that the force of Bataille's critique is avoided: price, intensive problematic vector in capitalism, exceeds value while being at the same time the positive ground, both of value and of the means by which the qualitative determinations of value are rendered from the ambiguous intensive signs of price. The economic system of our contemporary society can be discretely defined: it is the system composed of the market (intensive matrix of price) and the various realisations of price brought about by the immense array of sociopolitical apparatuses of capture.

NOTES

1. Bataille 1988.
2. Viveiros de Castro 2010, 13.
3. Bataille 1988, 18.
4. Bataille 1988, 20.
5. Derrida 1978, 327.
6. Famous essays by Michel Foucault (1998) and Jacques Derrida (1978) examine the paradoxical position of Bataille's discourse on this point.
7. The implication of Marx in Bataille's critique is made explicit in a classic piece by Jean Baudrillard: 'This critique is a non-Marxist critique, an *aristocratic* critique, because it aims at utility, at economic finality as the axiom of capitalist society. The Marxist critique is only a critique of capital . . . a critique of exchange value, *but an exaltation of use-value*. . . . The Marxist seeks a *good use* of economy'. (Baudrillard 1991, 136).
8. Bataille 1988, 22–23.
9. Baudrillard 1991, 136.
10. There would appear to be a difference in the role played by singularities in the 'Structuralism' essay and *Difference and Repetition* respectively. In the former, they are identified with the empty positions in the structure between which differential relations hold; in the latter, they correspond to the differential relations themselves, appearing as a static form of potentiality, and actualised not by occupants of differential structures but by the qualities that pertain to quantitative diversity. This contrast cannot be discussed here but seems to involve the place given to the imaginary register in the 'Structuralism' essay, one that appears only marginally in *Difference and Repetition* at the end of the fifth chapter.
11. *A Thousand Plateaus* certainly also covers economic topics, but it does so more or less entirely on the grounds already presented in *Anti-Oedipus*.
12. Deleuze 1994, 256.
13. Deleuze 1994, 251.
14. Deleuze 1994, 215.
15. Deleuze 1994, 251.
16. Deleuze 2004, 177.

17. Deleuze 2004, 174.

18. Deleuze 1994, 252.

19. As Henry Somers-Hall (2012, 224–33) has shown, Deleuze's account here draws on and radicalises that of Geoffroy St. Hilaire. Alongside Geoffroy's influence, however, a suite of embryologists are also invoked, as is the work of a lesser-known contemporary of Deleuze, Raymond Ruyer (see Roffe, forthcoming).

20. Deleuze 1994, 221; on this, see also the following remark in the 'Structuralism' essay: 'Every structure presents the following two aspects: a system of differential relations according to which the symbolic elements determine themselves recipro-cally, and a system of singularities corresponding to these relations and tracing the space of the structure' (Deleuze 2004, 177).

21. Deleuze 2004, 187.

22. Althusser 2009, 188–89.

23. A full version of this account would also have to insist upon a fifth point, namely the various ways in which the virtual and intensive conditions of a given state of affairs are covered over or 'cancelled out' in the differentiated product: 'An economic structure never exists in a pure form, but is covered over by the juridical, political and ideological relations in which it is incarnated. One can only *read*, find, retrieve the structures through these effects' (Deleuze 2004, 181). This is one reason why Althusser turns to the notion of symptomatic reading; for Deleuze, it indexes the perennial significance of the Kantian theory of transcendental illusion. The same point also plays a key role in *Anti-Oedipus*. Unfortunately, there is no room for this additional discussion here. For a treatment of the same texts that does incorporate this element, see Roffe 2017.

24. It is, moreover, quite easy to construe Althusser's attempt to develop a non-Hegelian reading of Marx in terms nearly identical to those of Deleuze's own project in *Difference and Repetition*. See, for instance, Morfino (2015), which mentions Deleuze not at all, but whose outline is strikingly consonant with the latter's.

25. Deleuze 1994, 186.

26. Deleuze 2004, 179.

27. Deleuze 1994, 186.

28. Deleuze 1994, 193.

29. Deleuze 1994, 193.

30. Cited at Deleuze 1994, 186.

31. Deleuze 1994, 186.

32. Deleuze 1994, 186.

33. Deleuze 2004, 191, see also 188.

34. Deleuze 1994, 124.

35. Buchanan 2008, 57.

36. Deleuze and Guattari 1983, 155.

37. Deleuze 1994, 256.

38. Deleuze and Guattari 1983, 105.

39. Deleuze and Guattari 1983, 224.

40. Deleuze and Guattari 1983, 247.

41. In his landmark study of *Anti-Oedipus*, Eugene Holland presents the three formations as, respectively, (1) noneconomic and nonpolitical, (2) noneconomic but political, and (3) economic and political (see, notably, the Greimas-inspired diagram and the subsequent discussion [Holland 1999: 59f]). While this appears to contradict what I will say here, Holland uses the category of the economic to designate processes of production. For this reason, I would wager that his analysis and the one that I am sketching here are complementary. Beyond this, Holland's ongoing work on Deleuze and political economy seems to me to be the very cutting edge of work being done in this area, and everything that appears here would need to be considered in its light.

Holland's book also advances the immensely thought-provoking claim that Bataille's work is central to Deleuze and Guattari's construction and in particular that of antiproduction (see Holland 1999: 62). This obviously has bearing on the current discussion, but cannot be directly considered for reasons of space; it will be the object of future work.

42. I take this title from Marshall Sahlin's landmark *Stone Age Economics* (Sahlins 1972).

43. Deleuze and Guattari 1983, 156.

44. Deleuze and Guattari 1983, 154.

45. Deleuze and Guattari 1983, 156.

46. Deleuze and Guattari 1983, 146.

47. Viveiros de Castro 2014, 127.

48. Viveiros de Castro 2014, 132.

49. Deleuze and Guattari 1983, 148.

50. Deleuze and Guattari 1983, 156.

51. Deleuze and Guattari 1983, 147.

52. Deleuze and Guattari 1983, 186.

53. Clastres 2010, 198.

54. Deleuze and Guattari 1983, 146.

55. Deleuze and Guattari 1983, 180.

56. Deleuze 1983, 43.

57. Deleuze and Guattari 1983, 197.

58. Deleuze and Guattari 1983, 194.

59. Deleuze and Guattari 1983, 209.

60. Deleuze and Guattari 1983, 213.

61. Deleuze and Guattari 1983, 197.

62. Clastres 2010, 204.

63. Samuelson 2009, 10.

64. Deleuze 1994, 235.

65. Wray 2000, 2; 6. See also the following remark in *A Thousand Plateaus*: 'As a general rule, it is taxation that monetarizes the economy' (Deleuze and Guattari 1987, 443).

66. Deleuze and Guattari 1983, 337.

67. Christian Kerslake (2015) has analysed in detail Deleuze and Guattari's account of two forms of money, and its transformation between *Anti-Oedipus* and *A Thousand Plateaus*.

68. Deleuze and Guattari 1983, 227. See too Holland 1991, 82–83.

69. '[U]sury is most reasonably hated, because it gets wealth from money itself, rather than just what money was provided for. For money was introduced for the sake of exchange, but interest makes money itself grow bigger. That in fact is how it got its name. For offspring (*tokos*) resemble their parents, and interest (*tokos*) is money that comes from money. And so of all the sorts of crafts of wealth acquisition this one is the most unnatural' (Aristotle 2017, I.11; 1258b1).

70. On this point, see Holland 1991, 58f.

71. Deleuze and Guattari 1983, 263.

72. Deleuze and Guattari 1983, 249.

73. Note that this is distinct from the issue of 'monetisation' that Deleuze and Guattari invoke—'In a certain sense, capitalist economists are not mistaken when they present the economy as being perpetually "in need of monetarization," as if it were always necessary to inject money into the economy from the outside according to a supply and a demand' (Deleuze and Guattari 1983, 239)—which concerns the introduction of purchasing power, not the supplementation of the sum of money qua material token.

Note too that the general economy that the production of money itself opens onto for Bataille is not to be confused with the wasting *of* money, for instance in the 'holiness of the romanticism of gambling' (Bataille 1992, 84).

74. Deleuze and Guattari 1987, 461.

75. In what follows, I present one version of the argument that is elaborated at length in Roffe 2016.

76. Deleuze and Guattari 1983, 241. For a related analysis of price as sign, while relying on Pierce rather than Deleuze, see Muniesa 2007.

77. Deleuze and Guattari 1983, 156.

78. Marx 1972, 161; 162.

79. Deleuze and Guattari, 1983, 156.

REFERENCES

Althusser, L. (2009). 'The Object of *Capital*'. Translated by B. Brewster, in *Reading Capital*, New York: Verso, 77–222.

Aristotle (2017). *Politics*. Translated by C. D. C. Reeve. Indianapolis: Hackett.

Bataille G. (1988). *The Accursed Share, Vol 1. Consumption*. Translated by R. Hurley. New York: Zone Books.

Bataille, G. (1992). *On Nietzsche*. Translated by B. Boone, London: Athlone.

Baudrillard, J. (1991). 'When Bataille Attacked the Metaphysical Principle of Economy'. Translated by S. Kendall, *CTheory* 15(1–3), 135–38.

Buchanan, I. (2008). *Deleuze and Guattari's* Anti-Oedipus: *A Reader's Guide*. London: Bloomsbury.

Clastres, P. (2010). *Archeology of Violence*. Translated by J. Herman. Los Angeles: semiotext(e).

Deleuze, G. (1983). *Nietzsche and Philosophy*. Translated by H. Tomlinson. London: Athlone Press.

Deleuze, G. (1994). *Difference and Repetition*. Translated by P. Patton. New York: Columbia University Press.

Deleuze, G. (2004). 'How Do We Recognise Structuralism?' In *Desert Islands and Other Texts*, ed. D. Lapoujade. Translated by M. Taormina. New York: semiotext(e), 170–92.

Deleuze, G., and Guattari, F. (1983). *Anti-Oedipus*. Translated by R. Hurley, M. Seem and H. R. Lane. Minneapolis: University of Minnesota Press.

Deleuze, G., and Guattari, F. (1987). *A Thousand Plateaus: Capitalism and Schizophrenia*. Translated by B. Massumi. Minneapolis: University of Minnesota Press.

Derrida, J. (1978). 'From a Restricted to a General Economy: A Hegelianism without Reserve'. In *Writing and Difference*. Translated by A. Bass. London: Routledge, 317–50.

Foucault, M. (1998). 'A Preface to Transgression'. In *Aesthetics, Methodology and Epistemology*, ed. J. Faubion. Translated by R. Hurley. New York: The New Press, 1998, 69–87.

Holland, E. (1991). 'Deterritorializing "Deterritorialization": From the "Anti-Oedipus" to "A Thousand Plateaus"'. *SubStance* 20(3), 58f.

Holland, E. (1999). *Deleuze and Guattari's* Anti-Oedipus: *Introduction to Schizoanalysis*. New York: Routledge.

Kerslake, C. (2015). 'Marxism and Money in Deleuze and Guattari's *Capitalism and Schizophrenia*: On the Conflict between the Theories of Suzanne de Brunhoff and Bernard Schmitt'. *Parrhesia* 22, 38–78.

Marx, K. (1972). *Theories of Surplus Value*, Part 3. London: Lawrence and Wishart.

Morfino, V. (2015). 'The Concept of Structural Causality in Althusser'. *Crisis and Critique* 2(2), 87–107.

Muniesa, F. (2007). 'Market Technologies and the Pragmatics of Prices'. *Economy and Society* 36(3), 377–95.

Roffe, J. (2016). *Abstract Market Theory*. Basingstoke: Palgrave.

Roffe, J. (2017). 'Deleuze's Concept of Quasi-Cause'. *Deleuze Studies* 11(2), 278–94.

Roffe, J. (forthcoming). 'The Egg: Deleuze between Darwin and Ruyer', in *Deleuze and Evolutionary Theory*, ed. M. Bennett and T. Posteraro. Edinburgh: Edinburgh University Press.

Sahlins, M. (1972). *Stone Age Economics*. Chicago: Aldine Atherton.

Samuelson, P. (2009). *Economics*, 19th ed. New York: McGraw-Hill.

Somers-Hall, H. (2012). *Hegel, Deleuze and the Critique of Representation*. Albany: State University of New York Press.

Wray, L. R. (2000). 'Modern Money'. In *What Is Money?* ed. J. Smithin, New York: Routledge, chapter 3 (np).

Viveiros de Castro, E. (2010). 'The Untimely Again'. In *Archeology of Violence*, P. Clastres, ed. Translated by J. Herman. Los Angeles: semiotext(e), 9–52.

Viveiros de Castro, E. (2014). *Cannibal Metaphysics*. Translated and edited by P. Skafish. Minneapolis: Univocal.

Chapter 13

A Modification in the Subject of Right

Deleuze, Jurisprudence and the Diagram of Bees in Roman Law

Edward Mussawir

A conception of law as founded on jurisprudence can do without any 'subject' of rights. —Gilles Deleuze[1]

I would like to explore in this article, one perhaps underacknowledged aspect to the convergence of interests that in recent times have come under the banners of 'antihumanism' and 'nonanthropocentrism'. I am thinking simply of the activity of *jurisprudence*. A lot of debate concerning the position of nonhuman animals with regard to law today still centres only on a single category: that of the subject of rights. It is here, we are led to believe by moral philosophers and the proponents of animal rights for instance, that we find an unshakable prejudice at the heart of law. Being blind up to now to the needs and capacities and indeed rights of various classes of nonhuman beings, we are supposed to have cast our jurisprudential construct of the 'subject' too narrowly. The human has been privileged over the animal, the transactional has been privileged over the ecological, the artificial over the natural, and so on. And it is as if all that stood in the way of rectifying the plight that animals—representatives of an objectified, commodified and overall mistreated natural world—would experience under the laws of modern liberal democracies, was the weight of this monumental juridical edifice of the 'subject': a figure which is treated no longer as a mere abstraction of legal science which it might have remained, but as a category which is at once moral and metaphysical, supposedly separating, at the heart of our legal culture, all of those who 'count' for law from those who don't.

The concept of legal subjectivity, however, far from being a quality foreign to or denied to nonhumans animals, in fact finds itself distinctly shaped by the attempts to include them within particular legal institutional forms. It is not a question here necessarily of the problematic philosophical construct that has tended to tie the category of the 'subject of rights' to an image of 'man'. We hardly need any further proof of how the centrism of the human, white, male, meat-eating subject of law operates to exclude, to oppress, to marginalise, to alienate its 'others'. Yet when one takes on the daunting task today of decentring the image of the human from the prevailing imagination of law—for instance in the name of animal rights or ecological justice—one often only discovers a rampant inflation to the currency of this category of the 'subject', as though one could increasingly no longer imagine any value under the law for a being other than through holding the position of a subject or in the possibility of being 'granted' or having 'recognised' some form of legal subjectivity. It hardly matters whether legal rights are attributed by virtue of any likeness to the 'image of man'. The category of the subject itself becomes the abstract form under which every call for a previously unrecognised capacity to hold rights in general must be made. In this way, a humanist ideology of law redoubles itself by the same force that animals, nature and so on come to claim the position of subjects. A whole humanist vocabulary of inalienable freedoms, rights of nature, inherent dignity of persons before the law and so forth finds itself rediscovered in relation to these newly recognised subjects. All the while, the distinct jurisprudential meaning of animals, arising from finite juridical problems and relations, are sidelined in favour of a new politico-metaphysical redemption: a wholesale liberation of nonhuman animals from the category of legal 'things' to which they have been unfairly consigned.

What I would like to suggest in this chapter is that we might find a way to counter some of the difficulties faced by the movements of antihumanism and nonanthropocentrism in law today through the detour of certain technical jurisprudential questions. As Gilles Deleuze has pointed out, not only is it possible to observe—in the practice of jurisprudence and case law—a conception of law that can do without any totalising 'subject' of rights, but we can also develop a philosophy of the subject that 'presents a conception of law founded on jurisprudence'.[2] We don't often pay enough attention in this sense to the cases, to the sets of jurisprudential problems, the procedural or institutional inventions, the subtleties of interpretation in which particular forms of legal subjectivity are embedded. But we also don't often pay enough attention to the operations in legal thought that secure for nonhuman animals a meaning and an activity that is in fact far more lively and even subversive than the ordinary circumstance of their having the status either of 'subject' or 'object'. If legal thought, as Deleuze suggests, is not about 'recognising' rights but 'inventing' them: then—rather than simply polemicising our discourse of rights in relation to nonhuman animals—we can begin to observe some of the ways in which nonhuman animals, in a technical sense, provide the outline for the invention and creation of law.

DELEUZIAN JURISPRUDENCE, THE ROMAN JURISTS AND THE QUESTION OF SOME BEES

The particular story that I would like to tell in this chapter is one that concerns the place of some *bees* in a fragment of Roman civil law: a statement concerning the interpretation of an ancient statute on reparation for unlawful damage—the *lex Aquilia* (c. 287 BCE)—by the classical jurist Ulpian.[3] The story is interesting because of the way the kind of distortion of 'facts' and 'rules' that attends the juristic expression in question comes forth and the unusual centrality of the bees to the technical operation that the jurist performs on his material. If it is possible to acknowledge the centrality that a type of animal can take as a technical element in the thought of the jurist, then we can begin to steer a clearer path through the difficulties posed by the calls to take the position of animals seriously in jurisprudence and more generally for the development of a nonanthropocentrism in law. My hypothesis here is that the bees leave an important trace of the creativity of jurisprudence in Roman law: a jurisprudence understood as Deleuze sees it, more as the *thought* of law, the immanent invention of right, than the abstract philosophical *representation* of it.

The topic of a 'Deleuzian jurisprudence' has been addressed in far more detail elsewhere.[4] Here, I am concerned with the possibility of demonstrating something of this activity of Deleuzian jurisprudence through a close analysis of the *Digest* fragment in question. It is helpful to make some remarks first of all about the affinity that Deleuze's thought on law—his emphasis on the 'case' and what he calls jurisprudence's emphasis on 'emissions of singularities and functions of extension'[5]—may have with the method and activity of the classical Roman jurists. It is common to think of jurisprudence today as a philosophically subsumptive and schematic activity. It is supposed to bring us from objective facts to legal principles; from concrete cases to general rules and vice versa. We tend to applaud it when it takes us from the solutions in individual cases to the principles and concepts that logically apply by analogy beyond them, or alternatively from what is posited as general, universal, *a priori*, to the particular instances that instead confirm it by way of example of the universality of what is given. In this way, practices of law—adjudication, legislation and so on—are supposed to claim the conceptual advantage of theory, abstraction, systematisation; while philosophy (moral, political and so on) gains the sense of an 'applied' science. What is striking however about Deleuze's remarks on law is that he invites us to consider an activity and a method of jurisprudence which is, I would say, a critique of this whole conception.

For Deleuze, a conception of law based on 'jurisprudence' is a pure *case-law*, not so much in the sense of a system of case-based precedent like in the adjudicative analogical model of the common law, but in terms of the creative construction and association of institutions forged out of concrete situations, more akin I would suggest to Roman juristic craft. In *Empiricism and Subjectivity: An Essay on Hume's Theory of Human Nature*, questions in the style of Roman casuistry become a lynchpin to Deleuze's reading of the Scottish philosopher and his attempt to rescue both philosophy and law from the pretensions of a naturalistic or dogmatic image. The determination of rules (of possession, etc.) in Hume's work always have to be 'corrected', Deleuze suggests, by 'a casuistics and a theory of the accidental'.[6] Cases in this sense are not just a collection of material 'facts' or contingent 'circumstances' over which claims are made in the name of law, the determination of which form lasting principles. They constitute a set of differences that activate the law on the terrain of its fundamental creativity, and through which alone it is possible to 'think' it. David Saunders remarks on the way in which Deleuze inverts the usual subordination 'of legal case to philosophical principle',[7] allowing the case to serve as the occasion for the immanent invention of principles rather than as the occasion for the mere application of them. We don't appeal to pre-existing principles, to pre-existing rights: we find ourselves in cases, situations. This, for Deleuze, is *life*.[8] And to speak of jurisprudence is to speak of the mode of invention, the artifices of the law, this 'topical' rather than 'axiomatic' practice of law,[9] that goes along with life. It doesn't subsume cases under principles. It starts, we could say, as the classical Roman jurists do, from the particular case (imagined or real) and ventures to go further toward its extreme singularity, its precise uniqueness for the thought of law. It 'dismisses the universal in favour of emissions of singularities'.[10] It embeds the principles in the vicinity of an increasingly unique set of circumstances and an increasingly particular, minor, subtle and technical refinement.

If we can see the Roman jurists through these Deleuzian eyes—we see the whole object of their art and the whole effort of the intellectual craft as being to continually refine, not the principles, but the cases: cases in which the facts are remodelled, the rules stretched to their institutional limits; a method that does not seek to describe or represent the law but to *isolate* it in its cases; to extract the peculiar juridical and institutional shape of things like a chemist isolates compounds from more complex composites.[11] With a kind of sober, antihumanitarian creativity the Roman jurists meticulously refrain from becoming moralists as much as legislators: not because, like modern formalists, they want to preserve the properly 'interpretive' vocation of the judge, but because—finding laws already bound up in the traditions of their ancestors—they delight in testing them and in seeing them re-emerge out of the depth of their science of 'cases'.

In the following analysis, I hope to show one of the ways that a jurisprudence of this sort allows a more sensitive appreciation for the action and autonomy that nonhuman animals can acquire with respect to law. We often think of an animal simply as part of a nature beyond law, or as a contingent external circumstance with no essential relation to the essence or grammar of legal formulation. But if it is possible—as the following analysis tries to make out—to encounter the animal as inseparable from a highly crafted case to which the thought of law is tied, it is also possible to view the legal action and autonomy of animals in a new light. The animal is more than a 'subject of right' or a 'metaphor' for the subjected place that nature occupies in relation to the law. In the hands of the Roman jurist, it becomes instead an artifice, a 'becoming' of thought, a diagram of right, a technical modification through which the law is singularly invented, tested, extended. In this way the intelligence of law is found less in the question of reaching toward a more inclusive, a more transcendent, more cosmological ethical view of the natural world and of the legal 'subject'. It is first of all a question of how the jurist, as a thinker, recruits an animal to serve in the inventive construction of law, in what we could call, along with Deleuze, certain 'singularities' or 'cases for jurisprudence'.[12] Even if this casuistry does not leave either the rule or the facts of the case unaltered, and even if the animal may appear with barely any resemblance to the image it ordinarily takes on in our social or cultural imaginary, we can at least observe the earnestness of the encounter that this animal has with the necessity of the thought of law that both bears as well as modifies it.

IF, WHEN MY BEES HAD FLOWN TO YOURS, YOU BURN THEM . . .

'If, when my bees had flown to yours, you burn them up, Celsus says that an action on the *lex Aquilia* lies'.[13]

Here is the fragment in which the classical Roman jurist Ulpian relates the opinion of Celsus on the application of the third chapter of the *lex Aquilia*, an ancient Roman plebiscite imposing reparation for certain kinds of unlawful harm, to the situation of the burning of some bees. The particular chapter of the *lex Aquilia* in question here deals with harm done to property (other than the killing of slaves and cattle) and imposed liability on whoever had unlawfully 'burned, broken or spoiled'[14] the property of another. The fragment is included in Justinian's Digest among a series of case-scenarios in which Ulpian explores the meaning of various parts of this statute.

Among these cases, the statement in relation to the bees stands out as being particularly unusual. What do the formulations 'my bees', 'to yours' and 'you burn them' mean exactly? The reference to any actual or likely state of affairs seems especially tenuous or opaque. Is Ulpian speaking of one to two bees or a whole swarm? Does 'to yours' refer to the bees joining and merging with your own swarm or hive of bees? Or does it just mean flying onto your property or settling into your trees? What is the precise context and motive for 'burning' the bees? If there is a particular or typical case intended by this example, we find it to be unusually difficult to envisage. Bees, we might be told by naturalists, don't typically fly off and join another swarm on their own accord. But if all that is meant by the statement is that the bees flew off from one person's property and onto a neighbour's property, then why—putting possible corruptions of the text aside—would the writer not bother to waste a word to specify that fact? And at the end of the day, if the intended case is so truncated and so poorly defined, what is the point of including it within a commentary on the extent of the application of the *lex Aquilia*? Can we dismiss it simply as a certain awkward phrasing of the point by the jurist? Can we just put it down to a poor understanding on the lawyer's part of the typical behaviours of bees and the general troubles and concerns of beekeepers?

No. To understand the position of the bees in this fragment, it is necessary to understand something of the jurisprudential context and in particular the juristic art in which they come to take on an activity, a role and a function. We can be easily forgiven for thinking that the facts here are simply poorly described. We can be forgiven for assuming that what the jurist should have been aiming to do is to elucidate by way of clear examples, the structure of the general rule of liability under the statute. The cases that it refers to, in this sense, should be commodious to the social purpose that the law is meant to serve. It should set out examples that are commonly encountered in practice and in which the rule can be distinctly understood and easily brought to mind. The case should, in short, reflect a set of facts, a social reality that the law aims to govern. And if there is obscurity in the way the facts of this case are described, it can only be the result of a missing piece, an error, a corruption of the text, or perhaps a deficiency in the skills of communication.

Now, such an interpretation leaves us in an unhelpful position for trying to think the position of the animal in law as anything other than a passive bystander. The animal may be included under one category here, excluded from another category there—all the while reduced essentially to a natural state of affairs that the law encounters as an external reality, an object of factual representation. And yet Ulpian's text about the bees can appear to us very differently when what we expect to see in it is not necessarily the laying down of a general rule and its application or explanation in a factual example, but rather the pursuing of a kind of scientific method of experimentation: a form of 'testing' the rule by bringing it into the vicinity of a tightly crafted case. In that case, the distortion that we find in the facts as described, can be the evidence not simply of some state of error or disrepair, but of a *thought* that persists on the page of law and which resists being reduced to the representation of some rule. When it comes to Roman jurisprudence—a work which amounts to little if not to an extreme care or exactness taken with the verbal forms and syntax of legal action—there is good reason to believe that the unusual form of words used by the jurist cannot be put down to any 'muddling' or 'mincing' of the terms. There is reason instead, at least at first, to treat things at face value and assume that when the legal literature gives us a case and an expression that appears distorted or not easy to locate in any objective reality, this may in fact be the *product* of—rather than a departure from—the precision required by this procedural literacy of the jurist. And when it's precisely an animal that accompanies this factual distortion, we can afford to read this not so much as an objectification of animal life, and of the natural world, but as a unique opportunity to recover something of the independence that this animal acquires and maintains in the thought and technique of law.

THE APIAN SHAPE OF POSSESSION

In what sense then are the words used in this fragment *exacting*? And what place do the bees play in that exactness? It is helpful to first outline a few of the problems that the animal has come to be associated with in Roman law. What we should have in mind here is not just the common understanding of the animal, either as nature or as metaphor, but a certain technical legal arrangement: a *juridical* concept that the jurist attempts to refine with all the tools at his disposal. Deleuze and Guattari emphasise that the animal is less a 'being' than a 'becoming' affecting a certain field. They refer in this way to the banality of 'imitating' animals but to the profoundness of certain affects and relations that constitute the becoming-animal of something or someone: cinema, a language, an author, a patient and so forth. Becoming-animal is not, as they say, 'content to proceed by resemblance' but constitutes a 'diagram, a problem'[15] outside any representation, imitation, metaphor, analogy. Far from bringing us back to the centrality of 'man', the register of Roman casuistry only confirms this diagrammatic conception of the animal more strongly. When bees are evoked in the passage by Ulpian, as we will see, it is neither to make them stand in for something else, nor to abandon the question of law to some natural or factual state of affairs. It is neither to treat them as subject or as object but to evoke, in a certain way, the distinct set of juridical relations already bound up with bees.

In the Roman juridical literature, like in many modern systems, as E. J. Cohn acknowledges, bees tend to 'furnish lawyers with attractive little problems'.[16] In particular they help trace the boundaries between various forms of ownership and possession. There is an extended passage, from which our fragment from Ulpian on the *lex Aquilia* appears to be an abbreviation, recorded in *Collatio* 12.7.10, in which explicit mention is made of the opposing juristic viewpoints on the legal nature of the bees: a distinction between the views of Proculus and Celsus. The bees seem here to animate the interpretive energies of the classical jurists. Proculus for instance thought that an action under the *lex Aquilia* did not lie because there was no property in fleeing bees. Classified as wild rather than domesticated animals, once these bees flew away from one's possession, they could be freely acquired and dealt with by others. Celsus, as the fragment confirms, thought on the contrary that the action did lie since bees were to be considered apparently not like other wild animals but like 'fruits'[17] and also, like doves, to have a mind to return (*animus revertendi*).

This discussion accords with other appearances of bees in the juridical texts where they come to test the contours of certain kinds of acquisition or occupation of property. Bees serve to qualify, in certain ways, the modes by which one is said to acquire or lose possession and ownership in things that are first considered no one's, *res nullius*. In *book 2* of Gaius's *Common Matters or Golden Things*,[18] for instance, the example of bees is used to navigate the boundary between two theories of acquisitive prescription: two theories on the question of when an individual is deemed to have acquired possession (of an animal) for the purpose of having an action against those who would interfere with that possession. First, the theory in which a wild animal will be considered 'ours' if it has been wounded to the point that it can be captured, so long as we are still in pursuit of it (the view favoured by Trebatius). Second, the view favoured by the majority of interpreters, according to Gaius, in which an actual capture is required in order to have a better title than any other would-be acquirer. Gaius notes then—somewhat obliquely in relation to this initial debate—that for bees which are treated as wild by nature, when 'a swarm flies away from our hive' it will still be considered 'ours so long as we have it in sight and its recovery is not difficult; otherwise, it is open to the first taker'.

Bees therefore evoke the idea of a form of possession that is not absolute. We have, with the bee, an animal that is always liable to return to nature, to regain its natural liberty and be claimed by the 'first taker', but also one which extends in a certain way beyond boundaries by the tendency of bees to return: a form of possession which can be maintained in a sort of pursuit in which other claims to the animal can be temporarily held at bay, and a shape of ownership that extends no further than this elastic, roaming possession. Yan Thomas explains the remarkable way in which the Roman jurists were capable in this area of filing a whole philosophical discourse on 'nature' and 'natural right' back within the narrow institutional frame of their civil law—a point also alluded to by Schulz when he explains that the *ius naturale* in classical Roman jurisprudence 'has nothing to do with legal philosophy, but is a thoroughly professional construction'.[19] They treated the so-called natural liberty that the wild animal is supposed to regain by fleeing capture as itself a neat but purely juristic outline for qualifying an institutional arrangement: namely the species of possession known as *pro suo* (an acquisition that is not derived from another) which could, along with a number of other modes of acquisition such as gift, bequest or dowry, accrue with the passage of time into a full ownership. Nature is not an external referent here. It doesn't provide a 'vague reference to the idea that institutions have to conform to an order that transcends them', as Thomas suggests.[20] It is only, like with Deleuze's reading of Hume, an association and a reflection of ideas put in the service of conventions, institutions: as a means of forging them and extending them beyond their immediate terrains.[21]

We get a clearer view of the significance of the bees in Ulpian's passage then when we acknowledge the originality to the institutional meaning and technical work that the jurist reserves for them. It is not necessarily anything natural to the bee that makes it suitable for the juristic construction in question. Rather the jurist carves out a highly original meaning for nature in the guise of some bees: its meaning as *institution*. From a species of animal the jurist makes a species of possession. Thus, when Ulpian refers to the example of bees (built upon the discussion of Celsus and Proculus) in the context of the *lex Aquilia*, the choice of animal is not random. What is important is that enough of this juridical and casuistic figure of the animal can be borrowed from the law concerning the acquisition of ownership for the purposes of articulating the interpretive limits of the *lex Aquilia*. But what is equally important is that this analysis at the same time is able to sufficiently distinguish itself from the other (possessory) context. It has to somehow avoid preempting or subsuming the whole jurisprudence on acquisitive prescription within the narrow point of statutory interpretation that the discussion of the *lex Aquilia* concerns. What is the jurist to make of an ambiguity over whether one still has any relevant form of possession or ownership over some bees that have flown away for the purposes of a law that requires payment to owners of property against those who, in the words of the plebiscite itself, have done 'damage by unlawfully burning, breaking or spoiling' (. . . *damnum faxit, quod usserit fregerit ruperit iniuria*)?[22] The answer is evidently not to step outside the institutional realm of law to consider such aspects as the natural propensity of bees, the economic implications for beekeepers and so on. Nor is it—one should add—to refer on the other hand the whole question of what can be considered 'property' subject to the protection in the *lex Aquilia* back to some naturalistic philosophy drawn in reverse from the casuistry of acquisitive prescription. The challenge is rather to meet the ambiguity one finds in the immediate institutional field with an adequate juridical abstraction drawn from another.

BURNED BEES: A PROCEDURAL ESTIMATION OF VALUE

It is worth mentioning at this point the interpretation of Ulpian's fragment that is offered by Bruce W. Frier in his two essays 'Bees and Lawyers' and 'Why Did the Jurists Change Roman Law? Bees and Lawyers Revisited'.[23] Frier puts Celsus's approach to the problem, which he champions, down to an astute understanding of the social value of beekeeping on the part of the jurist and a flexibility with respect to the function of the rules, maintaining that it matters less in the context of this problem whether the bees ' "belong" (in one sense or another) to their owner' than the fact that '*their owner is a beekeeper, and beekeeping is a desirable and productive activity*'.[24] Frier's point of view is built on a hypothesis about the nature of legal change and the flexibility of legal casuistry,[25] however it is also premised on certain assumptions about the attribution of values to legal things. From his perspective, what the fragment on the bees reveals primarily is that the Roman jurists, far from being caught in their own thoroughly professional and artistic insularity, were in fact influenced to a large degree by the broader social and economic contexts of their time. What the fragment shows us, in Frier's view, is the way the law evolves and establishes new principles to meet the needs of its society and changing circumstances. Even the Roman jurists, who are normally characterised by steadfastness in the independence of their craft, the strictness with which they held to their science and to the worth of their jurisprudence as an art for its own sake, can be depicted here by Frier as being directed, in the same way that any good common lawyer ultimately is, by judicious policy choices adopted in the penumbra of positive rules. Not even the pure artistic rigour of the Roman jurist can insulate itself from the need for law, at the end of the day, to be 'actually socially adequate for its time and place'.[26]

Now, this view ascribes both a naturalistic and an economic value to the bees, in the name of a contextual reading of the law, that is in fact found nowhere explicitly in the juristic writing itself. Frier's view is a straightforward one. Beekeeping was central to Roman economy. Bees have to fly free to some extent so that they become 'productive' animals for their owners. The law therefore finds good reason to treat them as a category of their own in order, unlike other wild animals, to 'protect them in their flight'.[27] It is a view that places significant stock in the universality of values tied to a determinate human economy in bees, but it is also one that potentially ignores the distinct independence that the animal can acquire in a *jurisprudence* that in fact has little interest in things as objects of nature, as economic means of production or as things-in-themselves. We should be wary in other words of dismissing too quickly the characteristic aversion that the jurists appear to show toward rationalities based merely in economic and public policy concerns. And we should be wary too of being over-confident in our own estimation of 'values' as to put more weight in the notion of beekeeping as a productive human activity, than to consider the detailed and detached technical reflection that the jurists themselves produced on as focused and as complex a procedural terrain as how value and loss were to be assessed under the *lex Aquilia*.[28]

Consider for a moment the much debated element of the third chapter of the law which provides for reparation according to the measure of 'how much the thing will be in the nearest 30 days' (*quanti ea res erit in diebus triginta proximis*). What did this mean? Did it mean the plaintiff could recover, in a similar way to the first chapter of the *lex*, the highest value that the damaged object had in the thirty days prior to the harm? Or did it mean the value of the loss as much as had accrued within thirty days following the harm? The modern interpretations of this provision are famously split. David Daube argued that it can't be the former since then the law would find no way to distinguish between minor injury to a thing and complete destruction of it.[29] Others thought that it did refer to the (highest) value that the damaged thing had in the thirty days preceding the damage, but found the need to qualify it with the suggestion that the law only covered damage to a thing that was either absolute or very serious, so that the value of such damage largely approximated the entire value of the thing itself.[30]

Even here, the debates are set on a rather confusing path, however, when they seek to interpret the law through methods of evaluation of 'things' divorced from the procedure and casuistry that takes hold of them. There is a tendency to see law as secondary to values tied somehow to the metaphysics of objects, rather than as creative of the very values that inhere in legal 'things'. It is true for instance that the Roman jurists did not think of a *res*, 'thing', as separate from the procedure in which it was held as an object of contestation. The term *res*, as Yan Thomas has also pointed out, is at once a 'thing' as well as a 'contested matter': the *value it represents in a proceedings*.[31] It is not the thing itself that must be valued then (a comparison of what it was worth 'before' and 'after' it was damaged). The thing is itself the identity in its value, an estimation: what this wrong as alleged represents in the estimation of the judge. The reference to thirty days seems likely to simply be a proximity to the wrong to which the imaginary time of reckoning is directed. When the jurist Paul remarks rhetorically for instance in Digest 9.2.24 (*Edict*, book 22): 'what wound are we to value, or to what time shall we reckon back?' in reference to the situation where a defendant had confessed under the *lex Aquilia* to wounding a slave but where the slave hadn't actually been wounded, he's not necessarily indicating that the thirty days are to be reckoned from the wrong backwards in time, but simply referring to the necessity for a judge to be able to put himself at an approximate point in time in order to estimate the value (of the thing, the injury) in question. The *res* means this thing the law understands as arising from having been 'burnt, broken, spoiled' as well as, at the same time, the estimate of the value this thing will be in the proceedings. In Paul's example, it doesn't mean the slave in him- or herself (who exists as a being and who could be valued as property), but the *wound* (which doesn't exist and therefore can't be valued at all). Through this contemporary debate, we can see just how far the reliance upon modern economic and metaphysical paradigms or contexts can tend to force and distort rather than explain the meaning of the legal text, and also just how far the technical jurisprudential register of *res*—far from reducing the bees to the status of commodity—remarkably insulates them from a commonplace naturalistic or liberal-economic view of their value. The casuistic thinking of Roman law refuses to accede to any objective, let alone social or economic, value of a thing derived from outside the legal procedure in which it is forged and temporarily held.

SEVERAL OR A SWARM? BEES AS A
DIAGRAM OF JURISPRUDENCE

Let's return then to the words of Ulpian's fragment and try to discern something of the nonanthropocentric function that the bees serve in the thought of the jurist. Faced with the unusualness of the expression in the fragment, Bruce W. Frier's approach is to try to fill in some missing pieces. He has a typical case in mind: a beekeeper's bees have flown off onto the property of his neighbour in search of pollen. The neighbour destroys them. Based on that typical case, it becomes possible to alleviate the ambiguity in Ulpian's bees which are flying simply from mine to yours. The first thing that has gone unstated, from Frier's viewpoint, is that the said bees must not have been, 'at least at the first instance', a full swarm but just one or two individual bees.[32] Celsus could scarcely have constructed a legal exception out of the bees in question on the basis, had they been a full swarm, of their inclination (like doves) to return, since—as he must have known—swarming bees are not accustomed to return but swarm precisely in order to find and establish a new colony.[33] What this means for Frier is that 'to yours' does not indicate some mixing of bee swarms (mine and yours).[34] Rather he suggests that a word has gone missing. The bees, the text should read, are flying to your *trees* or to your *property*. In Frier's view, it is necessary to reinsert these missing pieces in order to make the formulation of the rule more cogent and the text more readable.[35] The 'case' is something that the jurist is concerned to address at the level of social needs, more than as a tool sharpened precisely for pursuing a type of science.

It is possible however that what we are missing is not necessarily the elements of a mis-transcribed or corrupted text, but the key to a conception of jurisprudence—a creative practice of the law—that animates the jurist and renders the peculiar truncated formulation that we find in the text into a more necessary mode of expression. It may be possible that our focus should be placed not just on what would make the statement of the principle more logical, the factual situation referred to more typical or plausible, the rule contained in it more clear and certain. We can afford, along with Deleuze, to be sceptical of a 'dogmatic image of thought' that has tethered the act of thinking to a goodwill, a common-sense and good-sense on the part of the thinker, rather than to the radical singularity of an encounter.[36] We should be wary too of reading the work of the jurists as pursuing some unstated humanistic purpose: a form of social engineering aiming at valid human ends and fulfilling its conception of the Good through policy choices. Instead, we can focus on what must or must not be stated from a technical juridical point of view in order for the analysis to situate itself within certain precise jurisdictional limits. If, in the work of the jurist, the description of the facts of the case appear to have undergone some kind of distortion, to be wrought from some sort of misshapen mould, then we should avoid trying to simply beat it back into shape.[37] We should rather use that distortion as a lens through which to account for law as a technical medium that—despite the limitations in the resources that language provides it—acts in a definite way upon the world and maintains itself at a distance from any common-sense 'reality'.

To be more precise, the formulation 'my bees have flown to yours', may make better sense when we emphasise the basic legal point that what is precisely in question is the extent of what can be considered to be, for an action under the *lex Aquilia*, 'burnt, broken or spoiled'. For the moment, consider the words 'you burn them': equally unusual from the point of view of an ordinary description of the facts. This unusualness is clearly no accident however. And it is also separate from the question of whether we can find a suitable explanation for 'burning' bees from the historical record of beekeeping, as Ariana Pretto-Sakmann admirably explores, seeing it probably as some failure to apply some smoke in order to pacify and capture them.[38] Rather, we can see it, to borrow Alain Pottage's description, as a kind of jurisprudential 'stenography'.[39] The facts may appear 'surreal or bookish' according to Frier,[40] but they are at the same time the product of an attempt to focus the legal analysis. The bees are 'burnt' because if it were a question of 'poisoning' them as in the 'case of the poor man's bees', described in the thirteenth *Major Declamation* attributed to Quintilian,[41] or killing them or driving them away with 'smoke' as in Digest 9.2.49, the effect would be to leave problematised something that is decidedly not intended to be so: whether the act of the defendant was a 'direct' or an 'indirect' cause of the destruction.[42] The point is that 'burning' comes explicitly within the (already somewhat archaic) terms of the *lex Aquilia* and is not in question here. Our concern is sharply focused on what sort of *ownership* or *possession*, what shape of *dominium* is envisaged by the terms of the plebiscite when it speaks of reparation. It is on this focused legal terrain that the bees are meant to enter the picture.

It is a short step from there to acknowledge the technical work that the other oddly formulated words of the passage perform. It is apt for the jurist to emphasise that we are not dealing with the same question as—as mentioned previously—whether one has ownership in general over such things as wild animals and bees in particular. It is not technically about whether another person can validly claim them as their own when they have flown away from your direct control. The concern is narrower. It is about the precise form of ownership or possession or control that is capable, under the terms of the *lex*, of being subject to the infliction of such unlawful damage (*damnum facere*) as 'burning, breaking or spoiling'. The peculiar tightness of the phrase makes better sense when we acknowledge, borrowing Thomas Finkenauer's words, the 'concrete and associative' rather than 'schematic and rigid' nature of the thought of the jurist.[43] There is something that can afford to be bracketed out in the economy of the treatment. That is precisely the question: what form of ownership does one retain and acquire in bees? We don't get very far in the interpretation (we don't enrich it very much) to go via analogy from what would be a dogmatic position on this point in one area (they remain ours so long as . . .) to a solution which is based on that same dogmatic position applied to the *lex Aquilia* (they can be considered property subject to being unlawfully 'burned' . . .). The jurist would rather keep these sets of legal subtleties in both areas in play. He would rather discover the technical terrain upon which the precise question enclosed in the case—and only that question—can be addressed, than to subject both the case and the prior jurisprudence to the dogmatism of an abstract rule. This thought of law extracts from the figure of the bees a certain diagram—an abstract set of juridical relations and a distinct jurisprudential meaning—and puts it to work to sharpen its focus.

They have simply 'flown to yours'. Even if we can't exactly picture the whole distinct factual scenario alluded to here, we can understand something of the necessary juridical precision involved. The jurist is at extreme pains to avoid making, in a roundabout way, a judgement on an issue that strictly does not belong to the jurisprudence on the *lex Aquilia*. In just a few words, we are capable of following all of the precision of the jurist's thought. Are we supposed to surmise that they have flown to and merged with some bees that you already own, before you burned them? That they have flown onto your property? To your trees? Are we supposed—in order to understand the law as it is described—to picture a clear and distinct factual basis to the case? To extrapolate that the bees must not be a full swarm but only several individual bees, since otherwise they would not have the inclination to return? These concerns are actually beside the point. The crucial thing is that any of these terms tends to already say too much for the rigour of the analysis it demands from the jurist: it sets one on an inquiry into facts that are not strictly required and which don't help to distil the question of law. The suggestion by Pretto-Sakmann that 'to yours' (*ad tuas*) could be 'explained as a metonymy: a mention of bees for where bees reside, and thereby a reference to "land" or "property"' seems plausible.[44] But the bees can also afford to retain the even more independent shape they have acquired in jurisprudence. This shape is diagrammatic rather than figurative. When the jurist mentions the bees, it is the very concept of property (*dominium*) which is precisely in question. The reference takes a shape that can cover in one sense the actual animals themselves insofar as they are relevant to the case, and the distinct mode of possession or property which is elastic or amorphous enough to be capable of being extended from 'mine' to 'yours'. In this way the bees can offer a distinct diagram for interrogating the ownership or possession of things for which the *lex Aquilia* imagines reparation for unlawful harm, without enclosing the animal in any naturalising discourse, and without foreclosing anything in the lively casuistry, the set of cases, in which ownership in wild animals can supposedly be lost by one and acquired by another.

THE ANTI-HUMANISM OF JURISPRUDENCE

Can we call such a jurisprudence 'antihumanist' or even 'nonanthropocentric'? A typical rebuttal of the whole approach presented earlier would proceed as follows. Nothing here challenges the most basic Western anthropocentric views that Roman jurisprudence is, after all, a typical example of. The interests of no one other than humans have, for the Romans, featured in the legal estimation of value, harm, unlawfulness and so on. Nothing other than the Western, entrenched, self-ordained right of humans over the natural world and over the bees in question informs the values expressed in the passage from Ulpian. There is no question of the interests, the rights, of any animal. There is no theory of any subject of rights other than 'man'. There is no ecological perspective on justice that is broader than that defined by the narrow, private, even petty juridical interests of the claimants.

Ok. But let's not get carried away in the commonplaces. Let's not confuse the pettiness of the human interests in question, with the enduring structure and matter of the law itself, the call and demands that it makes on thought, and the place that a humanist ideal (a respect for the rights and freedoms of all humanity) and an anthropocentric vision (making 'man' the kind of standard for all rights) holds or doesn't hold in it. We shouldn't be too quick to dismiss the significance of the animal when it appears in juristic thought, even if that animal is—for the claimants and for the jurisprudential framing of their dispute—only the object of some banal economic claim over property. A humanistic philosophy doesn't just take stock preferentially of the claims of human subjects over others—in their profoundness as much as in their pettiness. It installs the very value of humanity, the idea that we are all human, united in our humanity and in the 'intrinsically moral powers of human reason', at the heart of the spirit of law.[45] Legal anthropocentrism, similarly, is not just the fact that law is composed and constructed by humans for needs that they understand as uniquely their own. Nor is it the typical condition of recognising and giving preference to the rights and interests and values of humans over those of other species. It is the projection of the very idea of 'man', the being and the ends and destinies of 'man', at the centre of the vision that law has of the world in general.

It goes without saying that the Roman jurists did not challenge legal institutions in which not only animals but many men and women were treated as the property of others. And of course it can be conceded that, in the example of the bees, the jurist is in no way interested in what may be the consequences of this or that interpretation on the bees themselves as concrete moral, ethical or legal subjects. This should not simply be considered a shortcoming, a lack of progress or sophistication in their legal philosophical conceptualisation. It represents a broader detachment of the thought of the jurist from the worlds of philosophy, rhetoric and politics; worlds which it is comfortable to treat as not its own. What we shouldn't be too quick to dismiss is the relevance of this thought for a project in law that today finds difficulty situating animals in a juridical language that is appropriate to their independence and power. If we can find a nonanthropocentric perspective in law, it need not be one that falsely stretches itself into the subject-positions of nonhumans—trees, rivers, animals, nature, the Earth or whatever—in order to represent the interests of beings that have up to now been disregarded, or valued only for what they represent for a man. The Roman law gives us a far more inventive vision. It studiously avoids the ideals of any naturalism, any transcendentalism, any abstract metaphysics, any higher-order field of rights and duties. It refuses to assess cases by anything other than the modifications these introduce to its technical constructions, its associative experiments, its diagrams of right.

In this casuistic conception of law, we can observe—at least momentarily in a fragment like Ulpian's—a remarkable centrality of the animal to the thought of law. There is a privilege given by the jurist to the shape this animal offers to the elegance and refinement of their juristic constructions, over and above the all-too-human rhetorical, social, political contexts of the dispute. How does one manage to make anything creative out of the ordinary and meaningless circumstances of litigation: the mundane situation in which one person makes a claim for reparation from another? What we see the jurist, Ulpian, doing—far from attempting to respond earnestly to all the circumstances of the litigants' situation from an all-encompassing conception of justice—is to isolate that part of the problem that alone concerns the thought of law. What we see is a disarming of the natural law philosophies that would posit, if not a universalism of man's dominion over the natural world—the rights to the products of his own industry and so forth—then at least some transcendent natural order to which humanity and its laws, just as much as the animal world, must conform. The image of this natural order we find instead diffracted beyond recognition under the 'topical' force of their civil law: modified (in our case) under the refinement of a precise juridical-institutional question concerning liability under the *lex Aquilia*. The interpretive ends may appear banal, even trivial, but the technique is highly original. There is truly no place left in the thought of the Roman jurists for a totalising and humanising philosophy of nature. Each case in their casuistry is an artifice for the invention of right, a rehearsal of the supremacy of a uniquely jurisprudential vision of law.

Within this lightness of the jurist's touch, the flourish of creativity and experimentation that sits effortlessly alongside a sober, technical appreciation for the forms and institutions of law, we can note the indispensable, modest and even intimate role played by the bees. Here are some animals which, for the narrow purpose that the jurist recruits them for, can uniquely test the limits of the institutions of the civil law and to extend these limits beyond their otherwise lifeless, sclerotic doctrinal terrain. The bees may not have rights. But they are themselves the technical *modifications* of right: bearers of an altered jurisdiction. It is only in the thought of law and not in the representation of it that we can see these bees released, as it were, both from the sterility of legal doctrine and from the naturalism and humanism that normally reduces them to metaphor and allegory.

ACKNOWLEDGEMENTS

I would like to thank the colleagues and friends at Griffith University and at the 2017 Conference of the Law Literature and Humanities Association of Australasia for their thoughts, questions and comments on earlier versions of this paper. Special thanks to Marta Madero who offered some invaluable insight and advice on ideas contained in this piece and to Mary Keyes whose close reading of an earlier draft helped give it shape. I would also like to express my gratitude to the editors of this volume, Simone Bignall and Rosi Braidotti, for all their care and work devoted to this text and the warm invitation to contribute.

NOTES

1. Deleuze 2006, 350.
2. Deleuze 2006, 350
3. Ulpian Digest 9.2.27.12 (*Edict*, book 18). For references to Justinian's *Digest* in English translation, refer to Watson 1985.
4. For a selection of interpretations of Deleuze's affinity for law and jurisprudence in recent years, see, e.g., Moore 2007; Lefebvre 2008; de Sutter 2009; Braidotti, Colebrook and Hanafin 2009; de Sutter and McGee 2012; Murray 2013.
5. Deleuze 2006, 350.
6. Deleuze 1991, 62. See also, for example, Deleuze 2001, 36: 'Hume raises unexpected questions that seem nevertheless familiar: To establish possession of an abandoned city, does a javelin thrown against the door suffice, or must the door be touched by a finder? To what extent can we be owners of the seas? Why is the ground more important than the surface in a juridical system, whereas in painting, the paint is more important than the canvas?'
7. Saunders 2012, 198.
8. Deleuze 2004b.
9. In a rare direct reference to Roman law, Deleuze and Guattari—drawing upon the work of Paul Veyne—describe Roman law as 'topical' as opposed to modern law which is 'axiomatic'. Roman law, they suggest, proceeds more by way of 'topics' than 'concepts'. (Deleuze and Guattari 2002, 568 [fn 44 and 50]). This general idea was made more well known in the 1950s by Theodor Viehweg 1993.
10. Deleuze 2006, 350.
11. On legal isolationism in Roman jurisprudence, see especially: Schulz 1936; and Watson 1995.
12. Deleuze uses this idea in an interview with Claire Parnet where the philosopher contrasts jurisprudence, the invention of right, as against the respect for human rights (Deleuze 2004b). For discussion, see especially Lefebvre 2008, 54–59; and Saunders 2012.
13. Ulpian Digest 9.2.27.12.
14. The actual terms are '*usserit fregerit ruperit iniuria*'. In Digest 9.2.27.13 Ulpian notes that the statute says '*ruperit* [break or rend asunder]; but almost all the early jurists understood the word to mean *corruperit* [spoil]'.
15. Deleuze and Guattari 2002, 233; 258.
16. Cohn 1939, 289.

17. Pretto-Sakmann critiques Frier's translation of *fructui* as 'source of profit', arguing that this ignores the fact that the term 'fruits' (*fructui*) is normally read as having a technical meaning in Roman law. The conclusion is that bees may have become an exceptional case because of a cultural tendency to view them sometimes more as 'crops' than as 'wild animals' (Pretto-Sakmann 2006, 491).

18. Digest 41.1.5.

19. Thomas 1991; Schulz 1946, 137.

20. Thomas1991, 219.

21. Deleuze 1991, 37–54.

22. This phrasing, given by Ulpian in quoting the third chapter of the *lex Aquilia* in Digest 9.2.27.5, is generally taken to be a genuine rendition of the original.

23. Frier 1982, 1994.

24. Frier 1982, 112.

25. Frier 1994, 143–45.

26. Frier 1994, 144.

27. Frier 1982, 112.

28. Nietzsche avers I think to this detachment of the juristic conception of value when, in his *Genealogy of Morality*, he makes reference to what he sees as the more 'calculating' more 'Roman' conception of law reflected in the provision of the Twelve Tables which said, in relation to the principle that a creditor could cut off a certain amount of flesh from the body of his insolvent debtor, that there was no fraud if he cut off more or less (Nietzsche 1998, 50–51). Thus, even at its origins, the Roman conception of law can be reflected in a resistance to the idea of value as a pure system of equivalence (the pettiness for example in the painstaking inventory of body parts and what they are worth), rather than as invention or transvaluation.

29. Daube 1936.

30. For selection of work addressing this theme, see Jolowicz (1922), Daube (1936), MacCormack (1970), Kelly (1971), Westbrook (1995) and Zimmerman (1996).

31. Thomas 1980; Thomas 2002.

32. Frier 1982, 111.

33. The assumption for Frier is that this 'returning' (*animus revertendi*) for the jurist is a natural rather than a distinctly juridical attribute of bees. This is ultimately what makes him privilege, in his reading of the fragment, the idea of several individual bees rather than a swarm, despite the obvious insignificance of a legal action brought for the destruction of just a few bees.

34. It would be interesting to consider how far such a misreading of the Roman law influenced the drafting of the present day German Civil Code which includes four rarely used sections (961–64) dealing solely with the unique legal situation of the ownership of bees, including a whole discussion of the combinations and permutations concerning the merging and intermixture of bee swarms.

35. Frier also notably appears to replace the final word of the *Collatio* fragment *fugiunt* with *remanent* (Frier 1994, 135). Thus, in Frier's reading, the bees, when they 'flee' or 'take flight' from the hand, should actually be said to still 'remain' at home rather than 'flee' or 'take flight' home.

36. Deleuze 2004a, 164–213.
37. As Pretto-Sakmann notes: 'Frier's interpretation is not entirely plausible in that it tries to make the bees' nature square with the law' (2006, 493).
38. 'In all probability', Pretto-Sakmann (2006, 494) concludes, 'the *ad tuas* text is a case of a swarm taking off, thus losing its *animus revertendi*. A neighbour rather inaptly tries to use smoke to pacify the swarm and capture it, or take the honey. The attempt at pacification fails. Fire and destruction ensue'. Smoke is mentioned by Ulpian in relation to killing bees in *Disputations, Book 9* (Digest 9.2.49) as not falling under the *lex Aquilia* since it appears 'to have provided the cause of their death' and not 'to directly to have killed them'.
39. Pottage 2014, 156.
40. Frier 1994, 143.
41. Sussman 1987.
42. This point is made by Dieter Nörr in 1986, 193.
43. Finkenauer 2011, 42
44. Pretto-Sakmann 2006, 494.
45. Braidotti 2013, 13.

REFERENCES

Braidotti, R. (2013). *The Posthuman*. Cambridge: Polity Press.
Braidotti, R., Colebrook, C., and Hanafin, P., eds. (2009). *Deleuze and Law: Forensic Futures.* London: Palgrave Macmillan.
Cohn, E. J. (1939). 'Bees and the Law', *Law Quarterly Review*, 55, 289–94.
Daube, D. (1936). 'On the Third Chapter of the *Lex Aquilia*', *Law Quarterly Review* 52, 253–68.
Deleuze, G. (1991). *Empiricism and Subjectivity: An Essay on Hume's Theory of Human Nature*. Translated by C. V. Boundas. New York: Columbia University Press.
Deleuze, G. (2001). *Pure Immanence: Essays on A Life*. Translated by A. Boyman, New York: Zone Books.
Deleuze, G. (2004a). *Difference and Repetition*. Translated by Paul Patton, London: Continuum.
Deleuze, G. (2004b). *L'Abécédaire de Gilles Deleuze, avec Claire Parnet*. Paris: DVD Editions Montparnasse.
Deleuze, G. (2006). *Two Regimes of Madness: Texts and Interviews 1975–1995*, ed. David Lapoujade. Translated by Ames Hodges and Mike Taormina. New York: Semiotext(e).
Deleuze, G., and Guattari, F. (2002). *A Thousand Plateaus: Capitalism and Schizophrenia*. Translated by B. Massumi. London: Continuum.
de Sutter, L. (2009). *Deleuze: la pratique du droit*. Paris: Michalon.
de Sutter, L., and McGee, K., eds. (2012). *Deleuze and Law*. Edinburgh: Edinburgh University Press.
Finkenauer, T. (2011). 'On Stolen Swine, Fished Fisherman, and Drowned Dogs', *Roman Legal Tradition* 7, 30–44.

Frier, B. W. (1982). 'Bees and Lawyers', *The Classical Journal* 78(2), 105–14.

Frier, B. W. (1994). 'Why Did the Jurists Change Roman Law? Bees and Lawyers Revisited', *Index: International Survey of Roman Law* 22, 135–49.

Jolowicz, H. F. (1922). 'The Original Scope of the Lex Aquilia and the Question of Damages', *Law Quarterly Review* 38, 220–30.

Kelly, J. M. (1971). 'Further Reflections on the "Lex Aquilia"', In *Studi in onore di Edoardo Volterra, Vol. 1*, ed. Luigi Aru, Milan: Giuffrè, 235–41.

Lefebvre, A. (2008). *The Image of Law: Deleuze, Bergson, Spinoza.* Stanford, CA: Stanford University Press.

MacCormack, G. (1970). 'On the Third Chapter of the Lex Aquilia', *Irish Jurist* 5(1), 164–78.

Moore, N. (2007). 'Icons of Control: Deleuze, Signs and Law', *International Journal for the Semiotics of Law* 20(1), 33–54.

Murray, J. (2013). *Deleuze and Guattari: Emergent Law*. London: Routledge.

Nietzsche, F. (1998). *On the Genealogy of Morality*. Translated by M. Clark and A. J. Swensen. Indianapolis: Hackett Publishing.

Nörr, D. (1986). *Causa mortis: Auf den Spuren eine Redewendung*. Munich: C.H. Beck.

Pottage, A. (2014). 'Law after Anthropology: Object and Technique in Roman Law', *Theory, Culture and Society* 31, 147–66.

Pretto-Sakmann, A. (2006). "You Can Never Tell with Bees": Good Advice from Pooh for Students of the *Lex Aquilia*', In *Mapping the Law: Essays in Memory of Peter Birks*, eds. A. Burrows and A. Rodger. Oxford: Oxford University Press, 475–96.

Saunders, D. (2012). 'Cases against Transcendence: Gilles Deleuze and Bruno Latour in Defence of Law', In *Deleuze and Law*, eds. Laurent de Sutter and Kyle McGee. Edinburgh: Edinburgh University Press, 185–203.

Schulz, F. (1936). *Principles of Roman Law*. Oxford: Clarendon Press.

Schulz, F. (1946). *History of Roman Legal Science*. Oxford: Clarendon Press.

Sussman, L. A., ed. (1987). *The Major Declamations Ascribed to Quintilian: A Translation.* Frankfurt-am-Main: Verlag.

Thomas, Y. (1980). 'Res, chose et patrimoine', *Archives de Philosophie du Droit* 25, 413–26.

Thomas, Y. (1991). '*Imago naturae*. Note sur l'institutionnalité de la nature à Rome', *Théologie et droit dans la formation de l'Etat moderne* (Collection de L'école Français de Rome 147). Palais Farnèse: École française de Rome, 241–78.

Thomas, Y. (2002). 'La valeur des choses: Le droit romain hors la religion', *Annales: Histoire, Sciences Sociales* 57(6), 1431–62.

Viehweg, T. (1993). *Topics and Law: A Contribution to Basic Research in Law*, Frankfurt-am-Main, P. Lang. [Originally published in German in 1953]

Watson, A., ed. (1985). *The Digest of Justinian, Vols 1–4*. Philadelphia: University of Pennsylvania Press.

Watson, A. (1995). *The Spirit of Roman Law*. Athens: University of Georgia Press.

Westbrook, R. (1995). 'The Coherence of the Lex Aquilia', *Revue internationale des droits de l'antiqué* 42, 437–71.

Zimmerman, R. (1996). *The Law of Obligations: Roman Foundations of the Civilian Tradition*. Oxford: Oxford University Press.

Chapter 14

Lines of Shite

Microbial-Mineral Chatter in the Anthropocene

Myra J. Hird and Kathryn Yusoff

At the Berkeley Pit, a Superfund site filled with acidic and metal-laden contaminated waste from copper mining in Butte, Montana, microbes have learned how to digest toxic waste. The artificial lake, which is a mile wide and a mile-and-a-half long, is breeding a new form of life that has scientists bioprospecting for unusual bacteria to fulfill evermore intricate forms of nonhuman labour, from antivirals to anticancer drugs. Among the new forms of life, one bacterial agent has been found with the ability to digest metal waste. Weirdly, this bacteria is found only in the rectum of geese and had evidently found its way into the pit after a mass die-off of migrating snow geese that had stumbled into the toxic lake, impacting its ecology. This chapter begins from the Butte Superfund site to map out the multidirectional and inhuman trajectories of the interstratum of life and nonlife. Attending to insistent and opportunistic bacterial innovation and the emerging science of mineralogical evolution, this chapter argues for a form of mineral-microbial heterogenesis; an interlocking stratum that has consequences for thinking the multipersectival dimensions of becoming across geologic and biologic strata in post-Anthropocene worlds.

LINES OF FLIGHT

In 1995, the postindustrial town of Butte, Montana, became the site of a massacre of sorts. One stormy night in November, tens of thousands of Canada geese touched down on Lake Berkeley on their migratory path between Canada and the southwestern United States. But the 'lake' that the geese unwittingly descended on is actually more of a waste dump. The profoundly misnamed lake is actually composed of some thirty billion gallons of highly acidic, metal-laden water that has accumulated in an old abandoned open-pit copper mine that contaminates almost seven hundred acres of territory.[1] While tens of thousands of Canada geese landed, fewer took off, leaving behind some 350 of their compatriots, whose corpses lay in the stagnant lake.[2] Fried in the acidic bath, the geese became a focal point for the quotidian forms of 'nonlife' that are being made readily available to organisms in the back-loop of late industrialisation. But the categories that we use to characterise such extinctions and recognise forms of biodiversity-loss stumble. Centrered around the priorities of the organism and mourning for the loss of winged flight, the narrative failed at first to register what survived beyond the death of the organism. Concentrating on the bacteria thriving in the anal tract of the geese, we want to disrupt and rework these attachments to life—to focus on the traversals between the always already interpenetrative terrains between biologic and geologic plateaus, between life and nonlife, between biological and mineralogical evolution.

The timeline for this catastrophic avian event stretches back more than 55 million years ago when the Rocky Mountains were formed from subducting tectonic plate and later glacier erosion during the Laramide Orogeny. The area is part of the great Continental Divide, stretching from British Columbia to the Rio Grande, which designates the hydrological divide for rivers emptying into either the Atlantic or Pacific oceans. *Les Montagnes de Roche* have supported human inhabitants since the last ice age, some twelve thousand years ago. Butte (now called Butte-Silver Bow) was established as a mining camp in 1864, when large copper deposits were found in the area. From the late 1800s and early 1900s, Butte drew miners from across America, helping to fortify the association of boom towns with 'wild west' living, complete with a countrywide reputation for its saloons and sex workers, and the forms of microbial and viral sexual transfers that accompanied humanity's extractive culture. In 1881, Marcus Daly discovered the rich copper deposits, and bought the rights to the site, which he then sold to H. H. Rogers and William Rockefeller in 1899. These two entrepreneurs established the Anaconda Copper Mining Company, which morphed—as the extractive industry so often does, changing hands and increasing profit again and again—into the Amalgamated Copper Mining Company, and then in 1977 into the Atlantic Richfield Company (ARCO) until its closure in 1980. After some $48 billion in profit from copper ore extraction, the final mining company abandoned the area, ceased pumping water from the pit and created the vast Berkeley Pit Lake, which in 1983 became the United States's largest Superfund site.[3] It's also a tourist attraction, where sturdy folk can pay $2 to survey the environmental devastation from a newly constructed heritage viewpoint. For another $2 they can buy a 'Mile High and Mile Deep', 'More Acid Than Woodstock' or 'Not Your Average Death Metal' bumper sticker or postcard. As with many domestic, nuclear and military Superfund sites in the United States that have become wildlife refuges or public parks, the heritage status negates the costly work of remediation and fixes the redesignation of waste as the threshold point of conversion in postindustrial landscapes.

The Berkeley Lake—which is more accurately a flooded mining pit—is as highly acidic as Coca-Cola (2.5 ph level). The oxygen dissolved in the water allows the purite and sulfide minerals to decay, releasing acid. And so the lifeless lake contains extraordinarily high concentrations of copper (187 ppm Cu in places), arsenic, cadmium, zinc and sulfuric acid.[4] Combined with 'acid-tolerant bacteria that thrive on iron and sulfur compounds [that] hasten th[e] [acidification] process ... when the pumps were shut down, the Berkeley Pit became an immense chemical transformer producing ever-greater amounts of toxic soup'.[5] And when the pit water reverse flows back into the surrounding groundwater and the lake reaches the water table in, scientists predict, 2020, all of this contamination will merge with the Silver Bow Creek, which in turn flows into the Clark Fork River.

LINES OF SHITE

And the story connecting the line of flight of these unfortunate Canada geese to this acidic liquid waste dump is yet more convoluted. In a stranger-than-fiction twist, it turns out that the bacteria specific to the anal tract of the geese have, in their chatter with the acidic soup ecology, been busily digesting the lake's metal waste. So this could be deployed as an example within an emerging narrative within techno-science Anthropocene literature: that of nature (in this case bacteria) in the service of toxic remediation. A line of flight leading to a line of shite becomes a line of humanity's redemption.

Enter Grant Mitmann, chemist and algae enthusiast. When, in the same year that the Canada geese died, Mitmann discovered some weird-looking slime on a rope he found in the mining pit/lake/waste dump, this strange organism turned out to be *Euglena mutabilis*, a resilient species of algae. Mitmann merged his efforts with those of two other sleuthing chemists, Andrea and Don Stierle. The Stierles had been hunting for microbes with antiviral or anticancer properties, when Andrea discovered a 'thick, gooey, black organism' that appears to very effectively metabolise contaminating metals in the waste lake.[6]

And now we are in the familiar territory of the Anthropocene: the bacteria largely constituting the Canada geese shite appear to provide a cozy tale of 'man' harnessing nature through industrialisation, and then sustaining his dominance by 'putting nature to work' to clean up his mess. While not likely counted in the roster of entepreneurial geo-engineering, these numberless microscopic critters are nevertheless as modest as they are relentless in creating and transforming the livable planet.[7]

Of the growing number of examples, perhaps Deepwater Horizon is the most familiar. This 2010 oil rig disaster in the Gulf of Mexico exemplifies Ulrich Beck's theory that techno-science produces the accidents that this same techno-science is relied upon to resolve.[8] An estimated 4.9 million barrels of oil gushed up from the underwater oil pipe, covering some 112,000 kilometres[2] of the ocean's surface, and the massive plume of hydrocarbons reached a depth of 1,100 metres.[9] As sure as the human culpability for this environmental disaster was debated, a concurrent narrative thread identified local marine microorganisms as the solution: man would once again supervise these bacterioplankton in disappearing the hydrocarbon plume.[10] In a widely reported public lecture at the University of Southern Mississippi titled 'Can Mother Nature Take a Punch?: Microbes and the BP Oil Spill in the Gulf of Mexico', microbiologist Terry Hazen answered largely in the affirmative, recounting that bacteria preadapted to the natural presence of hydrocarbons in their ecosystem had thronged to the plume like 'oil-seeking missiles'.[11] In the apparently never-ending tale of technological innovation, replete with the possibilities of disaster to provide new opportunities, narratives of the Anthropocene often read like technofix writ large; a techno-fix planet. Ecomodernisation, the 'good' Anthropocene, biomimicry, rewilding and geoengineering all seek to reinscribe control within environments gone awry. Even in the shit, it seems that the god complex is as robust as ever. If the narrative of the fix is familiar, then the ability to deal with the eternal return of the environmental remainder, and *its* trajectory, seems shortsighted in its perspectivism.

We might, then, trace an aeons-old *temporal* line of flight from subducting tectonic plates to minerological sedimentation to anthropogenic extraction to avian migration and death, to bacterial clean-up, traversed by a *material* line of flight from inorganic ancient rock to copper to the labouring bodies of miners and sex workers to the contaminated fallout of mining extraction to Canada geese and their shit to bacterial proliferation and differentiation. And traversing all of these grand plateaus are the planet's most prolific, industrious, interfacing, and diversifiying drivers of evolution: from the accumulation of untold billions of bacterial corpses that moved the tectonic plates to the microflora occupying the Canada geese's anal tracts, and now—we cross our fingers—that are digesting our toxic legacy.

LINES OF MINERALISATION

While Anthropocene pundits shape stories of human evolution around lines of coal and the extractive legacies of seams and bands of copper, silver and gold (and more recently rare earth minerals and lithium), it might seem prescient to mention the lowly bacterial 'chatter' with the stratum that disrupt the stratigraphic thinking that characterise both the organisation of thought in continental theory (as 'plateaus' in Deleuze and Guattari, 'formations' in Foucault, and 'strata' in sociology) and the temporal sequencing of epochs in geology. While the conceptualisation of 'plateaus' offers a way to become cognisant of forms of social and political stratification that hold together, in various densities, the molecular processes that subtend strata and constitute them, understood as a uniform 'plane of composition' a plateau or strata reinforces dominant delineations between biocentric life and inhuman materials. While Deleuze and Guattari proposed planes of becoming that were understood to integrate a range of forces to generate politics and sociality, which differentiate to produce different stabilities, bacteria can be understood in these terms as agents of absolute difference, able to deterritorialise the integrity of stratification through a few rounds of monstrous coupling. Seemingly able to enter into a relation with both other forms of life and nonlife, bacteria produce movement across and with the strata in radically nonlinear ways that produce and destabilise materiality and life in nonstructural forms and far beyond a focus on the organism. It's not just that bacteria have a 'nonhuman expressivity', they integrate planes of expression into new epochs and material forms. That is, in stratigraphic parlance, bacteria make the planes. And by doing so, bacteria challenge thinking that has a biologic granularity, which positions the inhuman as a more permanent, solidified or stratified plane through its distinction with life. If no such distinction can be made then the concept of stratification implodes.

Scrape away a little of the humanist hubris in Anthropocene discourses and the era of industrialisation has a bacterial foundation that is less about great white men and more about a super organism that digests binaries as a matter of course, across aeons of time. The photosynthesising capabilities of cynobacteria that extracted energy and matter from the sun and carbon dioxide rich atmosphere 2.5 billion years ago led to the formulation of lignite plants that characterised the carboniferous and its coal stocks, and (we're now thinking) bacteria's new found ability to metabolise fossilised lignite that ended the deposition of coal seams.[12] The 'great acceleration' read from a bacterial vantage point is far more a case of the microcosmos relentlessly doing its thing—playing the long game of experimenting in diversification— with humanity naively hitching a ride in short-time.

And what a ride it has been. In a paper by Anthropocene Working Group scientists, Mark Williams et al. argue that the geological record preserves evidence for two fundamental stages in the evolution of Earth's biosphere, a microbial stage that they date from approximately 3.5 to 0.65 Ga, and a metazoan stage evident by c. 650 Ma. In addition to these two stages of the biosphere they add a 'new' third stage of evolution; 'characterised by: (1) global homogenisation of flora and fauna; (2) a single species (*Homo sapiens*) commandeering 25–40% of net primary production and also mining fossil net primary production (fossil fuels) to break through the photosynthetic energy barrier; (3) human-directed evolution of other species; and (4) increasing interaction of the biosphere with the technosphere (the global emergent system that includes humans, technological artefacts, and associated social and technological networks)'.[13] These changes in the biosphere, the authors suggest, could persist over geologic timescales. The argument that there are three stages that represent the evolution of the biosphere—1 (microbial), 2 (metazoan), and 3 (anthropocene)—frames the activities of humans as a major geologic force within the earth, organised in a comparative mode to microbial and metazoan life. While this is a useful acknowledgement of the impact of humans on earth processes (in keeping with the political force of the Anthropocene), such an anthropocentric organisation can quickly become conflated with a sequential understanding of impacts. Although the authors are careful to argue for a difference in kind, in terms of evolutionary development, rather than a succession of planetary states, the placement of protagonists matters to what kind of imaginary of planetarity we end up with. From a mineral evolutionary point of view, the succession of planetary states is exactly what is needed in an account of evolutionary change, but crucially it needs to be an account that acknowledges the various co-survivals of life-forms (microbial and metazoan) as well as charting their extinctions or eclipse. The subtle patternation of human agency and its representation should mean that agentic action of humans is understood in its nonagentic formations. Another way to say this would be to acknowledge that humans may initiate and accelerate the development of waste-forms, but they rarely control those forms and *their* formations.[14]

The point is that while the assertion that humans have transported organisms around the globe and as such have initiated a vast array of globalisations that have transformed the earth, that we have commandeered the stockpiles of stored solar energy from the earth, as well as creating vast intricate biological, chemical and technological geographical networks is all undoubtedly correct, humans are by no means the only globalisers, nor the most agentic in the mass balance of planetary terms.[15] That humans *come after* the evolutionary stage of bacteria becomes an argument that bacteria have been put in their evolutionary place by a more commandeering agent. As such, all sorts of eco-innovators and green entrepreneurs try to utilise bacteria as 'carbon workers'[16] in plans to clean up spills, waste—via the bacteria in the anal tracts of geese in our example—or leftover plastic, the giddy assertions of 'putting bacteria to work' articulate a certain misplaced ability for geologic overlording.[17]

But microbial and mineralogical evolution is not a tale about 'biotic innovators', and their unexpected utility in munching waste as a psychic amelioration to the weight of dead birds (as the tale of Butte might subsequently be told), but, perhaps, something more akin to a story about how organism-orientated relations are often a distraction to an understanding of the relations of wasting and exposure that cohere around human detritus (chemical, metallurgic, organic and otherwise) in the Anthropocene.[18] Waste matters, and bacterial traversals disaggregate the arrangements of geochemical matter (in its material and epistemic catgeories) that form the analytical apparatus of the Anthropocene. This is not just an argument about the primacy of the duration of microbial interactions in the context of the planet, but points to the foundational need to readdress the categorisation of 'life' and mammalian organisms as the primary mode of attention within an epoch whose precarity stems precisely from a neglect of nonlife processes.[19]

Take, as another illustration, the origins of sexual indifference,[20] which occurred only 1.2 Ga (billion) ago, as an emergent force within an earth that is estimated to be 4.5 Ga old. That the origins of life are estimated at 3.8 Ga years old is another way to say that sexual reproduction (and by extension, sexual difference) is a very recent story in the earth's history and by no means its most endurant form of biological or geological attachment.[21] The Great Oxidation event—at 2.45 Ga years photosynthesis evolves over 1 Ga before a fragile sexual reproduction—subtended multicellular life and skeletal biomineralisation, and irreversibly transformed Earth's near-surface mineralogy. As well, estimate that 70 percent of the diversity of species on Earth arose indirectly from biological changes of the atmosphere and oceans.[22] The point here is not a competitive slide across billions of years to the present, but an impetus to organise a conceptual and material perspectivism that does not forget its origins, nor how those 'origins of sociable life'[23] continue to organise and fete the possibilities of traversals across the different materially arranged earths (that are as contingent as the organisms that occupy and rearrange its surfaces).

In collaboration with recent work on mineral evolution[24] and microbial ontologies[25] that suggest that microbial life has been fundamentally more than just 'involved' in the evolution of the Earth through geologic time, when the bacteria in the anal tracts of the unfortunate Canada geese are metabolising our toxic legacy, they are reminding us that plateaus are not stable: minerology does not serve as a background that stages the biological events of life. From this view of conjoined microbial and mineralogical evolution, '[t]he question of life's origin is in essence a problem of information transfer from a geochemical environment to a highly localized volume'.[26] Earth's prebiotic environment possessed a varied inventory of raw materials to be sure; an atmosphere, oceans, rocks and minerals, and a diverse suite of small organic molecules. But much more than this, the processes by which the Hadean Earth was transformed into a living world required the selection, concentration, and organisation of specific organic molecules into successively more information-rich localised assemblages. In this view, life's origins can be modeled as a problem in emergent chemical complexification and not a story about the various endgames of organisms (including humans).

LINES OF THEORY

Given enough time, everything becomes disgestable to bacteria. The politics of life and nonlife, we might argue, are fundamentally contaminated (or made anthropogenically incoherent) through bacterial agency. Conceptualised within a Deleuzian framework of 'a thousand plateaus', the trajectories that emerge as cogent, get refigured through the single arrow of escape; the bacteria from the rectum of the geese; the potentialities of the aquatic acid soup; the creative innovation of the sexual and nonsexual co-minglings of the microorganism; the 'happy accident' of the new progeny. If Deleuzian lines of flight are liberatory acts of escape from a relatively stable grid of stratigraphic restraint, they nonetheless privilege the time-space of particular biocentric forms as the operative agents of evolution phenomena. This misses those agents and processes that continually traverse the plateaus across deep time and deep carbon. Another way to say this would be that there is a parallel universe of bacterial-earth relation that is not just contaminating and coproducting strata (the already there of the inhuman), but it is constantly refiguring what strata actually is, and its temporal organisation. In bacterial formation, stability can be the several billion years of bacteria-archaea experiementation with undersea alkaline vents or the time taken to conjugate with geese shite. In the foci on entanglement in the work of making the environmentally new (and thus captivating), the potentialities of the present are already preconstituted in the plateau through a purely biological scene of apprehension. What has potential is understood as what is within the temporal domain of the vital, even as it might be recognised as an inhuman or nonhuman force. But, if we shift the perspectives into a geologic mode, or more properly, a geologically informed biological mode, the plateaus begin to shift as coherent planes in the narrative of what's going on. Because what's going on is far more stretched in time than the immanent plane acknowledges, pulled across an evolving geo-chemical conversation between organisms (bacterial) and minerals across aeons of time.

In other words, *the plateau cannot hold*, and the stratigraphic imaginary needs to be fundamentally reworked though all its theoretical, epistemic and material suppositions. In fact, sections of *A Thousand Plateaus* extend a non-linear and 'molecular' framework for conceptualising processes of complex organisation in the mode of time Deleuze and Guattari name as 'Aîonic'.[27] Thus plateaus—as discrete forms of organisation or stratification—not only come undone as their elements trace lines of flight that induce them to escape the ordered forms in which they participate; but at the same time a plateau (any structure or ordered form of composition) is itself always-already comprised as shifting particulate or molecular forms that over time have broken free from other stratified forms, and which combine and associate with elements from other strata and so enter into new complex assemblages to produce new formations, contaminating and transforming structures in complex and nonlinear ways. The coproducing processes of becoming as complex assemblage, involving both living and nonliving forces, clarify how the 'plateau' is actually 'not a plan(e) of organisation, development, or formation, but of involuntary transmutation'.[28] Another way to look at this, we suggest, is to put the conversation between bacteria and rocks front and centre as the most enduring relation in processes of stratification; and thus in the formation of the politics of nonbinary (not to mention sexuate) forms of chatter through organic and inorganic forms of life and nonlife. For example, casting a geologic eye back to the emergence of complex life and the indirect link now suggested between the recycling of continents by plate tectonics and the evolution of life, it is this very conversation in the background between bacteria and rocks that led to the formation of these continents, not to mention the consolidated and breathable atmosphere. Schwarzmann and Volk have shown that microbes facilitate rock weathering by as much as one thousand times.[29] And Lowman and Armstrong's research goes even further, suggesting that while the earth's major concentric layers—the liquid core, the convecting mantle and the outer crust—were formed by the same kinds of processes found on other (silicate-rich) planets, the broad aspects of the Earth's geology as it is now—continents, ocean basins, the oceans themselves, sea floor spreading and related processes—are the product of fundamentally biogenic processes, acting on a crustal dichotomy formed by several enormous impacts on the primordial Earth.[30] The fundamental structure of the Earth, not just its exterior and outer layers, thus appears to have been dominated by water-dependent—and thus life dependent—plate tectonic processes. The Earth's continental plates, that is, may well have moved as a consequence of the buildup of the bodies of uncountable billions of bacteria.

If we can even begin to imagine bacteria as the orogeny of continental plates, then it follows suit that they at least have some part in nation-building and regulating the role of the state as a geophysical entity (this is geopolitics operationalised through the harnessing and practising of geopower by bacteria in ways that set the possibilities for human colonisation and configurations). This, indeed, is a far more realistic relay—from Earth's crust and ocean formation, to continents, to isolated life-forms, to species, to hominid, to race—than the blithely accepted nonlife to life to complex (human) life to technology to the Anthropocene. At the very least, in accepting the formation of commons as a (bacterially informed) geologic process, we might begin to see how the borders and boundaries of the social are both prefigured and rendered proto-political through this bacterial-mineral conversation.

The kinds of geophysical work that constitutes the mineral-bacteria chatter we are outlining here suggests a different kind of geopolitics that both disrupts the biopolitical in its focus on biocentricism (focused on the organism) and challenges the new political geologies of the Anthropocene in their anthropocentricism. The case for bacteria as the superagents of earth formation is not just a plea from the margins of life, but rather suggests that the foci of agency matters in how materialism is both understood as a practice, and in terms of the categories of explanation for what's going on (in terms of agency and time).[31] And, what's going on seems to suggest that life in its current apprehensions is a big distraction to the more prescient dynamics with nonlife (which conditions and constrains the politics of life). If the Anthropocene and the formation of new mineraological formations[32] hitherto unseen and distinct to an anthropomorphic trace present a new material empirics, humans are not alone in these conversations with the evolution of strata. Rather than distinct plateaus of life and nonlife it is the *to* and *fro* between minerality and bacteria solutions that characterise the particular ordering of both biological and geological life in their political and nonpolitical forms (as biopower and geopower). As Hazen and Sverjensky argue, 'mineral surfaces may have contributed centrally to the linked prebiotic problems of containment and organisation by promoting the transition from a diluted prebiotic "soup" to highly ordered local domains of key biomolecules'.[33] Whether in the deep sea trenches where bacteria convert the upwards injections from the deep earth into mineral forms or in the eruptive crusts where extremophiles 'make safe' the conditions for life through a process known as chemotrophy, the energetic traversals of bacteria make strata seem much less stratified. Another way to say this is to acknowledge that the transformation of the material, mineralogical, metallurgic basis of the Earth by bacteria has temporal consequences for understanding the geochemical basis of the Anthropocene, but also more widely for understanding processes of materiality beyond biocentrism and theories of stratification.

In the view of a planetarity of microbial-mineralogical evolution, bacteria take central stage as the protagonists of geochemical origination in the longer story of the evolution of the earth. Hazen and Ferry suggest that there are three eras to the Earth's history: first, the 'Era of Planetary Accretion' (>4.55 Ga) with the initial diversification of minerals in meteorites; second the 'Era of Crust and Mantle Reworking' (4.55 to 2.5 Ga) sequence of geochemical and petrologic processes, including volcanism and degassing, fractional crystallisation, assimilation, regional and contact metamorphism, plate tectonics, and associated large-scale fluid–rock interactions, which produced the first continents and ultimately resulted in an estimated 1500 different mineral species; and third, the 'Era of Biologically Mediated Mineralogy' (>2,5 Ga to Present).[34] At the cusp of the Era of Crust and Mantle Reworking and the era of Biologically Mediated Mineralogy sits plate tectonics and the material mediation of bacteria. Hazen and Ferry argue that life has not just transformed the near-surface environment—the oceans and atmosphere—but that it has transformed the rocks as well. They estimate that two-thirds of all known mineral species are the consequence of the earth's transformation by living organisms. Their theory of mineral evolution suggests that framing mineralogy in a historical context by concentrating on its evolutionary characteristics, advances the premise that the geosphere and biosphere have coevolved through a sequence of deterministic and stochastic events (albeit set within a longer history of the earth as initially devoid of life forces). As Paul Gillen explains, 'The biological origin of some minerals has long been recognised but not generally acknowledged as a sign of a symbiotic relationship almost as old as Earth. Mineral evolution contends that life and minerals have been complementary phenomena since life began'.[35]

Mineral evolution is of course an evolutionary theory—it explains why phenomena change in the way that they do—but it is not a Darwinian theory. It is in fact a more powerful type of evolutionary theory, since it claims to be able to do two things for minerals that Darwinian selection cannot do for living things: provide a causal account of their origin and make some probable predictions about their sequencing.[36] The implications of this, Paul Gillen argues, is that the 'distinction between life and nonlife therefore appears not as a clear division but as a tangled chemical continuum'.[37] As Hazen suggests:

> There's a growing awareness of the dramatic changes in Earth's mineralogy over the past 4.5 billion years. Remarkably, that epic 'mineral evolution' story is as much about life as it is about rock. We now realize that minerals and life co-evolved.[38]

LINES OF CATASTROPHIC FLIGHT (CONCLUSIONS)

Under the title, 'Mineral Fodder', Hazen argues that 'we may think we are the first organisms to remake the planet, but life has been transforming the earth for aeons' and a very specific form of life at that.[39] Bacteria intuit the possibility of movement in sexual and asexual terms, across a myriad of plateaus. Bacteria work at the interjunction of pure difference that the focus on life and the organism obscures. In the process of traversal between radically different entities, bacteria operate as something like a Deleuzian 'difference operator' for the organisation of complex forms, as a kind of nonhuman agency which has the systemic role of 'relating difference to difference' at the complex interface of an encounter between plateaus.[40]

Numerous possible modes of attachment exist that are dependent on a whole range of geochemical factors. As those factors shift, such as the available energy or mineralogy on the earth's surface or nitrogen balance, new modes of attachment and combination become possible. As Hazen and his colleagues reflect:

> Human ingenuity has led to a host of crystalline compounds that never before existed in the solar system, and perhaps the universe. Thus, from a materials perspective (and in contrast to Earth's vulnerable biodiversity), the Anthropocene Epoch is an era of unparalleled inorganic compound diversification.[41]

Prior to this human perturbation, and its great explosion of minerality, the most significant 'punctuation event' in the diversity of crystalline compounds on Earth followed the Great Oxidation Event. Hazen et al. estimated that as many as two-thirds of Earth's more than 5,000 mineral species arose as a consequence of the biologically mediated rise of oxygen at −2.4 to 2.2 Ga.[42] By comparison, 'the production of more than 180,000 inorganic crystalline compounds … reflects a far more extensive and rapid punctuation event. … Human ingenuity has led to a host of crystalline compounds that never before existed in the solar system, and perhaps in the universe. Thus, from a materials perspective (and in contrast to Earth's vulnerable biodiversity), the Anthropocene Epoch is an era of unparalleled inorganic compound diversification'.[43] In geologic terms, humans are niche proliferators, rapidly increasing the concentrated diversification of minerals but with little ability to understand the complex dynamics of that production over time in concert with life-forms. Understanding mineral and biological evolution as a complex and shared event, entwined with other evolving systems 'including the nucleosynthesis of elements and isotopes, the prebiotic synthesis of organic molecules, biological evolution through Darwinian natural selection, and the evolution of social and material culture'[44] suggests that the politics of

nonlife shares some common traits with the politics of life. How this complex, evolving mineral-biological system is punctuated with well-known
biological traits such as extinction[45] is crucial to how the 'events' of the
Anthropocene are understood (and how what gets to count as an event shapes
a set of material interventions and expectations). That is, we need to notice
proliferation of mineral evolution as a trajectory, one that affords numerous
potentialities for other life forces in becoming agentic.

What we are proposing here is not just a conversation between bacteria
and rock through time, but one across and within the understanding of territory and its material and temporal conceptualisation. Recent research on
'deep-down' organisms suggests that concentrating on the surface activities
of mineral exchange, such as the carbon imaginaries that shape contemporary climate change and petrochemical cultures, are woefully inadequate
in their conceptualisation of the range and scope of the kinds (and places) of
exchanges taking place.[46] Subsurface water, for example, is estimated to be
one hundred times as great in volume as all the available fresh water in the
rivers, lakes and swamps combined. This water, ranging in ages from seven
years to two billion years, defines the scope and range of deep life. Research
suggests that the deep terrestrial subsurface is home to one quintillion simple
(prokaryotic) cells. Some estimates suggest that the deep biosphere could
contain up to one-third of Earth's entire biomass (see Deep Life work of the
Deep Carbon Observatory). These overlooked and understudied 'microbial
dark matter' are similar to their astronomical counterparts, as they evade
detection and vastly outnumber the microbes that are visible.

Rethinking biological evolution within geologic processes requires a
repositioning of the foci of engagements (in their proto-organic and nonorganic forms), as well as an understanding of the diachronistic potentiality
of geologic time and those organisms (bacteria, for example) that are more
accomplished time travellers. What we are proposing here, in these lines of
shite, is not simply that geology be understood in an asymmetric relation to
life (as context, stage and forerunner), but that geology and life are already
involved in a complex inter-evolutionary relation that preceeds and exceeds
human activities but nothcless hitches an evolutionary ride on its material
practices. Perhaps it is time that stratified theoretical conceptualisations
loosened up and recognised how the resident (bacterial) chatter down the
aeons mobilises and remakes the territory in decidedly more creative ways.
In stretching the imaginary of potentialities through an understanding of
mineralogical evolution, a conversation with geology in the Anthropocene
starts to look decidedly less bio- and anthro-centric and less stratigraphically
constrained.

NOTES

1. Dobb 2000.
2. Zhang 2016.
3. Robbins 2016; Associated Press 2017.
4. Robbins 2016.
5. Dobb 2000, np.
6. Dobb 2000; Robbins 2016.
7. Hird 2009.
8. Beck 1992.
9. Kimes et al. 2014; Beyer et al. 2016.
10. Hazen et al. 2010.
11. Cited in Kirgin 2011, np; see Clark and Hird forthcoming.
12. See Ward and Kirschvink 2015; and Nelsen et al. 2016 for rebuttal to these ideas.
13. Williams et al. 2015.
14. Hird 2012; 2013a.
15. Hird 2009.
16. Gabrys 2013.
17. See, for example, Carrington 2018.
18. Hird 2017.
19. Hird 2010.
20. And multicellular organisms; see Colebrook 2012.c
21. Hird 2009; 2013b.
22. Hazen and Sverjencksy 2010.
23. Hird 2009.
24. Hazen 2013.
25. Hird 2009.
26. Hazen and Sverjensky 2010.
27. See, for example, the sections 'Memories of a Spinozist, 1' and 'Memories of a molecule' in Plateau 10 of *A Thousand Plateaus*, titled '1730: Becoming-intense, becoming-animal, becoming-imperceptible . . . '.
28. Deleuze and Guattari 1987, 269.
29. Schwarzmann and Volk 1991.
30. Lowman and Armstrong 2002.
31. Yeager 2008.
32. Hazen et al. 2017.
33. Hazen and Sverjensky 2010, np.
34. Hazen and Ferry 2010.
35. Gillen 2016, 217.
36. Ibid., 219.
37. Ibid., 222.
38. Hazen 2017, np.
39. Hazen 2017.
40. Deleuze 2004, 97.

41. Hazen et al. 2017, 606.
42. Hazen et al. 2008.
43. Hazen et al. 2017, 606.
44. Hazen and Eldredge 2010.
45. Hazen et al. 2013, 79.
46. Borgonie and Lau 2017.

REFERENCES

Associated Press. (2017). 'At Least 3,000 Geese Killed by Toxic Water from Former Montana Copper Mine', *The Guardian*, https://www.theguardian.com/us-news/2017/jan/23/geese-die-montana-toxic-mine-epa. Accessed 22 April 2018.

Beck, U. (1992). *Risk Society: Towards a New Modernity*. Cambridge: Polity Press.

Beyer, J., Trannum, H., Bakke, T., Hodson, P., and Collier, T. (2016). 'Environmental Effects of the Deepwater Horizon Spill: A Review'. *Marine Pollution Bulletin*, 110, 28–51.

Borgonie, G., and Lau, M. (2017). 'Life Goes Deeper', *Aeon*, https://aeon.co/essays/deep-beneath-the-earths-surface-life-is-weird-and-wonderful. Accessed 23 April 2018.

Carrington, D. (2018). 'Scientists Accidentally Create Mutant Enzyme That Eats Plastic Bottles', *The Guardian*. https://www.theguardian.com/environment/2018/apr/16/scientists-accidentally-create-mutant-enzyme-that-eats-plastic-bottles. Accessed 23 April 2018.

Clark, N., and Hird, M. J. (forthcoming). 'Microontologies and the Politics of Strata'. In *Geographies of Power*, M. Coleman and J. Agnew, eds. Northampton, MA: Edward Elgar Publishing.

Colebrook, C. (2012). 'Sexual Indifference'. In *Theory in the Era of Climate Change*, T. Cohen, ed. Ann Arbor, MI: Open Humanities Press, 167–82.

Deleuze, G. (2004). 'The Method of Dramatisation'. In *Desert Islands and Other Texts 1953–1974*, D. Lapoujade, ed., M. Taormina, trans. New York: Semiotext(e).

Deleuze, G., and Guattari, F. (1987). *A Thousand Plateaus.* Minneapolis: University of Minnesota Press.

Dobb, E. (2000). 'New Life in a Death Trap: Will Algae Blooming in an Acidic, Poisonous Montana Mine Lead Us to an Answer for Superfund Sites?' Discover, http://discovermagazine.com/2000/dec/featnewlife. Accessed April 22, 2018.

Gabrys, J. (2013). 'Plastic and the Work of the Biodegradable'. In *Accumulation: The Material Politics of Plastics*, J. Gabrys, G. Hawkins and M. Micheal, eds. London: Routledge, 208–27.

Gillen, P. (2016). 'Notes on Mineral Evolution: Life, Sentience, and the Anthropocene', *Environmental Humanities* 8(2), 215–34.

Hazen, R. M. (2013). 'Paleomineralogy of the Hadean Eon: A Preliminary Species List'. *AJS Online* November 313(9), 807–43.

Hazen, R. M. (2017). 'New Exhibit Opens in Vienna, Showcases Mineral Evolution on Earth'. Deep Carbon Observatory. https://deepcarbon.net/feature/new-exhibit-opens-vienna-showcases-mineral-evolution-earth#.WO-TTRIrIUE.

Hazen, R. M., Downs, R., Kah, L., Sverjensky, D. (2013). 'Carbon Mineral Evolution', *Reviews in Mineralogy and Geochemistry* 75(1), 79–107.

Hazen, R. M., and Eldredge, N. (2010). 'Themes and variations in complex systems', *Elements* 6(1), 43–46.

Hazen, R. M., and Ferry, J. (2010). 'Mineral Evolution: Mineralogy in the Fourth Dimension', *Elements* 6, 9–12.

Hazen, R. M., Grew, E., Origlieri, M., Downs, R. (2017). 'On the mineralogy of the "Anthropocene Epoch"', *American Mineralogist* 102(3), 595–611.

Hazen, R. M., Papineau, D., Bleeker, W., Downs, R. T., Ferry F., McCoy T., Sverjensky D., Yang, H. (2008). 'Mineral evolution', *American Mineralogist* 93, 1693–1720.

Hazen, R. M., and Sverjensky, D. A. (2010). 'Mineral Surfaces, Geochemical Complexities, and the Origins of Life'. *Cold Spring Harbor Perspectives in Biology*, 2(5), a002162. http://doi.org/10.1101/cshperspect.a002162.

Hazen, T. E. A., Dubinsky, T. Z., DeSantis, G. L., Andersen, Y. M., Piceno, N., Singh, J. K., Jansson, A., Probst, S. E., et al. (2010). 'Deep-Sea Oil Plume Enriches Indigenous Oil-Degrading Bacteria,' *Science* 330(8), 204–208.

Hird, M. J. (2009). *The Origins of Sociable Life: Evolution after Science Studies.* Houndmills, Basingstoke: Palgrave.

Hird, M. J. (2010). 'Indifferent Globality'. *Theory, Culture and Society*, 27 (2–3), 54–72.

Hird, M. J. (2012). 'Knowing Waste: Toward an Inhuman Epistemology'. *Social Epistemology*, 26(3–4), 453–69.

Hird, M. J. (2013a). 'Waste, Landfills, and an Environmental Ethics of Vulnerability'. *Ethics and the Environment*, 18(1), 105–24.

Hird, M. J. (2013b). 'Digesting Difference: Metabolism and the Question of Sexual Difference'. *Configurations*, 20, 213–38.

Hird, M. J. (2017). 'Burial and Resurrection in the Anthropocene: Instrastructures of Waste'. In *Infrastructures and Social Complexity: A Routledge Companion*, P. Harvey, C. Bruun Jensen and A. Morita, eds. London: Routledge, 242–52.

Kimes, N. E., Callaghan, A.V., Suflita, J. M., Morris, P. J. (2014). 'Microbial transformation of the Deepwater Horizon oil spill—past, present, and future perspectives', *Frontiers in Microbology*, 18 November 2014, https://doi.org/10.3389/fmicb.2014.00603

Kirgin, H. (2011). 'Oil-Eating Bacteria Feasted on Oil from Deepwater Horizon's Broken Well Says Scientist', *GulfLive*, http://blog.gulflive.com/mississippi-press-news/2011/07/oil-eating_bacteria_feasted_on.html. Accessed October 11, 2016.

Lowman, P., and Armstrong, N. (2002). *Exploring Earth, Exploring Space.* New York: Cambridge University Press.

Nelsen, M. P., DiMichele, W. A., Peters, S. E., and Boyce, C. K. (2016). 'Delayed Fungal Evolution Did Not Cause the Paleozoic Peak in Coal Production',

Proceedings of the National Academy of Sciences of the United States of America, 113(9), 2442–47.

Robbins, J. (2016). 'Hordes of Geese Die on a Toxic Lake in Montana'. *New York Times*, https://www.nytimes.com/2016/12/12/science/snow-geese-deaths-montana. html. Accessed April 22, 2018.

Schwarzmann, D., and Volk, T. (1991). 'Biotic Enhancement of Weathering and Surface Temperatures on Earth Since the Origin of Life'. *Palaeogeography, Palaeoclimatology, Palaeoecology (Global and Planetary Change Section)*, 90, 357–71.

Ward, P., and Kirschhvink, J. (2015). *A New History of Life: The Radical New Discoveries about the Origins and Evolution of Life on Earth*. London: Bloomsbury Press.

Williams, M., Zalasiewicz, Z., Haff, P. K., Schwägerl, C., Barnosky, A., and Ellis, E. (2015). 'The Anthropocene Biosphere'. *The Anthropocene Review* 2(3), 196–219.

Yeager, A. (2008). 'Microbes Drove Earth's Mineral Evolution'. *Nature*, November 14, 2008. doi:10.1038/news.2008.1226.

Zhang, S. (2016). 'The Goose-Killing Lake and the Scientists Who Study It'. *The Atlantic*. https://www.theatlantic.com/science/archive/2016/12/berkeley-pit-geese/510089/ Accessed February 4, 2018.

Index

About the Contributors

Simone Bignall is senior lecturer in politics, based in the College of Humanities at Flinders University in Australia. Her book publications include *Postcolonial Agency: Critique and Constructivism* (Edinburgh 2010); *Deleuze and the Postcolonial* (with Paul Patton); *Agamben and Colonialism* (with Marcelo Svirsky); and *Deleuze and Pragmatism* (with Sean Bowden and Paul Patton). She is currently completing a book on *Posthuman Desire* and a project titled *Excolonialism: Ethics after Enjoyment*.

Sean Bowden is senior lecturer in philosophy at Deakin University, Australia. He is the author of *The Priority of Events: Deleuze's* Logic of Sense (EUP 2011), and the co-editor of *Deleuze and Pragmatism* (Routledge 2015—with Simone Bignall and Paul Patton) and *Badiou and Philosophy* (EUP 2012—with Simon Duffy). His work has appeared in the *European Journal of Philosophy*, *Angelaki, Critical Horizons*, *Journal of Speculative Philosophy*, *Deleuze Studies* and elsewhere.

Rosi Braidotti (FAHA, 2009; MAE, 2014) is distinguished university professor and founding director of the Centre for the Humanities at Utrecht University (2007–2016). Publications include *Nomadic Subjects* (Columbia University Press, 2011); *Nomadic Theory: The Portable Rosi Braidotti* (Columbia University Press, 2011); and *The Posthuman* (Polity Press, 2013). Braidotti has also recently co-edited *Conflicting Humanities* (with Paul Gilroy, Bloomsbury, 2016) and *The Posthuman Glossary* (with Maria Hjavajova, Bloomsbury, 2018). See details at www.rosibraidotti.com.

Elizabeth de Freitas is professor in the Education and Social Research Institute at Manchester Metropolitan University. Her research focuses on philosophical and anthropological investigations of mathematics, science and technology, pursuing the implications and applications of this work in the learning sciences. She also studies the material and social semiotics of education, seeking new research methods that can address biosocial and biopolitical entanglements. She has published five books and over fifty chapters and articles.

Gregory Flaxman is associate professor in the Department of English and Comparative Literature at the University of North Carolina–Chapel Hill. He is author of *Gilles Deleuze and the Fabulation of Philosophy* (Minnesota, 2011) and editor of *The Brain Is the Screen* (Minnesota, 2010). His co-authored book on cinematic thinking is forthcoming from the Edinburgh University Press.

Myra J. Hird is professor and Queen's National Scholar in the School of Environmental Studies, Queen's University, Canada (www.myrahird.com), and a Fellow of the Royal Society of Canada. Professor Hird is Director of the *genera Research Group* (gRG), an interdisciplinary research network of collaborating natural, social, and humanities scholars, and Director of *Waste Flow*, an interdisciplinary research project focused on waste as a global scientific-technical and socio-ethical issue (www.wasteflow.ca). Hird has published nine books and over seventy articles and book chapters on a diversity of topics relating to science studies.

Suzanne McCullagh is a visiting assistant professor at Miami University. Her work focuses on ways of conceiving of ethical and political action and community. She is particularly interested in how certain concepts (empathy, solidarity, political space, responsibility, collective action, and capacity to act) are open to contestation and modification by ecological thinking which alters who and what is subject to empathy and solidarity, has a capacity to act, or is a participant in political space. She is currently co-editor of a volume entitled *Minor Ethics: Deleuzian Variations*.

Edward Mussawir is a lecturer in the Griffith Law School in Queensland, Australia. His research covers various themes in jurisprudence including jurisdiction, judgment, legal personality, the legal status of animals and the work of Gilles Deleuze. Dr Mussawir is the managing editor of the *Griffith Law Review: Law, Theory, Society*. He teaches civil procedure and legal theory.

Thomas Nail is an associate professor of philosophy at the University of Denver. He is the author of *Returning to Revolution: Deleuze, Guattari and Zapatismo* (Edinburgh University Press, 2012), *The Figure of the Migrant* (Stanford University Press, 2015), *Theory of the Border* (Oxford University Press, 2016), *Lucretius I: An Ontology of Motion* (Edinburgh University Press, 2018) and *Being and Motion* (Oxford University Press, 2018). He is also co-editor of *Between Deleuze and Foucault* (Edinburgh University Press, 2016). His work has appeared in *Angelaki*, *Theory & Event*, *Philosophy Today*, *Parrhesia*, *SubStance*, *Deleuze Studies*, *Foucault Studies* and elsewhere.

Jussi Parikka is professor at the Winchester School of Art (University of Southampton) and Docent of Digital Culture Theory at the University of Turku. His books include the award-winning *Insect Media* (2010); *Digital Contagions* (2007, 2nd ed. 2016), *A Geology of Media* (2015); *A Slow, Contemporary Violence: Damaged Environments of Technological Culture* (2016); and *What Is Media Archaeology?* (2012). Parikka has edited various books, recently *Writing and Unwriting (Media) Art History* (2015, with Joasia Krysa) on the Finnish media art pioneer Erkki Kurenniemi. He is also the co-editor of *Across and Beyond:—A Transmediale Reader on Post-digital Practices, Concepts, and Institutions* (Sternberg Press, 2016, co-edited with Ryan Bishop, Kristoffer Gansing and Elvia Wilk).

Andrej Radman has been teaching design and theory courses at TU Delft Faculty of Architecture since 2004. A graduate of the Zagreb School of Architecture in Croatia, he is a licensed architect and recipient of the Croatian Architects Association Annual Award for Housing Architecture in 2002. Radman received his master's and doctoral degrees from TU Delft and joined Architecture Theory Chair as assistant professor in 2008. He is an editor of the peer-reviewed journal for architecture theory *Footprint*. His research focuses on new-materialist ecologies and radical empiricism. Radman's latest publication, co-edited with Heidi Sohn, is *Critical and Clinical Cartographies: Architecture, Robotics, Medicine, Philosophy* (2017).

Daryle Rigney is Ngarrindjeri, an Indigenous nation located along the lower River Murray, Coorong and Lakes in southern South Australia. He is professor of Indigenous Strategy and Engagement at Flinders University and a member of the International Council of the Native Nations Institute at the University of Arizona. His academic and community work currently focuses on international developments in Indigenous governance following colonisation. Daryle has published widely and influentially on this subject.

Jon Roffe is a lecturer in philosophy at Deakin University in Melbourne. An editor of a number of volumes on twentieth-century French thought, he is the author of *Badiou's Deleuze* (Acumen 2012), *Abstract Market Theory* (Palgrave 2015), *Gilles Deleuze's Empiricism and Subjectivity* (EUP 2016), and the forthcoming two volume *The Works of Gilles Deleuze* (re-press). He is also the co-author of *Lacan Deleuze Badiou* (EUP 2014) and *Practising with Deleuze* (forthcoming).

Iris van der Tuin is professor of theory of cultural inquiry at Utrecht University and Director of Education in the School of Liberal Arts. As the chair of New Materialism: Networking European Scholarship on 'How Matter Comes to Matter' (2014–2018) van der Tuin has developed an international network of over 150 scholars sharing an interest in bridging the humanities and the natural sciences for global challenges today. Some of her book publications are *New Materialism: Interviews and Cartographies* (Open Humanities Press, 2012) with Rick Dolphijn, the monograph *Generational Feminist: New Materialist Introduction to a Generative Approach* (Lexington Books, 2015) and *Gender: Nature* (Macmillan Interdisciplinary Handbooks, 2016). Iris is editor of the book series *New Materialisms* of Edinburgh University Press with Rosi Braidotti and editor of the journal *Somatechnics* with Holly Randell-Moon.

James Williams is honorary professor of philosophy at Deakin University. He has published widely on recent French philosophy, including books on Deleuze, Lyotard and poststructuralism. His latest books are *A Process Philosophy of Signs*, (Edinburgh University Press, 2016) and *The Egalitarian Sublime* (Edinburgh University Press, 2019). His past and current work can be found at http://www.jamesrwilliams.net.

Kathryn Yusoff is professor of inhuman geography in the School of Geography at Queen Mary University of London. Her work engages with feminist theory, black geographies and dynamic earth events. Recent publications include a special issue on 'Geosocial Formations and the Anthropocene' (with Nigel Clark in *Theory, Culture and Society)* and *A Billion Black Anthropocenes or None* (University of Minnesota Press, 2018). She is currently finishing a book on 'Geologic Life', which examines how geologic forces subtend social and racial relations.

Printed in Great Britain
by Amazon

44194651R00182